BEST-KEPT SECRETS OF

BERLIN

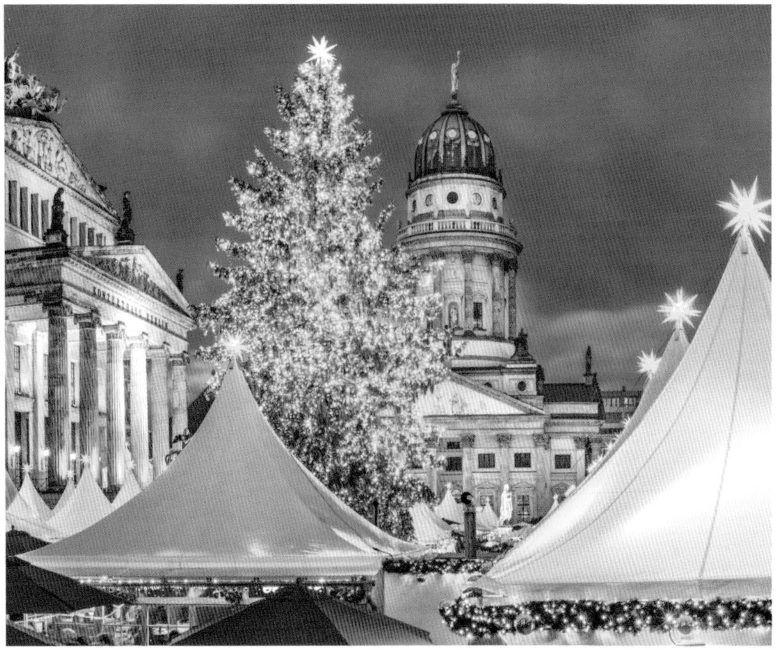

Publisher and Creative Director: Nick Wells
Commissioning Editor: Polly Prior
Editorial Assistant: Taylor Bentley
Art Director: Mike Spender
Layout Design: Jane Ashley

Special thanks to: Catherine Taylor, Claire Rogers, Amanda Leigh

FLAME TREE PUBLISHING
6 Melbray Mews
London SW6 3NS
United Kingdom

www.flametreepublishing.com

First published 2020

20 22 24 23 21
1 3 5 7 9 10 8 6 4 2

A CIP record for this book is available from the British Library upon request.

Courtesy of **Shutterstock.com** and © the following photographers: andersphoto: 102; Anticiclo: 117; anyaivanova: 105; N.M.Bear: 106; Gordon Bell: 32; Glen Berlin: 94; Gary Blakeley: 98; Bildagentur Zoonar GmbH: 168; Holger Boehm: 7, 62; bonchan: 153 (right); bonoc: 52; S.Borisov: 1, 56; Dante Busquets: 155; daisytrail: 99; ebenart: 92, 134, 150, 166; edella: 35; Electric Egg: 137, 142; JJFarq: 100; Thiago Figueredo : 108; Mariia Golovianko: 13, 58, 119; hanohiki: 3, 19, 65, 163; josefkubes: 48; Sergey Kelin: 97; Sergey Kohl: 8, 25; Patryk Kosmider: 6, 20; Kraft_Stoff: 160; TK Kurikawa: 18; laranik: 46, 47, 95, 107, 189, 192; kristof lauwers: 101; lindasky76: 72; Alessandro De Maddalena: 115; meunierd: 34, 37, 159; Mickis-Fotowelt: 175; Mistervlad: 75; mlcakm: 31; multitel: 59; NG-Spacetime: 80; Oscity: 22; Sergiy Palamarchuk: 66; Peeradontax: 91; pixelshop: 171; paul prescott: 152; Massimiliano Pieraccini: 76; posteriori: 45; ravelview: 49; Volker Rauch: 81; Ugis Riba: 83; RODKARV: 70, 181; Brian S: 84; SAKhanPhotography: 61; Tobias Schenk: 5, 177; Pavel Sepi: 124; Claire Slingerland: 17; Ralf Siemieniec: 157; Werner Spremberg: 147; struvictory: 172; Takako Picture Lab: 125; TeleMakro Fotografie: 183; Rudolf Tepfenhar: 53; tourpics_net: 71; Tupungato: 82; turtix: 9; VanderWolf Images, Germany: 16; wewi-photography: 113. Courtesy of **SuperStock.com** and © the following photographers: AGEFotostock: 138, 167; ArTono: 140; Andrea Astesiano/age fotostock: 74; F1 ONLINE: 169; Peter Erik Forsberg/age fotostock: 129; Siegfried Grassegger/imageBROKER: 96; Juergen Held/Prisma: 5, 93, 121, 127, 187; Jürgen Henkelmann/imageBROKER: 116, 131; Danuta Hyniewska/age fotostock: 64; imageBROKER: 136; Guido Koppes/age fotostock: 120; Javier Larrea/age fotostock: 79; look photos: 128, 133, 135, 148, 178; Iain Masterton/age fotostock: 28, 156; giovanni mereghetti/Marka: 14; Lothar Steiner/imageBROKER: 173; MIVA Stock: 161; Olaf Protze/age fotostock: 44; Sergi Reboredo/age fotostock: 55; Thomas Robbin/imageBROKER: 174; Phil Robinson/age fotostock: 122; Michael Weber/imageBROKER: 139; Jannis Werner/age fotostock: 43 ; Westend61: 26, 141, 149, 185, 186; Julie Woodhouse/imageBROKER: 38, 54, 68, 69. Courtesy of **Getty Images** and © the following photographers: Bildagentur-online/Universal Images Group: 36, 73, 112, 130, 143, 153 (left); Ulrich Baumgarten: 103; DEA Picture Library/De Agostini: 23; fhm: 67; John Freeman/Lonely Planet Images: 15; Sean Gallup: 4, 77, 89, 180; Gwengoat: 29, 85; Claudio de Sat/500px: 42; Schöning/ullstein bild: 88, 90, 154, 182; ©fitopardo.com: 109; Schlemmer/ullstein bild: 114

ISBN 978-1-83964-184-8

Printed in China | Created, Developed & Produced in the United Kingdom

BEST-KEPT SECRETS OF
BERLIN

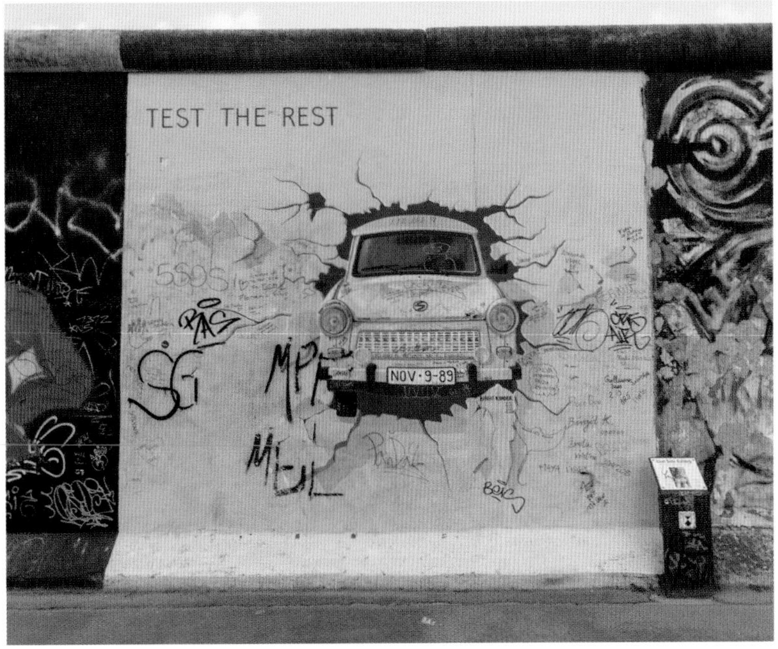

CHRIS MCNAB

FLAME TREE
PUBLISHING

CONTENTS

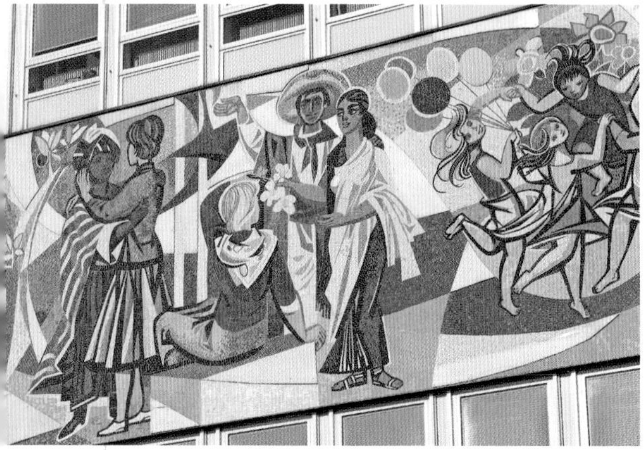

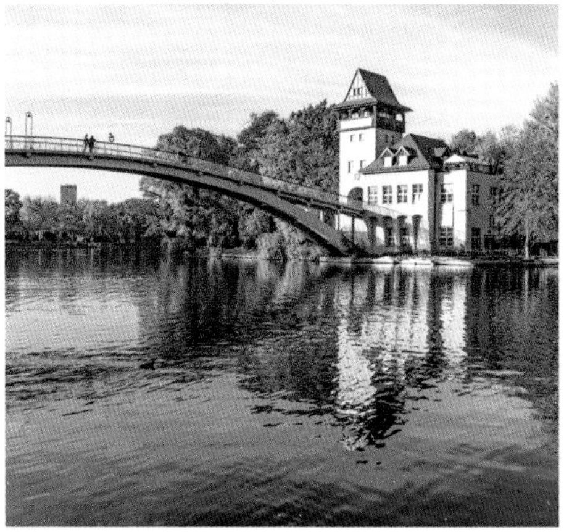

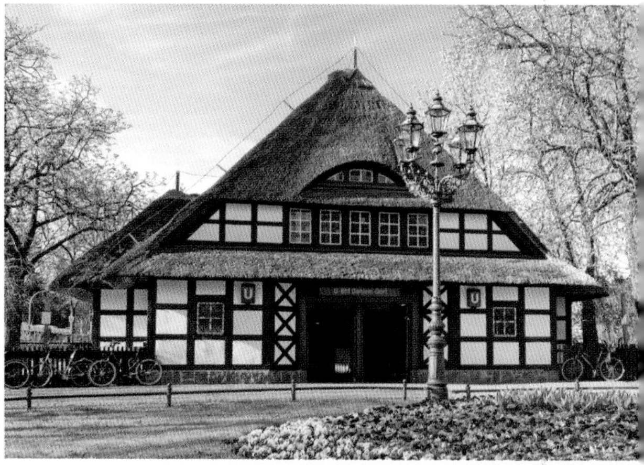

INTRODUCTION

Looked at purely in terms of its location, Berlin has a certain amount of geographical fortune on its side. Sitting on the Northern European Plain, which is characterized by both fertility and flatness (the latter makes it suited to transcontinental trade routes), Berlin is 180 km (112 miles) south of the Baltic Sea. The Spree River runs through the heart of the city, this 400-km (250-mile) waterway linking out to the Havel, the Oder and the Elbe, integrating Berlin into a vast water transport network that has served the city well commercially. The climate is firmly temperate and the surrounding landscape pleasant, with extensive lake systems ringed by lush pine forests.

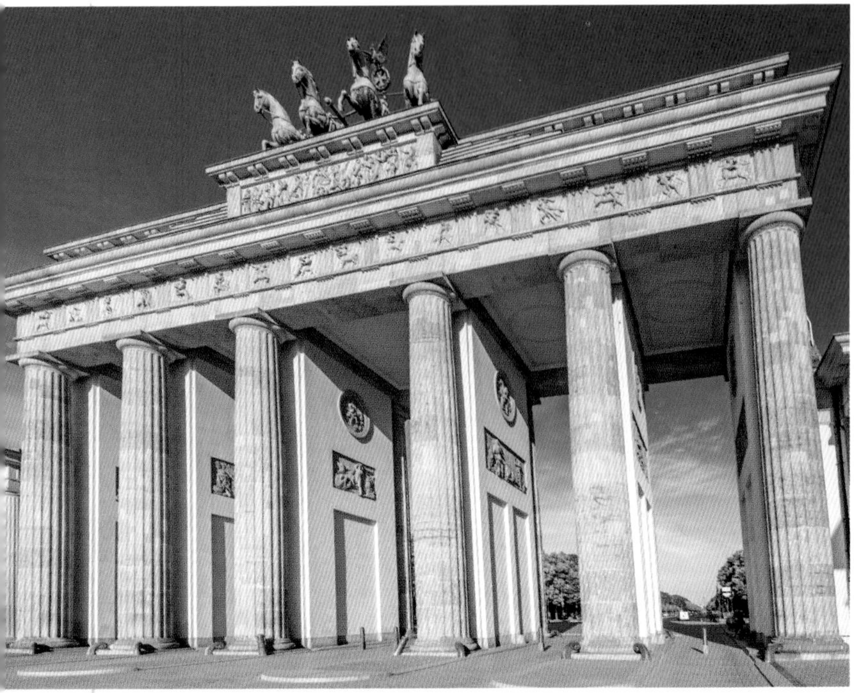

With nature alone on its side, Berlin had at least the physical preconditions for growth and influence. But, unlike other great European cities such as Rome and Athens, which achieved splendour well before the birth of the Christian era, Berlin began its ascent quite late in historical terms. The official birth of the city is laid down in the year 1237, when the two fortified trading towns of Berlin and Kölln, sitting either side of the Spree near what is today Alexanderplatz, unified as a single city, Berlin-Kölln. Berlin's first four centuries were politically dominated by the House of Hohenzollern, who established Berlin-Kölln as their capital, from which they ruled as the electoral princes of Brandenburg.

Berlin saw respectable commercial and cultural growth during these first centuries before, in 1618–48, the Thirty Years' War drew the city into its malign orbit. Not for the last time in its history, Berlin was virtually destroyed by war, but the city quickly staggered back to its feet. Under the galvanizing rule of Frederick William, the 'Great Elector' (1620–88; r. 1640–88), Berlin began a period of economic rejuvenation. William improved the city's defences and taxation system, and strongly encouraged the settlement of war refugees into the city, boosting the population with enterprising new groups of citizens. Under the Great Elector, and his son Frederick III (1657–1713; r. 1688–1713 as Elector of Brandenburg) – who was crowned the King of Prussia (as Frederick I; r. 1701–13) in 1701 – Berlin's population expanded to 61,000 citizens, from 12,000, between 1640 and 1712.

Berlin was now a royal residence city. It was a time of cultural, architectural and scientific self-confidence; two institutions established during this time were the Academy of Arts (1696) and Academy of Sciences (1700). This trend continued through the eighteenth century, especially under Frederick II, known as Frederick the Great (1712–86; r. 1740–86), despite the rise of Prussian militarism. Frederick, a true intellectual warrior, oversaw a broad programme of civic improvements and investment in the arts, making Berlin a locus for some of the greatest thinkers and artists of the age, and for some of its most impressive buildings. The nineteenth century continued Berlin's status as the new 'Athens of the North', but this was an era punctuated once more by war and revolution, including the Napoleonic occupation of the city in 1806–08 and the bloody bourgeois Revolution of 1848. This post-Napoleonic Berlin would increasingly become a hotbed of political radicalism, given expression by indigenous thinkers such as Georg Hegel (1770–1831), Friedrich Schleiermacher (1768–1834) and Karl Marx (1818–83). Industrialization, militarism and nationalism found their perfect expression in the unification of Germany under the Prussian Prime Minister Otto von Bismarck (1815–98) in 1871, Germany's constitutional monarchy headed by a Kaiser. Berlin, chosen as the capital of this new state, was now a very different animal

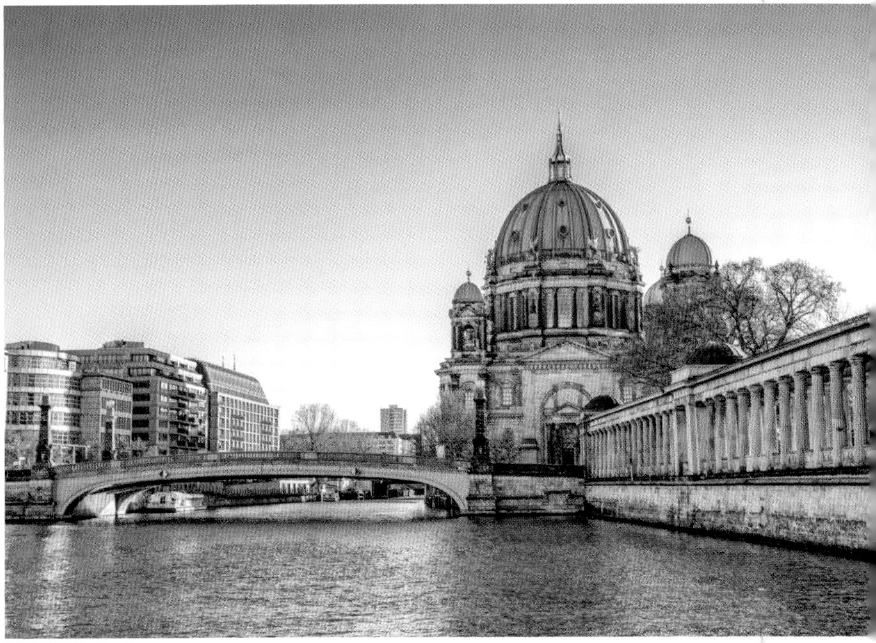

from the small town of five centuries ago. With a population of 826,000, Berlin was now the centre of a world power. Despite the rich history charted above, it is perhaps unavoidable that Berlin is most closely associated with the events of the twentieth century. During this century, the German capital saw the most extreme swings of fortune imaginable, from being the epicentre of European fascism to a model of enlightened tolerance, from absolute destruction to affluence and modernity, from divided ideologies to a generally unified liberalism. This history has been told so extensively that only the broadest brushstrokes will be given again here.

Between 1914 and 1918, Germany was plunged into a four-year world war (the First World War) terminating in German defeat, which not only brought the country and the capital

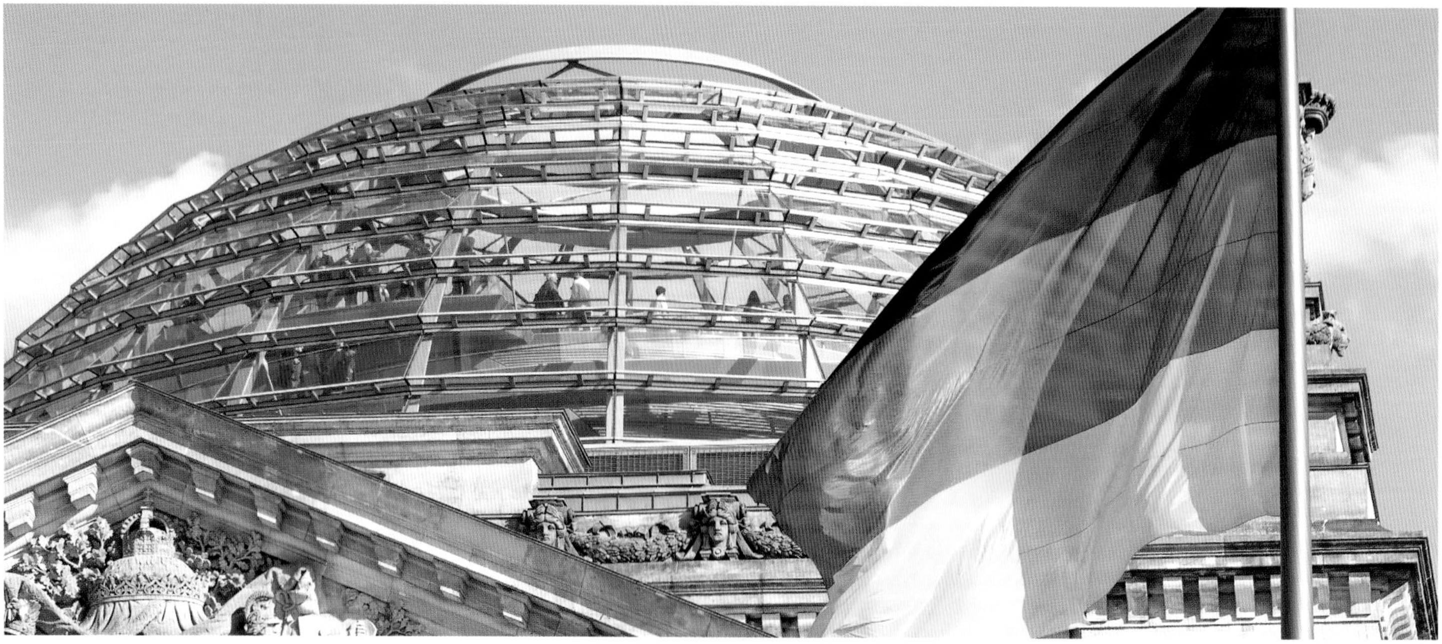

to its knees economically, but also laid the foundations of the turbulent era of the Weimar Republic (1919–33). Berlin was wracked by political violence, unemployment and the rise of Nazi fascism under Adolf Hitler (1889–1945) who, through a mix of street brutality and democratic process, became the leader, subsequently the dictator, of the 'Third Reich' in 1933. Under Hitler, fascism throttled Berlin's previously cosmopolitan culture. The Nazi take on art, architecture, politics and race – Berlin's *Kristallnacht* (Night of Broken Glass) on 9 November 1938 was but a taste of the horrors that awaited its Jews – was brutal, nationalist in its worse sense, and militaristic. But, for a time, Berlin appeared to prosper under Hitler's rule, after a decade of depression and mass unemployment, making it all the easier for Hitler to lead the country into another world war in 1939.

On 13 April 1945, Hitler committed suicide in his bunker below the Reich Chancellery. Berlin lay smashed around him, the bodies of 100,000 civilians killed in the final battle for the city adding to the 52,000 who died there through three years of Allied bombing. The victorious US, British, Soviets and French divided Berlin into zones of occupation, the Western Allies in the west of the city, and the Soviets to the east. In March 1948, the three Allied occupation zones in the west were unified into a single economic zone, precipitating a demonstrative pushback from the Soviets. A one-year Soviet blockade of the city (June 1948–May 1949), broken by the Allies via an airlift, was just a foretaste of the ideological fissures that would dictate the next 50 years of Berlin's history. With the building of the Berlin Wall in the 1960s, Berlin would be quite literally divided, its streets and people split between the Berlin of the communist German Democratic Republic (GDR) in the east and that of the capitalist, democratic Federal German Republic (FDR) in the west. Berlin had become the frontline of the Cold War.

In 1989–90, Soviet communism collapsed, the Berlin Wall was pulled down, and Berlin and Germany were reunified. It was a seismic moment in modern history, and for several days Berlin compelled the attention of the world. We cannot say that since 1990 the reunited Berlin has not faced its fair share of problems, particularly in relation to housing, urban planning, employment and social tensions. Yet the new Berlin, as we shall see in our journey through its landmarks and districts, is the truly thriving and dynamic capital of a resurgent Germany. The city is now tolerant, inventive and multicultural, known throughout Europe for its intellectualism, youthful hedonism, architectural confidence and entrepreneurial spirit. Its attractions for the traveller seem near endless, certainly well beyond the limits of this book. In addition to some of the world's greatest museums, palaces, art galleries, research centres, universities and cultural centres, Berlin also offers the gastronomy, nightlife, shopping and cultural curiosities to make any trip a pleasure as well as an education. Little wonder that it is in the top 10 list of most popular European cities, with 13.5 million visitors every year, well in excess of its own 3.7 million population. Berlin is everything a capital city is meant to be, its history speaking from every corner, but also looking emphatically towards the future. At its root, there is an optimism to Berlin, a sense of regeneration still underway. We hope that this book will give you a new, or renewed, impulse to explore this city.

A note on organization: this book divides the city into focused areas of exploration, roughly divided between the Tiergarten, Centre (Mitte), City North Central, City South Central, City West and the Suburbs. At an administrative level, Berlin is divided into 12 *Bezirke* (districts): Charlottenburg-Wilmersdorf; Friedrichshain-Kreuzberg; Lichtenberg; Marzahn-Hellersdorf; Mitte; Neukölln; Pankow; Reinickendorf; Spandau; Steglitz-Zehlendorf; Tempelhof-Schöneberg; and Treptow-Köpenick. Districts are in turn divided into *Ortsteile* (subdistricts or quarters). Each entry in the book provides information about the specific district, quarter or other locator, providing a means for you to navigate around the city's most famous, or famously hidden, landmarks.

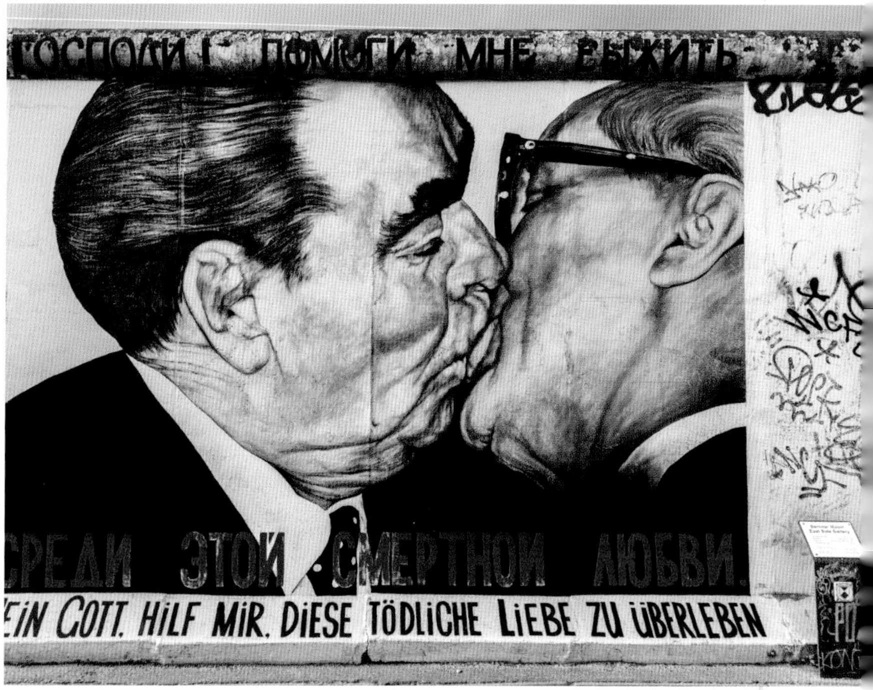

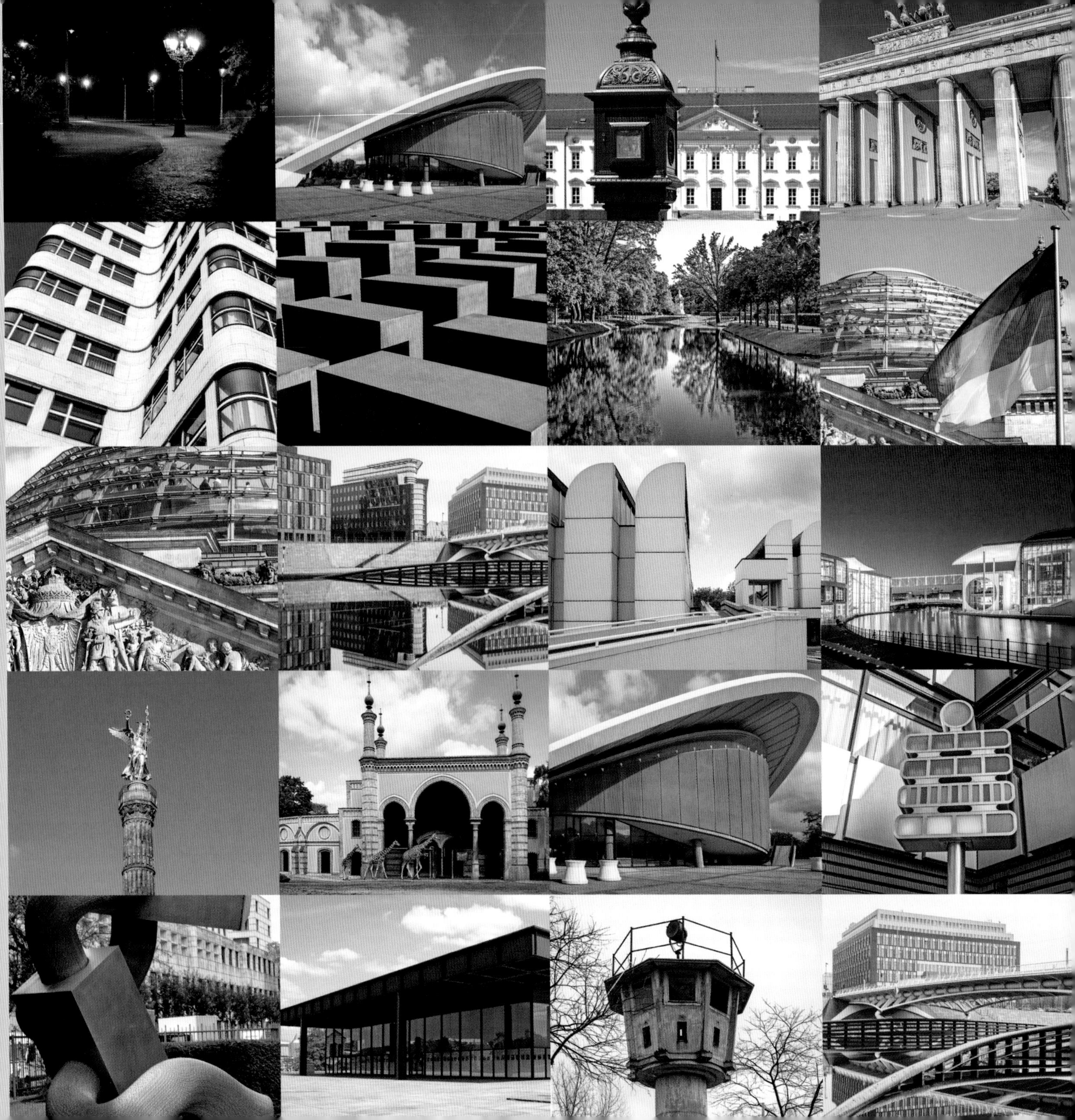

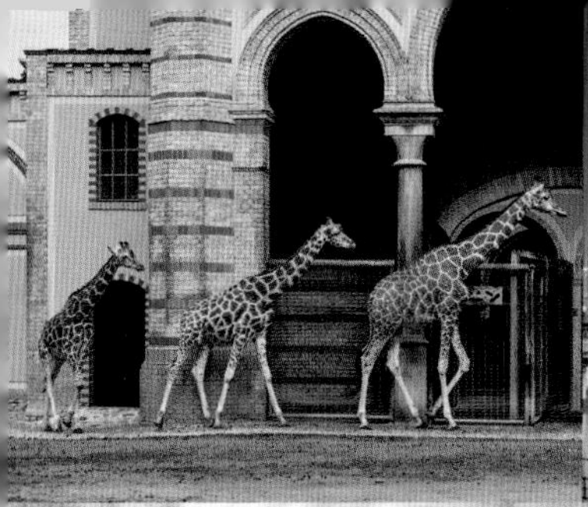
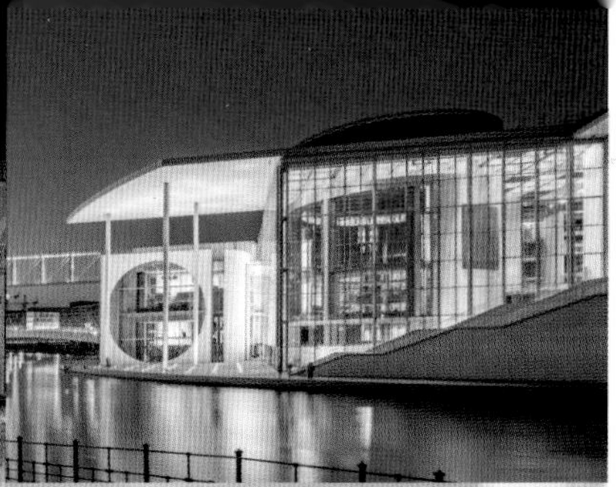
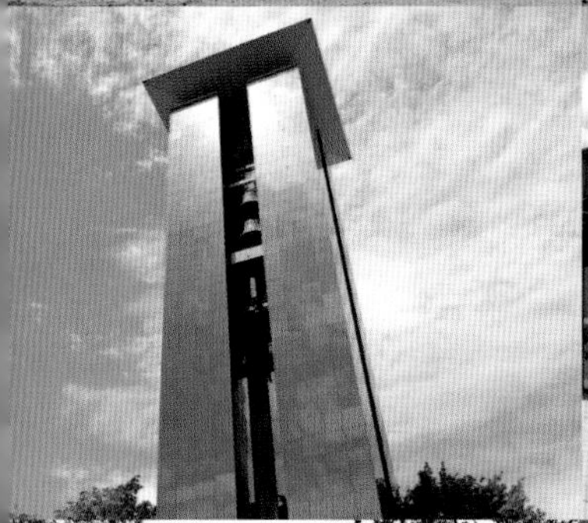
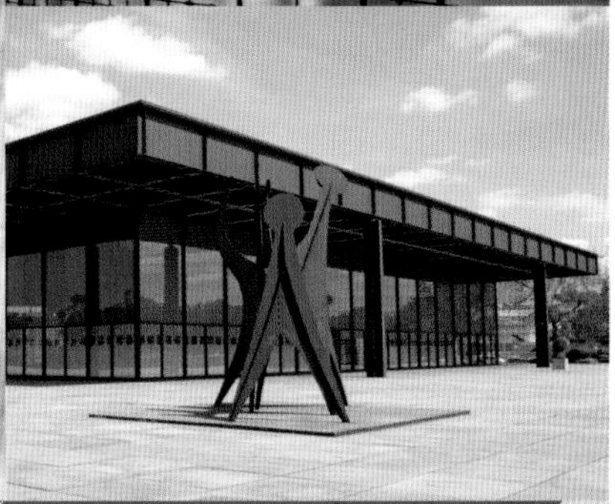
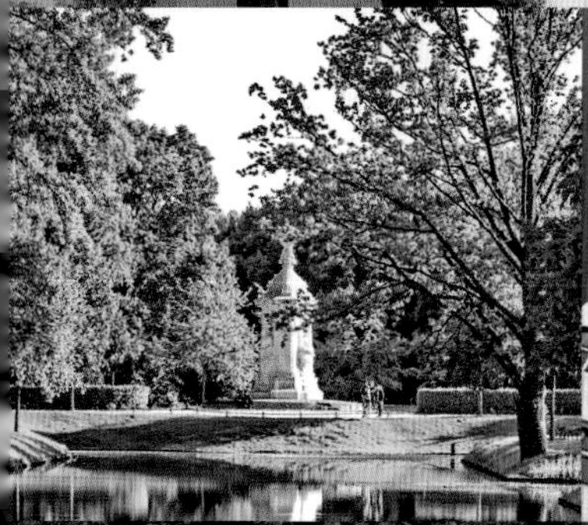
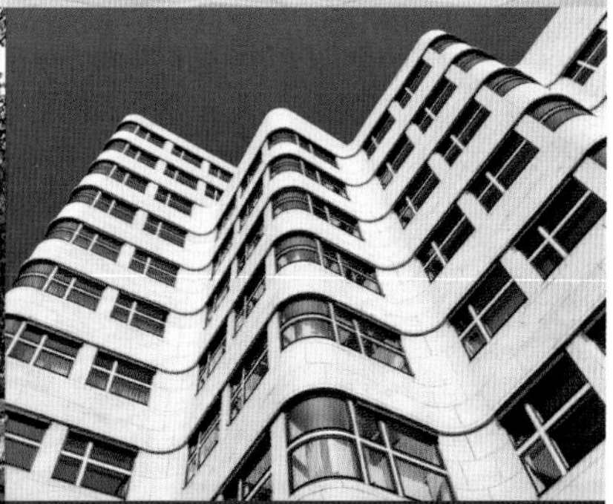
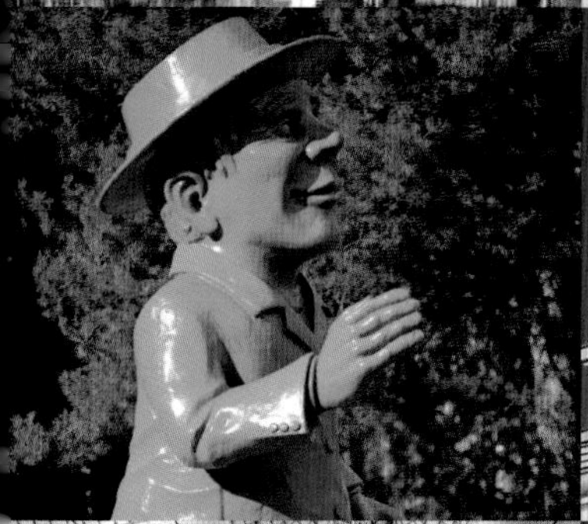
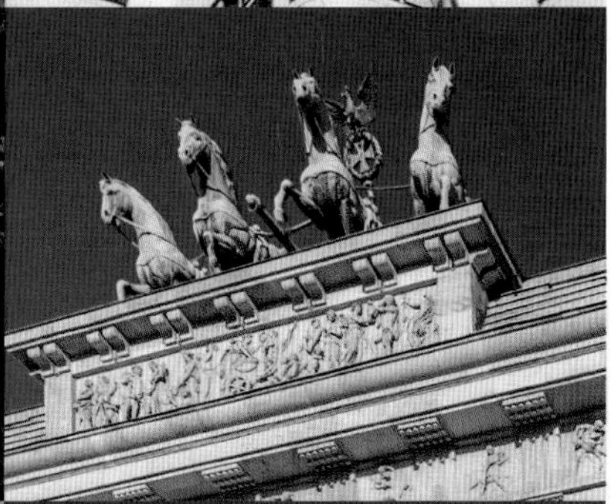
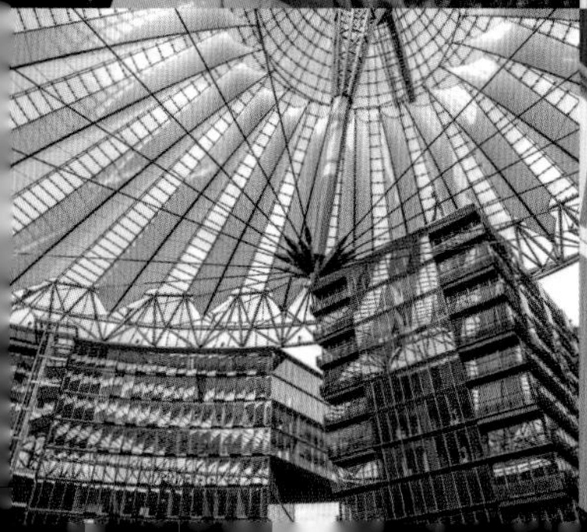
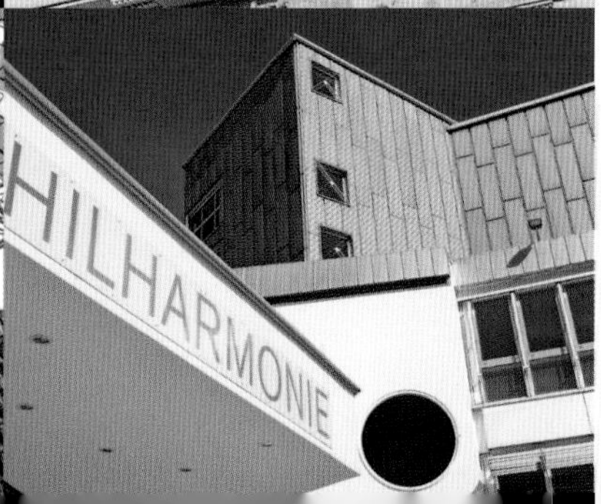

TIERGARTEN

Let's start our journey through Berlin not in its humming urban streets, but in the tranquillity, light and shade of the Tiergarten. Much like Central Park is to New York, the Tiergarten is Berlin's refuge, an expanse of 210 hectares (520 acres) that, since the sixteenth century, when it was established as a hunting ground for royals and nobles, has retained a sense of ordered peace, despite some periods in which history rode roughshod over its beauty.

The park that we see today is the product of intensive post-war rebuilding, replanting and landscaping. It is a place to lose oneself, in trees, lakes, distinctive gardens, bridges and monuments, but also some of the big attractions of the city, such as Berlin Zoo. Its character shifts gracefully with the seasons. In summer, it is a place of drifting boat rides, deep shadows on bright fields and picnics on the grass; in winter, its beauty is accentuated by coatings of ice or layers of muting snow, and sometimes the lakes freeze so hard that people can ice-skate upon them. Whatever the time of year, the Tiergarten is somewhere both to explore and to have some moments of peace from the bustling city, the noise of those streets muted by the trees.

CHESTNUT TREES

Tiergarten

Chestnut trees blossom by the side of a mirror-like pool in the Tiergarten. At the end of the Second World War, only a handful of the 200,000 trees that had once covered the Tiergarten remained, the gaunt survivors usually hacked down for firewood. Yet between 1949 and 1959, a total of 250,000 trees were donated or bought for the restoration of the park, meaning that today the Tiergarten has returned to a state of luscious tranquillity. Other major tree types in the park include linden, oak, maple and plane.

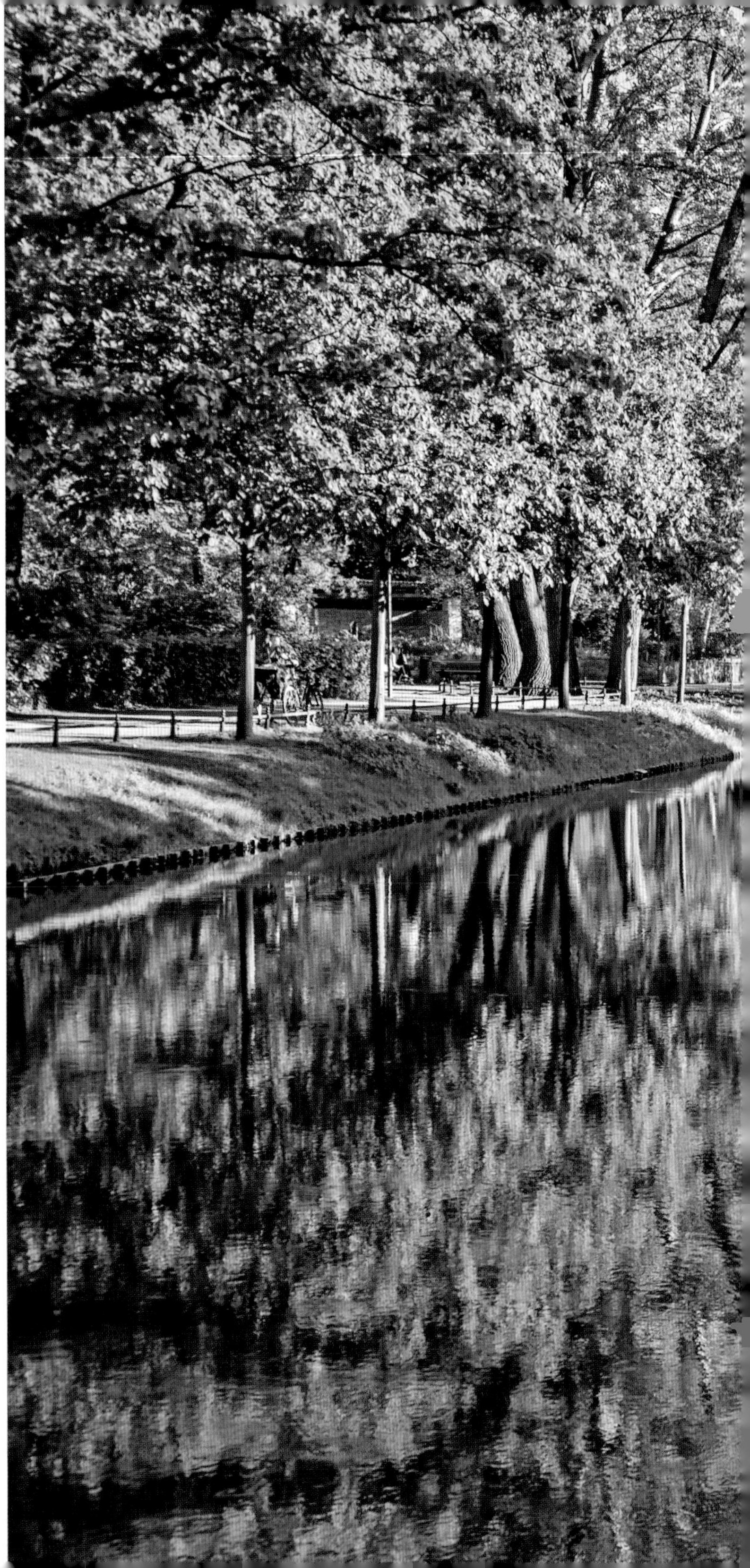

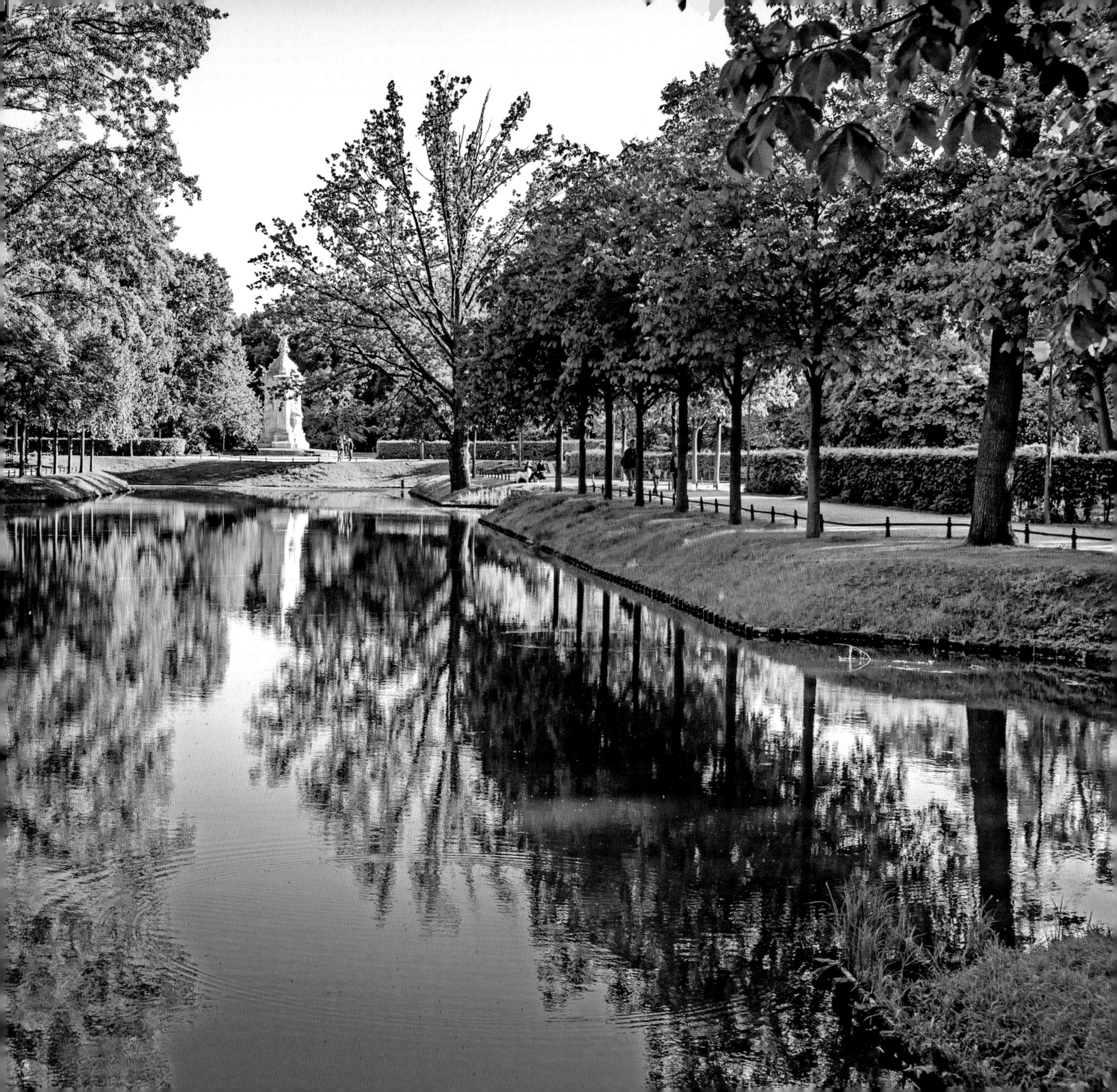

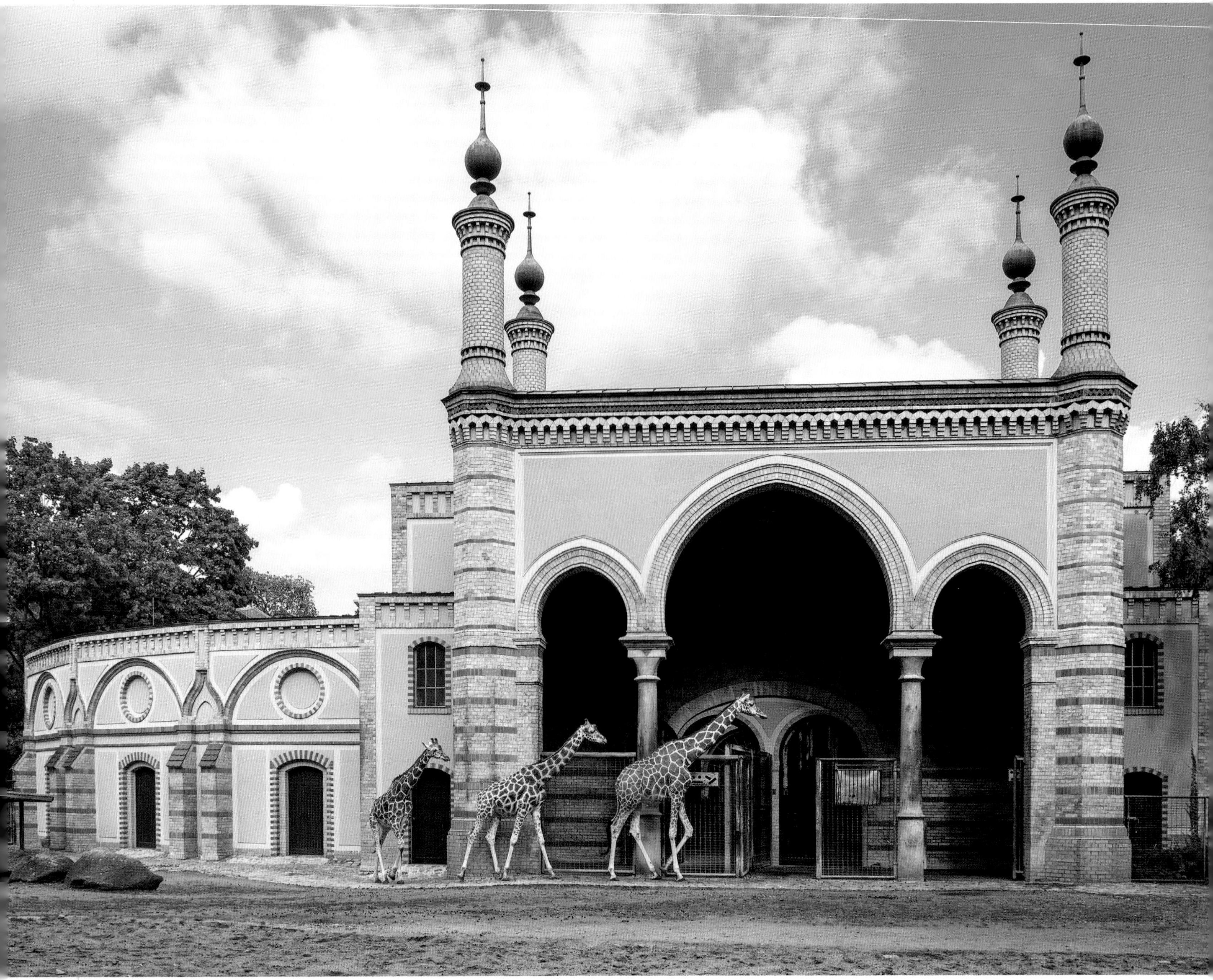

GIRAFFE HOUSE

Zoo Berlin, Tiergarten

With a nostalgic exoticism built into its design, the Giraffe House is a memorable landmark within the Zoologischer Garten Berlin (Berlin Zoological Garden), the 35-hectare (86.5-acre) animal park in the Tiergarten. Giraffes first arrived in the zoo in 1864, and the building to house them was constructed in 1889, although the zoo itself dates back to 1844, to which an aquarium was added in 1913. During World War II, the majority of the animals in the zoo were tragically killed, but impressive post-war reconstruction has made the zoo one of the city's most popular landmarks, with around 3.5 million visitors every year.

MENGENLEHREUHR

Budapester Straße, Tiergarten

The Mengenlehreuhr (Set Theory Clock), also known as the Berlin-Uhr (Berlin Clock), was installed on 17 June 1975, the Berlin Senate having commissioned the engineer and designer Dieter Binninger (1938–91) to produce a public piece of art to sit outside the Europa Centre mall. To the uninitiated, it appears as little more than a bank of coloured lights, yet it is actually a fully functioning clock, each bank of lights representing a different block of time. Each light in the uppermost red panel, for example, represents a five-hour increment, while those below give individual hours.

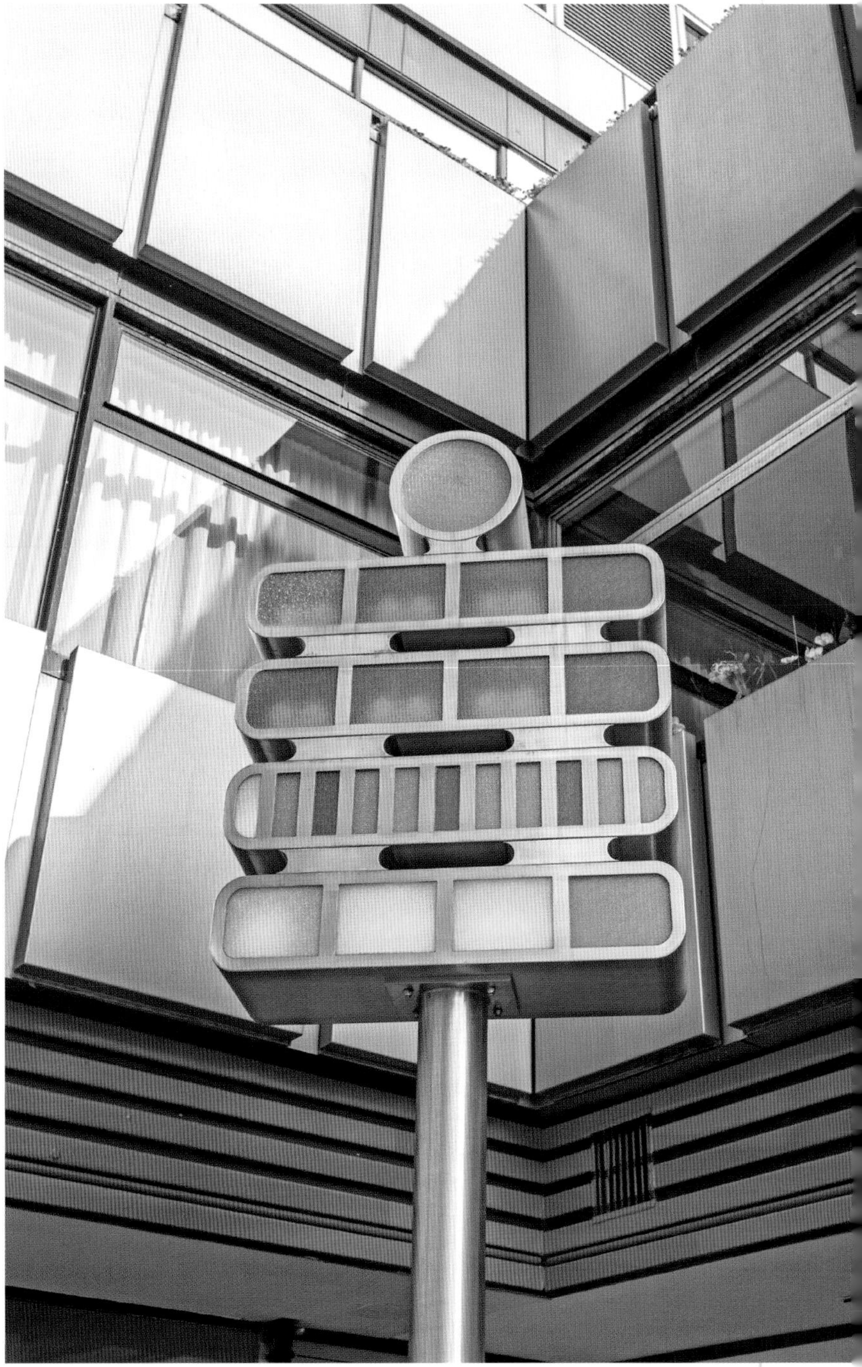

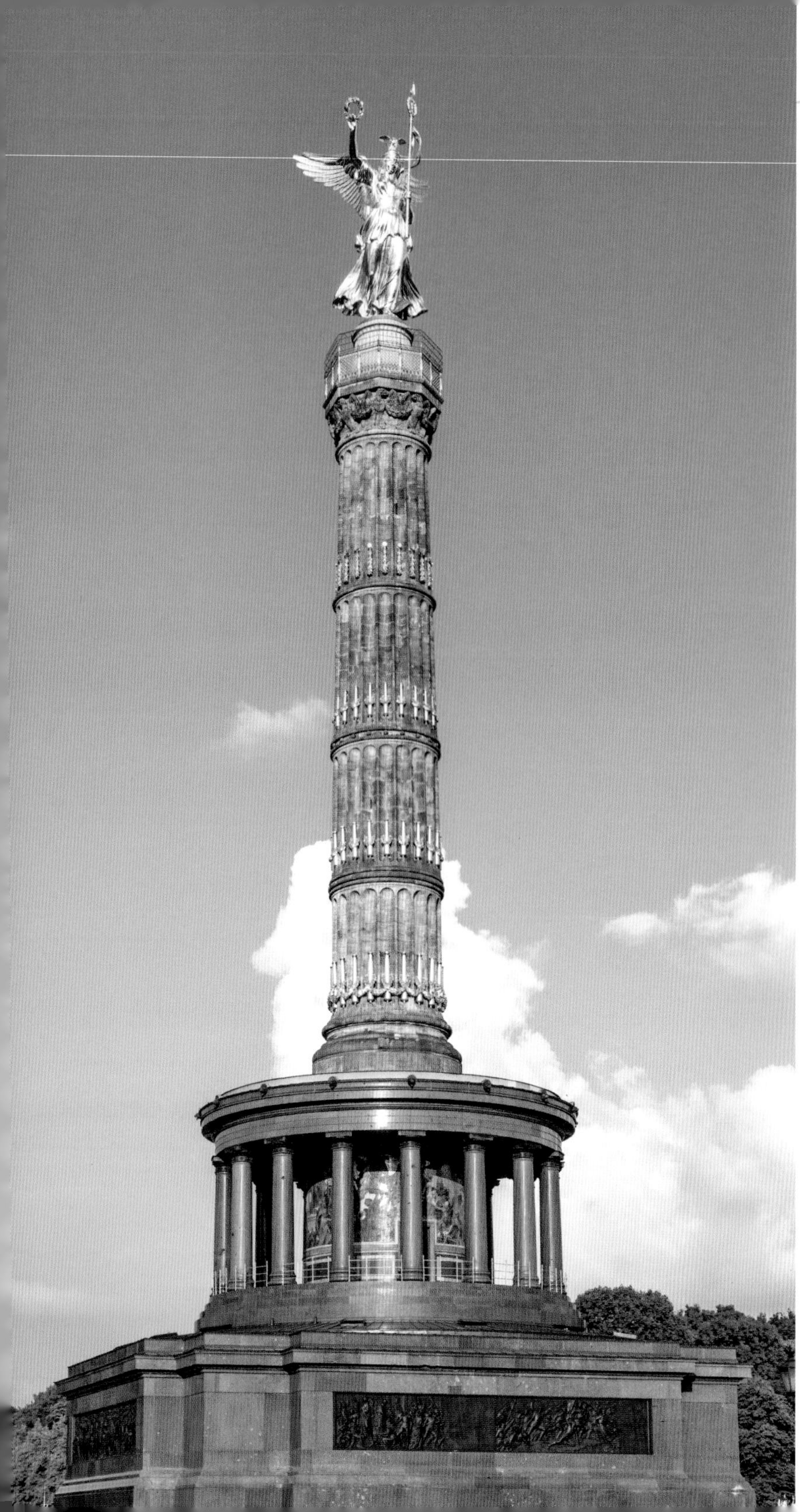

SIEGESSÄULE

Main Roundabout, Tiergarten

Imperial and triumphant, the Siegessäule (Victory Column) towers 67 m (220 ft) above the Tiergarten, the viewing platform at the top providing distant views across the city around it. The monument was commissioned following the Prussian victory in the Danish–Prussian War of 1864, although the duration of its building – it was finally inaugurated on 2 September 1873 – meant that, by that time, Prussia had also racked up further victories against Austria and France. The monument originally stood in Königsplatz (now Platz der Republik), at the end of the Siegesallee (Victory Avenue), but it was moved to its current site by the Nazis in 1939, a relocation that spared it destruction in the Second World War.

GASLATERNEN-FREILICHTMUSEUM

Ecke Klopstockstraße, Tiergarten

Evoking the magical illumination of a past era, ornate gas lamps throw out their spectral yellow light across the paths of Tiergarten Park. The lamps are part of the Gaslaternen-Freilichtmuseum (Open-air Gas Lantern Museum), a functioning collection of some 90 antique gas lamps manufactured between 1826 and 1956. The lamps have their own unique identities and craftsmanship, some being graced with redolent nicknames – Wilmersdorfer Witwe (Wilmersdorf Widow) and Bullenbein (Copper's Leg) are two notable examples.

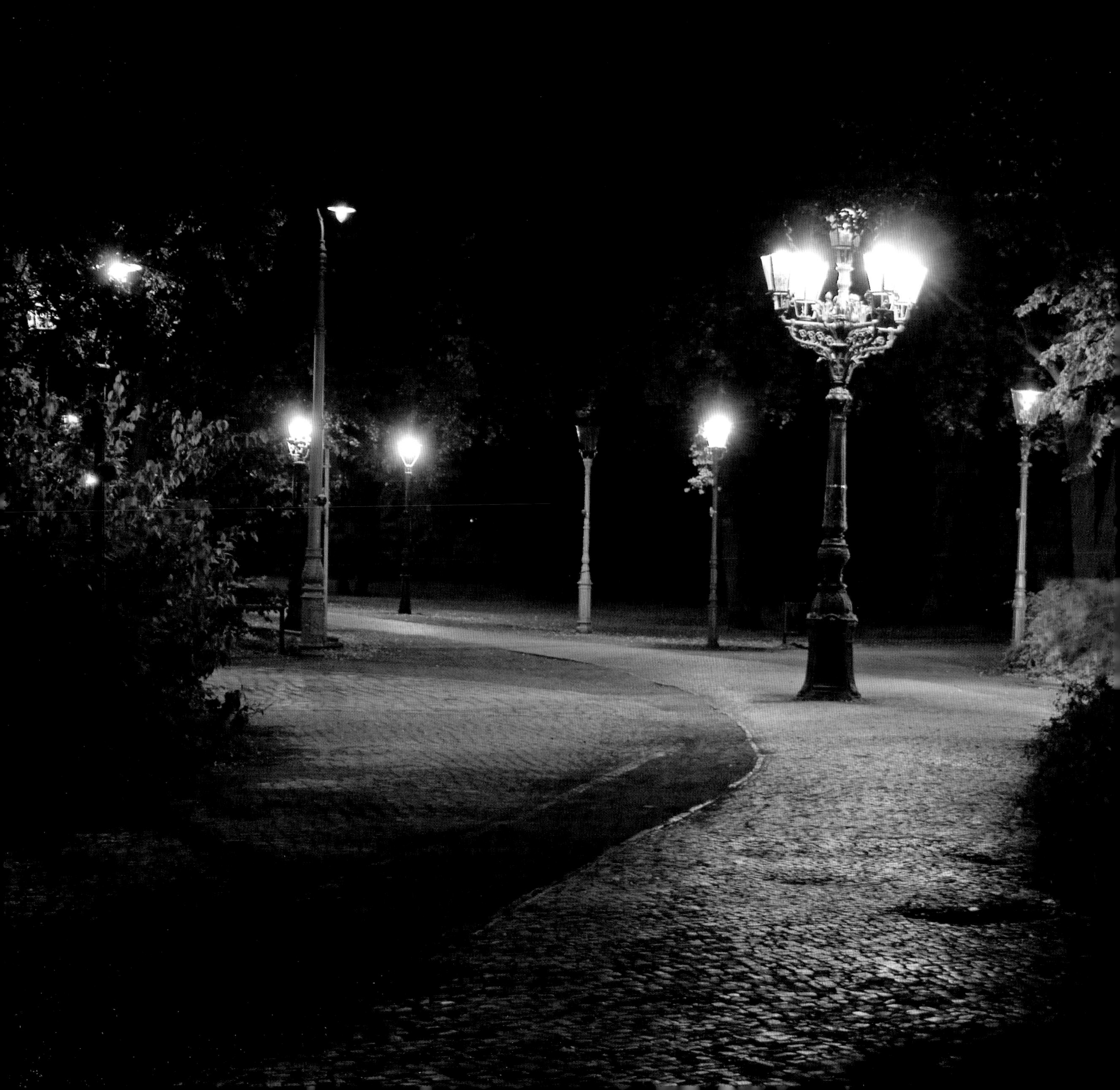

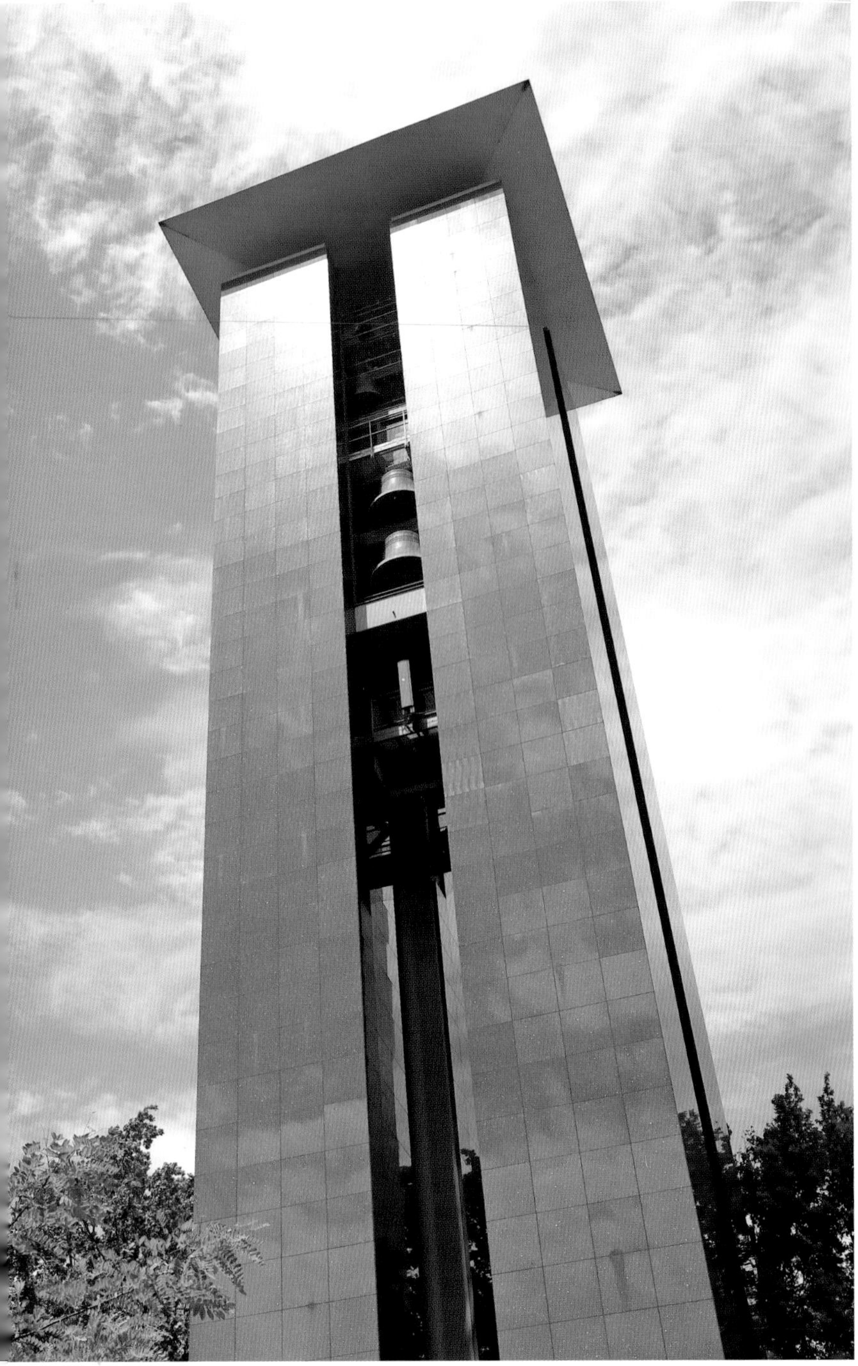

CARILLON

Tiergarten Park

An extraordinary piece of both architecture and musicality, the Carillon is a freestanding 42-m (137-ft) tower that houses a total of 68 bells, ranging from delicate high-pitched small bells through to a sonorous monster weighing 7.8 tonnes (7.7 long tons). To play the bells, the musician (or, more properly, the 'carillonneur') uses a 5½-octave keyboard, sending sparkling classical tunes floating through the trees of the park. The instrument was actually given to the city by Daimler-Benz AG in 1987 to mark the 750th anniversary of Berlin, and globally the instrument ranks as the fourth largest carillon.

HAUS DER KULTUREN DER WELT

John-Foster-Dulles-Allee, Tiergarten

The Haus der Kulturen der Welt (HKW; House of the World's Cultures) is visually arresting at first glance, a winged design created by US architect Hugh Stubbins (1912–2006), a former assistant to the great Bauhaus architect Walter Gropius (1883–1969). The building was originally a US-sponsored Congress Hall, opened in September 1957, and a venue for cultural and intellectual pursuits, especially music and theatre. Its proceedings were interrupted for six years following a roof collapse on 21 May 1981, but following its reopening the building became the headquarters of the HKW.

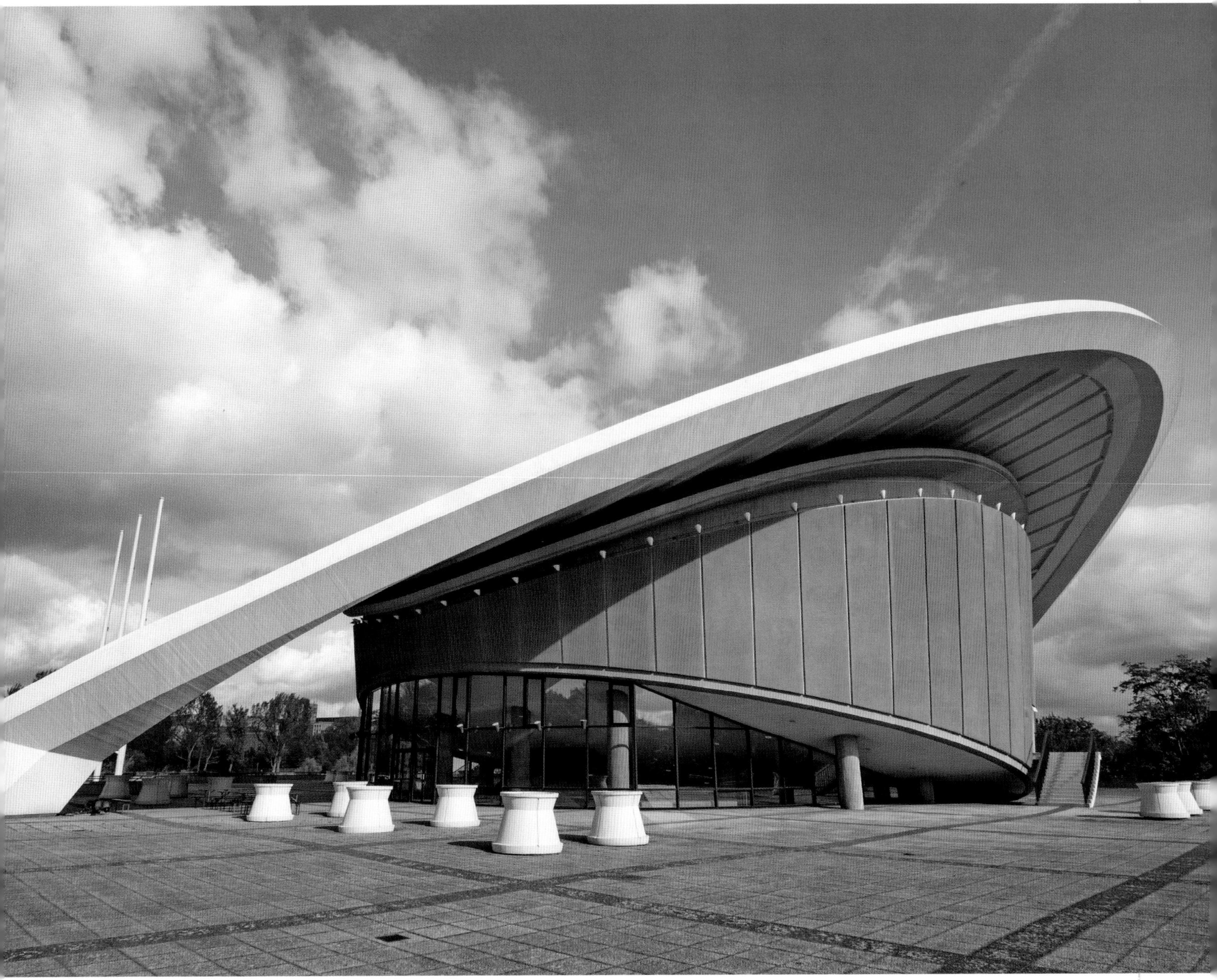

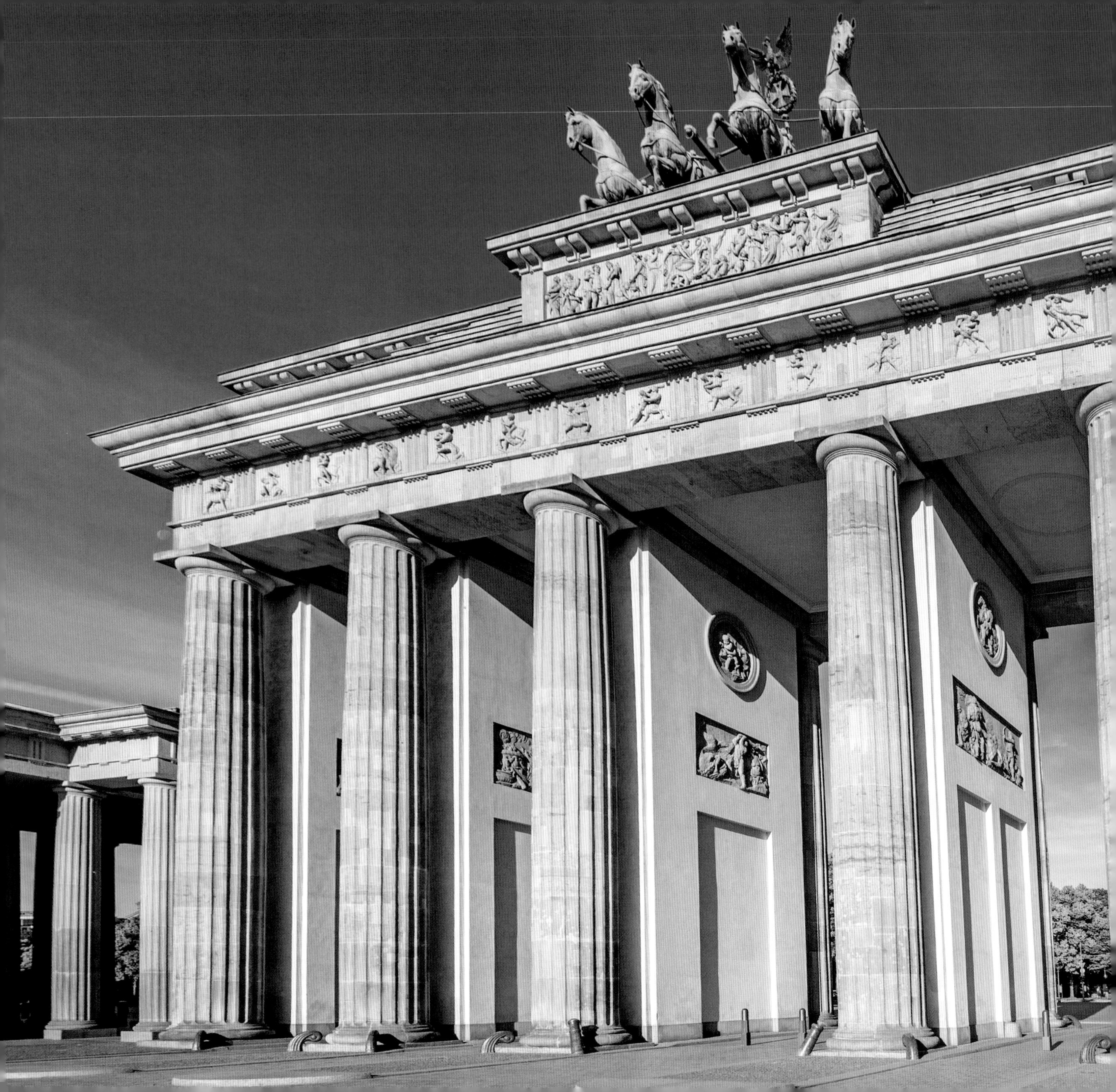

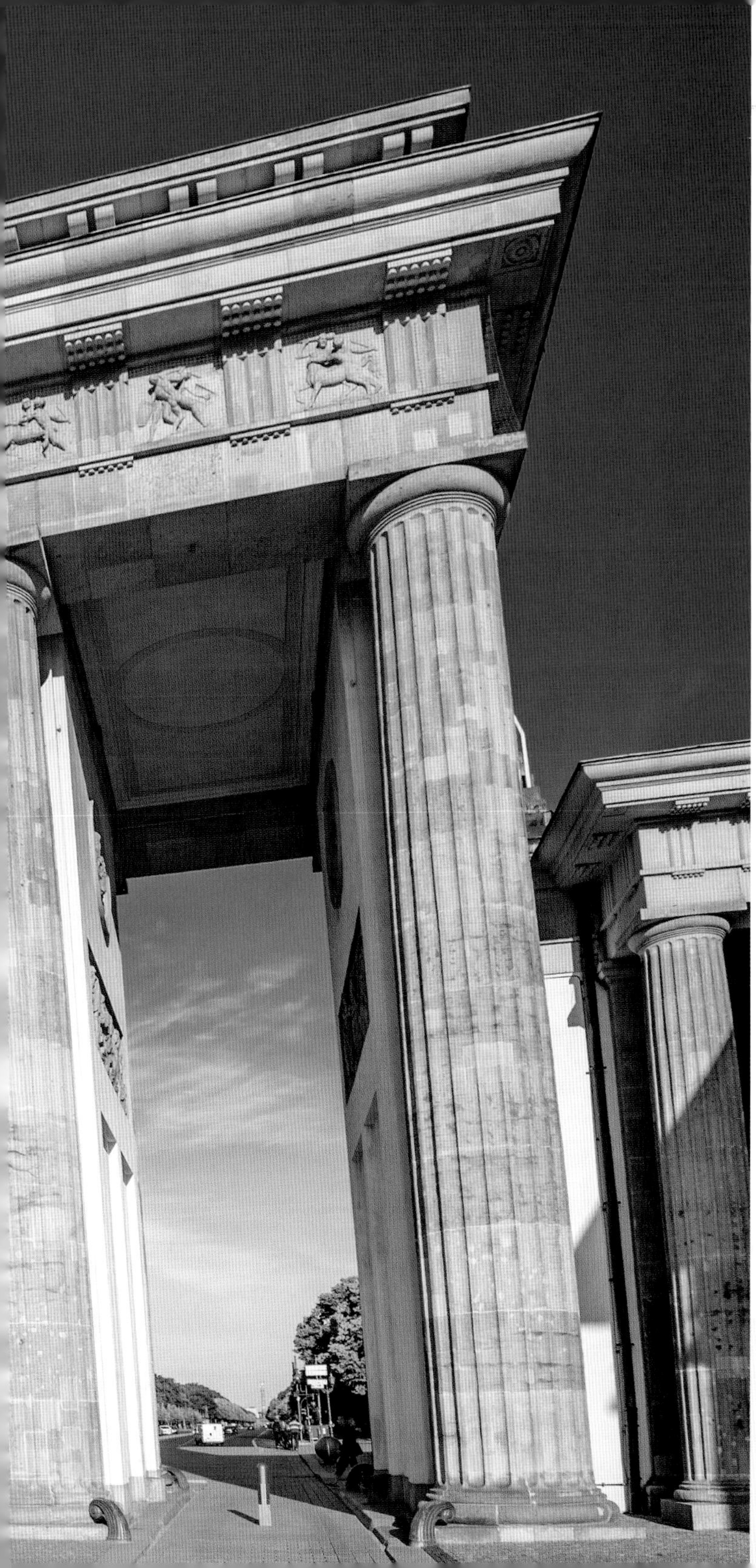

BRANDENBURGER TOR

Pariser Platz, Tiergarten

The Brandenburger Tor (Brandenburg Gate) is undoubtedly one of Berlin's defining landmarks; history has marched beneath its columns. Commissioned by Frederick William II of Prussia (1744–97), the gate was built between 1788 and 1791, designed by the Court Superintendent of Buildings, Carl Gotthard Langhans (1732–1808). Based directly on Classical Greek architectural models, the pillared gate is surmounted by a dynamic quadriga (four-horse chariot) sculpted by Johann Gottfried Schadow (1764–1850). Over its two centuries, the Brandenburg Gate has fully witnessed, indeed participated in, the ebb and flow of great political and social movements.

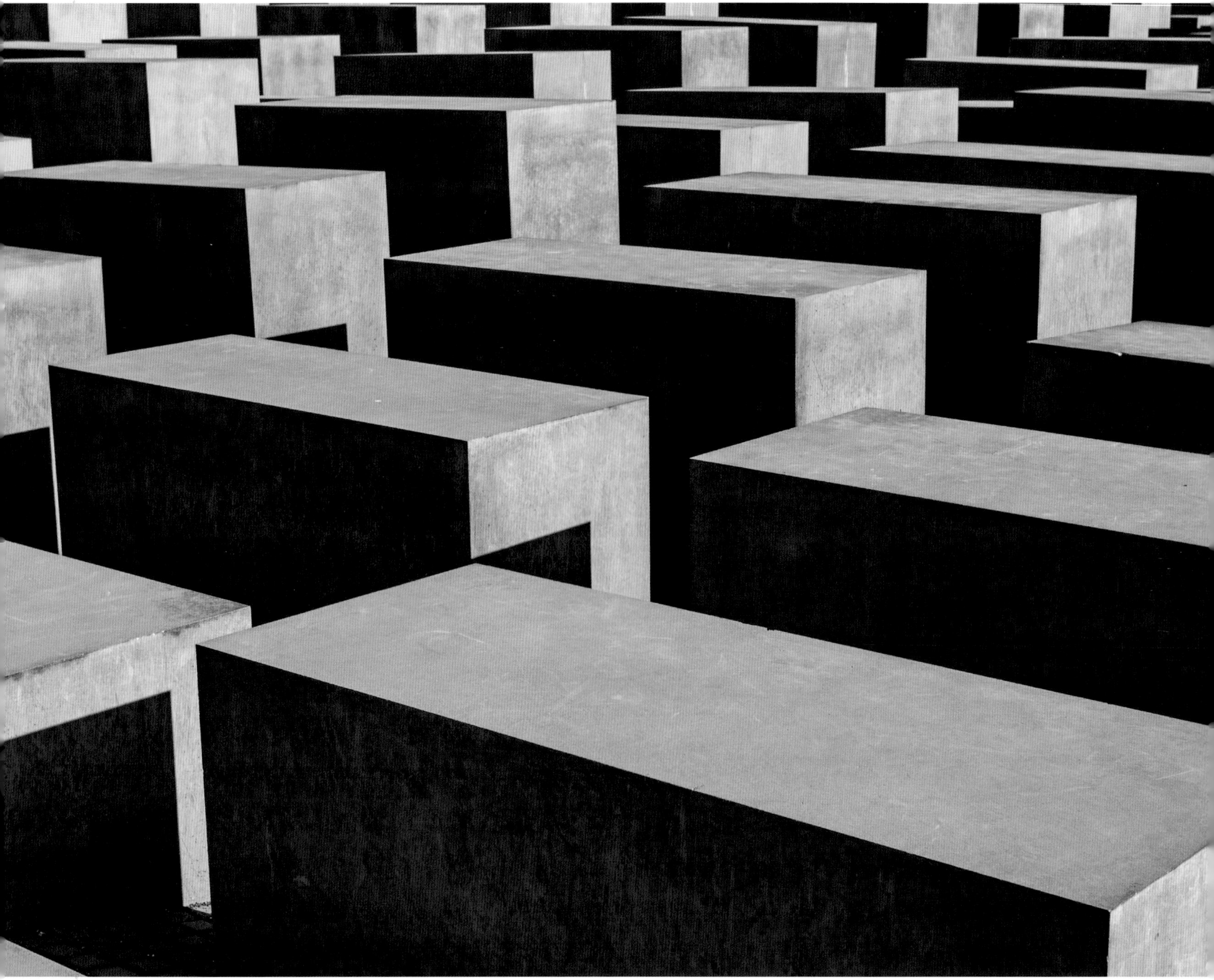

DENKMAL FÜR DIE ERMORDETEN JUDEN EUROPAS

Cora-Berliner-Straße, Tiergarten

The Denkmal für die ermordeten Juden Europas (Memorial to the Murdered Jews of Europe), also the Holocaust-Mahnmal (Holocaust Memorial), is an act of sombre national memory, confronting the ravenous human costs of Germany's descent into Nazism during the 1930s and 1940s. Designed by architect Peter Eisenman (b. 1932) and engineering company BuroHappold, the memorial is a 19,000 sq m (200,000 sq ft) area, blocked out with 2,711 concrete 'stelae' (referring to the funerary slabs of ancient Greece). With some blocks reaching up to 4.7 m (15 ft 5 in) in height, the visitor wandering between them can experience a fearful, lonely sensation.

BAUHAUS-ARCHIV

Klingelhöferstraße, Tiergarten

The 'shed roofs' Bauhaus-Archiv (Bauhaus Archive) demonstrates the classic Bauhaus approach of fusing industrial functionality with artistic sensibility. The original design of the building was done by no less than the founder of the Bauhaus Movement, Walter Gropius, but planning delays meant it was actually built and heavily modified by Gropius' associate Alex Cvijanovic (1923–2019) between 1971 and 1978. As a state archive for art, architecture and design, plus a Museum of Design, the Bauhaus Archive is a locus for international innovation.

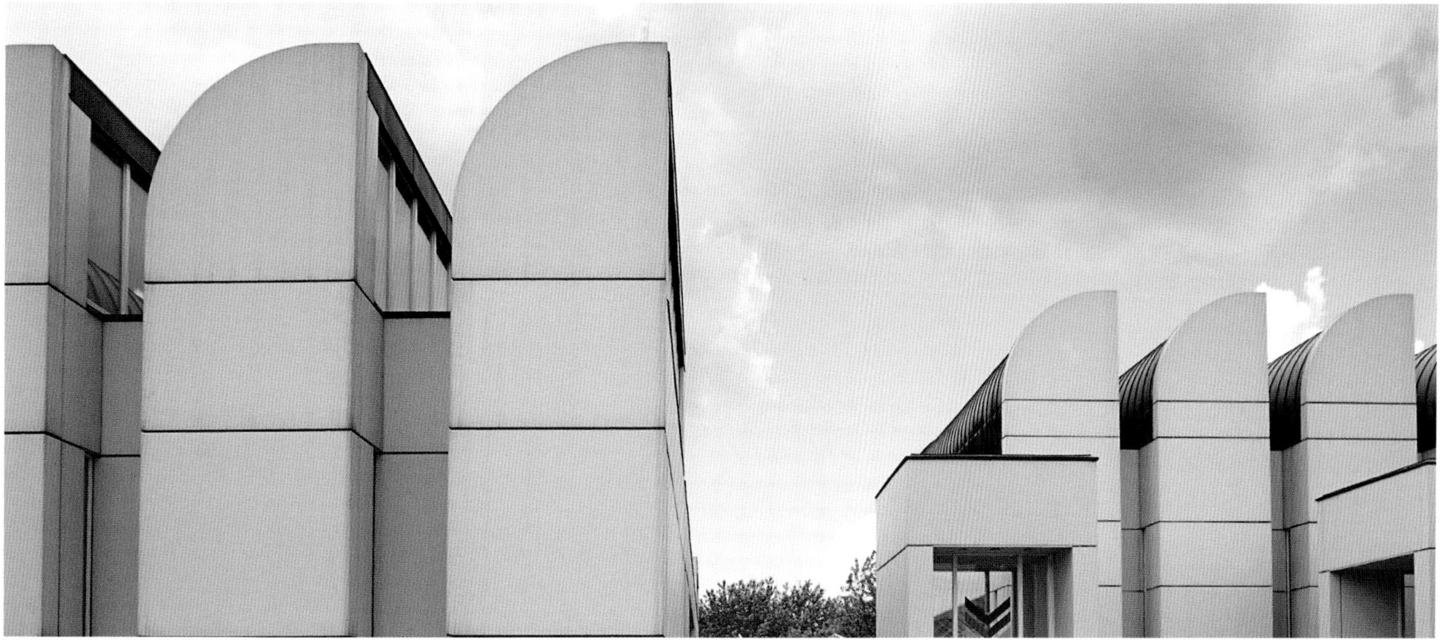

REICHSTAG BUILDING

Platz der Republik, Tiergarten

The Reichstag is at the heart of modern German history and governance. First built between 1884 and 1894, and modelled on the Memorial Hall in Philadelphia, the grand domed building was designed by Paul Wallot (1841–1912) as a home for the German Parliament. Parliamentary functions came to an end with the great Reichstag fire of 27 February 1933, a pretext for the establishment of the Nazi dictatorship, but the ruin was resurrected following German reunification, transformed into a space of political openness by the glass dome over the main hall of the Bundestag.

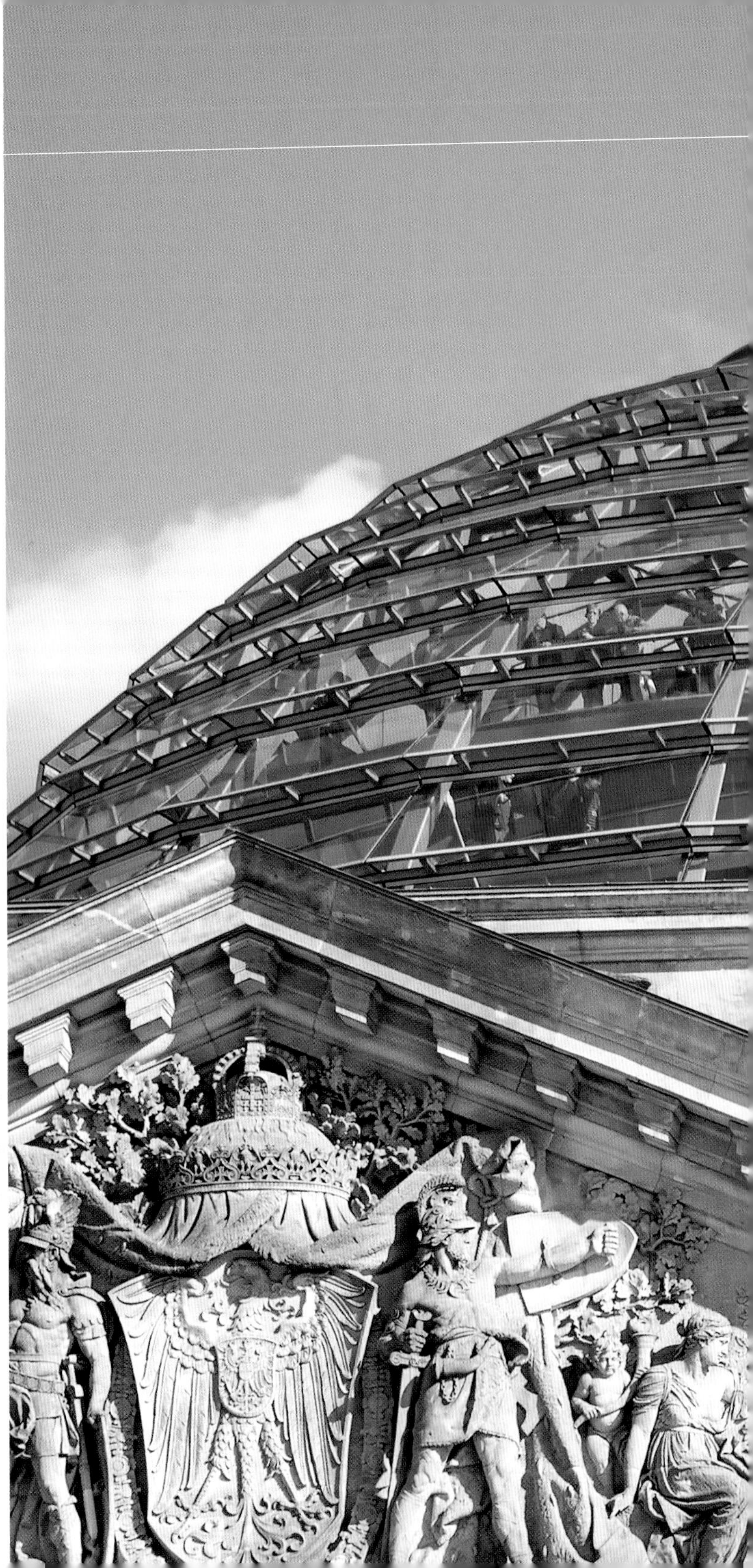

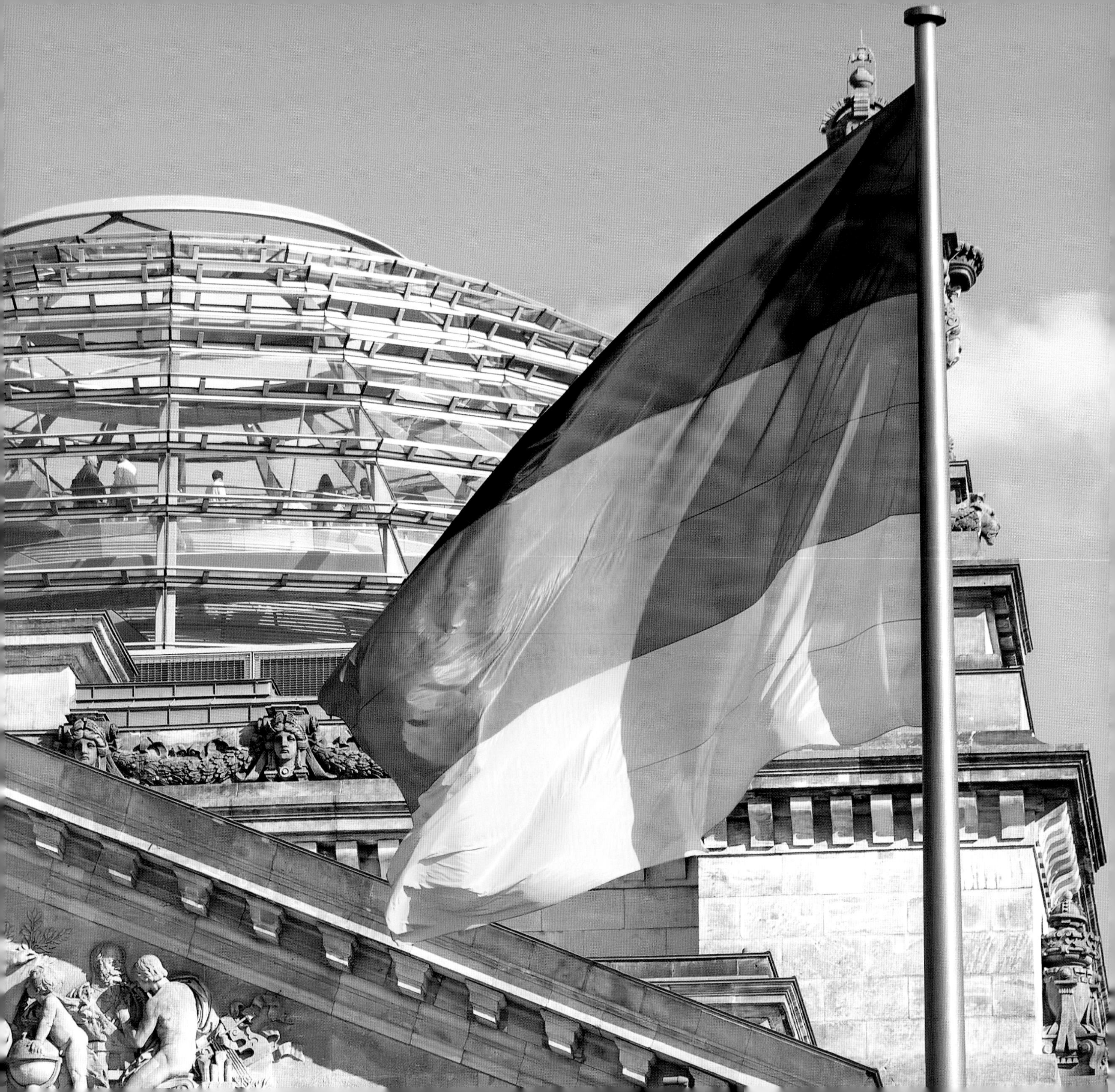

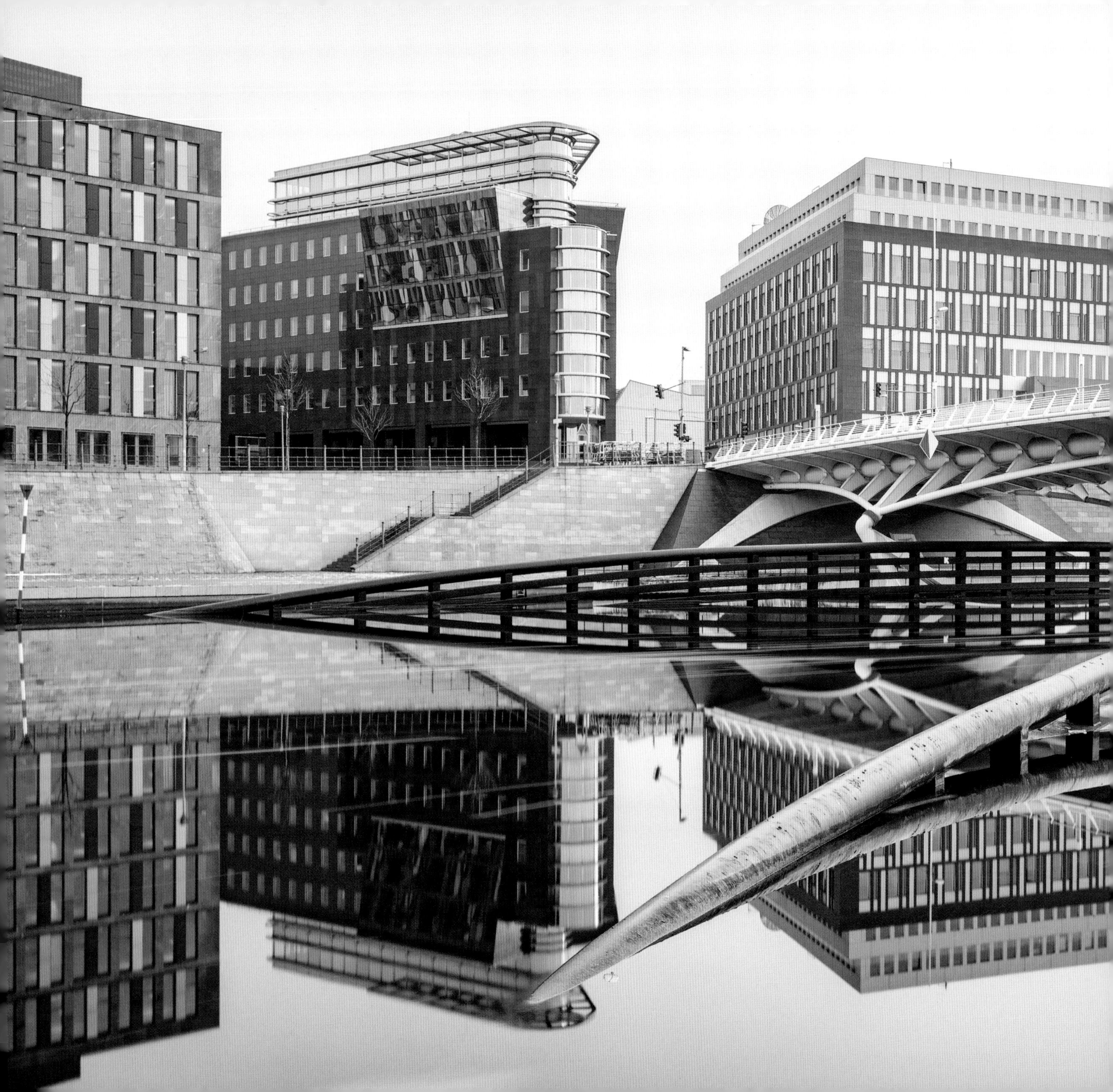

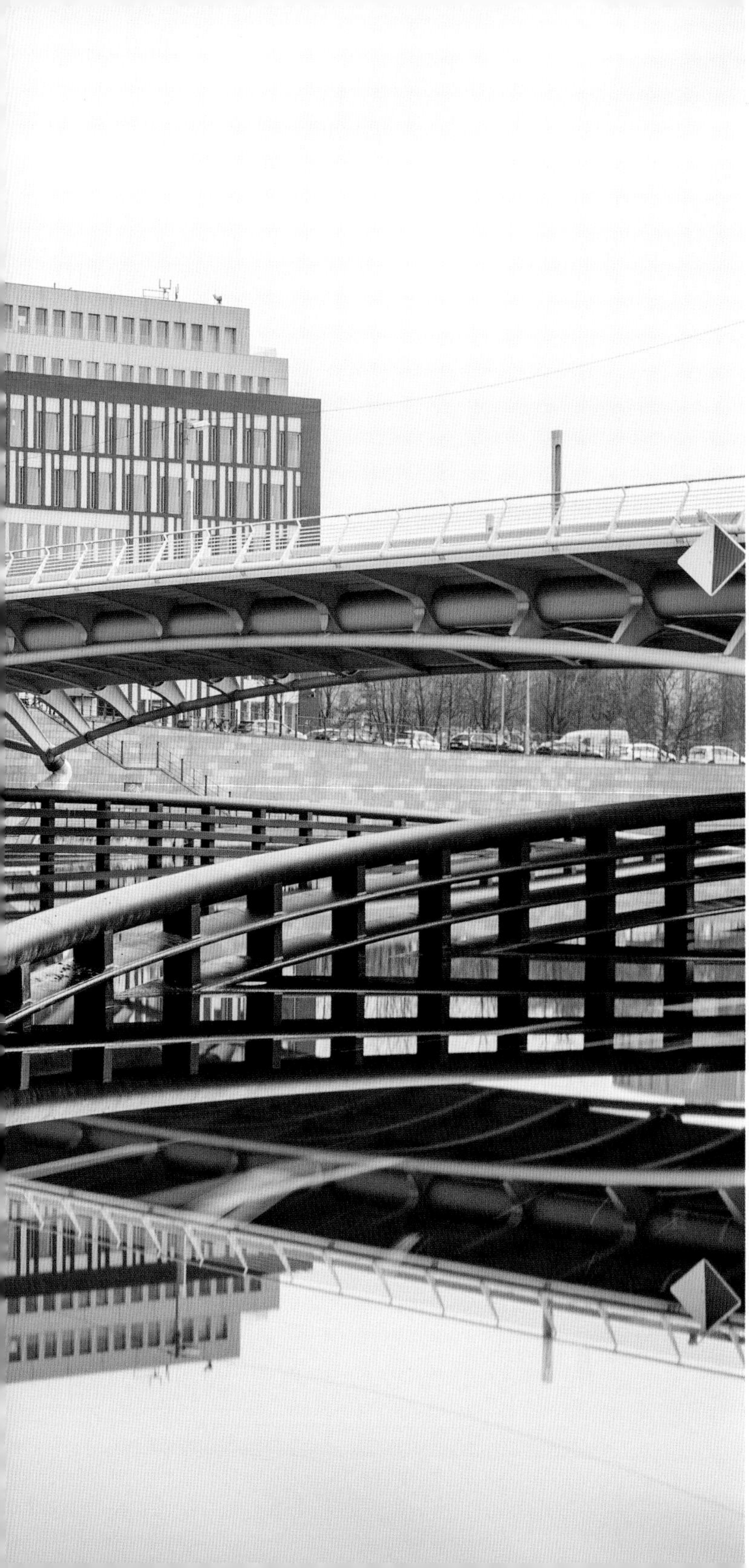

KRONPRINZENBRÜCKE

River Spree, Tiergarten

The Kronprinzenbrücke (Crown Prince Bridge) straddles the River Spree, joining the quarters of Mitte and Tiergarten. Its origins lie back in the early eighteenth century, with the construction of a wooden bridge near the present location, but its great predecessor was the cast iron, timber and granite three-arched bridge constructed between 1877 and 1879, named after the German crown prince, Frederick William (1831–88). This bridge was severely damaged in the Second World War, then actually torn down in 1972 by East Germany, but a new bridge was built between 1992 and 1996, which stands today as a symbol of reunification.

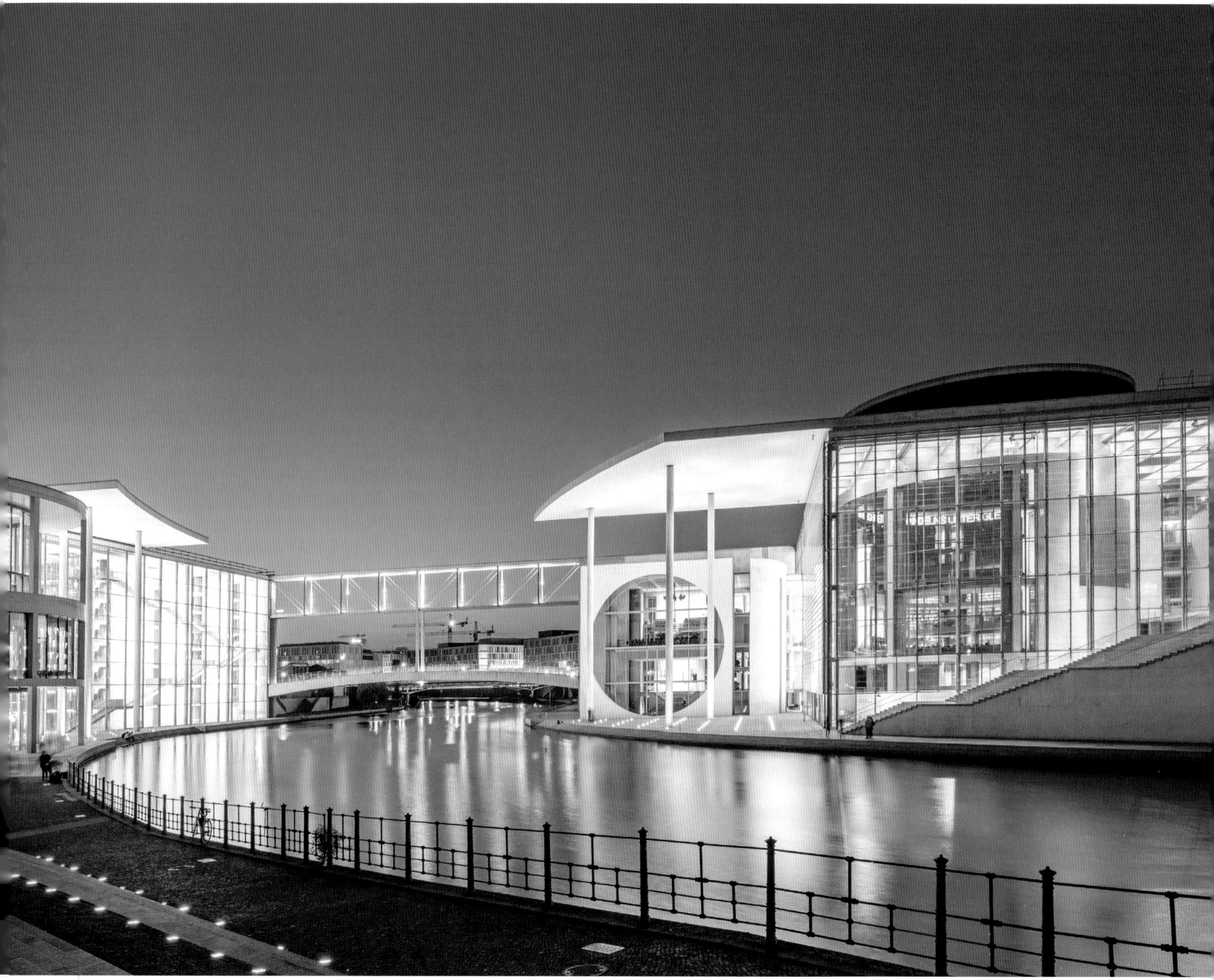

PAUL-LÖBE HAUS AND MARIE-ELISABETH-LÜDERS HAUS

River Spree, Tiergarten

Unified by the vision of Munich-based architect, Stephan Braunfels (b. 1950), the Paul-Löbe Haus and Marie-Elisabeth-Lüders Haus are governmental buildings, on opposite sides of the Spree but linked by a footbridge. The former building, named after SDP politician and Reichstag President (1925–32) Paul-Löbe provides offices and conference rooms for parliamentary personnel and committees. The Marie-Elisabeth-Lüders Haus, its title remembering one of the founder members of the women's rights movement in Germany, is a scientific services centre for the nearby Parliament.

SCHLOSS BELLEVUE

Spreeweg, Tiergarten

This stately neo-classical palace acts, since 1994, as the official residence of the Bundespräsident (German Federal President). It was built in the 1780s, its official function being, from 1786, as a private residence for Frederick the Great's youngest brother, Prince Ferdinand of Prussia (1730–1813). Over the subsequent 100 plus years of history, the building has variously been a royal residence, a school and the State Museum of Ethnology. The object seen in the foreground here is a vintage *Feuermelder* (fire alarm), one of 11 such alarms around Berlin, lovingly restored to its original condition.

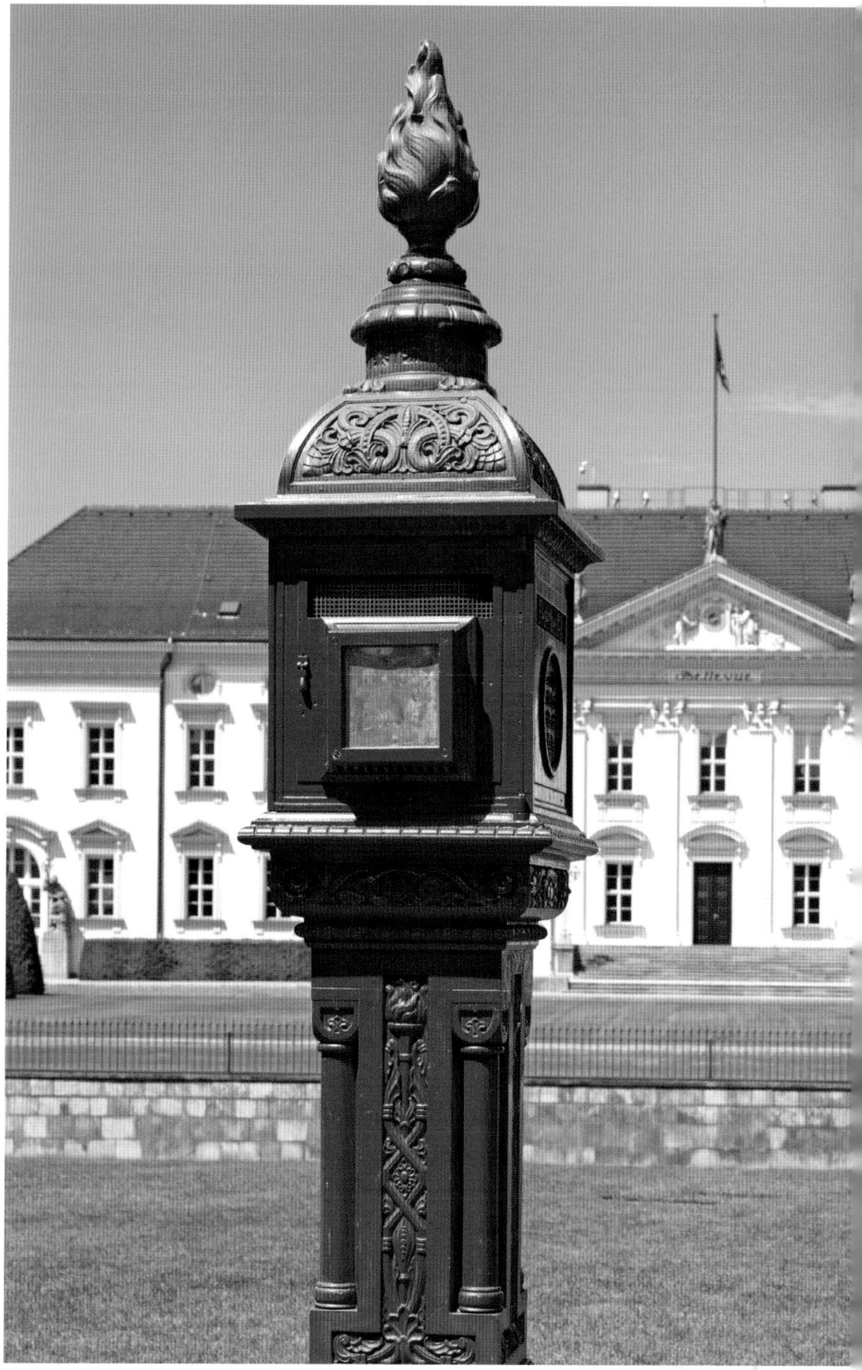

SHELL-HAUS

Reichpietschufer, Potsdamer Platz

An undulating wave of limestone, glass, steel and bronze, the Shell-Haus (Shell House) broke new ground in Berlin's architectural styles, and represented a notable diversion in vision for the normally conservative architect, Professor Emil Fahrenkamp (1885–1966) of the Düsseldorf Academy of Art. The structure was a commission by the Rhenania-Ossag Mineralölwerke AG, a subsidiary of the Shell oil company, and it was raised between 1930 and 1932. Damaged during the war, the building was given listed status in 1958 and then was restored to former glories during the 1990s.

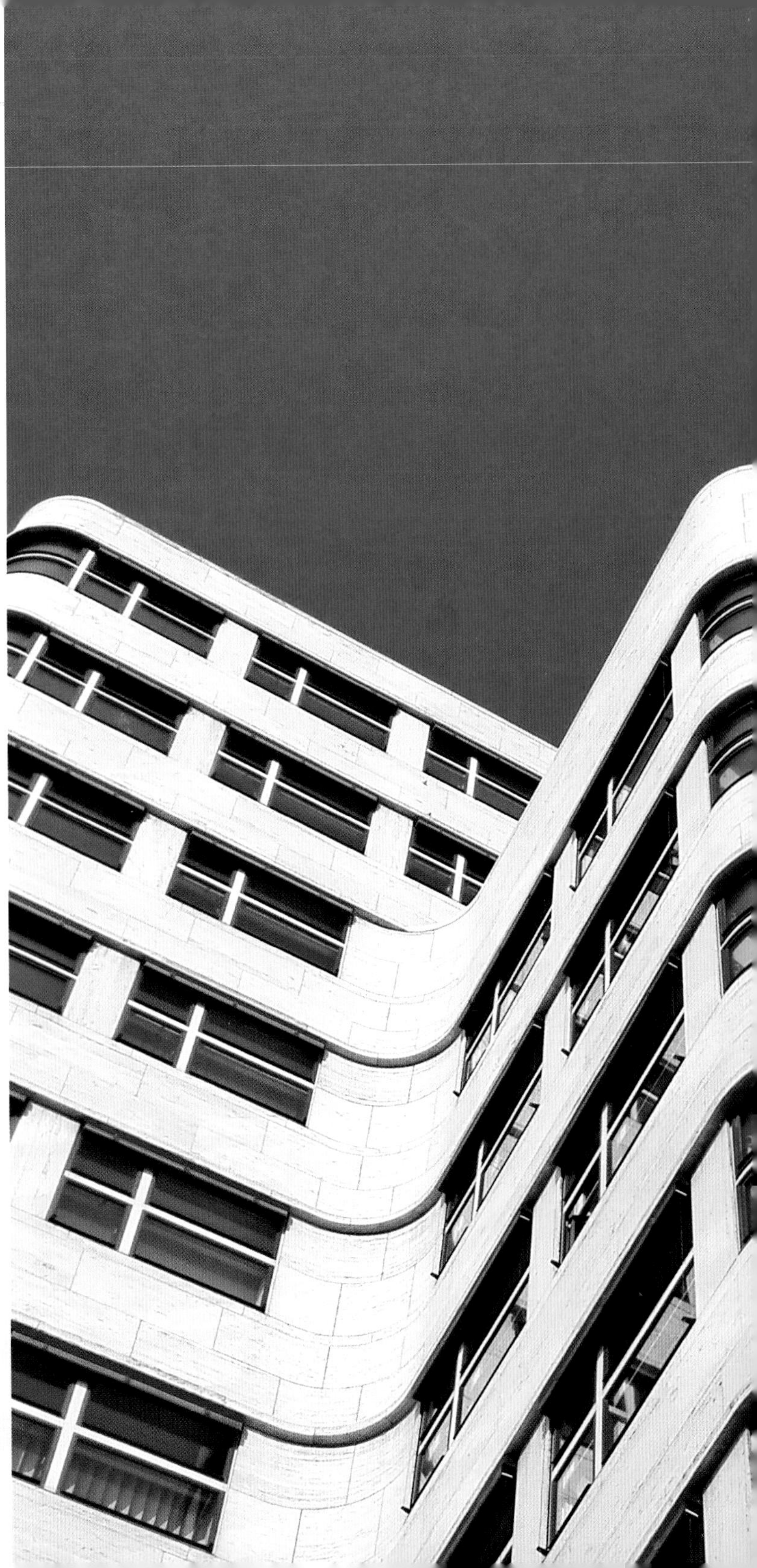

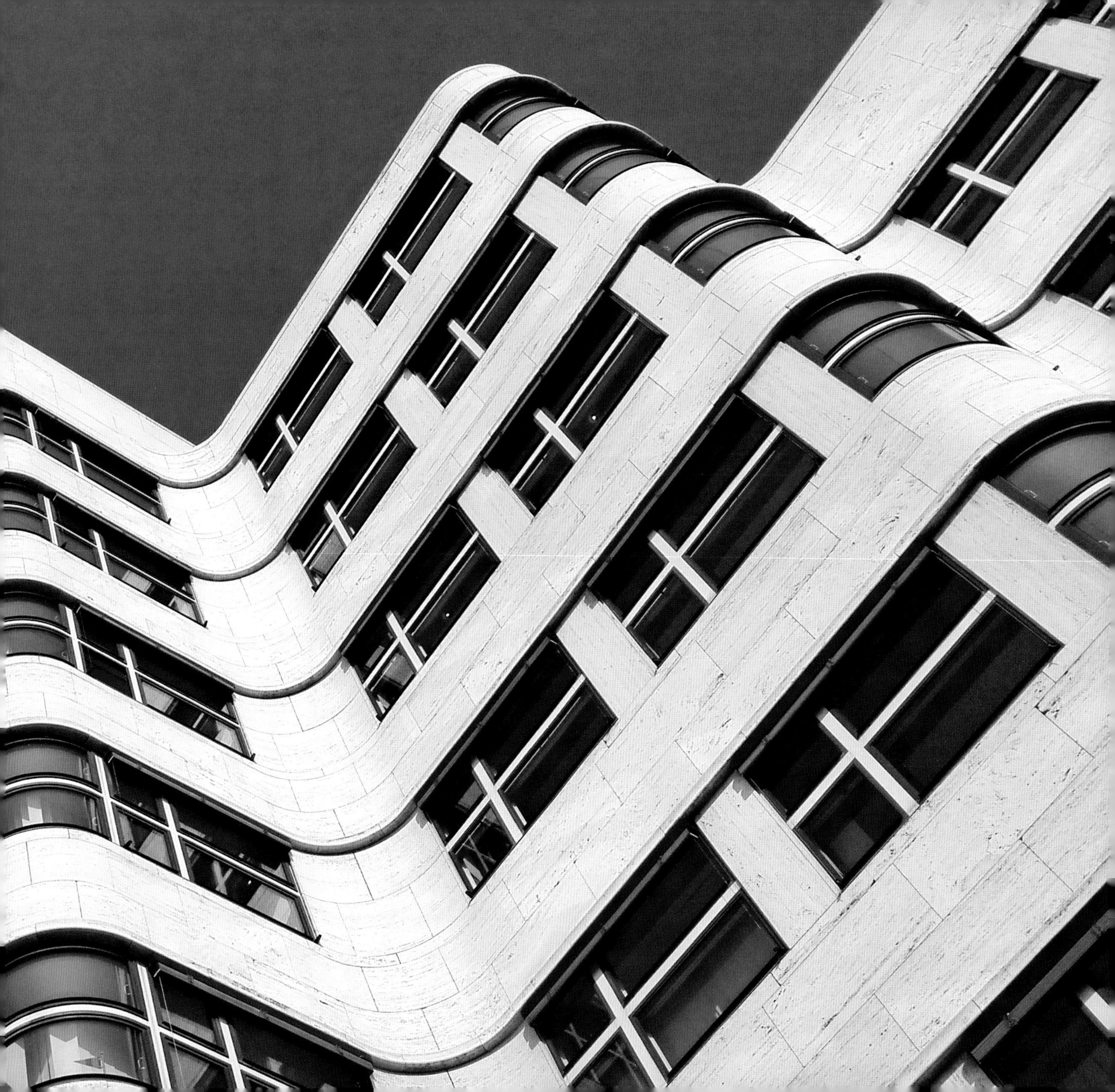

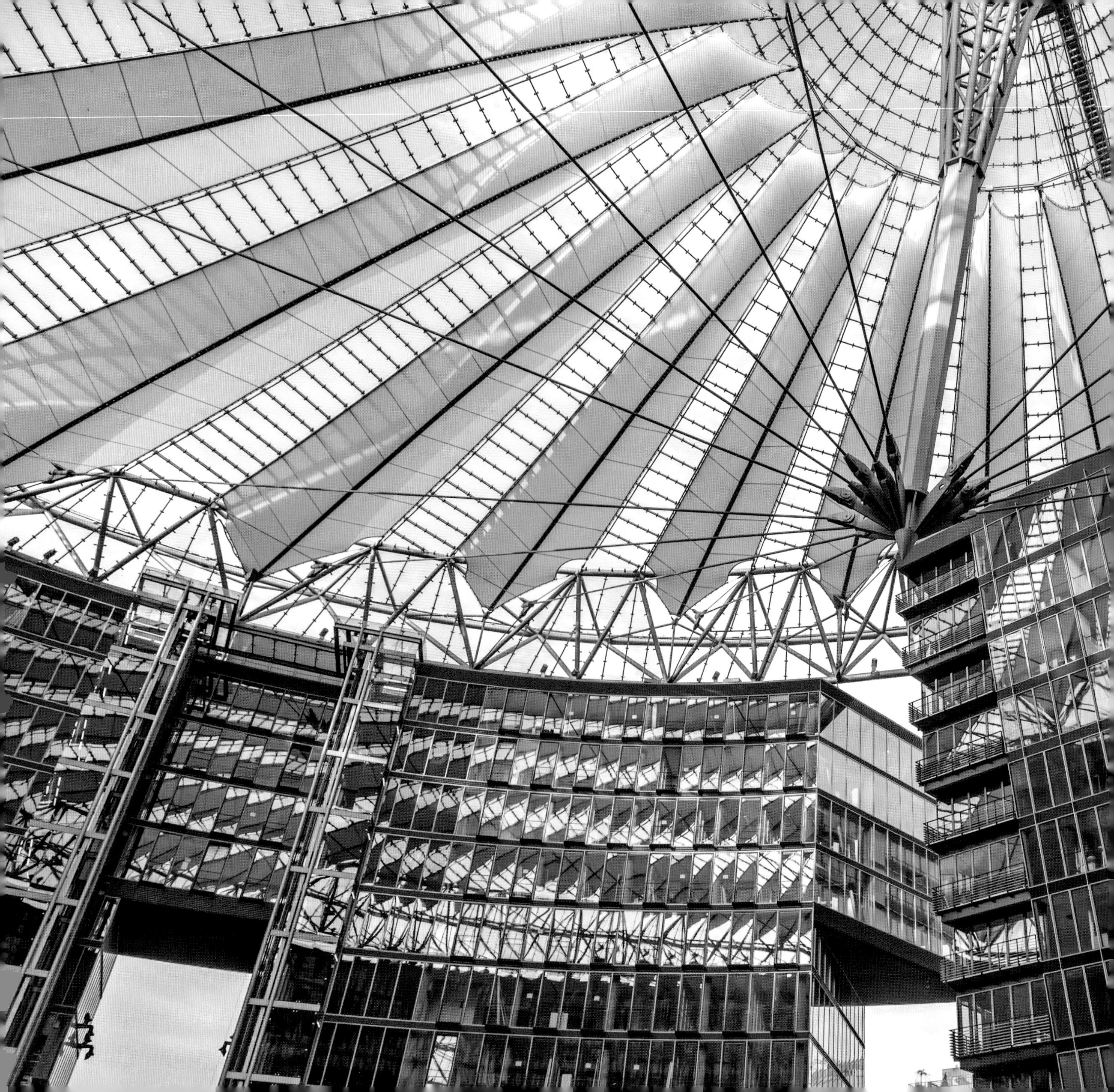

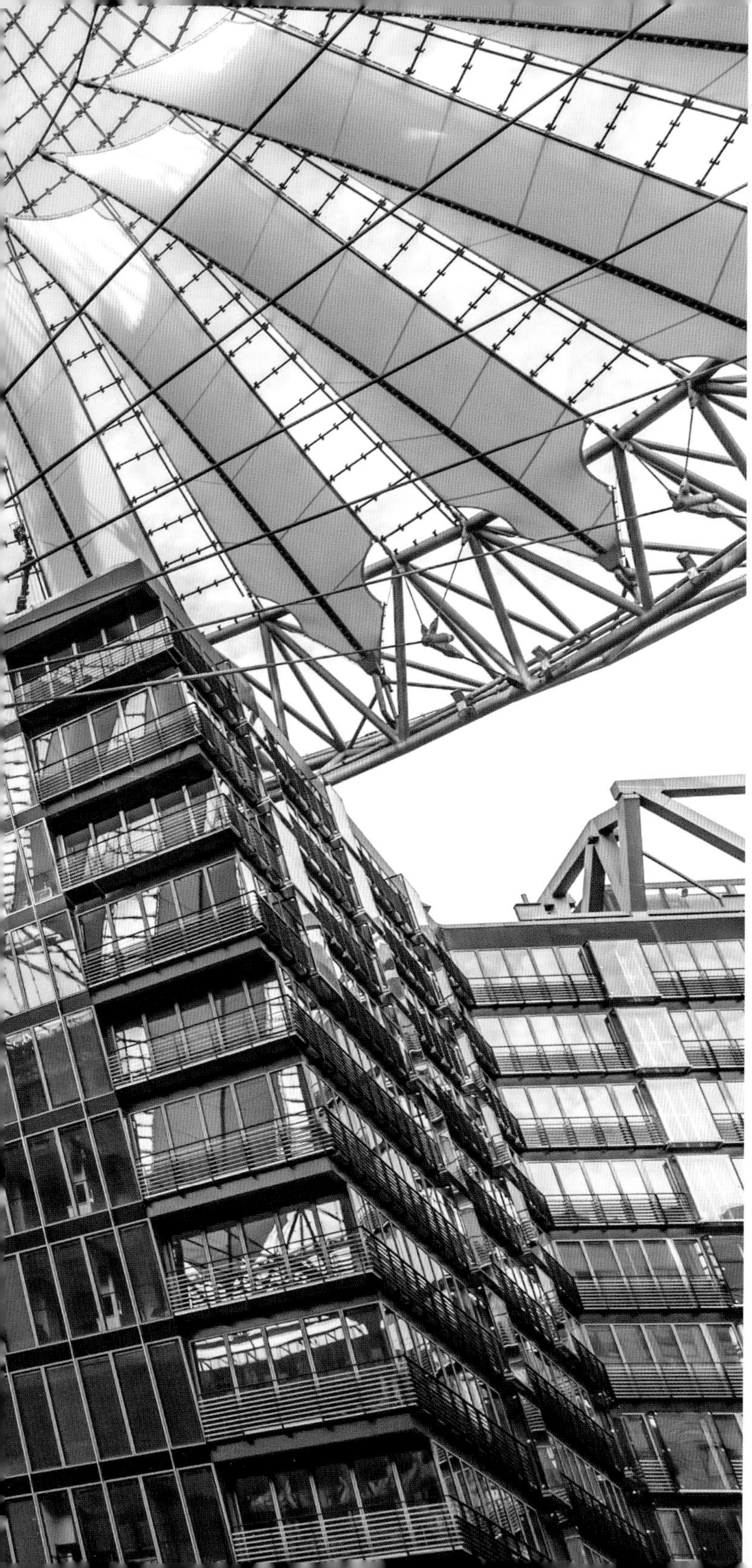

SONY CENTRE

Potsdamer Straße, Potsdamer Platz

As much a vision in light as physical materials, the Sony Centre in the Potsdamer Platz is a building complex emerging from the mind of architect Helmut Jahn (b. 1940). Here we see the central plaza, which has a glass roof supported by spoke-like beams, creating the impression of a giant tent. At night, both the roof and the surrounding buildings are illuminated in a tapestry of bright colours, creating a warm wonderland effect that raises the visitor's eye upwards, as they sit in one of the cafés and restaurants around the plaza.

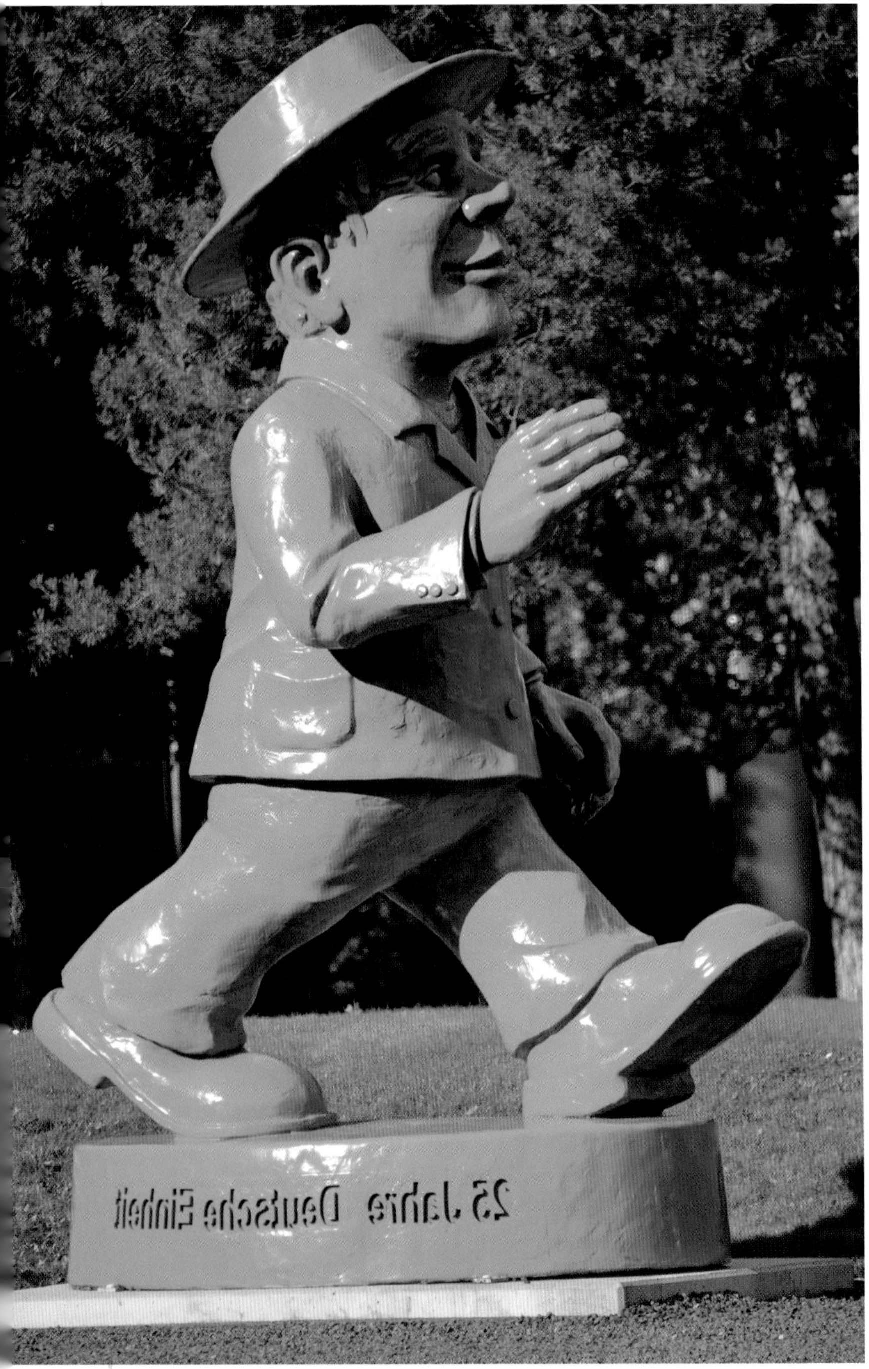

AMPELMANN

Potsdamer Platz

Designed by traffic psychologist Karl Peglau (1927–2009) during the 1960s, Ampelmännchen traffic signal figures – familiar and friendly, with the behatted 'walk' figure jauntily striding – became much-loved icons of life in East Berlin. After reunification, it seemed that the figures might simply disappear, but instead they were resurrected by the Ampelmann company under Markus Heckhausen, channelling the designs into a world of new products. The statue here was created by artist Ottmar Horl (b. 1950) as part of an exhibition celebrating 25 years of German reunification.

GRENZWACHTURM

Erna-Berger-Straße, Potsdamer Platz

This forbidding concrete BT-6 Grenzwachturm (watchtower) was erected in 1971, one of more than 200 such structures built by the communist GDR to keep a keen eye over the border between east and west and over nearby government ministries. It was designed to give a 360-degree viewing platform at tree-top height. Once inside the viewing area, accessed by two iron ladders that visitors can climb to this day, the soldiers inside did eight-hour shifts of vigilance, firearms at the ready to shoot any who tried to make the crossing.

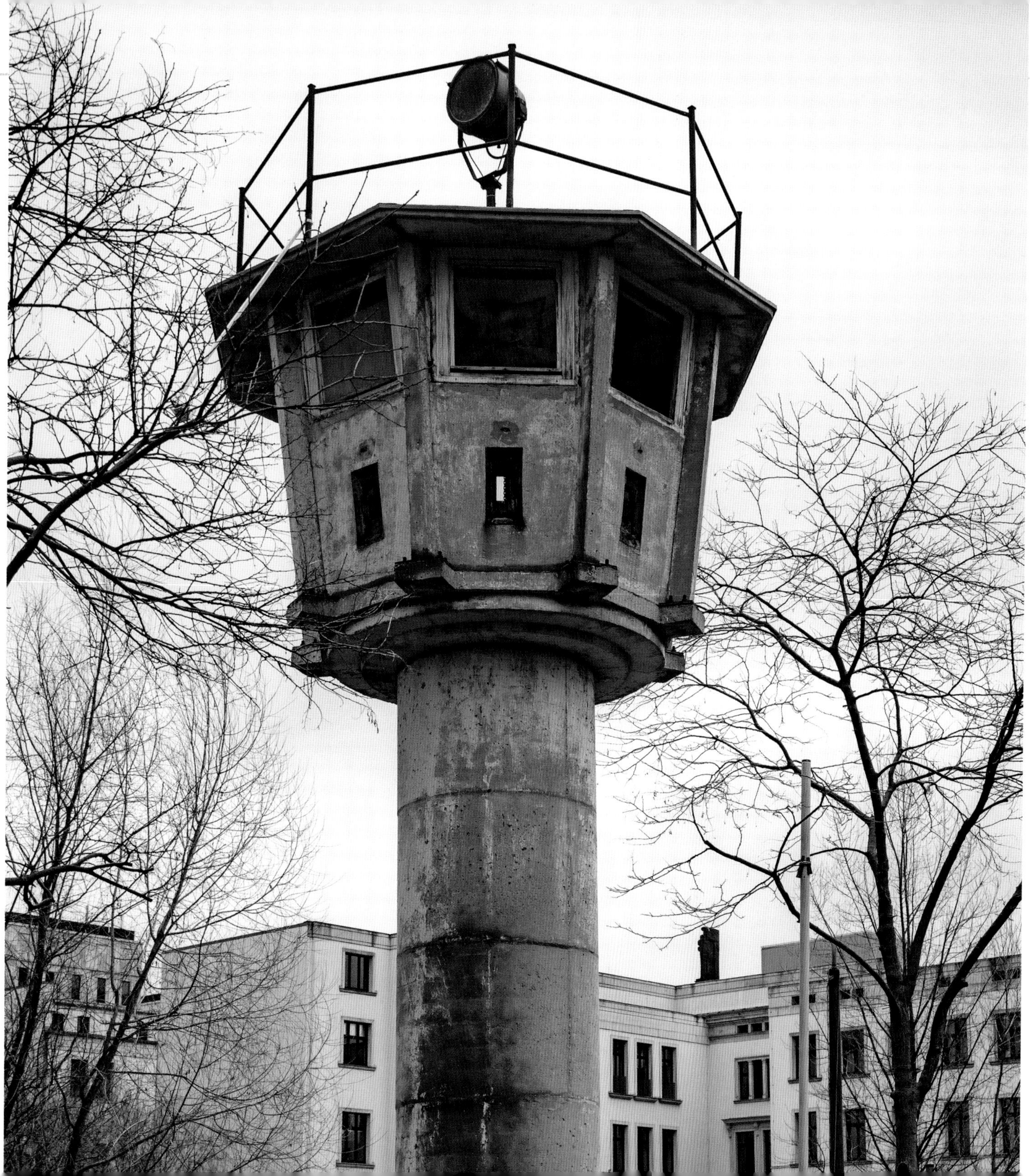

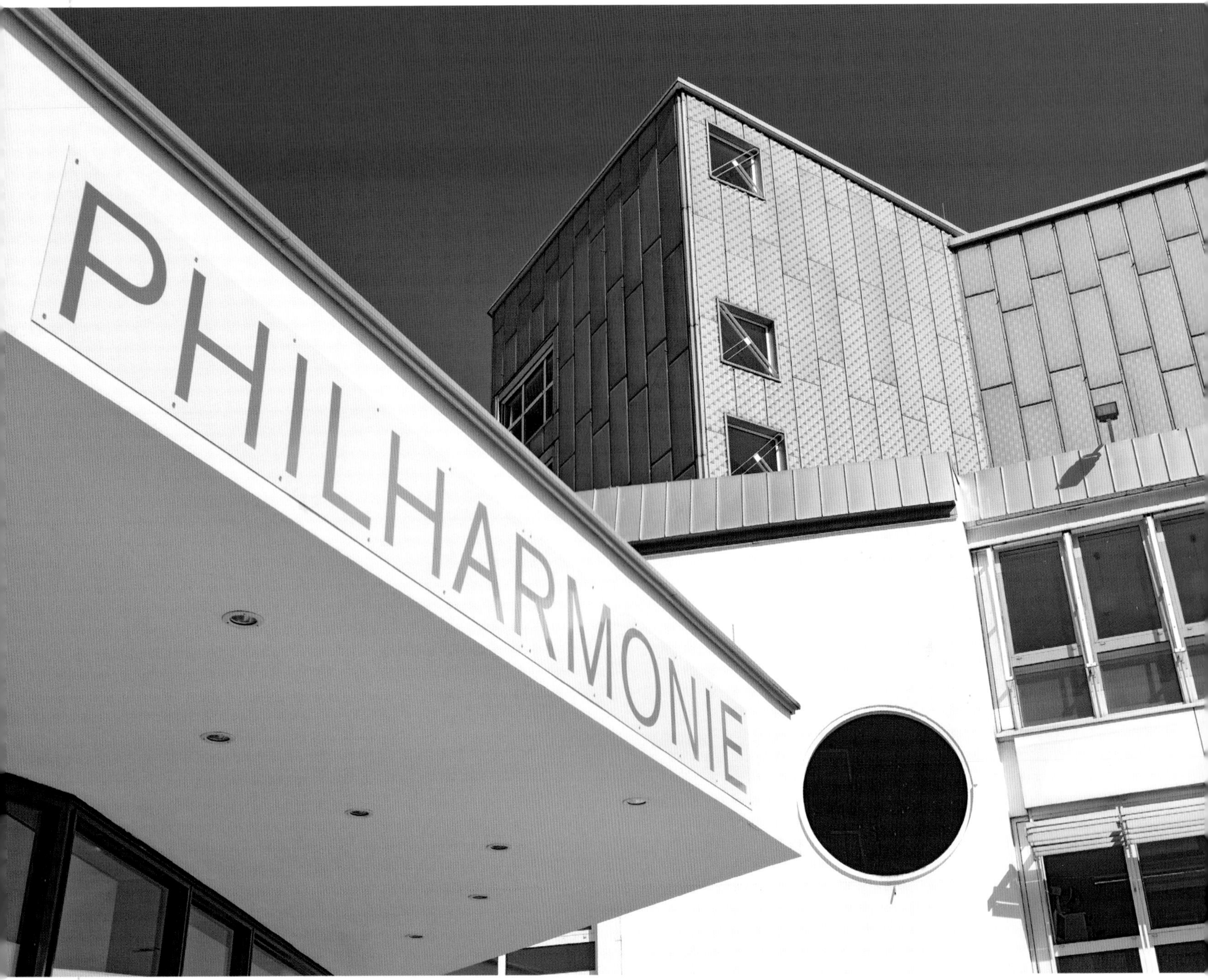
PHILHARMONIE

BERLIN PHILHARMONIE

Herbert-von-Karajan-Straße, Kulturforum

From the outside, the Berlin Philharmonie concert hall shows the architectural innovation for which the 1960s is known, the curious tent-like profile being the vision of expressionist architect Bernhard Hans Henry Scharoun (1893–1972). It is the physical home of the Berlin Philharmonic Orchestra, one of the world's leading orchestras, and has two primary venues – a 2,440-seat Großer Saal (Grand Hall) and a 1,180-seat Kammermusiksaal (Chamber Music Hall). When the Philharmonie opened on 15 October 1963, the great conductor Herbert von Karajan (1908–89) led the moment musically with Beethoven's Ninth Symphony.

HERCULES

Reichpietschufer, Potsdamer Platz

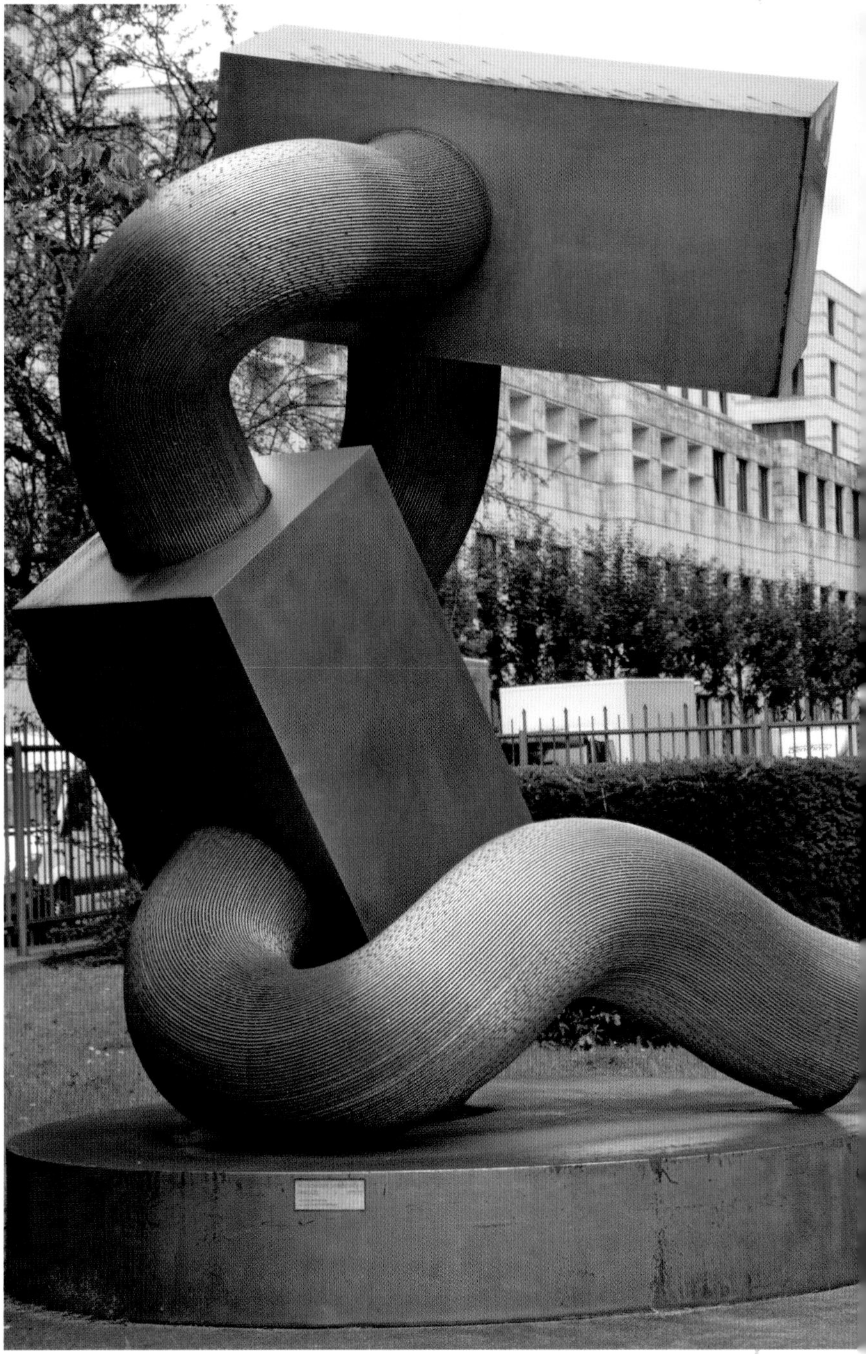

Created by the husband-and-wife sculpting team, Brigitte Matschinsky-Denninghoff (1921–2011) and Martin Matschinsky (b. 1921), Hercules evokes industrial strength and power, the connectors between the blocks suggesting giant, sinewy limbs. Brigitte and Martin are also known for their statue 'Berlin' on the Tauentzienstraße, which can be seen later in this book on page 152. Hercules sits in the grounds of the Wissenschaftszentrum Berlin für Sozialforschung (WZB Berlin Social Science Centre), an organization founded in 1969 to research important social and political issues.

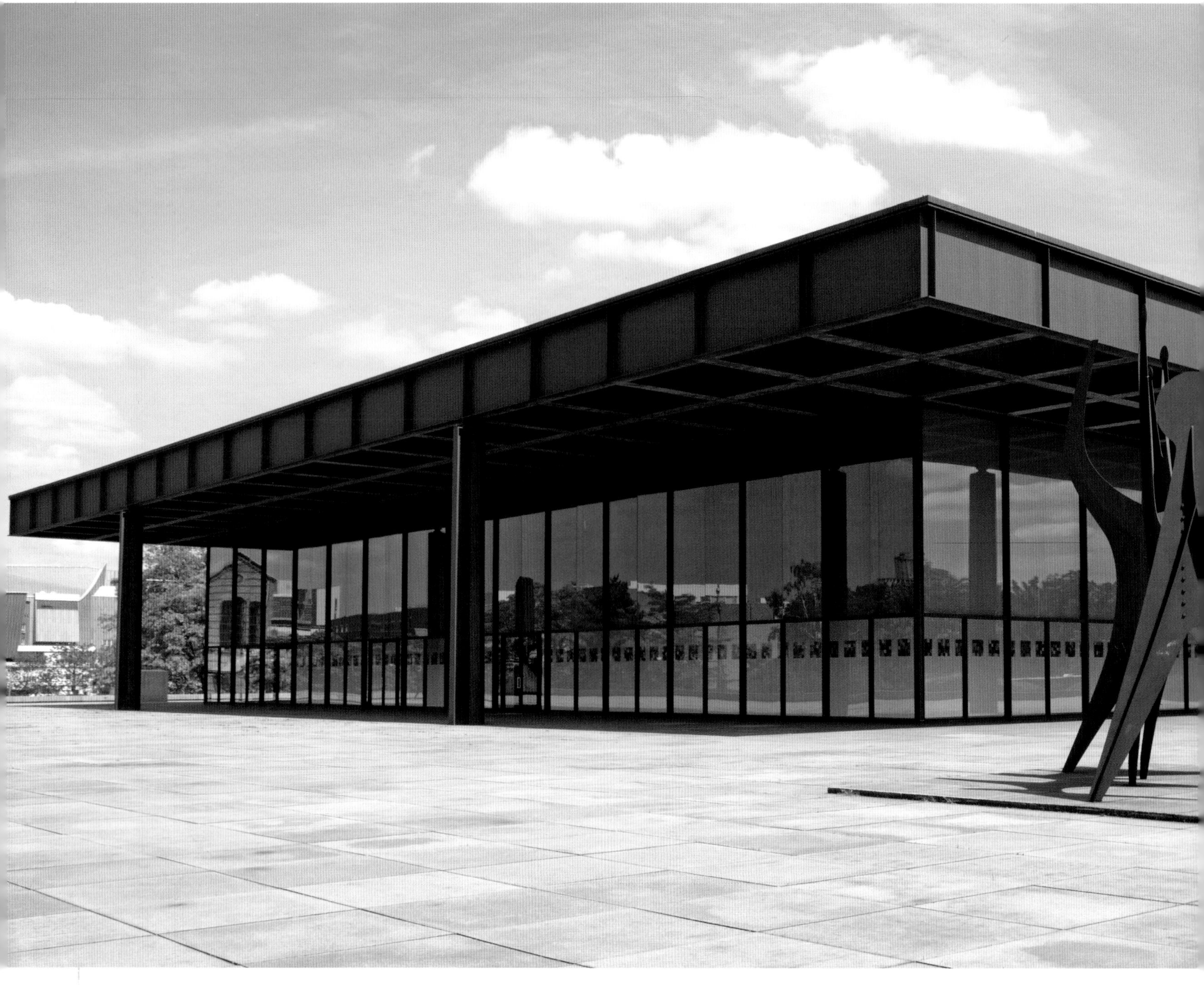

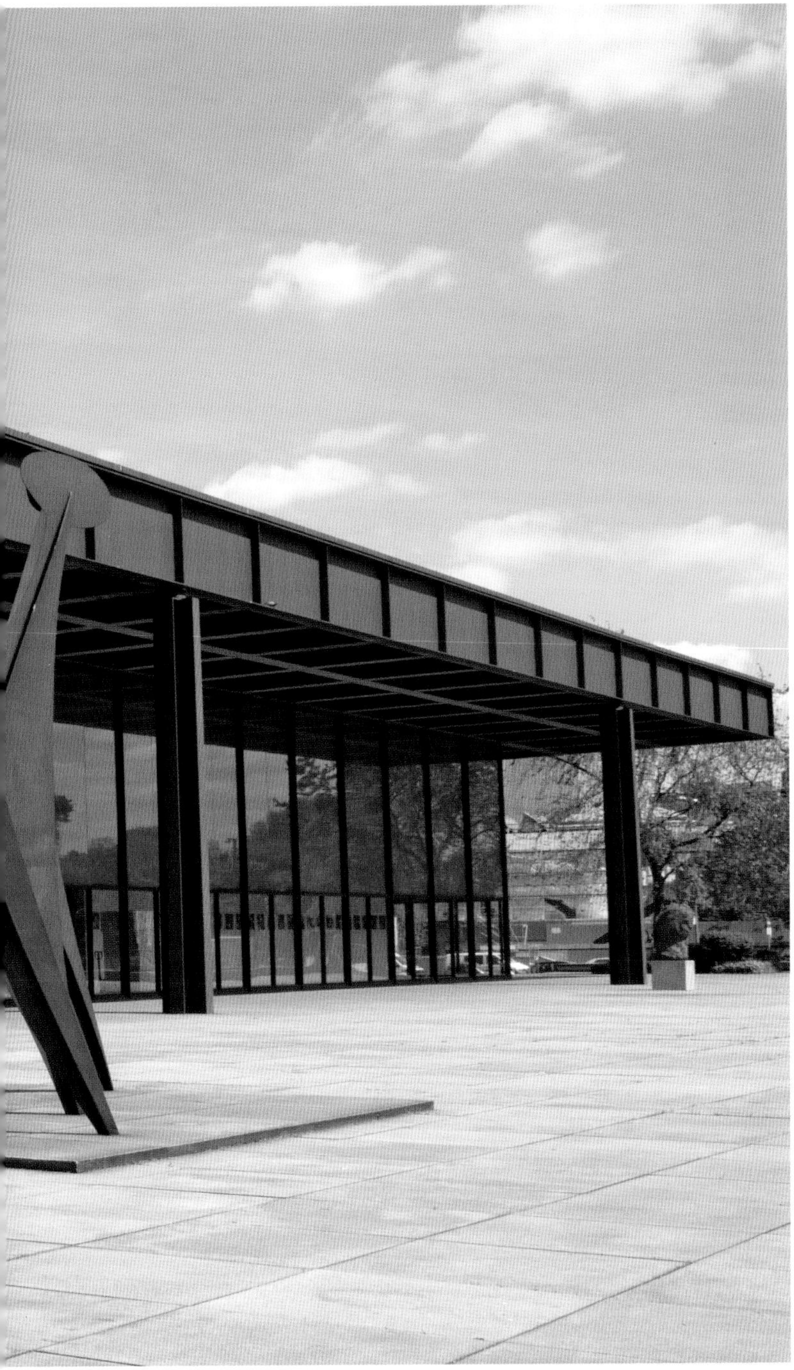

NEUE NATIONALGALERIE

Potsdamer Straße, Kulturforum

The Neue Nationalgalerie (New National Gallery) opened in 1968 as a landmark venue for the display of modern art. In keeping with the collections inside, the building itself represented future thinking, being a low glass pavilion created by none other than the great Ludwig Mies Van Der Rohe (1886–1969), who built upon some of his previous unrealized ideas to create this space of air and light. Inside, the museum displays work from many of the defining artists of the twentieth and twenty-first centuries, including Otto Dix, Pablo Picasso, Ernst Ludwig Kirchner, Andy Warhol, Paul Klee, Max Ernst, Salvador Dalí, Francis Bacon, Edvard Munch, Gerhard Richter, Richard Serra and Thomas Schütte.

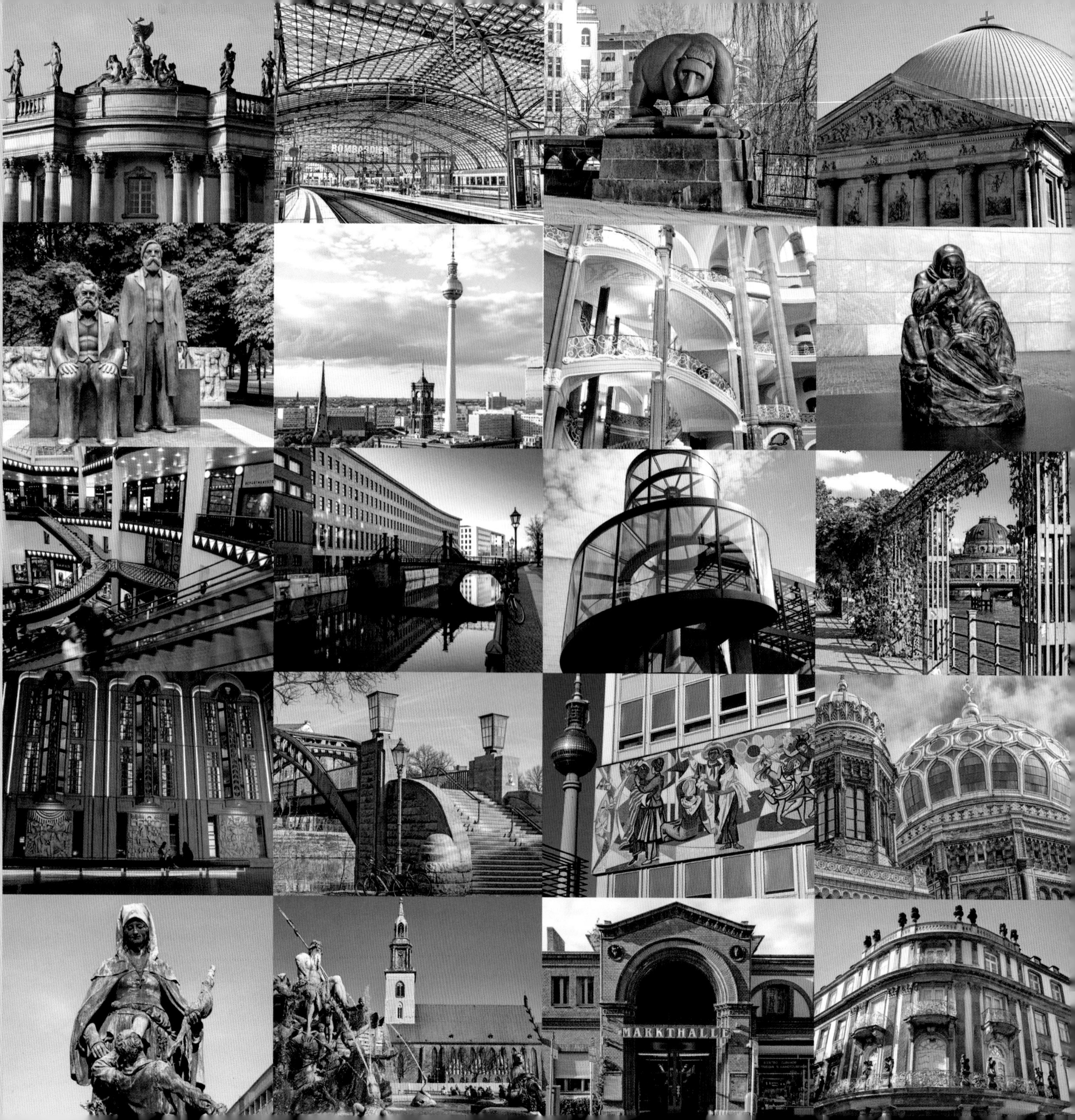
BOMBARDIER
MARKTHALLE

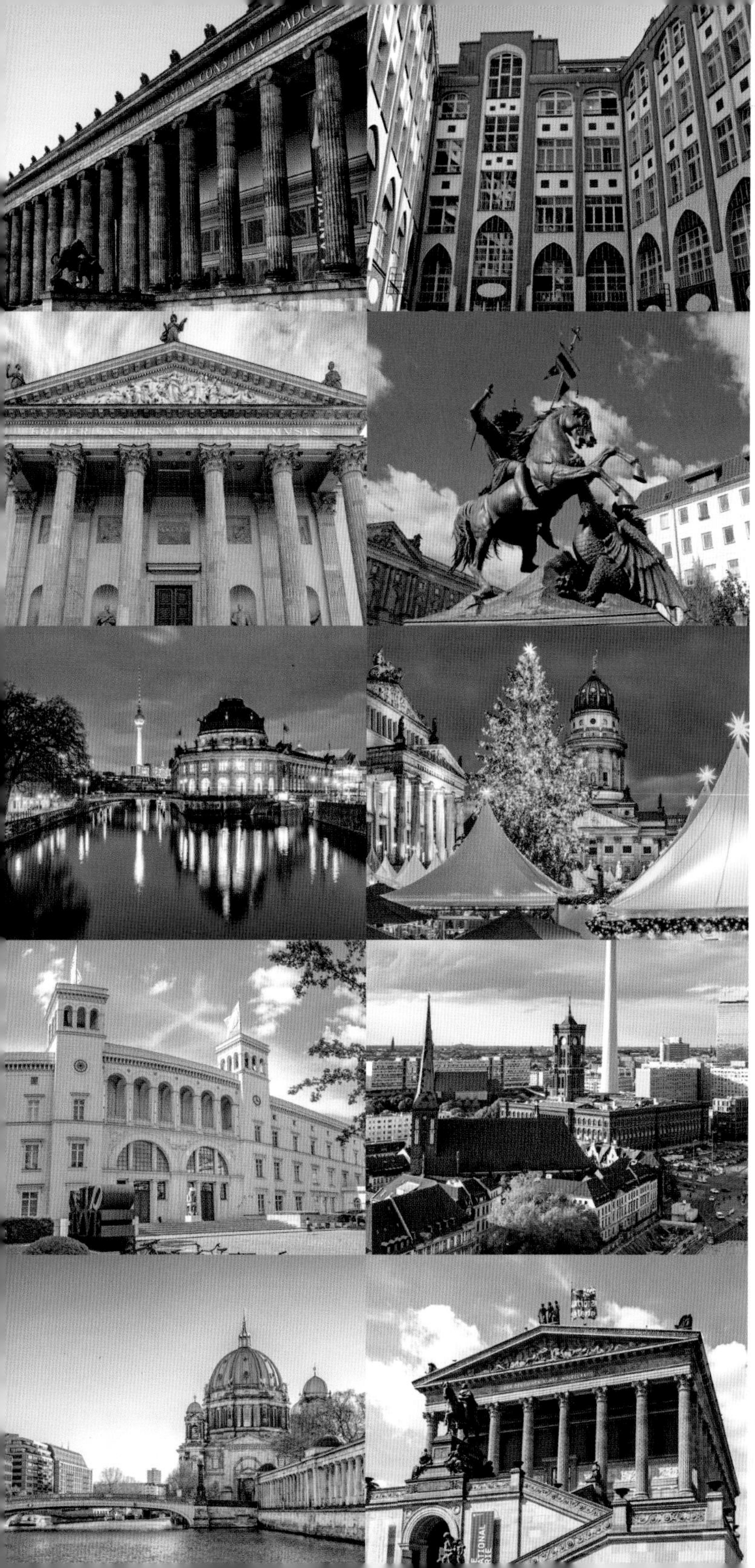

MITTE

The Mitte district of Berlin is in many ways the cultural and physical heart of Berlin, not only home to many of the city's great monuments and buildings, but also culturally diverse and expressive. It consists of six subdistricts, specifically Mitte proper, Tiergarten, Hansaviertel, Moabit, Wedding and Gesundbrunnen. Here is where much of Berlin's visible history survives, not least because this is the site of the first small settlements along the Spree, which over time burgeoned into a capital city.

For those who want culture and history, Mitte has an almost inexhaustible supply of attractions, from the imperial and political authority of the government quarter through to the educational concentration on Museum Island. The museums in the area frequently put on special exhibitions with quirky topics, from spying to the history of computers, and art galleries proliferate, showing every conceivable artistic genre and style. The district is also dotted with points of evidence referring to the Cold War, including concrete watchtowers. Yet Mitte is also a centre for shopping, eating and partying, with enough delights and attractions to hold anyone's attention for days at a time. Just remember to visit the rest of the city!

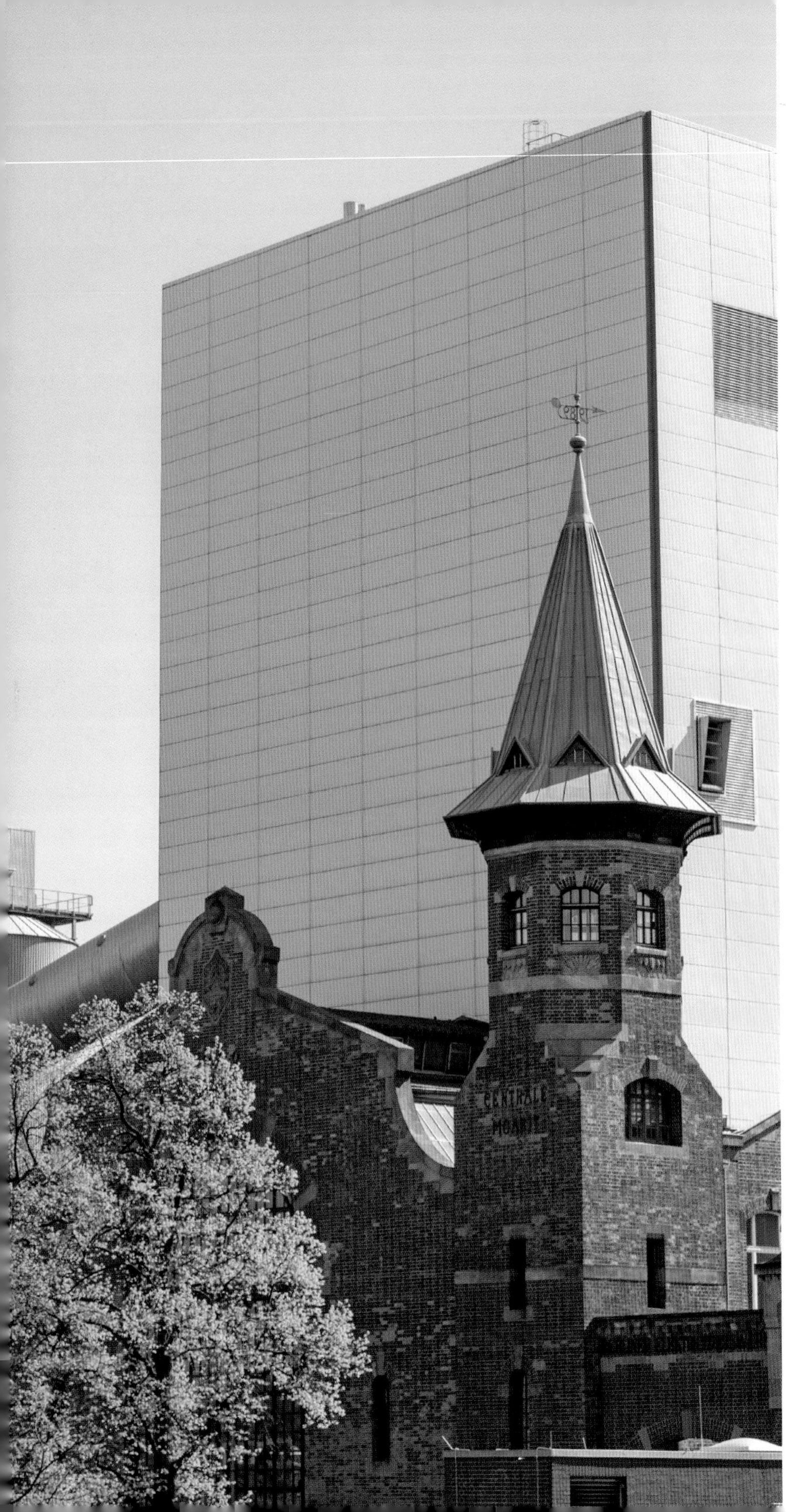

KRAFTWERK MOABIT

Friedrich-Krause-Ufer, Moabit

The old and new sit side-by-side in the Kraftwerk Moabit (Moabit Powerplant). The original powerplant, evidenced in the red-brick buildings in the foreground here, were built from 1899 to 1901 by Berliner Elektricitäts-Werke, and the technologies used in power generation were successively upgraded to keep up with the city's rapidly expanding demands for electricity. A major reconstruction of the site was undertaken in the 1980s, resulting in the demolition of many of the old buildings, apart from the listed examples still seen.

ARMINIUSHALLE

Arminiusstraße, Moabit

The Arminiushalle (Arminius Market Hall) is a historic building in the Moabit district, the fabric of the 1891 red-brick structure beautifully preserved to give a flavour of old Berlin. Such was the destruction in Berlin between 1943 and 1945, that few original market halls survived into the post-war period, hence the special value of this location. Inside, the hall is packed with cafés, restaurants, bars, shops and small businesses, making it a place to explore at leisure, discovering new attractions in every corner.

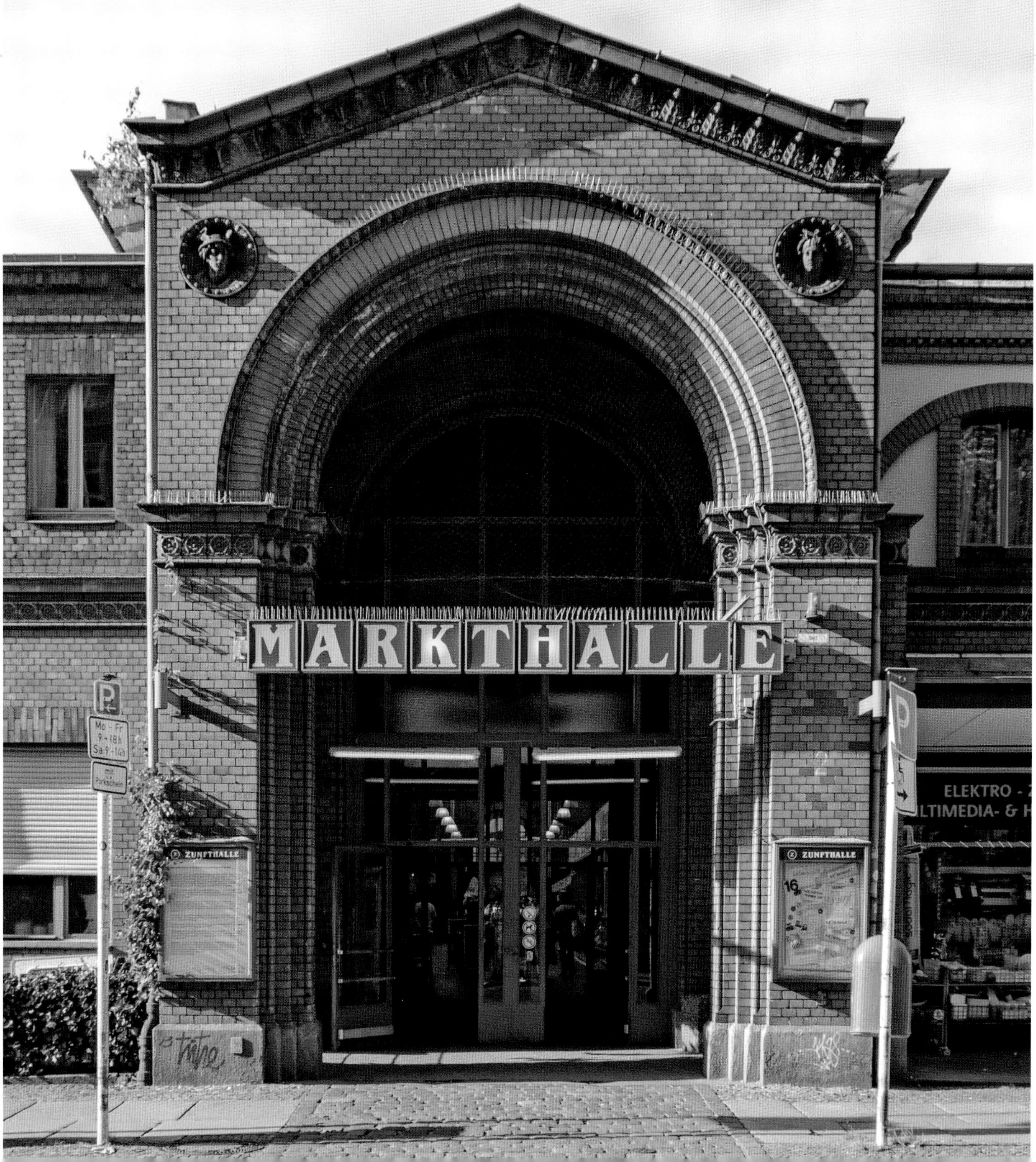
MARKTHALLE
ZUNFTHALLE
ZUNFTHALLE

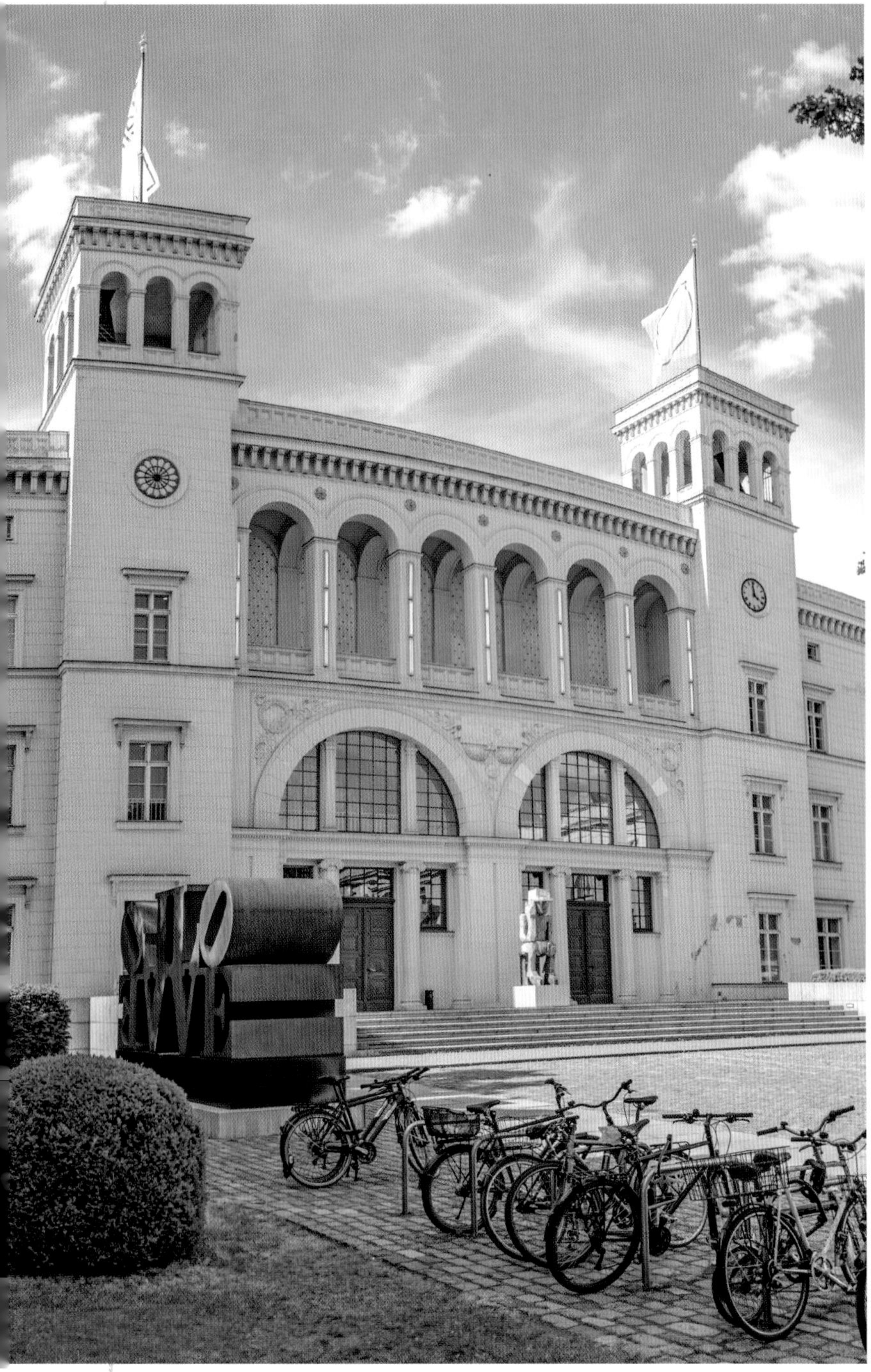

HAMBURGER BAHNHOF

Invalidenstraße, Moabit

Although the grand Hamburger Bahnhof is today, and has been since 1996, the Museum für Gegenwart (Museum of Contemporary Art), the building itself originally had a far more utilitarian purpose. It was originally a terminus on the Berlin–Hamburg Railway, built in 1846–47. Although by 1884 it had ceased to operate in that capacity, its opulent neo-classical style suited it to other purposes, and in 1906 it became the Royal Museum of Building and Transport. Severely damaged in the Second World War bombings, and awkwardly administered in the Cold War era, the building was finally refurbished in the 1990s to become the art museum we see today, housing many important collections.

BERLIN HAUPTBAHNHOF

Europaplatz, Moabit

The Berlin Hauptbahnhof (Berlin Central Station) opened on 26 May 2006, on the site of the station formerly known as the Lehrter Stadtbahnhof. It is an undeniably spectacular affair, referred to by some as a 'cathedral of transport'. The architect was Meinhard von Gerkan (b. 1935), although building realities during the 11 years of construction modified his plans somewhat. The defining feature is the 321-m (1,053-ft) long glass hall that covers the east–west rail lines; a 160-m (525-ft) long by 40-m (131-ft) wide concourse shields the north–south lines. The overall impression is of lofty heights and abundant natural light.

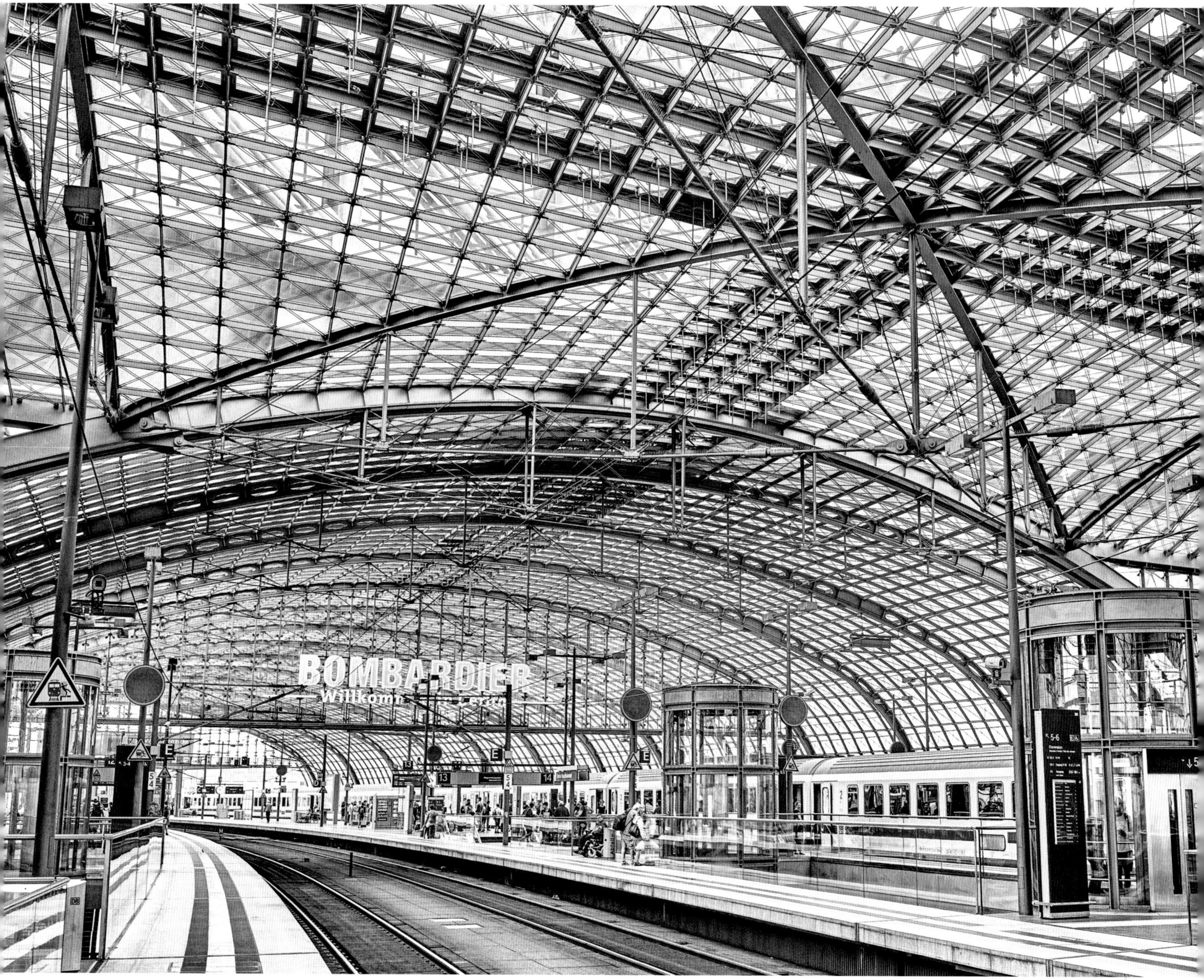
BOMBARDIER

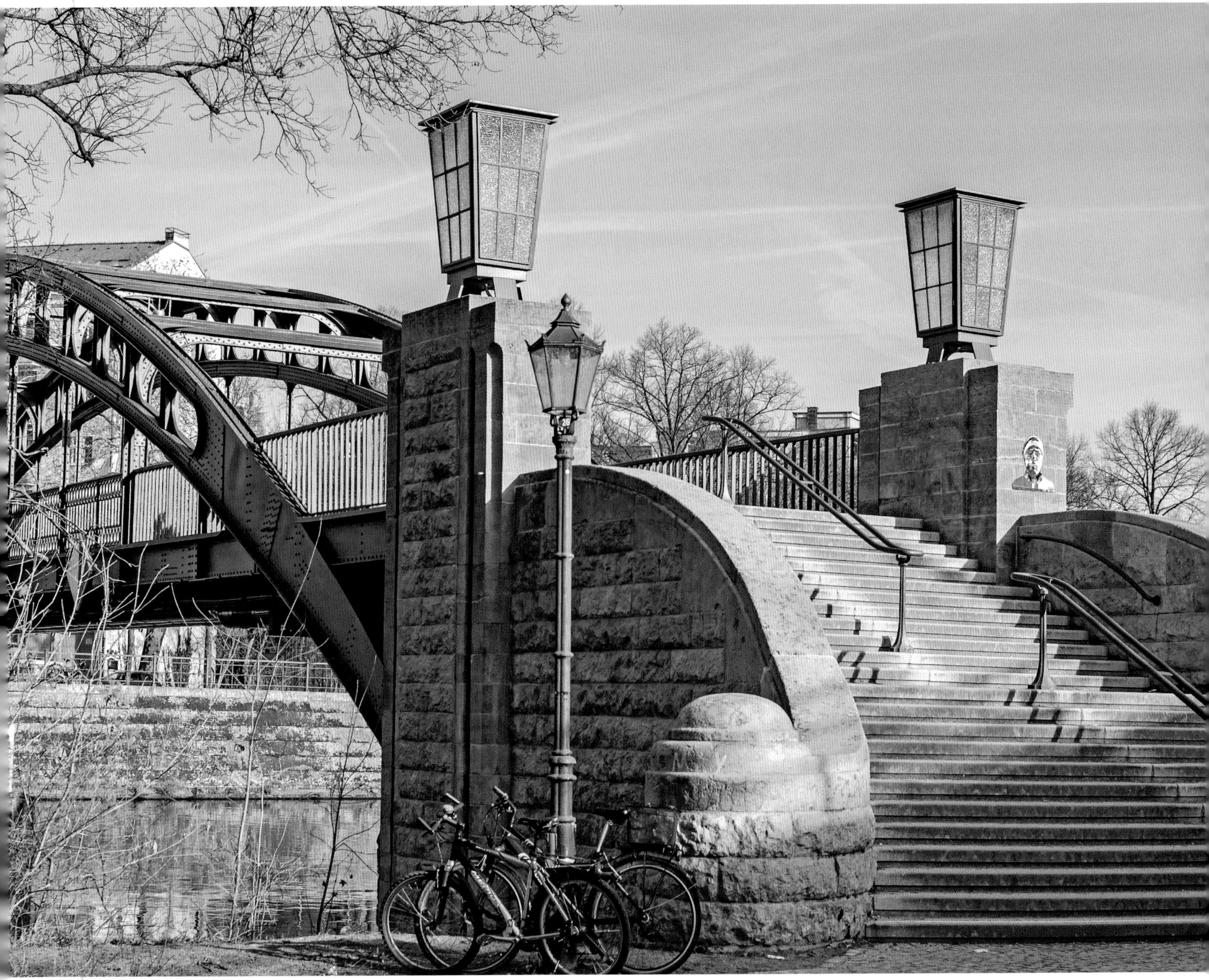

GERICKESTEG

River Spree, Moabit

The Gerickesteg pedestrian bridge across the Spree is a two-hinged arched bridge built during the first two years (1914–15) of the First World War, developed by the architect and urban planner Bruno Möhring (1863–1929). Its main span is of 52 m (170 ft), of a total length of c. 70 m (230 ft). During the dreadful days of the battle of Berlin in April 1945, German forces blew up the bridge to cut a crossing point for advancing Soviet troops, but the structure was restored in a major building project after the war.

MOABITER BRÜCKE

River Spree, Moabit

Another Spree crossing, the Moabiter Brücke (Moabiter Bridge) is a broad and strong stone construction, also known as the Bärenbrücke (Bear Bridge) on account of the four cast iron bear sculptures that grace its span. These were designed by sculptor Günter Anlauf (1924–2000), and installed in 1981. Berlin is a city of many bridges, mainly crossing the Spree, which runs on a south-east to north-west axis through the heart of the capital, and across the Havel to the east.

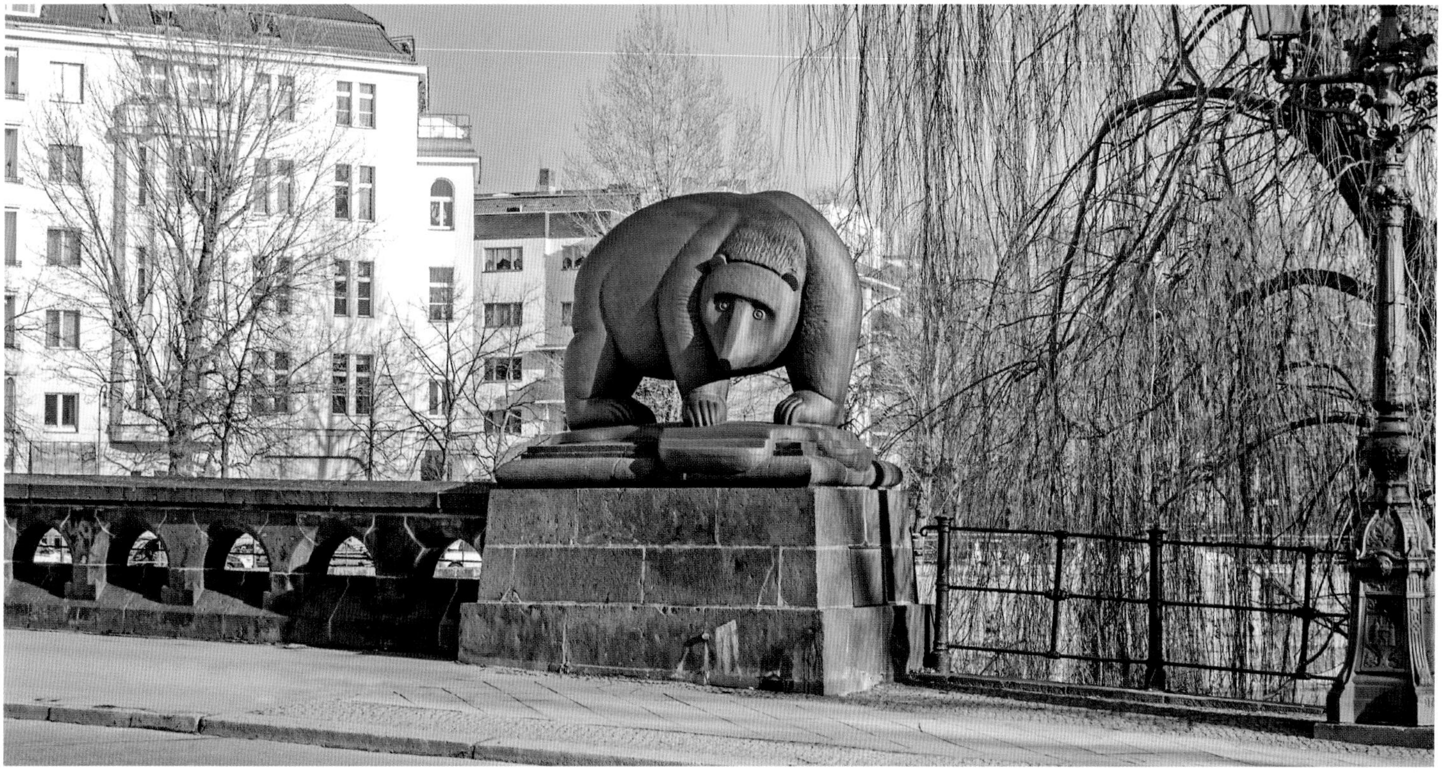

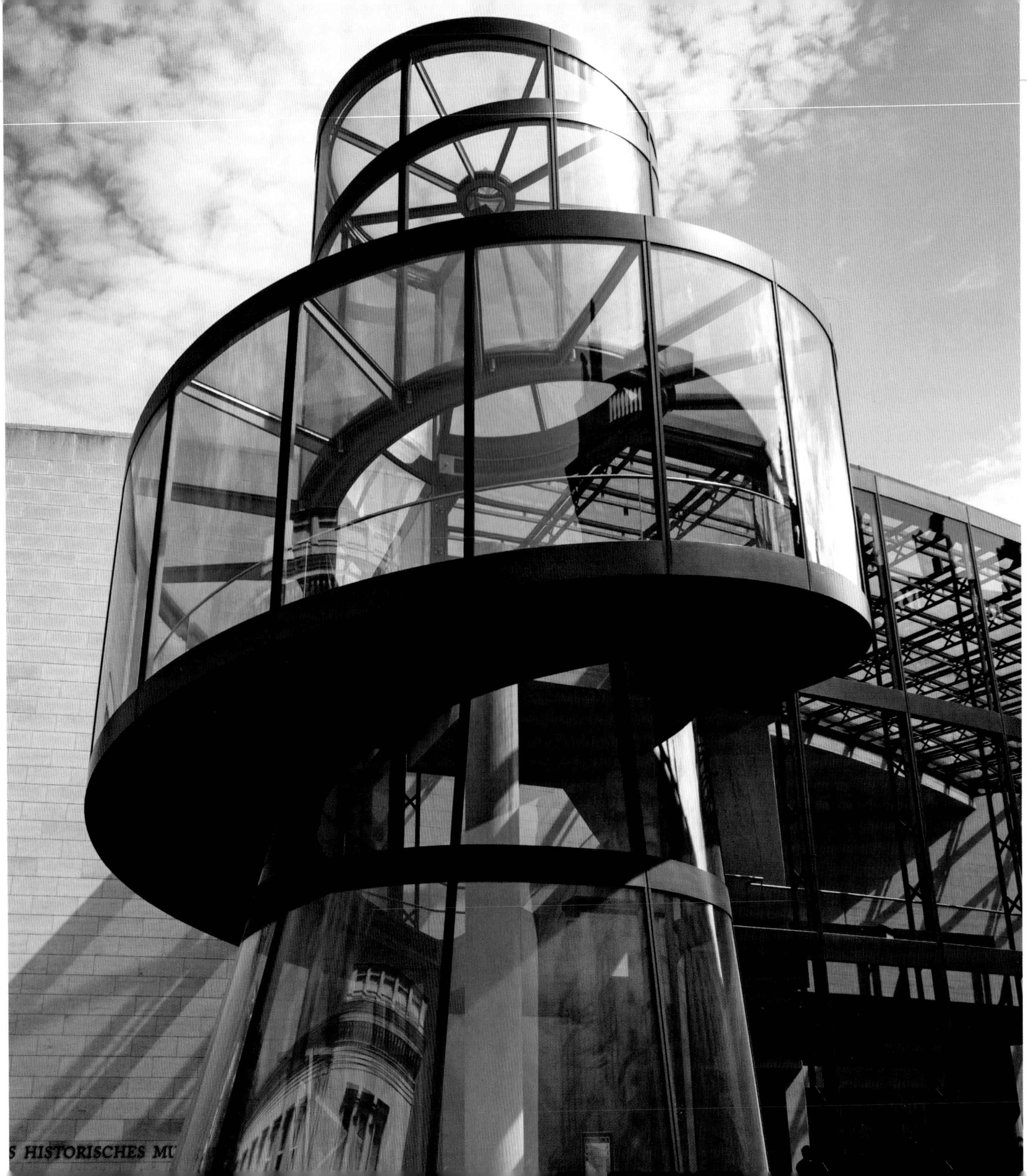
S HISTORISCHES MU

ZEUGHAUS

Deutsches Historisches Museum, Unter den Linden

The Zeughaus (armoury) building was originally a repository for weaponry and ordnance, specifically relating to artillery. It was built by Frederick III, Elector of Brandenburg (1657–1713), between 1695 and 1730, and subsequently (1875) became a military museum. As with so many of Berlin's historical buildings, the Zeughaus was seriously damaged during the Second World War, but it was restored in 1949–65 and became the Museum für Deutsche Geschichte (Museum of German History) in the GDR then, after reunification, the home for the modern Deutsches Historisches Museum (German Historical Museum).

PIETÀ

Neue Wache, Unter den Linden

In its nineteenth-century origins, the neo-classical Neue Wache (New Guardhouse) building was both a guardhouse for the Prussian royal family and a memorial to the German dead of the Napoleonic Wars and the Wars of Liberation. The guardhouse functions ceased in 1918, but it continued as the memorial, adding the dead of both world wars to its remembrance. Under the GDR, it became the Memorial to the Victims of Fascism and Militarism, while since 1993 it has been the Central Memorial of the Federal Republic of Germany to the Victims of War and Dictatorship. The statue 'Mother with her Dead Son' by Käthe Kollwitz (1867–1945), also known as the Pietà, stands in the centre of the memorial's chamber, a cold reminder of human cruelty.

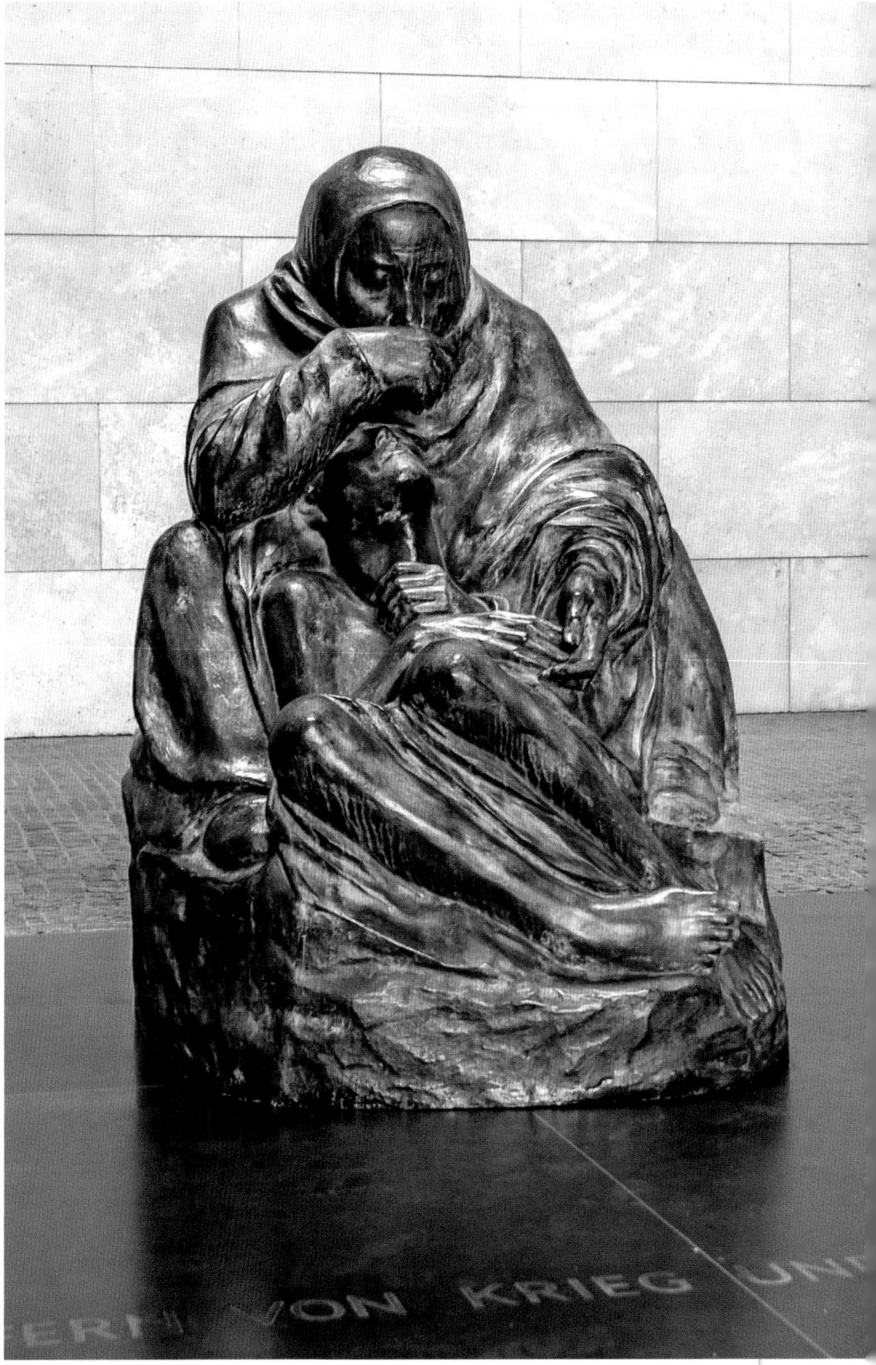

HUMBOLDT-UNIVERSITÄT ZU BERLIN

Unter den Linden

The Humboldt-Universität zu Berlin (HU Berlin; Humboldt University of Berlin) is one of Germany's most prestigious higher-education organizations. Today, it enrols some 32,000 students at any one time, with degree programmes in 189 disciplines, divided into nine faculties. Notable alumni include Otto von Bismarck, Dietrich Bonhoeffer, Paul Ehrlich, Fritz Haber, Elisabeth Jastrow, Karl Marx, Lise Meitner and Erwin Schrödinger, and some 55 Nobel Prize winners are affiliated with the university. Its doors first opened to students in 1810, and it subsequently had to negotiate both Nazi and communist regimes. Here we see statues atop the magnificent eighteenth-century Alte Bibliothek (Old Library), which today houses the law faculty.

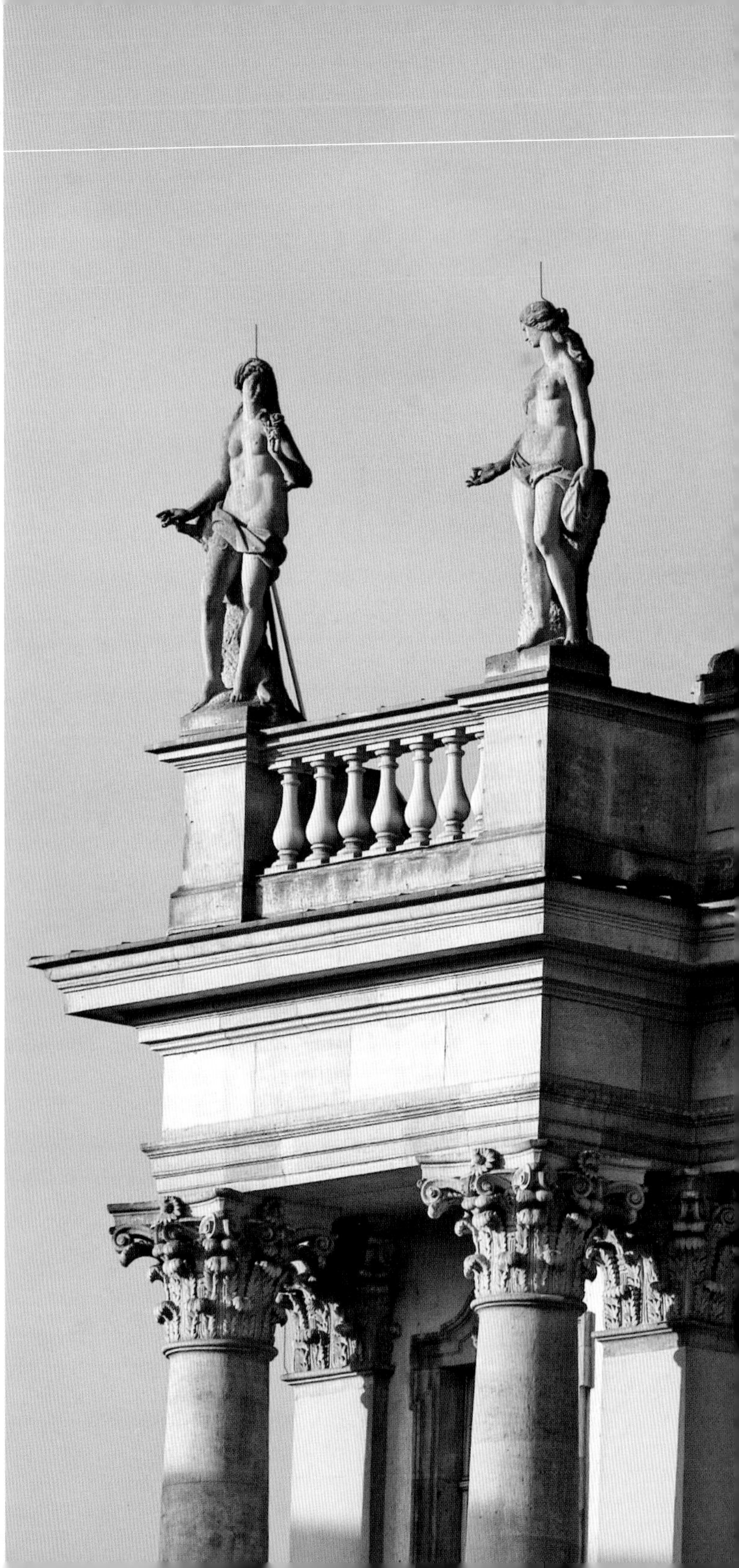

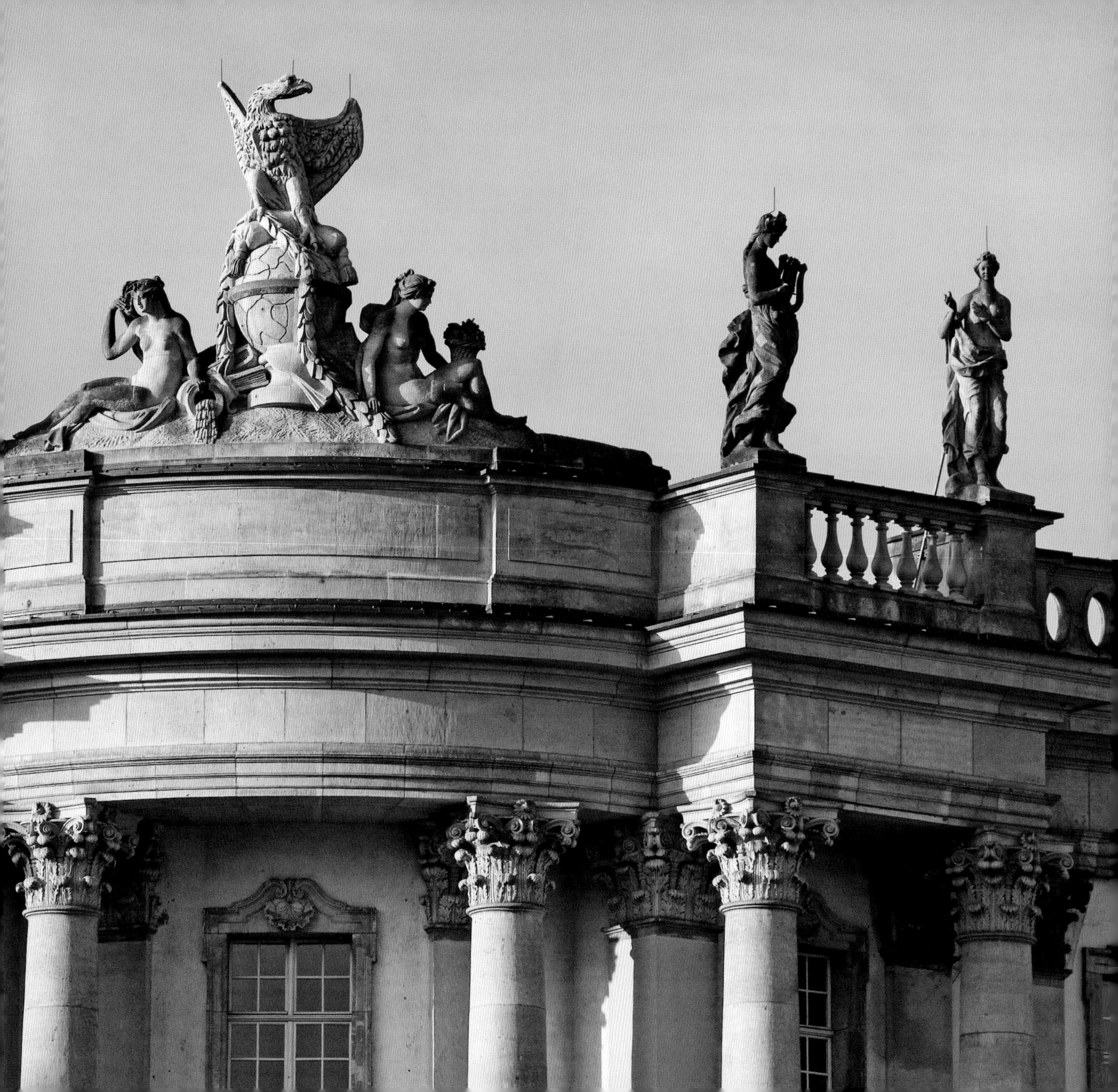

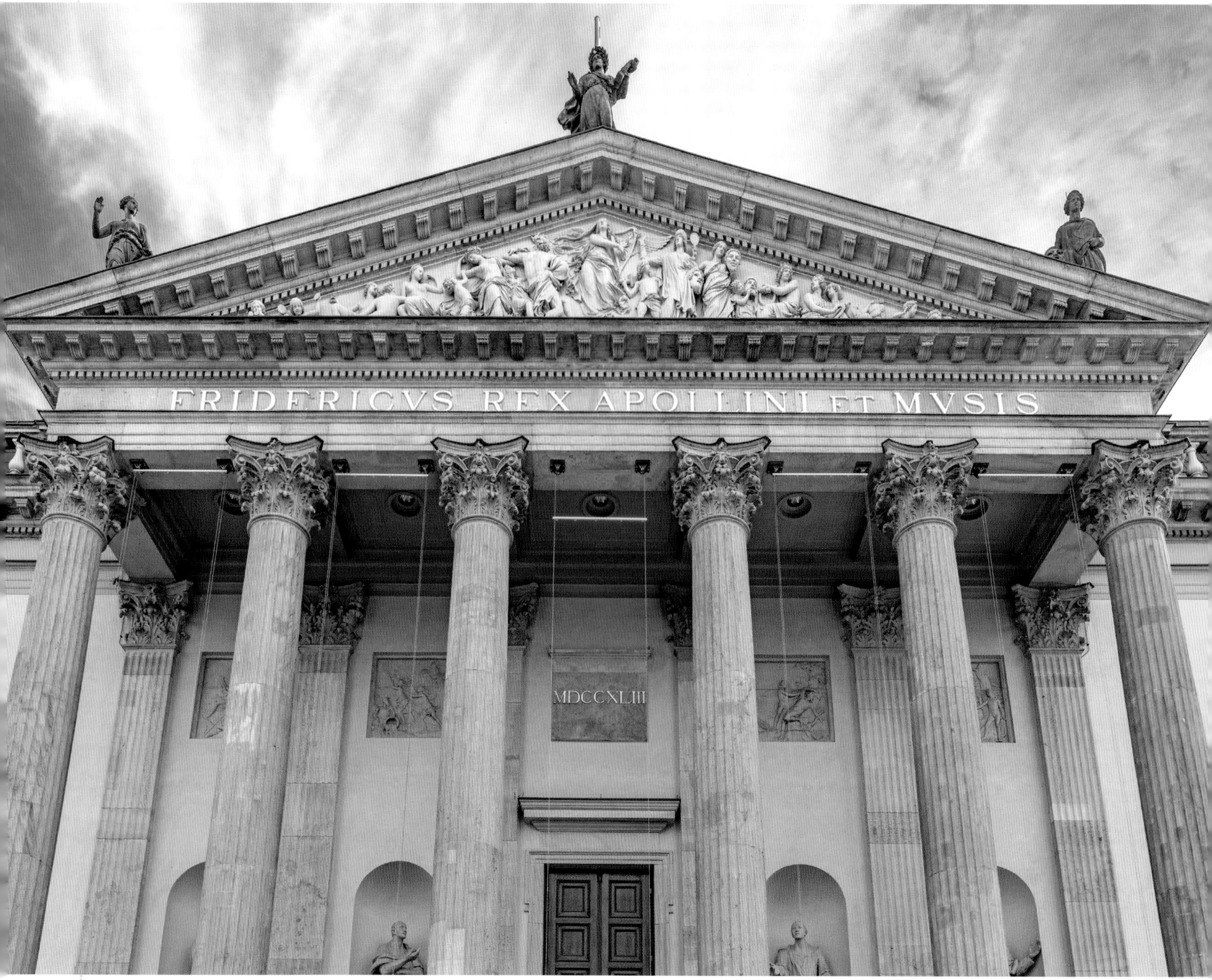
FRIDERICVS REX APOLLINI ET MVSIS
MDCCXLIII

STAATSOPER UNTER DEN LINDEN

Unter den Linden

The Staatsoper Unter den Linden (State Opera Unter den Linden) building carries with it a solid historical pedigree: it was commissioned as a court opera house by Frederick the Great as part of his Forum Fridericianum project and designed by architect Georg Wenzeslaus von Knobelsdorff (1699–1753), with construction taking place between 1741 and 1743. One hundred years later, in 1843, disaster struck when the opera house was gutted by fire. It was rebuilt under the direction of architect Carl Ferdinand Langhans (1782–1869), but had to be restored once again in the post-war years on account of bomb damage.

ST HEDWIG'S CATHEDRAL

Unter den Linden

St Hedwig's Cathedral wouldn't look out of place in Rome or Athens, and indeed was part of Frederick the Great's eighteenth-century Forum Fridericianum, an attempt to create an 'Athens on the Spree'. The most arresting external architectural feature is the cathedral's towering copper dome, greened by exposure to the elements, and internally the circular layout provides a pleasing harmony. St Hedwig's is a Catholic cathedral, the first built in Prussia after the Reformation, and later during the years of the Third Reich it became something of a centre for resistance to the spread of Nazi ideology.

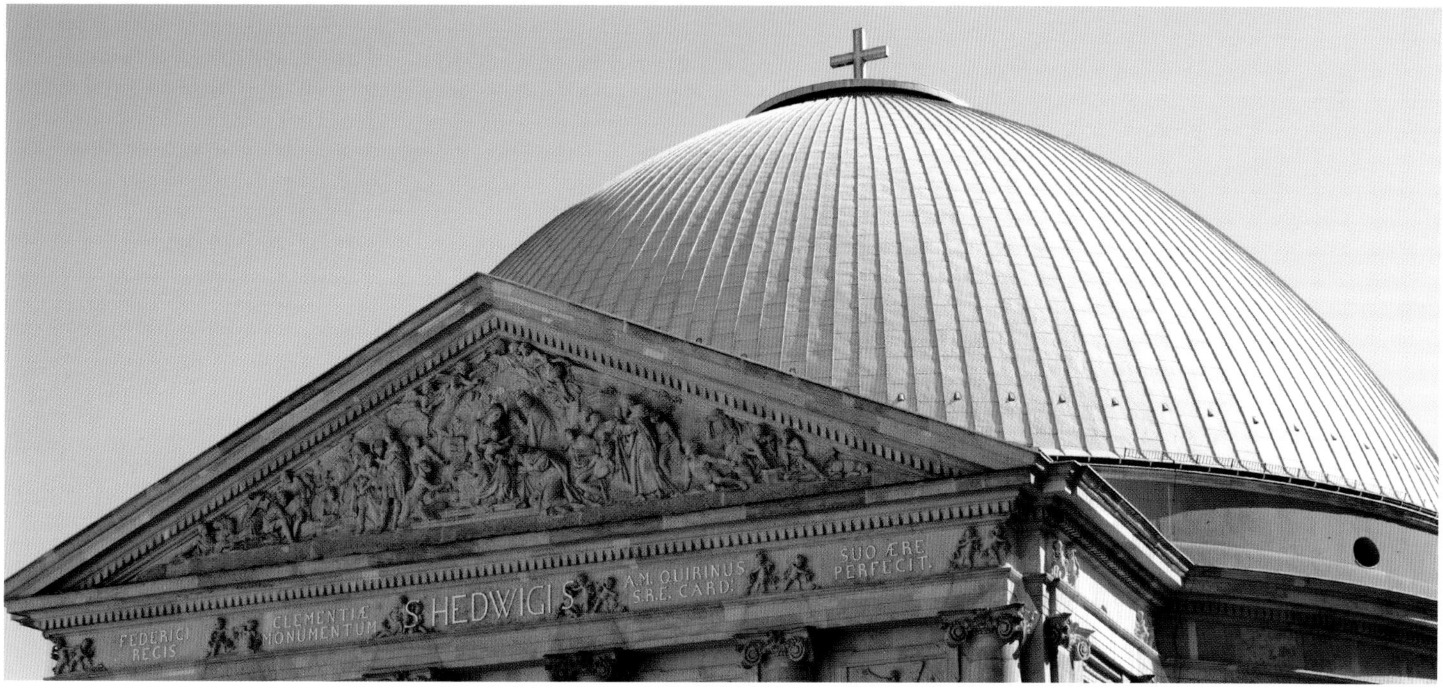

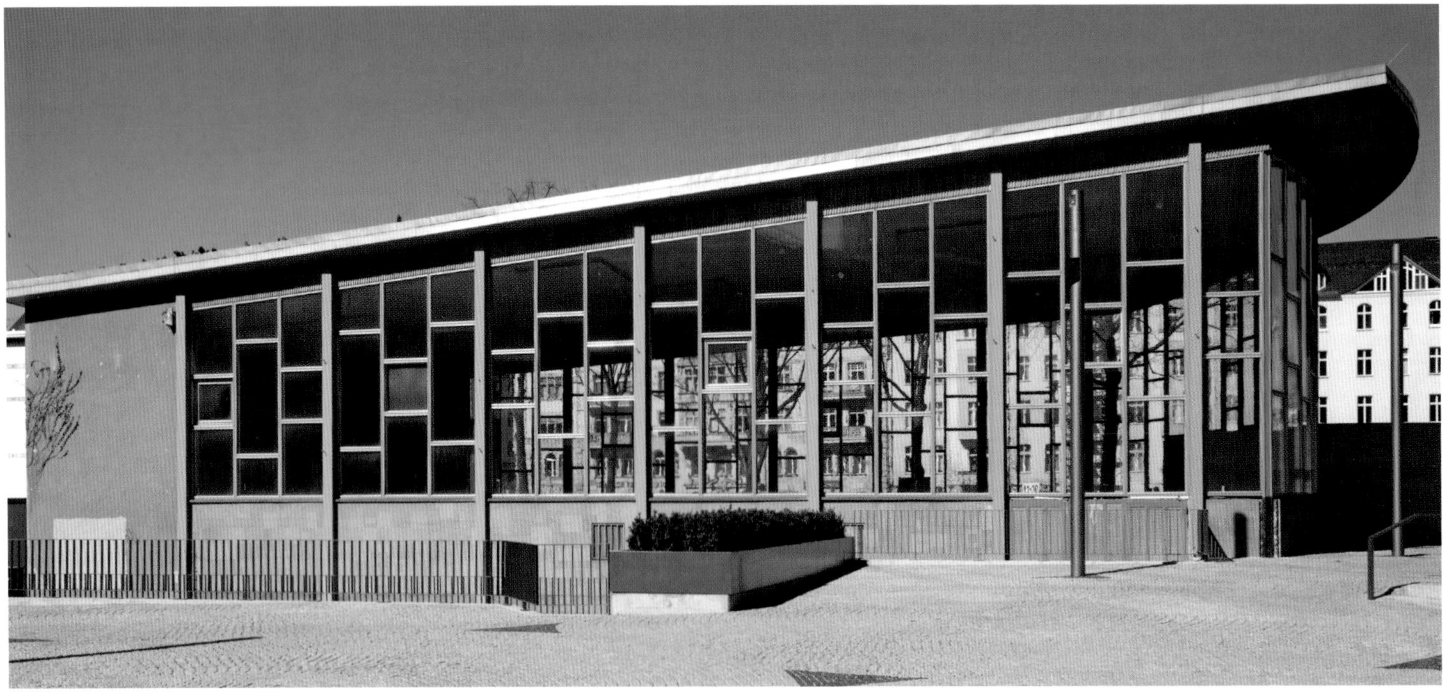

TRÄNENPALAST

Friedrichstraße, Mitte

The Tränenpalast (Palace of Tears) is a rather innocuous-looking building, but its name suggests the sadness of what occurred inside. It was a border crossing point between East and West Berlin at Berlin Friedrichstraße station, between the years of 1962 and 1989. Because transit at the crossing point was only permitted in the east-to-west direction, however, the building became the scene of many tearful and sometimes permanent goodbyes between families, friends and lovers, separated by physical and ideological borders. In 2008 the Tränenpalast became a federal memorial site, with a museum on the site from 2011.

QUARTIER 205

Friedrichstraße, Mitte

Perfectly representing modern commercial Berlin, Quartier 205 is a spacious complex between Friedrichstraße and Gendarmenmarkt. It was designed in the 1990s by Oswald Mathias Ungers (1926–2007), who worked heavily in French lime sandstone and architectural bronze, augmented with large areas of glass. Spread over eight floors, the complex includes not only extensive shopping and dining facilities, but also offices, gyms and residential spaces.

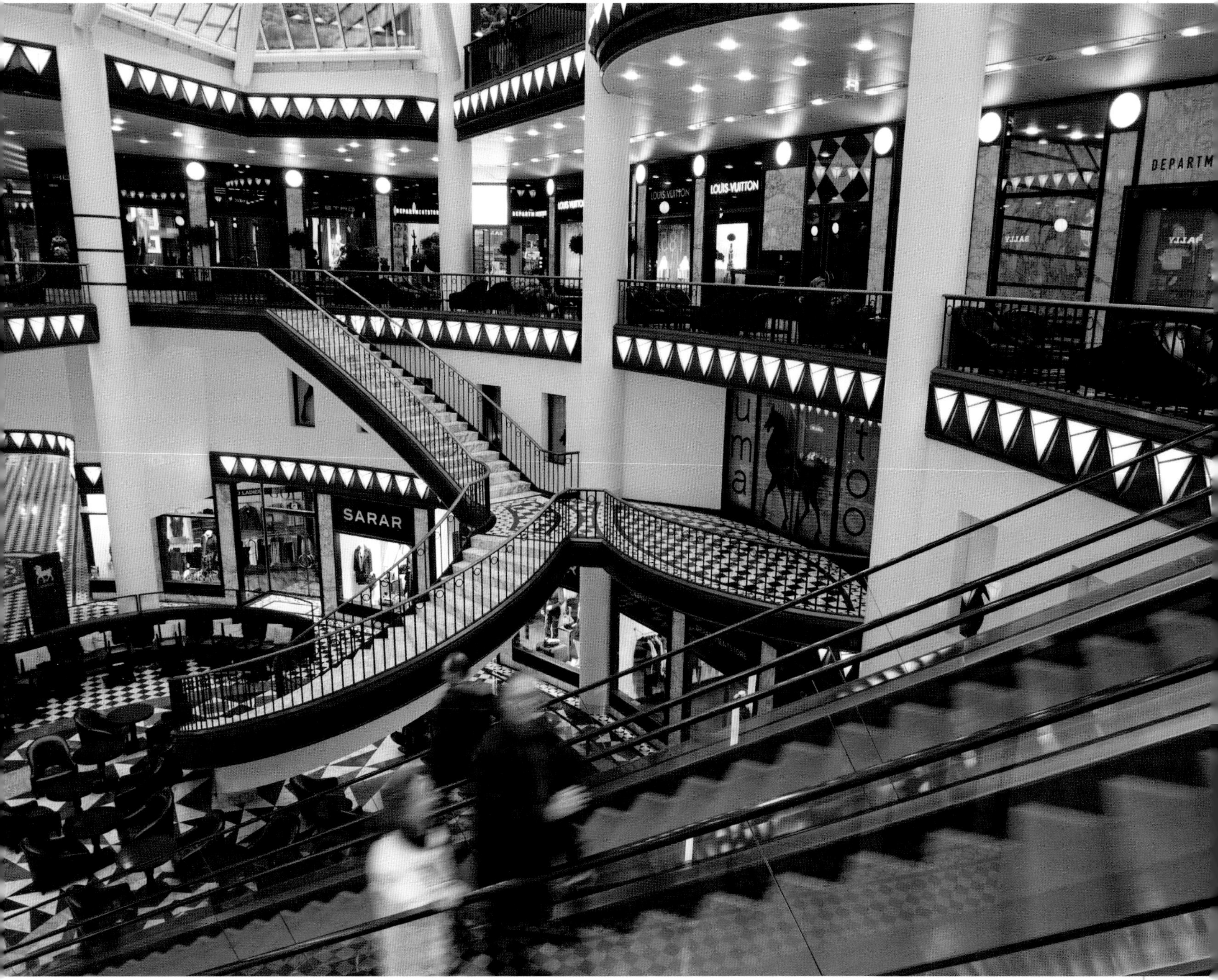
LOUIS VUITTON
LOUIS VUITTON
SARAR

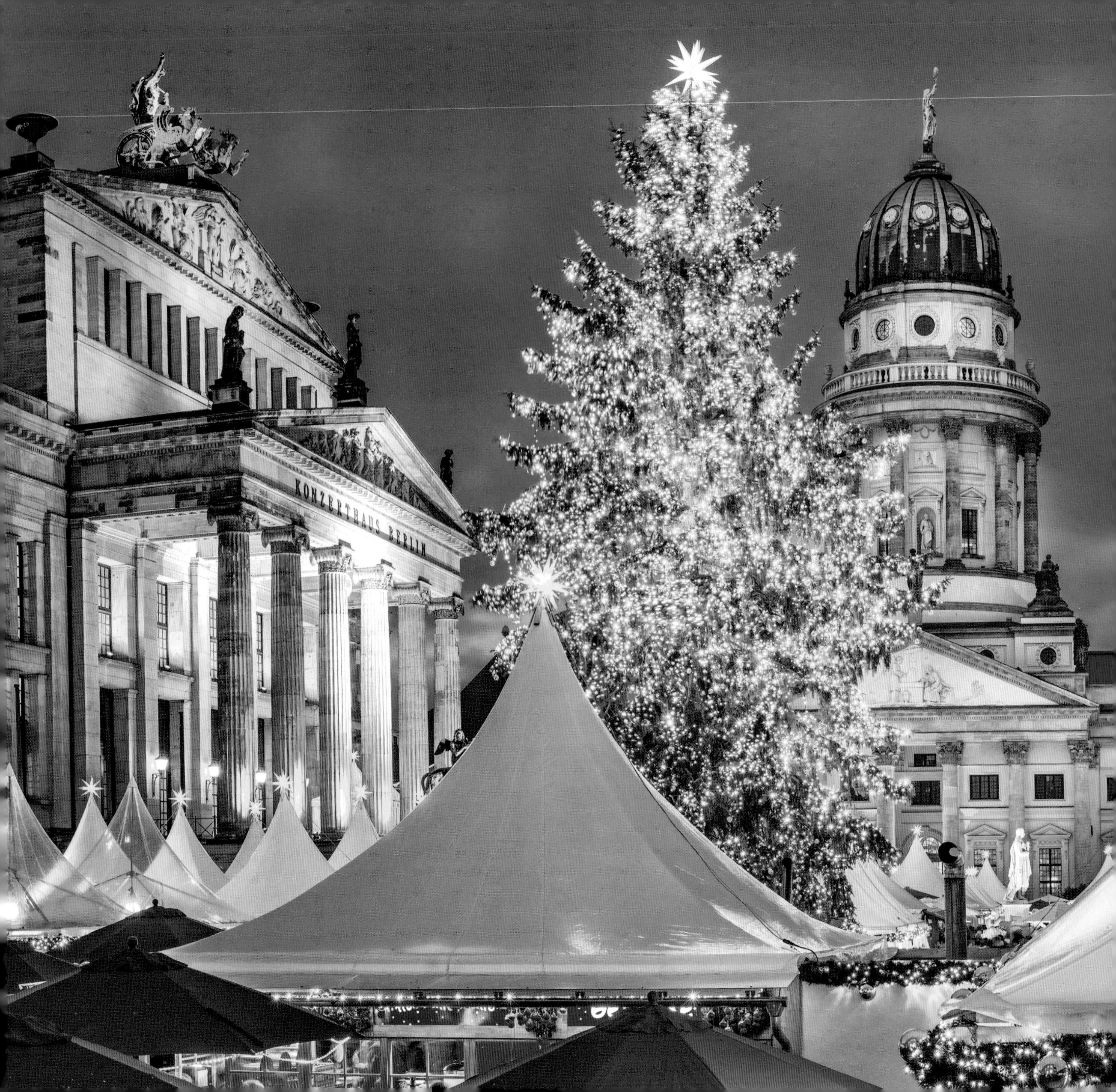
KONZERTHAUS BERLIN

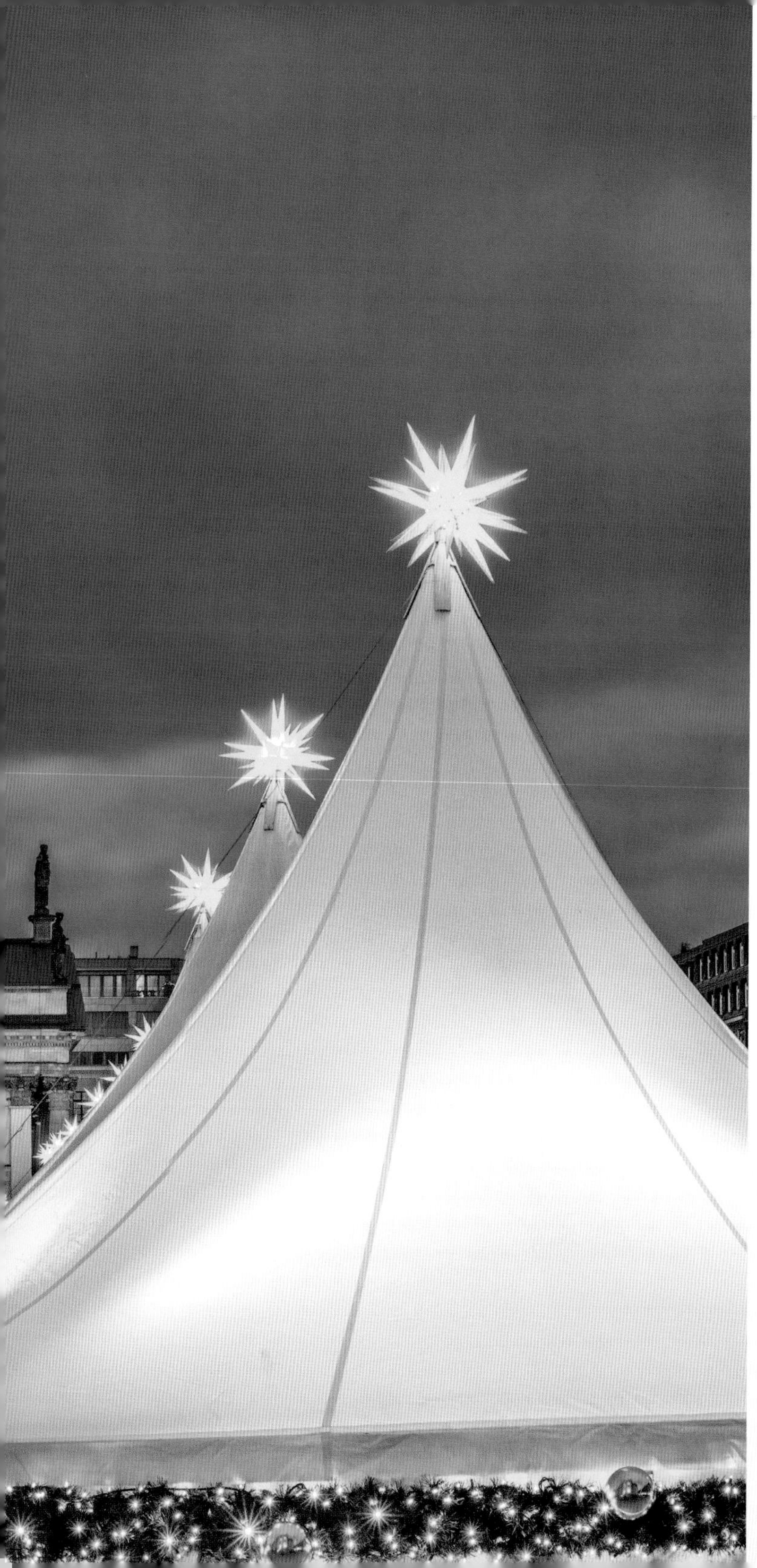

CHRISTMAS MARKET

Gendarmenmarkt

Germany is renowned for the magical nature of its Christmas markets, and Berlin is host to some particularly fine examples. Here we see the highly illuminated Christmas market at eighteenth-century Gendarmenmarkt, located between the Französischer Dom and Deutscher Dom, and widely regarded as one of the best such markets in the country. The market fills the neighbourhood with artisan stalls, traditional Christmas food vendors (lacing the air with fragrances for the hungry), artists showing their work and theatrical and musical entertainment.

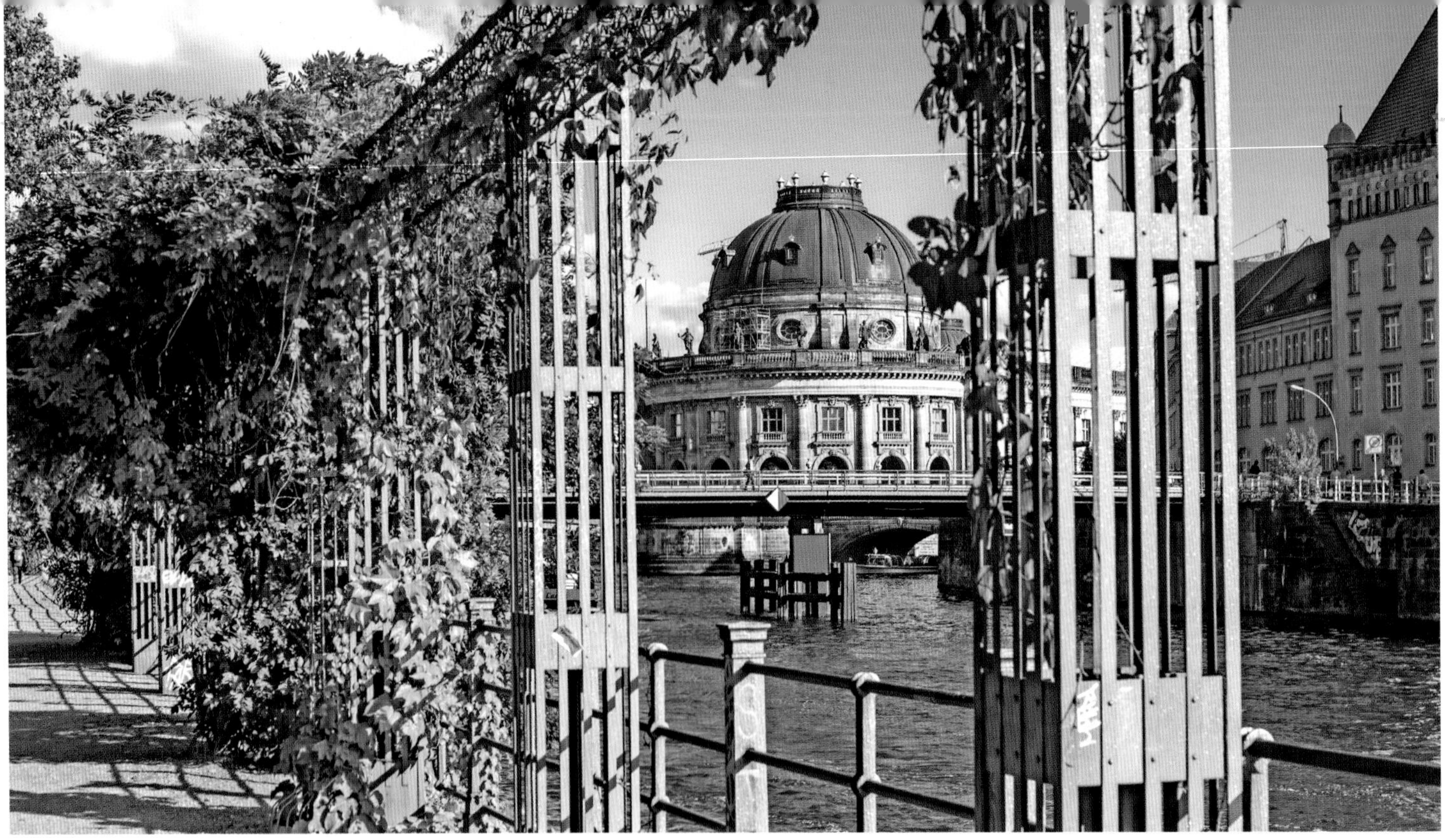

MONBIJOUBRÜCKE

River Spree

The Monbijoubrücke (Monbijou Bridge) provides a pleasant pedestrian crossing point over the Spree, connecting the nearby Monbijoupark with Museum Island. It is a listed bridge measuring 62 m (203 ft) long, and its surroundings are typical of the riverside culture of Berlin. The pace is leisurely and cafés and street music make for a relaxed and thoughtful atmosphere. The scene here looks towards the bridge, with the Bode Museum in the background, the whole scene framed by autumnal colours in the vegetation.

ALTE NATIONALGALERIE

Museum Island

One of the five museums on Museum Island, the Alte Nationalgalerie (Old National Gallery) is an internationally important home to collections of art from the eighteenth century to the early Modernist period in the twentieth century. The building itself was built between 1866 and 1876, its temple-like appearance heavily indebted to designs by Friedrich August Stüler (1800–65). Stüler died before realizing the project and it was completed under Carl Busse (1834-96). Artists and sculptors whose work is displayed in the museum include Caspar David Friedrich, Karl Friedrich Schinkel, Karl Blechen, Édouard Manet, Claude Monet and Johann Gottfried Schadow.

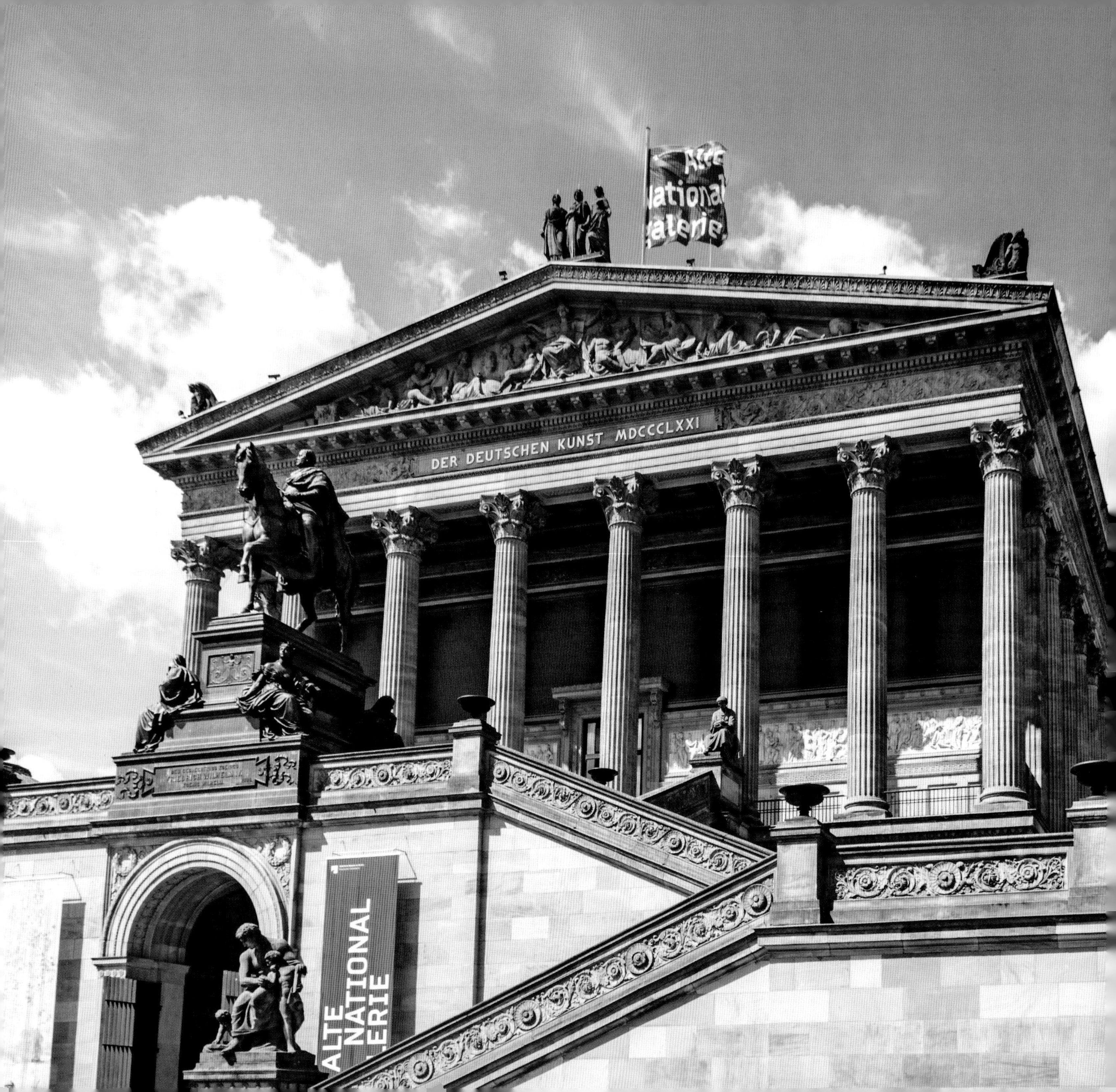
DER DEUTSCHEN KUNST MDCCCLXXI
ALTE
NATIONAL

MUSEUMSINSEL

Museum Island

The Museumsinsel (Museum Island) represents an unusual cultural concentration, with no fewer than five world-class museums clustered on the northern half of an island in the Spree in the Mitte district. The island began its growth in 1830 with the establishment of the Altes Museum (Old Museum), but expanded to its current five-museum configuration by 1930. In addition to the Altes Museum, the other institutions are the Pergamonmuseum (Pergamon Museum), Bode Museum, Neues Museum (New Museum) and Alte Nationalgalerie (Old National Gallery). Such is the cultural value of the buildings and exhibits, that in 1999 the Museum Island complex was given UNESCO World Heritage status.

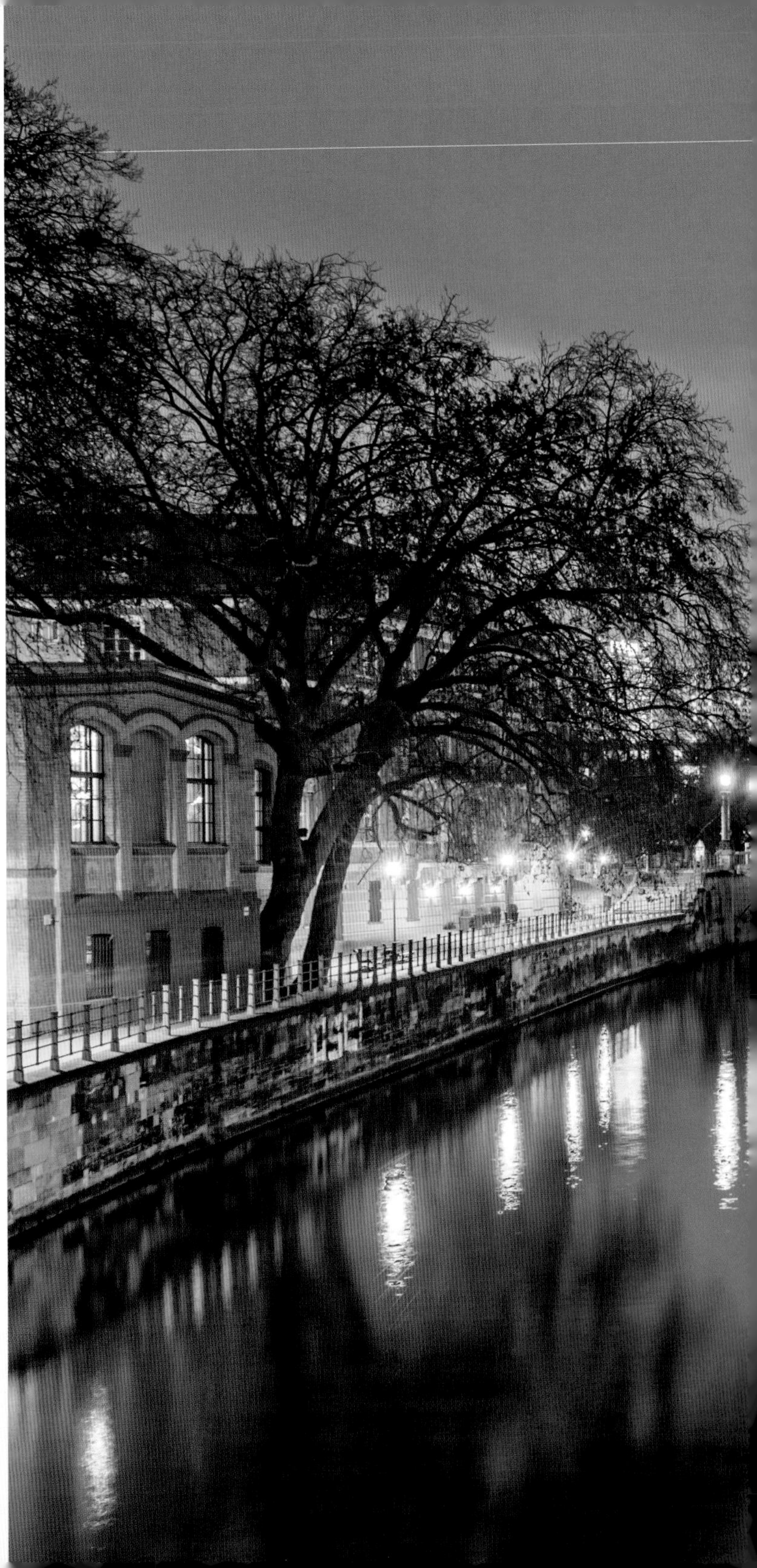

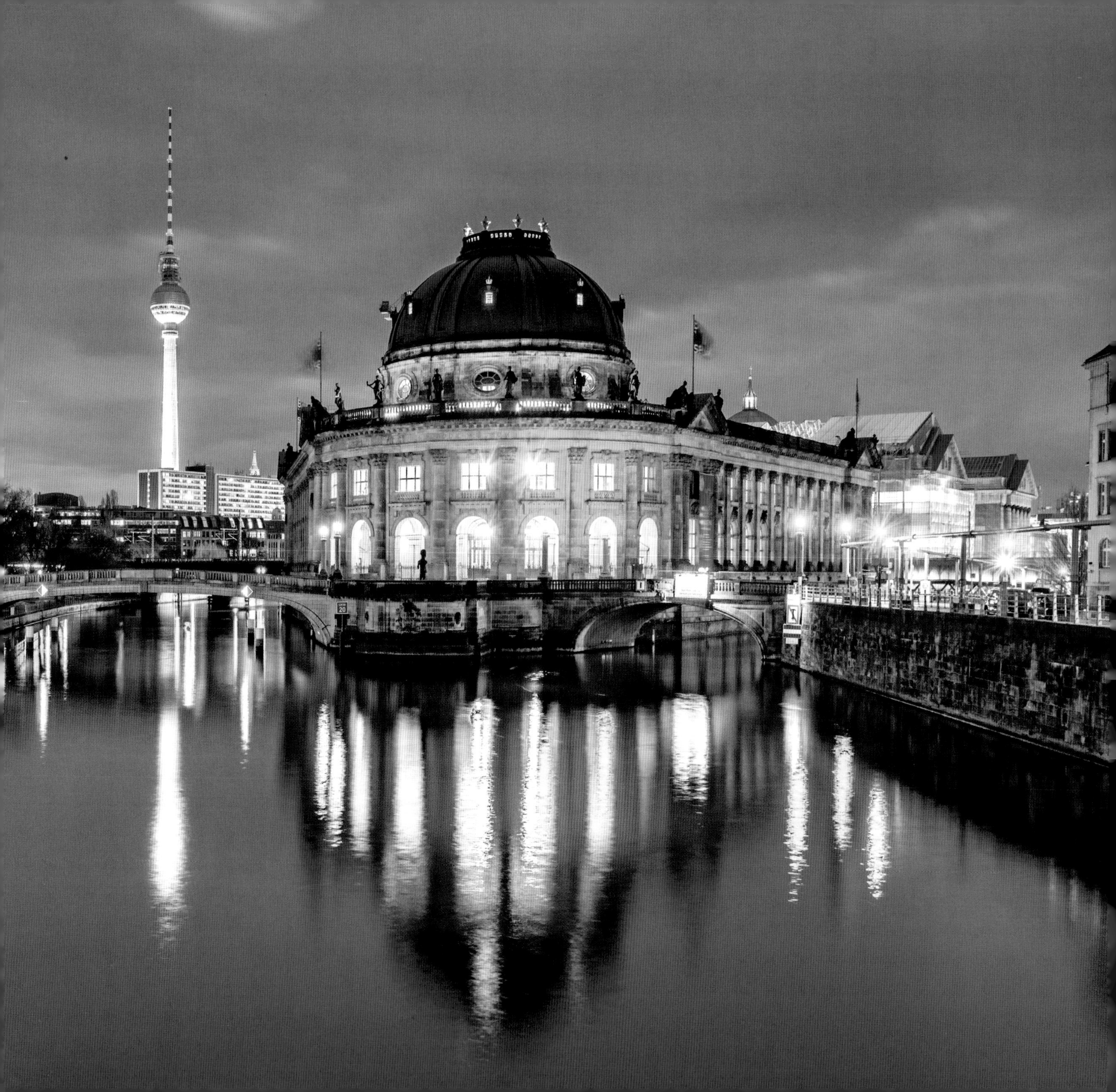

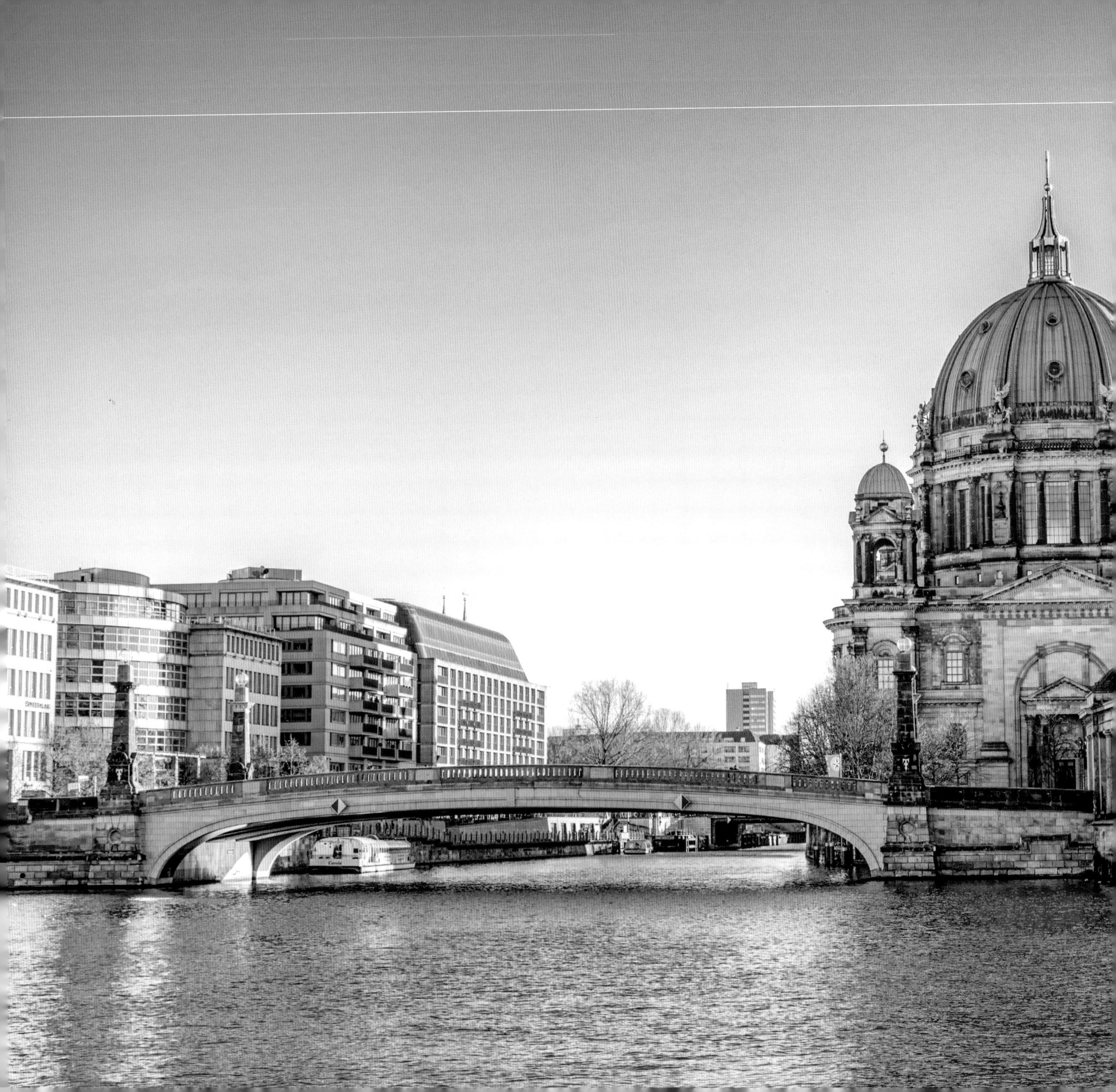

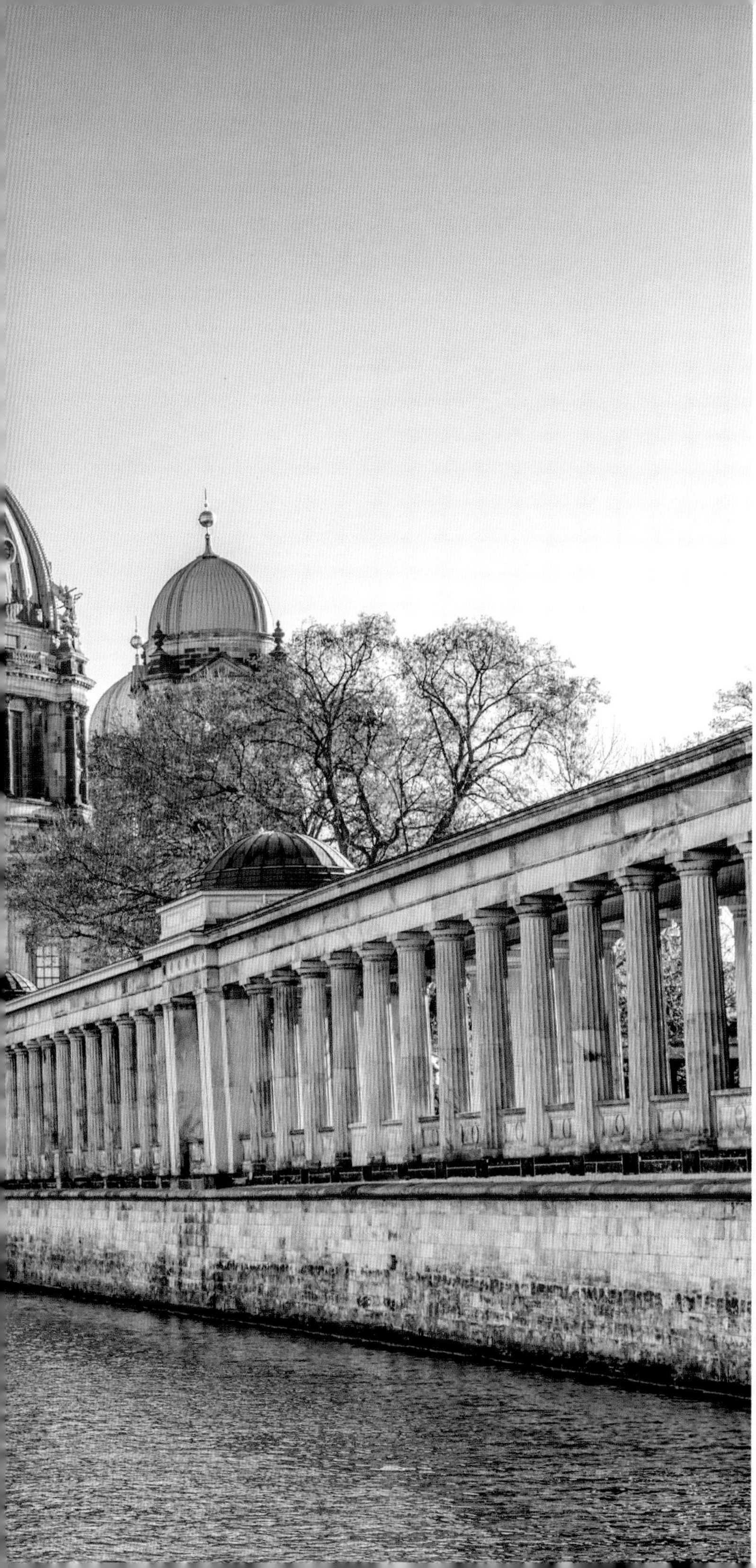

BERLINER DOM

Museum Island

The Berliner Dom (Berlin Cathedral) is technically a parish church, but historical service to various Prussian rulers and German emperors gives it the physical and spiritual status of a cathedral (it is referred to as the High Parish and Cathedral Church). The inspiring building that we see today, complete with monumental dome and four flanking towers, is very different from the smaller buildings that graced the site from the fifteenth century. Indeed, the whole building was pulled down in 1893 and rebuilt according to the vision of architect Julius Carl Raschdorff (1823–1914). This is largely what we see today, although changed somewhat by post-war renovations and restorations.

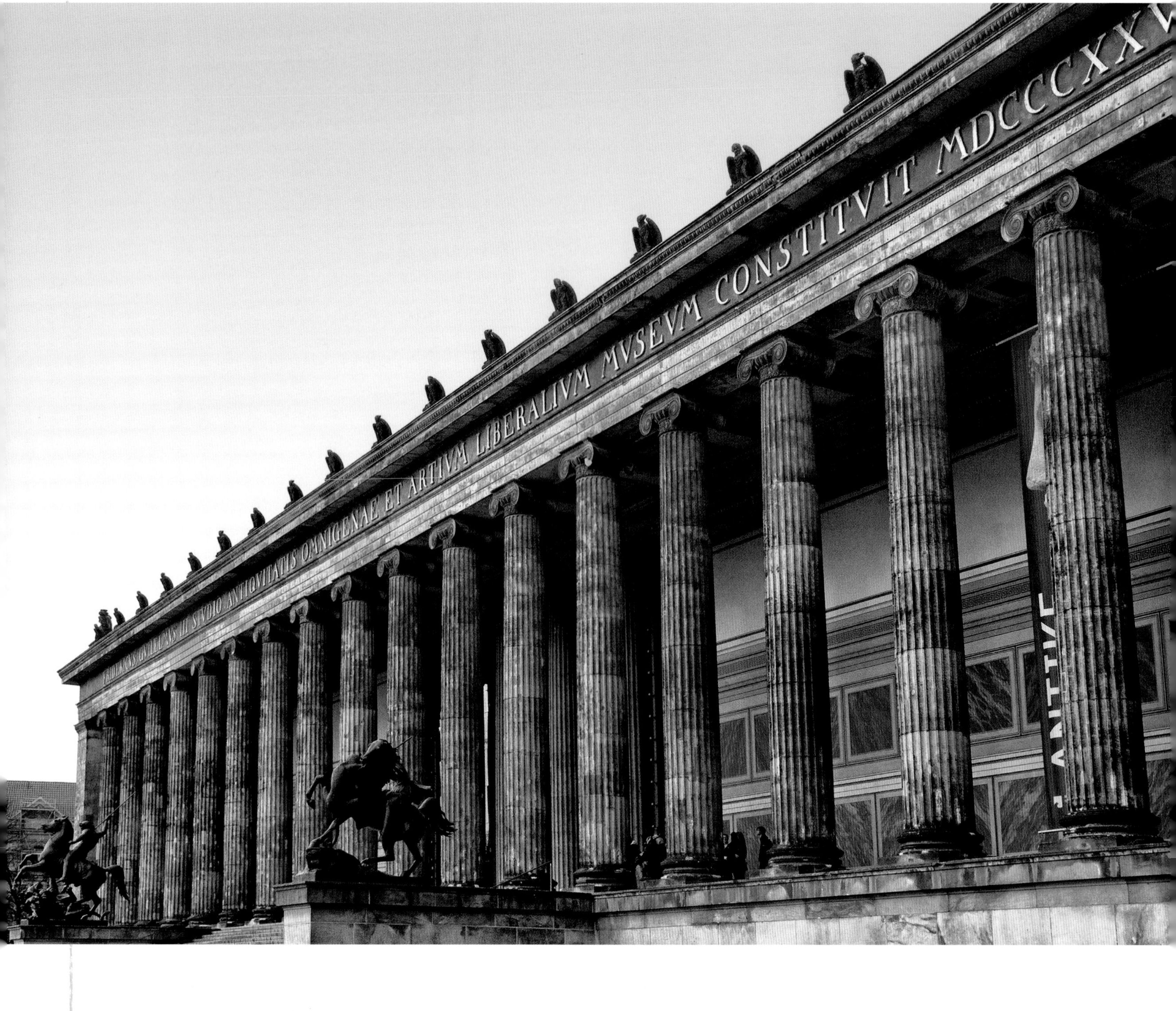
ANTIQVITATIS OMNIGENAE ET ARTIVM LIBERALIVM MVSEVM CONSTITVIT MDCCCXX

ALTES MUSEUM

Museum Island

Visitors to the Altes Museum (Old Museum) are first greeted by a pillared colonnade (18 pillars in total) that evokes the Athenian Parthenon in its grandeur. The setting is apt – passing through the colonnade and a light-filled rotunda, and climbing a great staircase, the visitor is transported back into more than 11 centuries of ancient Greek and Roman art, the oldest exhibits dating to the tenth century BC. Specialist collections include the most significant collection of Etruscan art outside Italy, plus a numismatic hoard of 1,300 ancient coins.

HUMBOLDT FORUM

Museum Island

The Humboldt Forum is a major new national museum in the former Berliner Schloss (Berlin City Palace) on Museum Island. The original palace was constructed in the fifteenth century, but was heavily redesigned in the eighteenth century. Wartime destruction was compounded by Soviet film-makers firing live artillery shells at the palace during the production of a post-1945 war movie, then completed when it was demolished by the GDR in 1950. The Palast der Republik (Palace of the Republic) that took its place in 1976 was also demolished in 2006–08. Full restoration of the palace, largely to its eighteenth-century appearance, began in 2013.

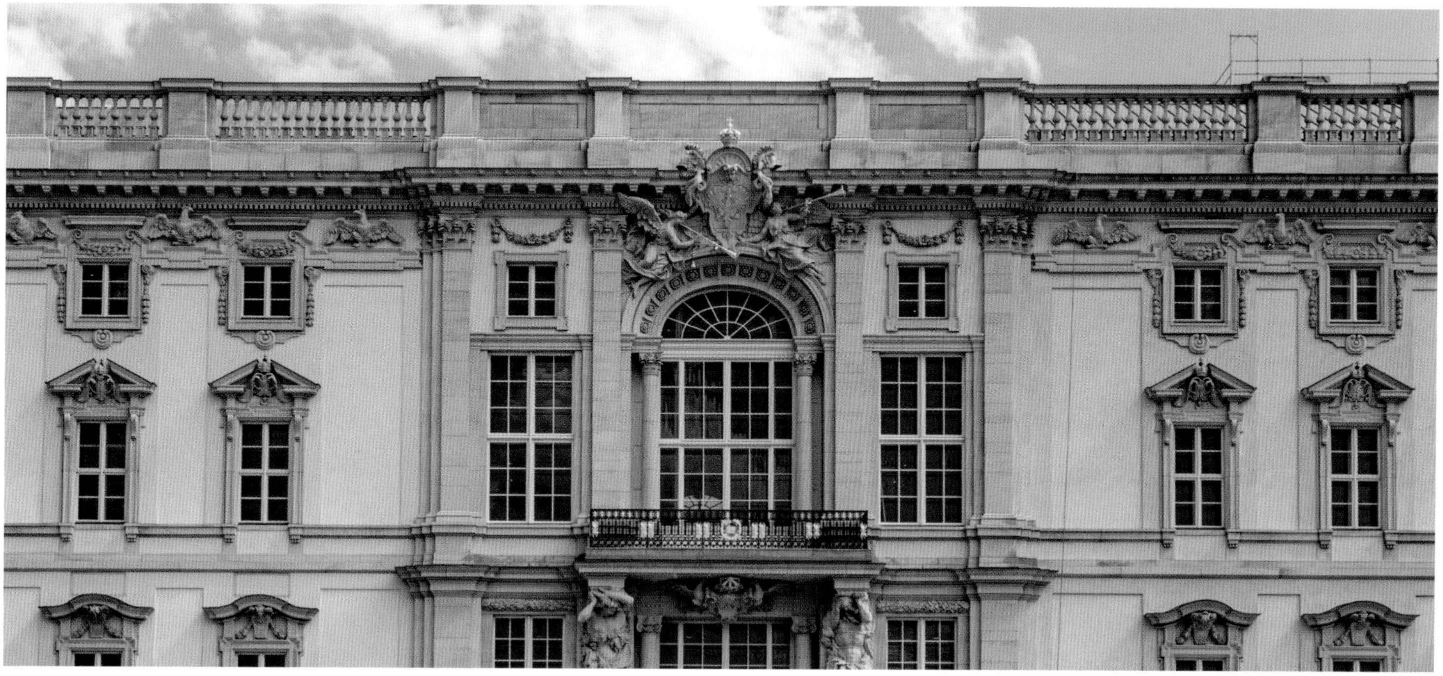

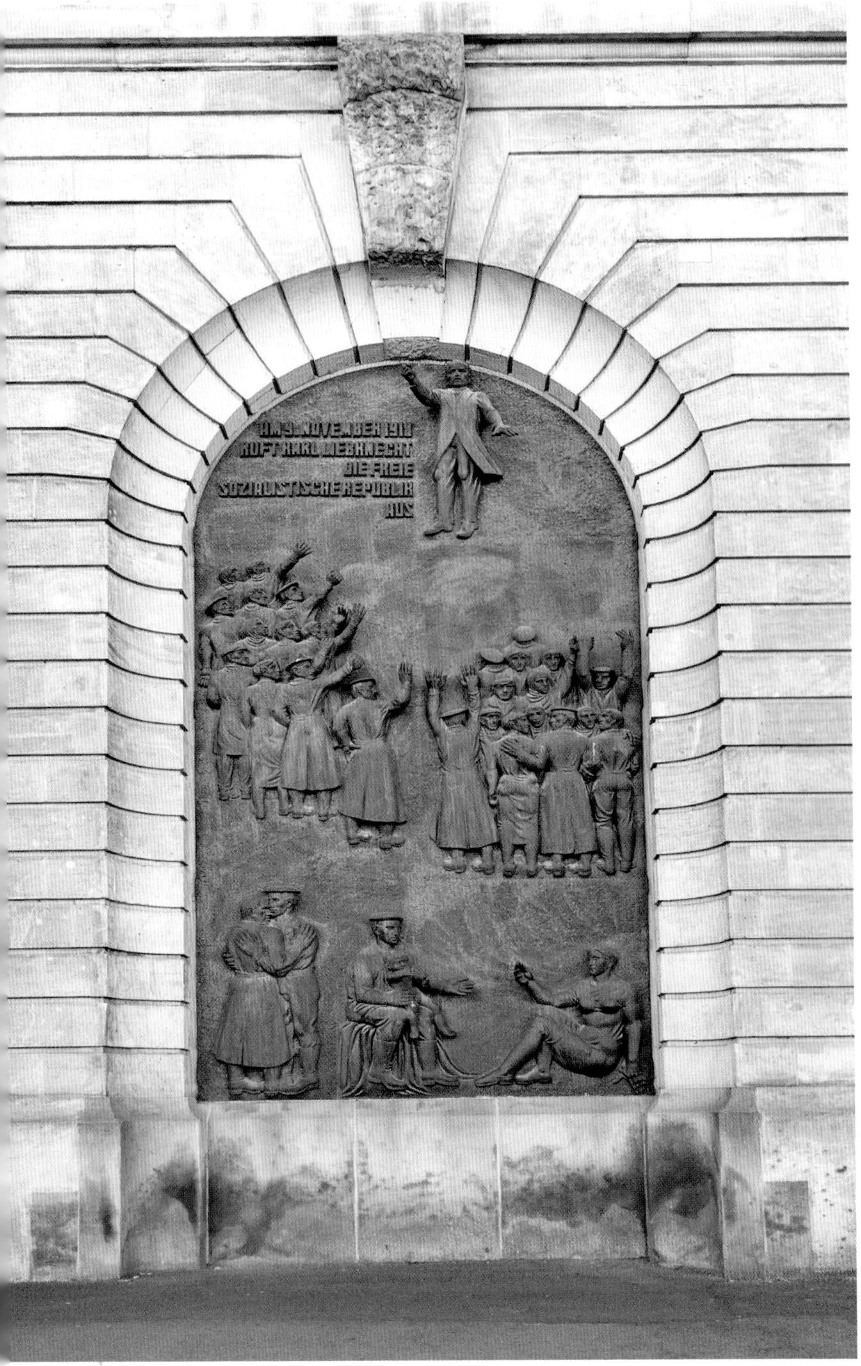

KARL LIEBKNECHT BAS RELIEF

Neuer Marstall, Museum Island

The name of the impressive neo-Baroque Neuer Marstall (New Stables) building refers to its original purpose in the early twentieth century, namely, of housing the royal horses and carriages. Today, however, it is the home of the Hanns Eisler Academy of Music and the Berlin City Library. The building is adorned with historically illuminating decoration. Here we see, on the north façade of the building, a GDR-era (1984) bas relief showing socialist politician Karl Liebknecht proclaiming a German socialist republic.

JUNGFERNBRÜCKE

River Spree

Berlin's bisection by the River Spree means that it is a city of bridges. The Jungfernbrücke (Jungfern Bridge) is the oldest survivor of these bridges, dating back to around 1701 and designed by one Martin Grünberg (1655–1706). It is a bascule bridge, meaning that it can be opened via a counterweight system to allow tall river traffic to pass through, although its active days are over and it is purely a pedestrian footbridge. This particular structure is the last of nine previous similar bridges, improved over earlier examples through the use of iron work.

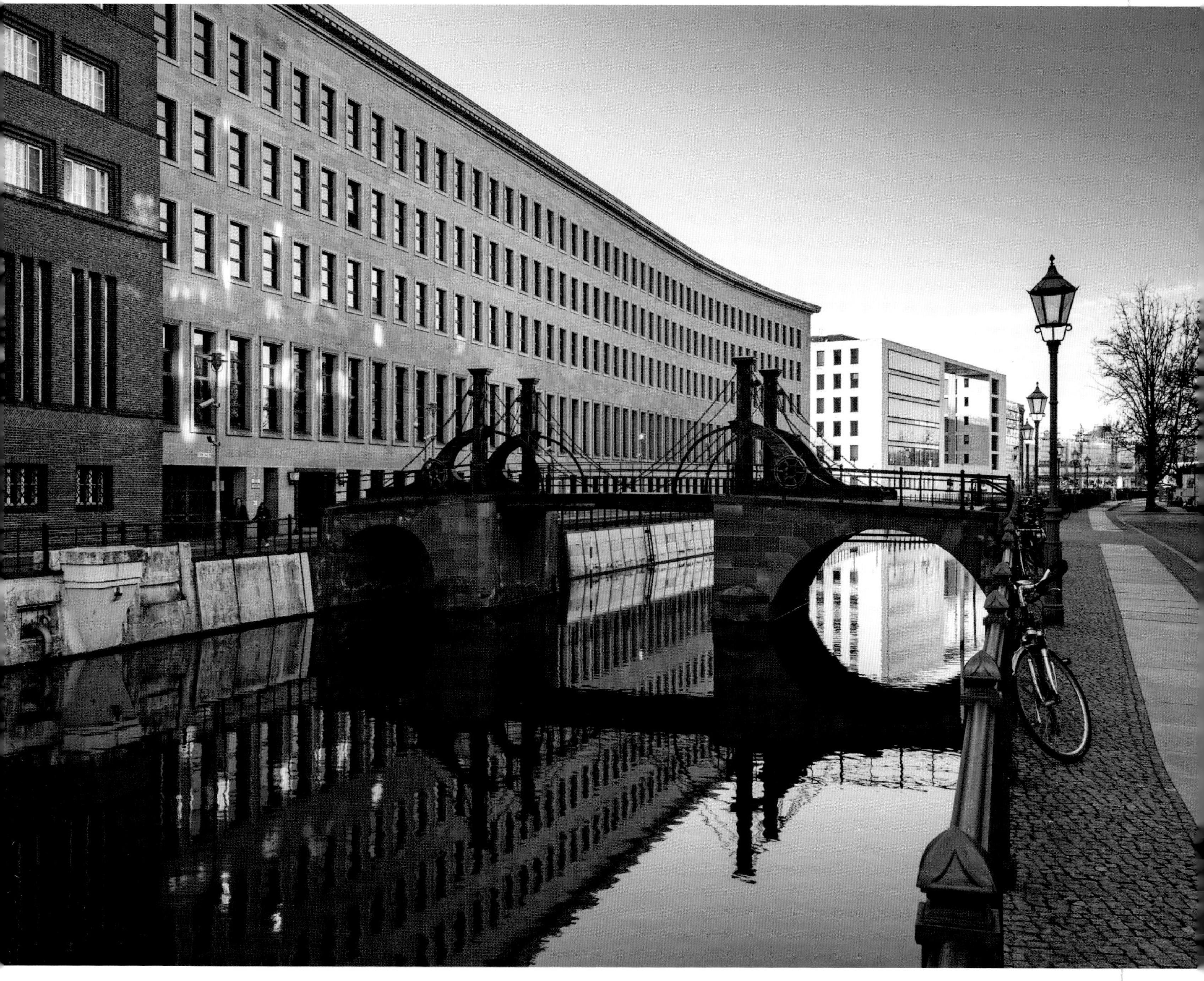

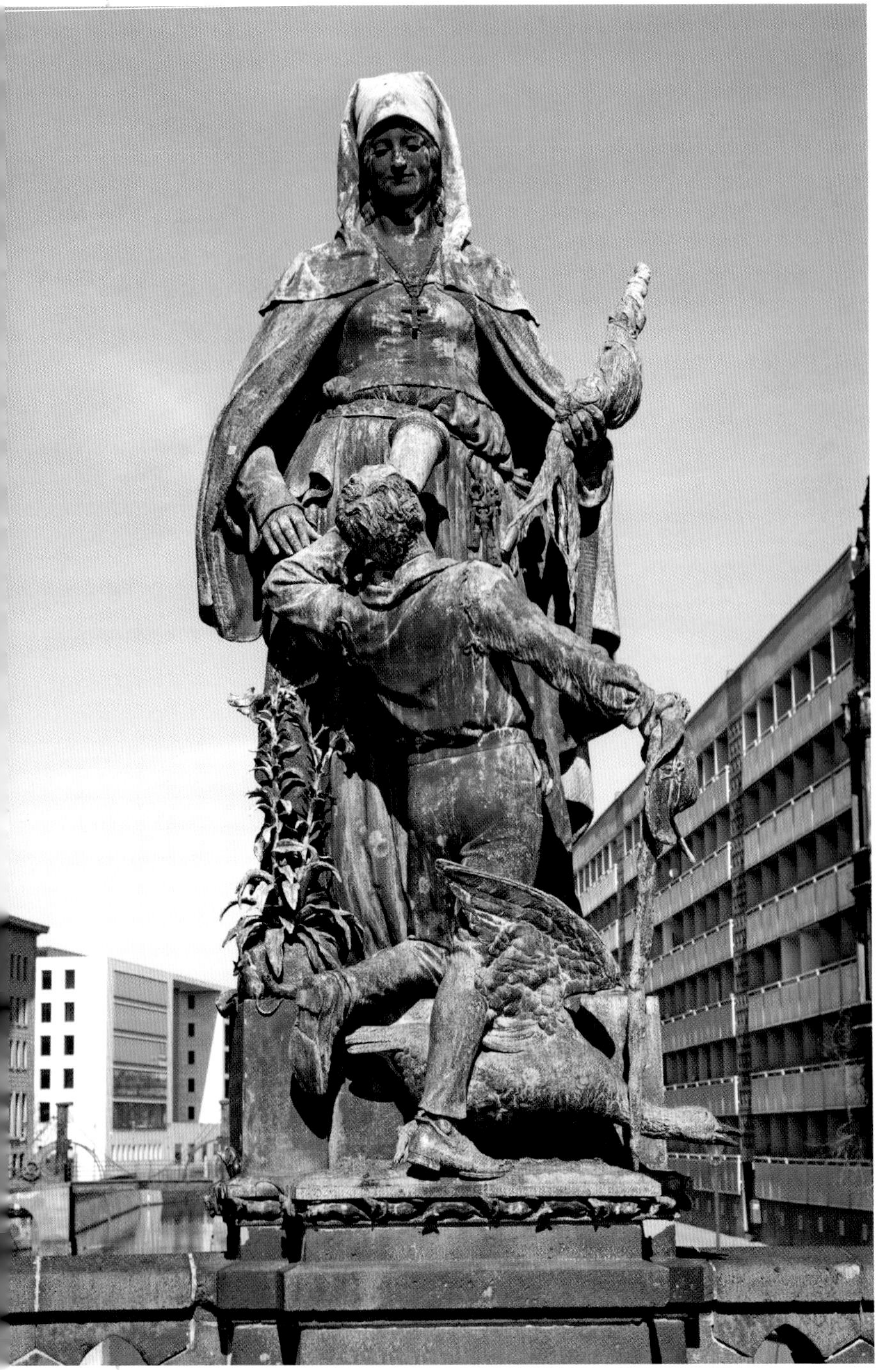

GERTRAUDENBRÜCKE

River Spree

Gertrude of Nivelles (in Belgium), although never officially canonized, is nevertheless regarded as a saint, albeit one with a curiously broad range of patronage. Not only can her guidance and protection be invoked by travellers, gardeners and those with mental illness, but they also extend to cats, or at least the protection of places against rats and mice. The Gertraudenbrücke (St Gertrude Bridge) features a 3-m (10-ft) bronze sculpture of Gertrude, with several nibbling rodents around the plinth. It is said that if you give one a quick rub as you pass, a wish will come true.

EPHRAIM-PALAIS

Poststraße, Nikolaiviertel

The Ephraim-Palais has been described as 'the most beautiful corner in Berlin'. Nestled near the banks of the Spree, the palace is certainly captivating, built in a perfectly balanced rococo style between 1762 and 1766 for Veitel Heine Ephraim (1703–75), the court jeweller and mint master of Frederick the Great. The most architecturally traumatic event in its history was its deconstruction in 1936–37 to make way for the extension of the Mühlendamm thoroughfare, but it was rebuilt between 1985 and 1987, and today is a museum space focused on the history of Berlin.

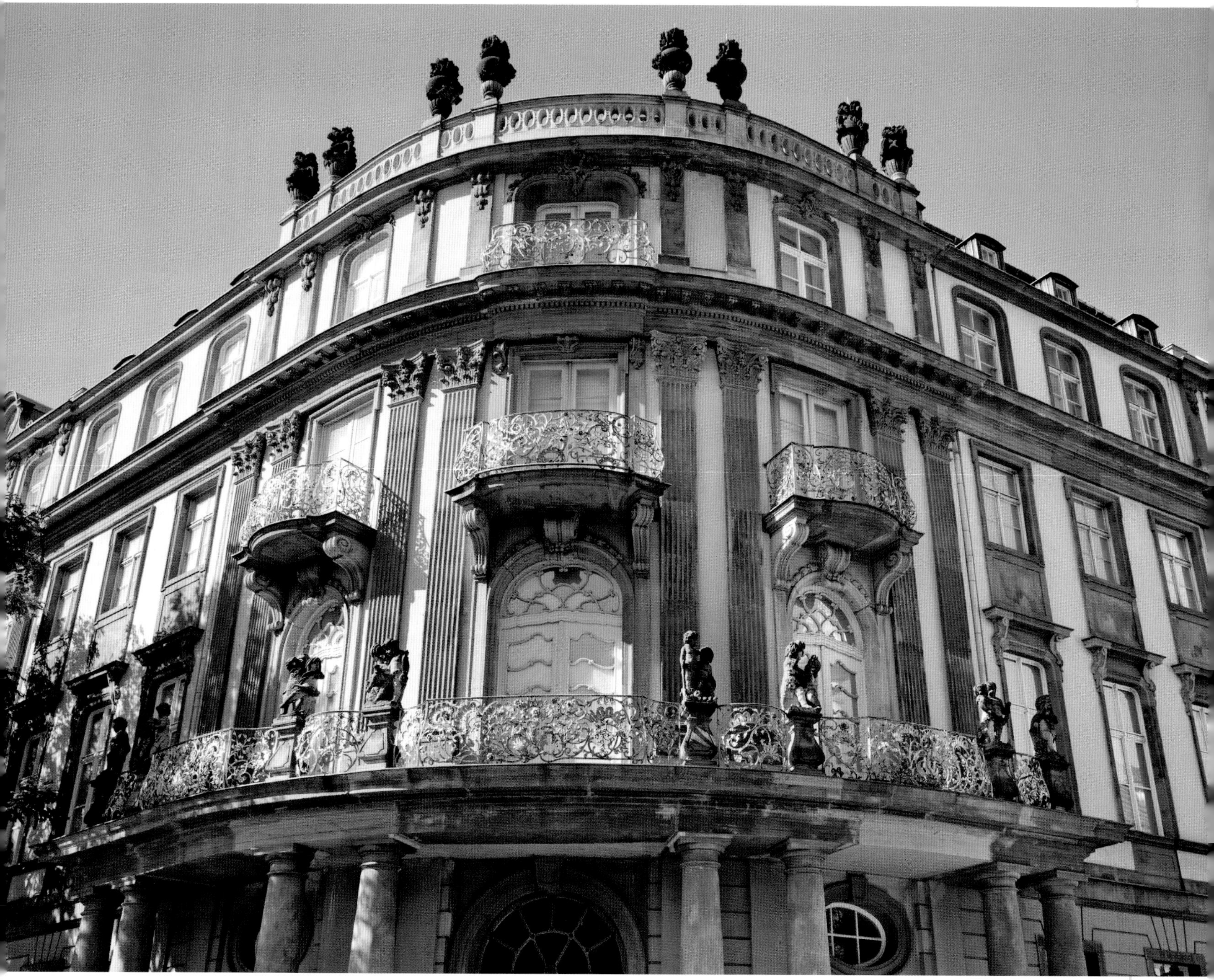

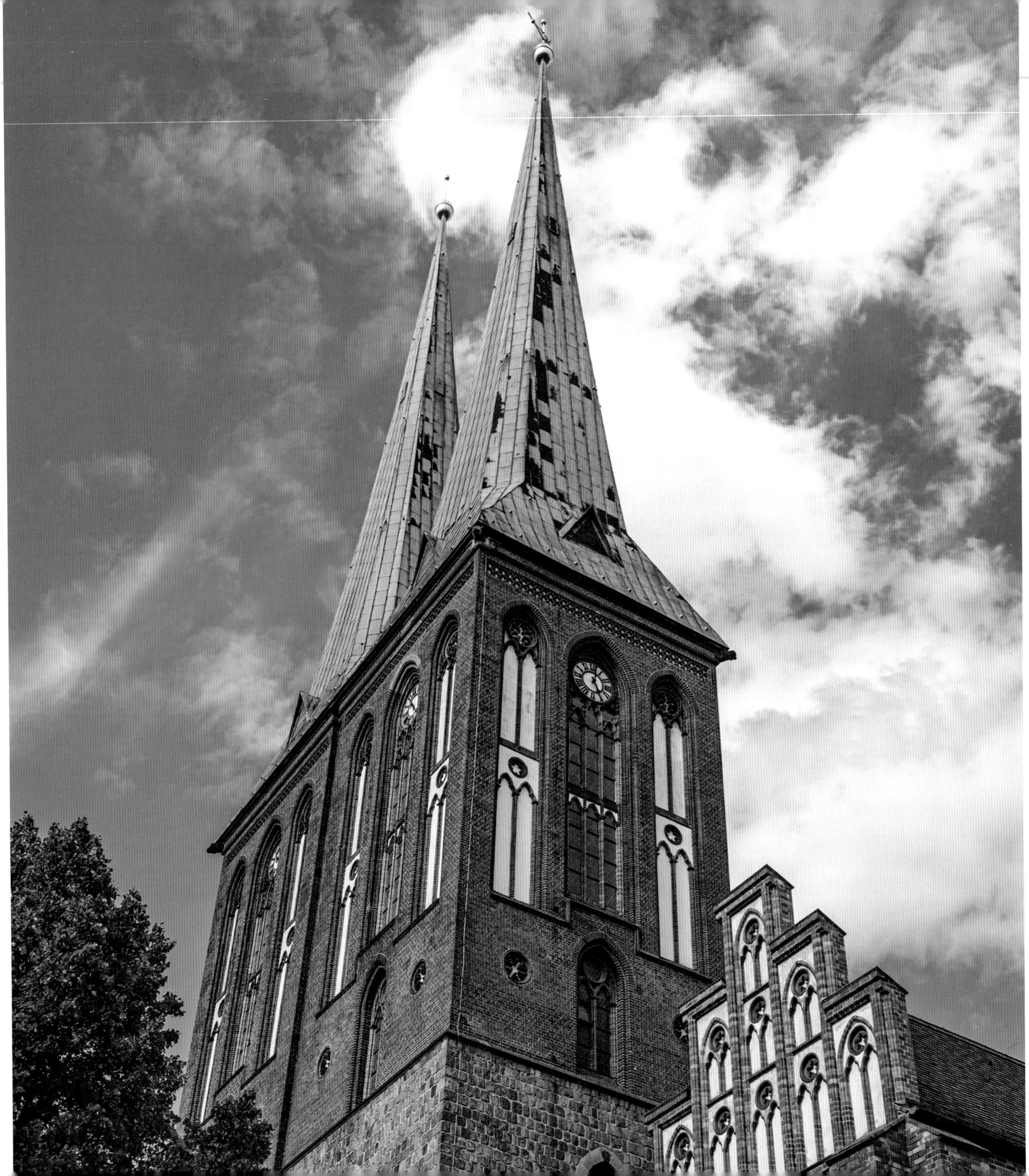

NIKOLAIKIRCHE

Nikolaikirchplatz, Nikolaiviertel

The Nikolaikirche (St Nicholas Church) is another example of a Berlin building that has risen from the ashes. Nearly eight centuries of active worship appeared to come to an end in the Second World War, when the above-ground church was completely destroyed by Allied bombing. It stayed as a ruin until 1984, when reconstruction began and it reopened in 2010 as a museum dedicated to explaining the history of both the church and the surrounding quarter. The external building is defined by its dramatic double spire, while the basement floors, which survived wartime destruction, are said to be the oldest existing rooms in Berlin.

WAPPENBRUNNEN

Nikolaikirchplatz, Nikolaiviertel

Nestled in front of the St Nicholas Church, the Wappenbrunnen (Coat of Arms Fountain) is a popular place to sit and take photographs. Although the fountain appears to be out of antiquity, it was actually created in 1987, based on an earlier design by Gerhard Thieme (1928–2018). A bear, the animal representing Berlin, sits in an ornate metal cage, clutching a coat of arms; other coats of arms adorn the octagonal base of the fountain. The fountain is also sometimes known as the Gründungsbrunnen (Fountain of the Founding), referring to the founding of Berlin.

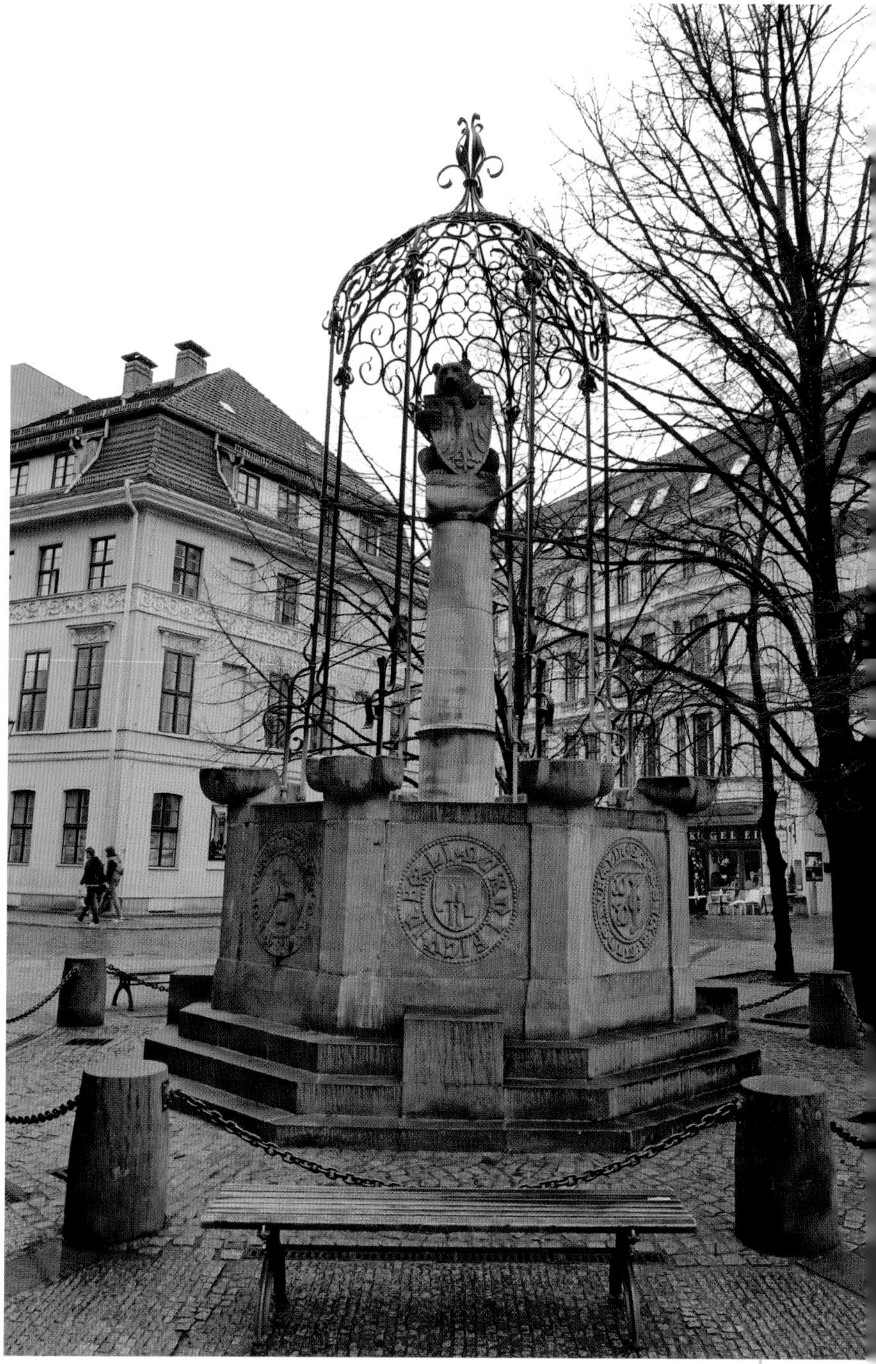

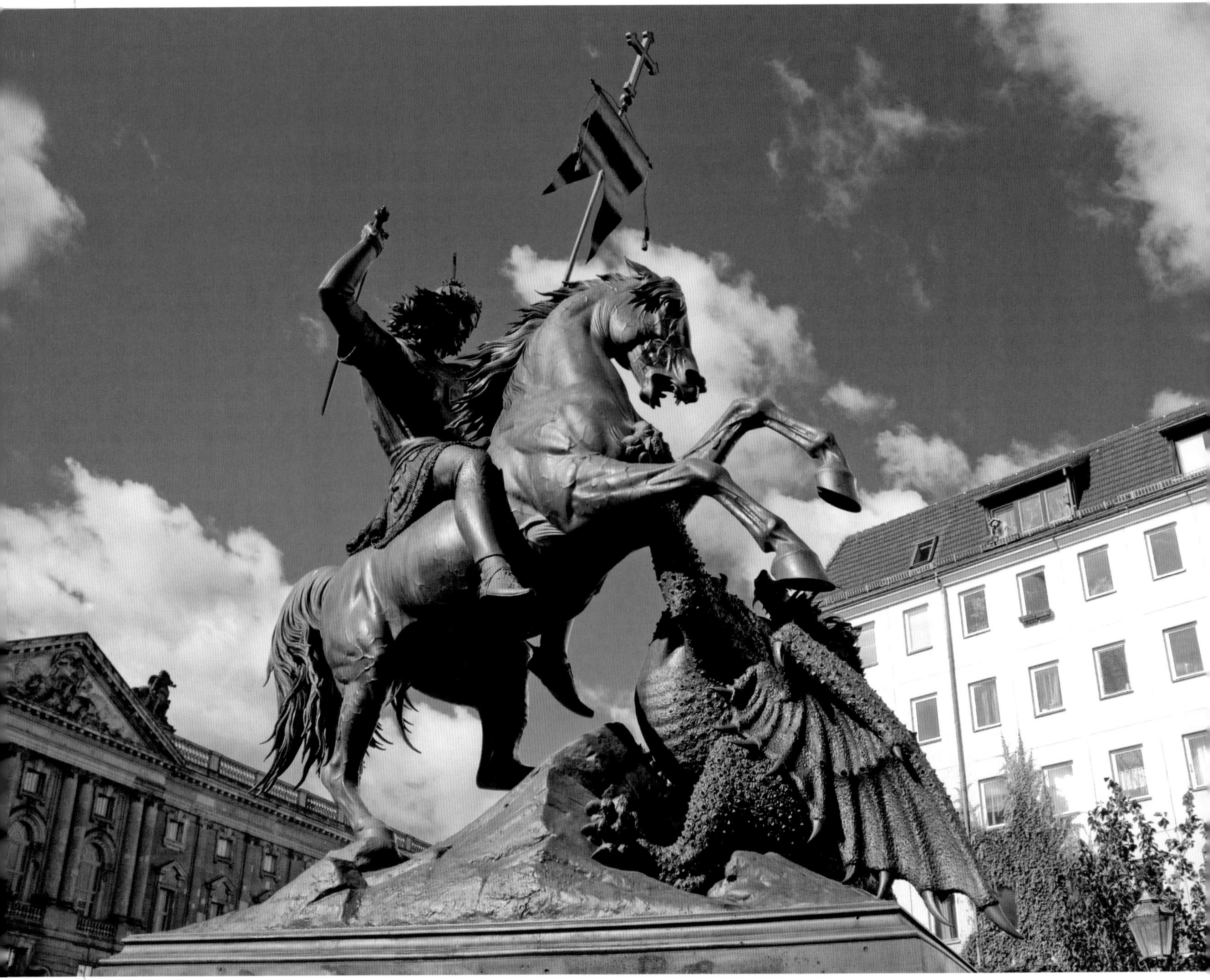

ST GEORGE FIGHTING THE DRAGON

Propststraße, Nikolaiviertel

With his sword raised and his horse rearing, St George fights the eternal battle against the dragon, in this sculpture that sits in the middle of Nikolaiviertel, on the Spree. The sculpture is made of bronze, and was unveiled in 1853, the product of the German sculptor August Karl Eduard Kiss (1802–65). Kiss was known for his monumental equestrian statues, particularly in Breslau, where his statues of Frederick the Great and King Frederick William III still stand. This particular statue was originally in the courtyard of the Berlin Palace, but was later moved.

FRANZISKANER-KLOSTERKIRCHE

Klosterstraße, Nikolaiviertel

The picturesque Franziskaner-Klosterkirche (Franciscan Friary Church) takes us back to the thirteenth century, the ruins all that are left of the monastery church for a nearby Franciscan order. It was an impressive edifice on its founding in 1250, 52 m (170 ft) long and 16 m (52 ft) wide, and it subsequently went through major periods of renovation and rebuilding in the intervening centuries. The ruins are the result of the church's destruction by Allied bombing on 3 April 1945; much of Berlin's ecclesiastical architecture was lost to the bombers.

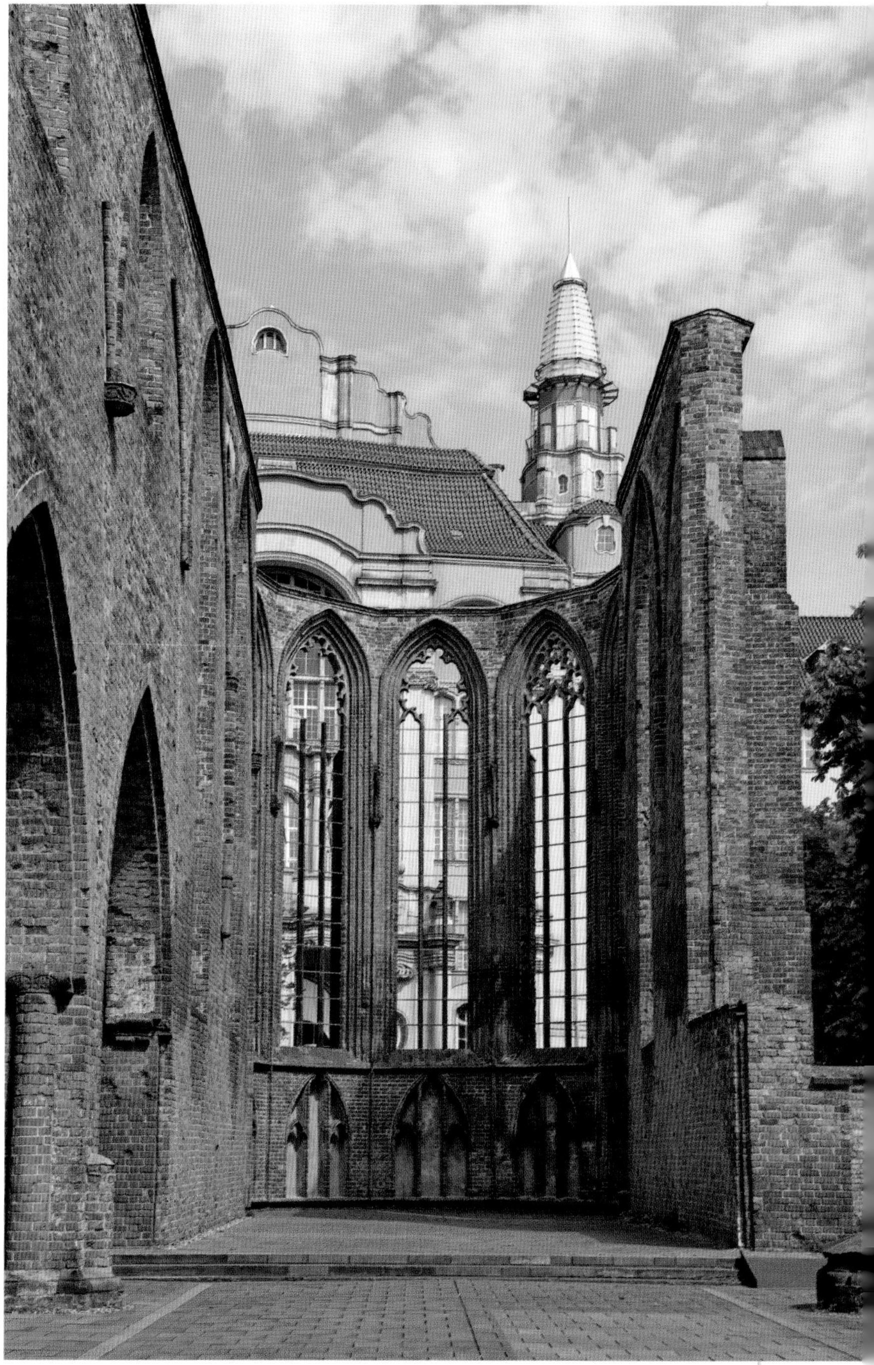

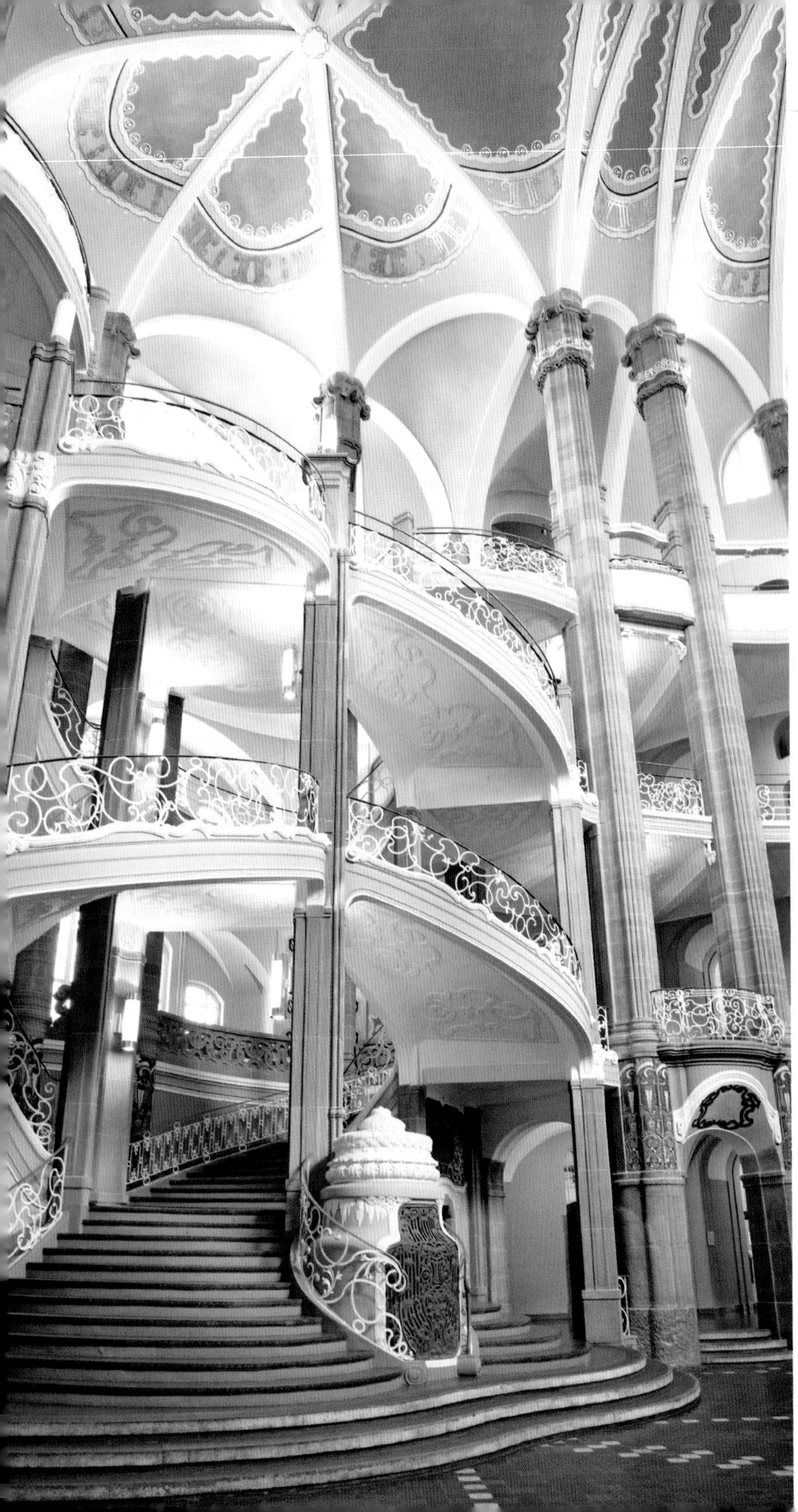

STADTGERICHT

Littenstraße, Nikolaiviertel

The Stadtgericht (Courts of Justice) are a long stretch of elegant buildings, constructed between 1896 and 1905. At the height of their majesty, the four complexes that composed the site measured 220 m (722 ft) in length, the buildings rising to five floors in height. In a familiar story, the building was heavily damaged during the Second World War, and restoration efforts are ongoing to this day. The photograph here shows a delicate but spectacular atrium, in the architectural Liberty style.

FERNSEHTURM

Panoramastraße, Alexanderplatz

As the fourth largest freestanding structure in Europe, at a dizzying 368.03 m (1,207.45 ft), the Fernsehturm (TV Tower), is a huge pin in the map of Germany, marking the centre of the capital. It was raised between 1965 and 1969 by the GDR, to improve the coverage of TV and radio broadcasts across the city. This it achieved, but it also came to be such a defining landmark that it was given monument status in 1979, which it still retains. Today owned by Deutsche Telekom, the structure receives more than one million visitors a year, who ascend to the elevated viewing platform.

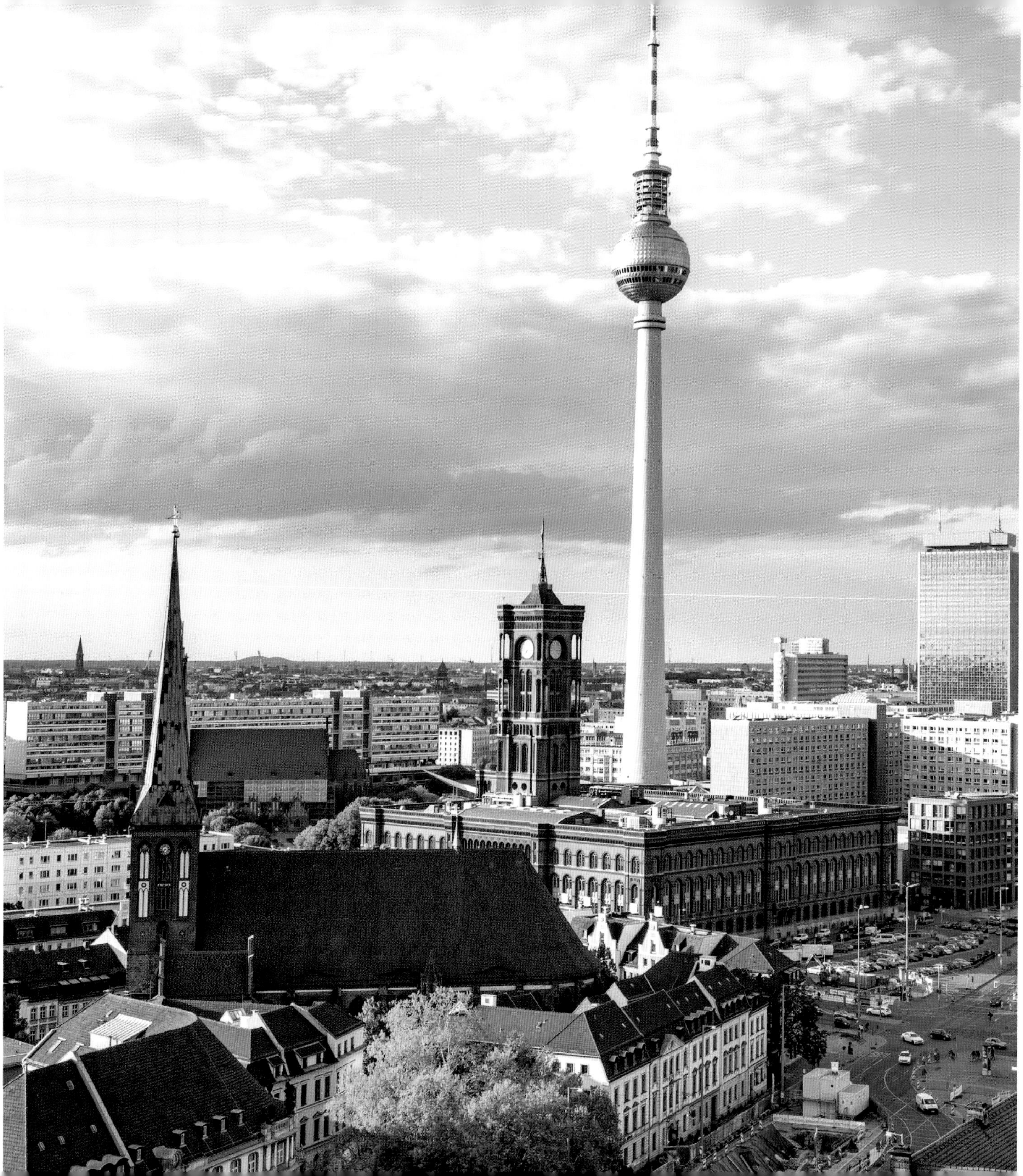

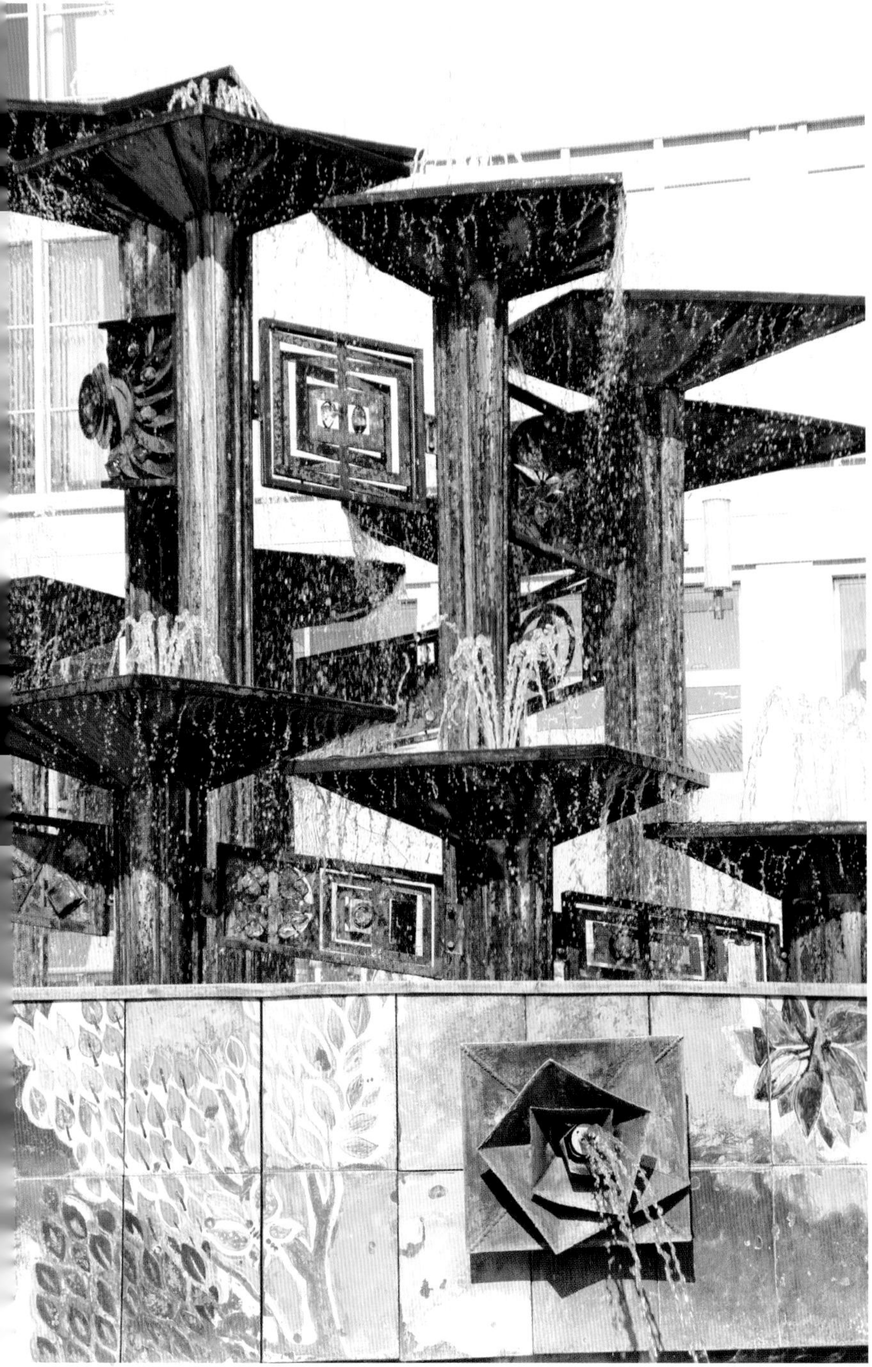

BRUNNEN DER VÖLKERFREUNDSCHAFT

Alexanderplatz

The Brunnen der Völkerfreundschaft (Fountain of International Friendship) was designed by Walter Womacka (1925–2010) in 1969–70 as part of a general civic redesign of the Alexanderplatz. It is a sizeable work: 23 m (75 ft) in diameter, a water spiral 6.2 m (20 ft) high cascading down 17 shells, constructed of copper, glass, ceramics and enamel. In true Womacka style, an enamel frieze wraps around the basin, showing highly coloured plant and animal motifs.

HAUS DES LEHRERS

Alexanderstraße, Alexanderplatz

From a distance, the Haus des Lehrers (House of the Teacher) appears much like many of the utilitarian buildings constructed in the GDR during the 1960s. Yet as you move closer, into focus comes the celebratory frieze that wraps around all four sides of the building, created by the artist Walter Womacka using 800,000 coloured tiles. Each side depicts different aspects of culture, technology and society, with a utopian and humanist energy. Restoration work on both the building and the damaged frieze began in 2002, and today the building provides high-grade office space.

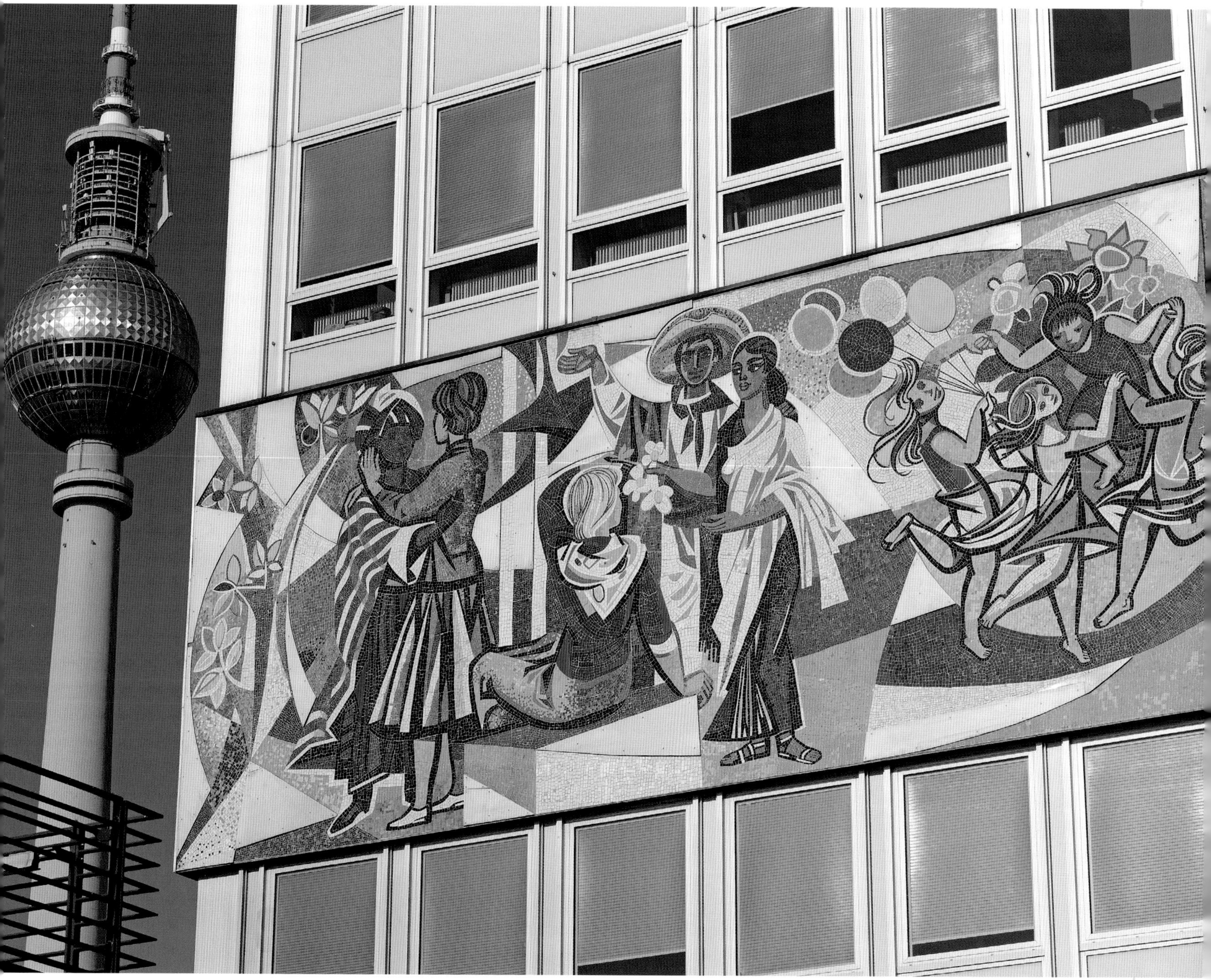

NEPTUNBRUNNEN AND MARIENKIRCHE

Karl-Liebknecht-Straße, nr. Alexanderplatz

With a historical heritage dating back to the thirteenth century, the red-brick and granite Marienkirche (St Mary's Church) on Karl-Liebknecht-Straße rivals the Nikolaikirche in age. At birth, and for the first three centuries of its existence, it was a Catholic church, although the Reformation moved it under the wing of Lutheran Protestantism. The grounds of the church feature a number of statues, including the Neptunbrunnen (Neptune Fountain) seen here, representing the Roman god Neptune and the four main rivers of Prussia.

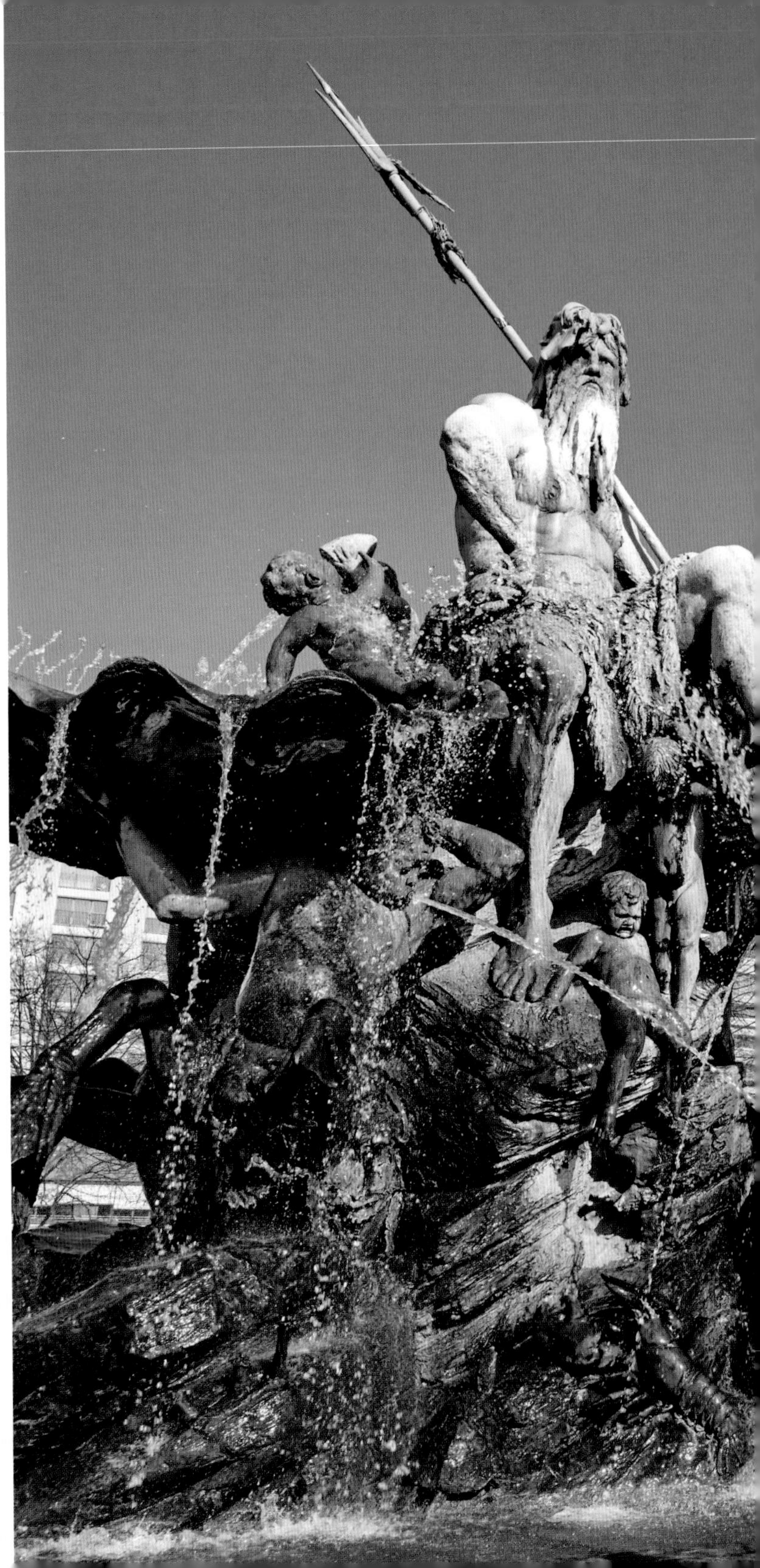

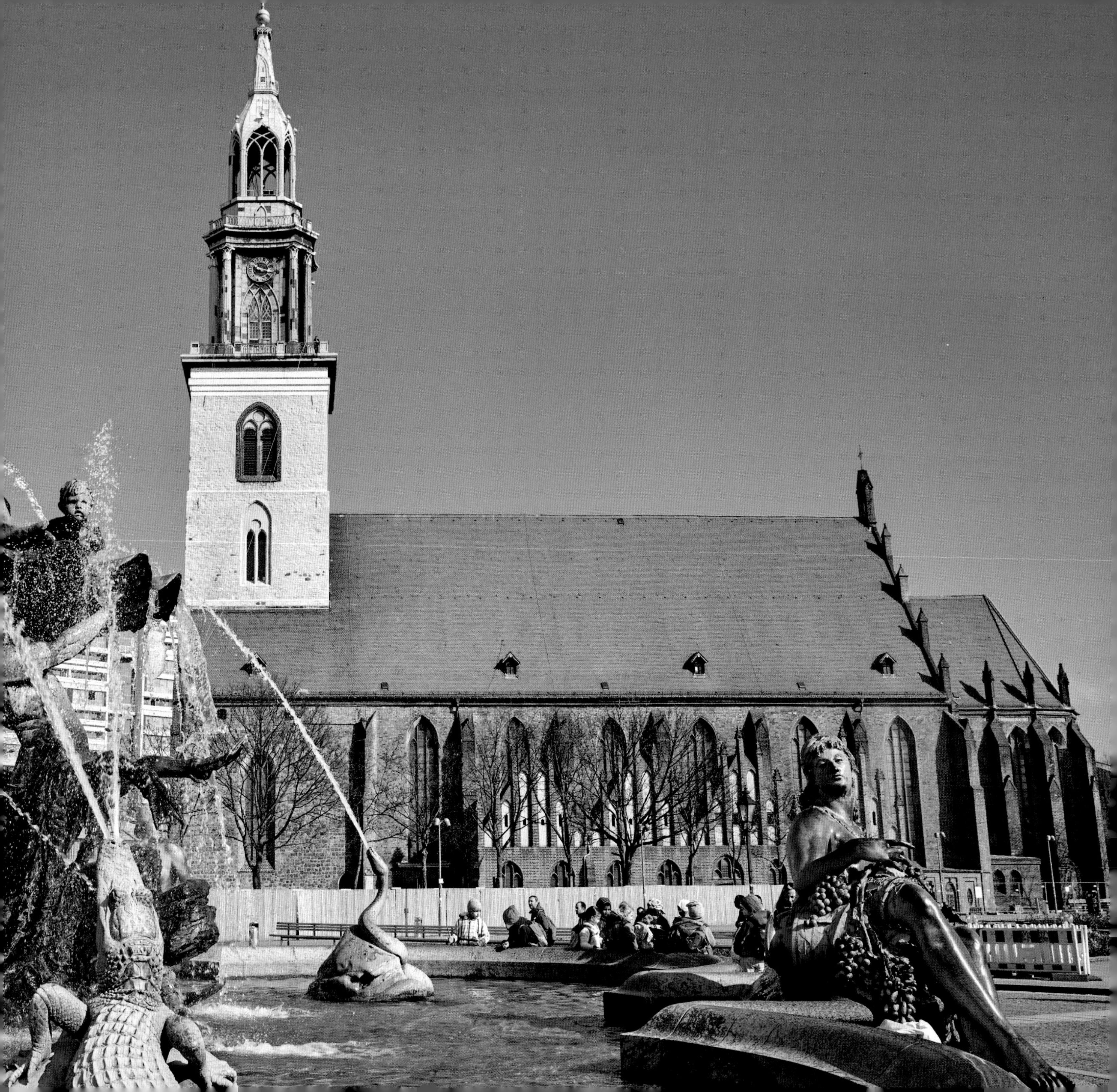

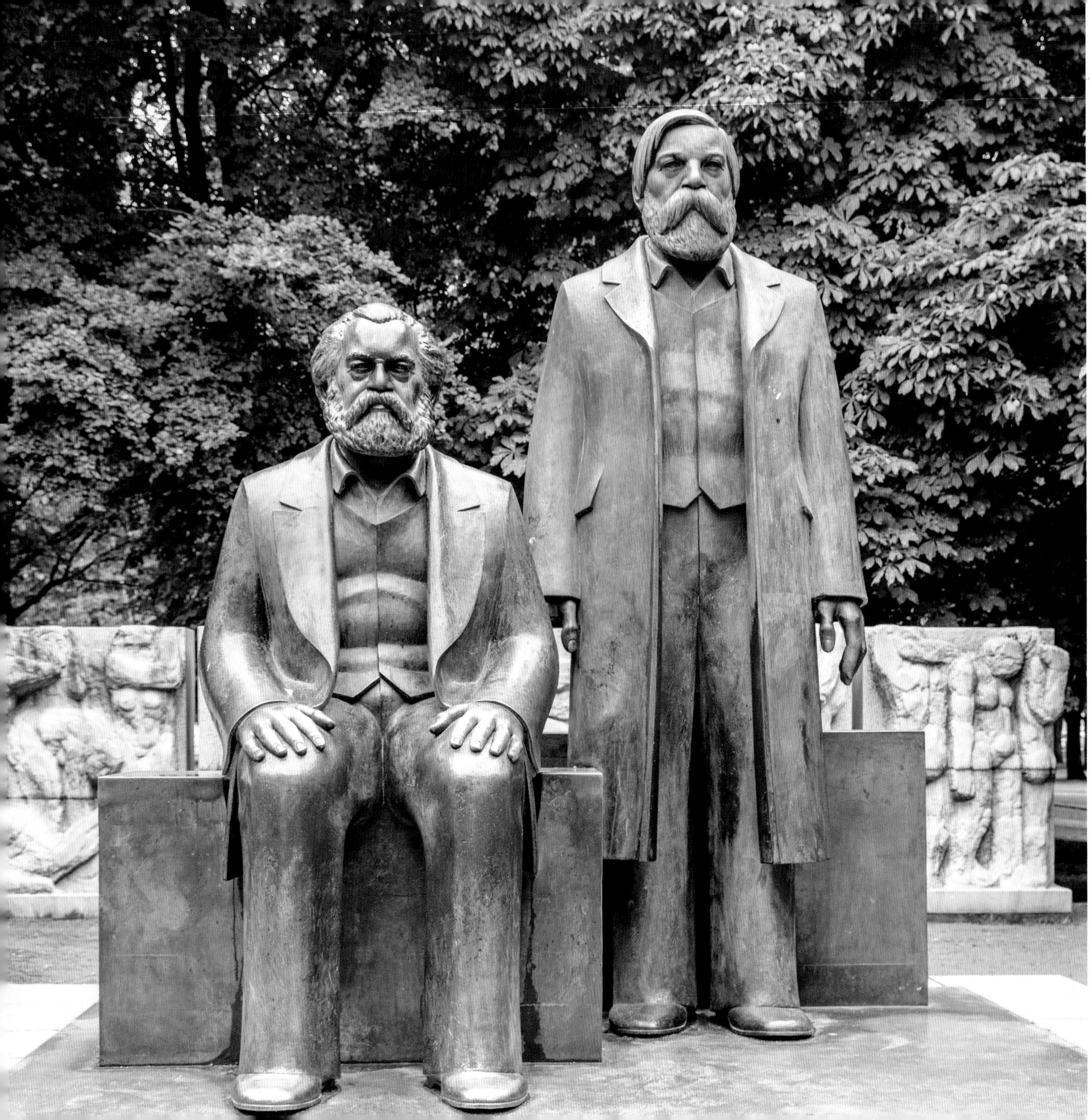

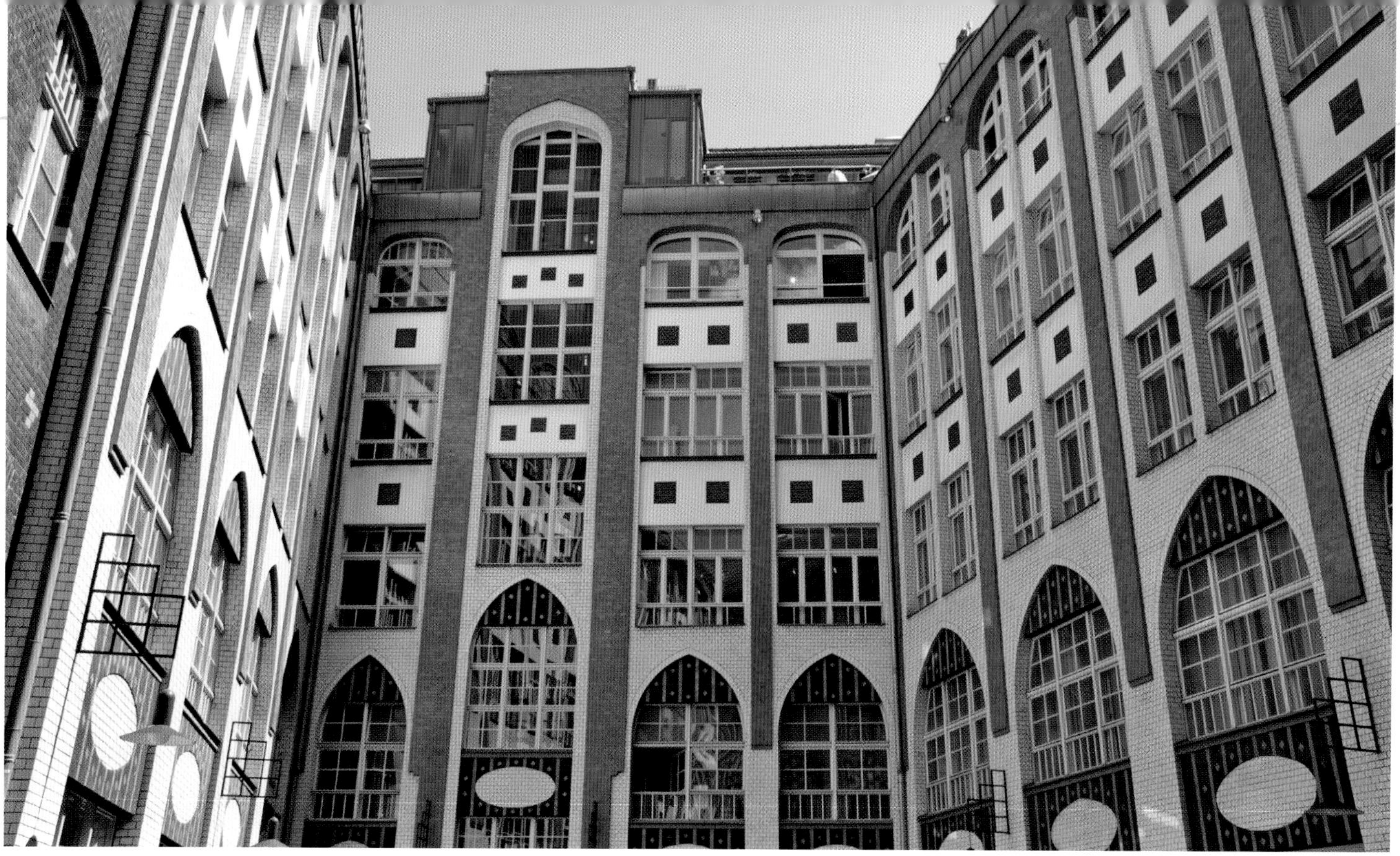

MARX-ENGELS FORUM

Karl-Liebknecht-Straße, Alexanderplatz

Two figures preside over the Marx-Engels Forum, a public park in the Mitte district of Berlin. Cast in bronze and designed by sculptor Ludwig Engelhardt (1924–2001), the oversized sculptures of Karl Marx (left) and Friedrich Engels, foundational personalities in the history of communism, form the park's political centrepiece, monuments to the ideology of the GDR, which established the park in 1986. Formerly, the park had been a densely populated part of the city, but one that was obliterated by wartime destruction.

HACKESCHE HÖFE

Rosenthaler Straße, Scheunenviertel

A magnet for tourists and locals alike, the Hackesche Höfe (Hackesche Courtyard) is a place to explore and discover. Rather than a single place, it is a courtyard complex designed and built by the architect Kurt Berndt (1863–1925), in what was already a burgeoning area of urban dynamism. August Endell (1871–1925), a pioneer within the German Expressionist movement, gave the complex a polished Art Nouveau finish, still resplendent after a 1997 restoration. The Hackesche Höfe is today a bustling area of cafés, restaurants, bars, shops and nightlife.

HAUS SCHWARZENBERG

Rosenthaler Straße, Scheunenviertel

Located beside the Hackesche Höfe, the Haus Schwarzenberg (Schwarzenberg House) delivers an abrupt aesthetic jolt. Having passed through a back alley, you enter a courtyard surrounded by buildings that appear trapped in the austerity and functionality of Cold War East Berlin. Yet here street art of every conceivable description – posters, graffiti, stencils, mosaics, installation art – covers almost the entirety of the wall surfaces, making the Haus Schwarzenberg an edgy space, hinting at rebellion and iconoclastic sentiments. The Haus contains a gallery, a shop selling electronic music and art books, a curious museum of automata, and also the poignant Anne Frank Zentrum.

NEUE SYNAGOGE

Oranienburger Straße, Spandauer Vorstadt

The Neue Synagoge (New Synagogue) leaps out from its surroundings courtesy of its Moorish architectural style, reflected in the golden-ribbed domes and oriental-style façade. Once, following its construction in 1866, the building was a thriving centre of Judaism, the largest place of Jewish worship in Germany, with a main hall holding 3,200 people. The malign effects of Nazism and war in the 1930s and 1940s led to the destruction of much of the building, but the façade remained, and the structure was rebuilt in 1988–91. Today the Neue Synagoge houses the Centrum Judaicum foundation.

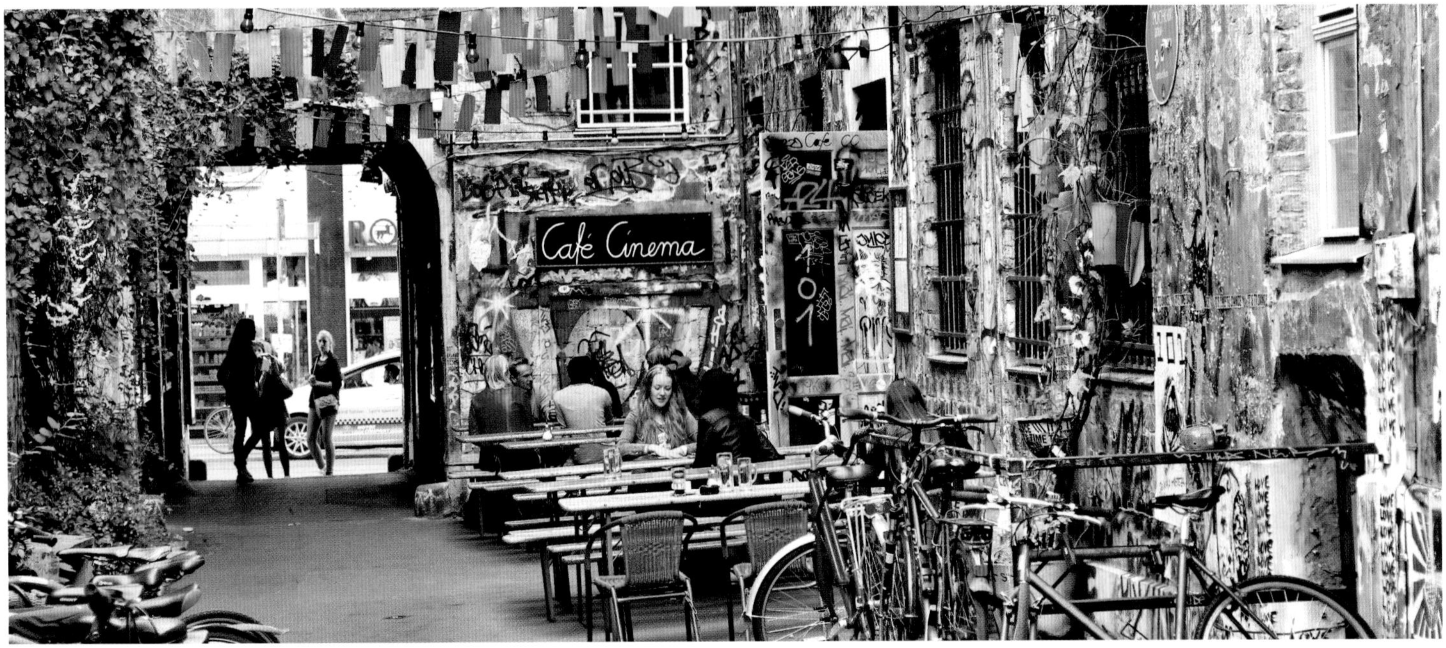

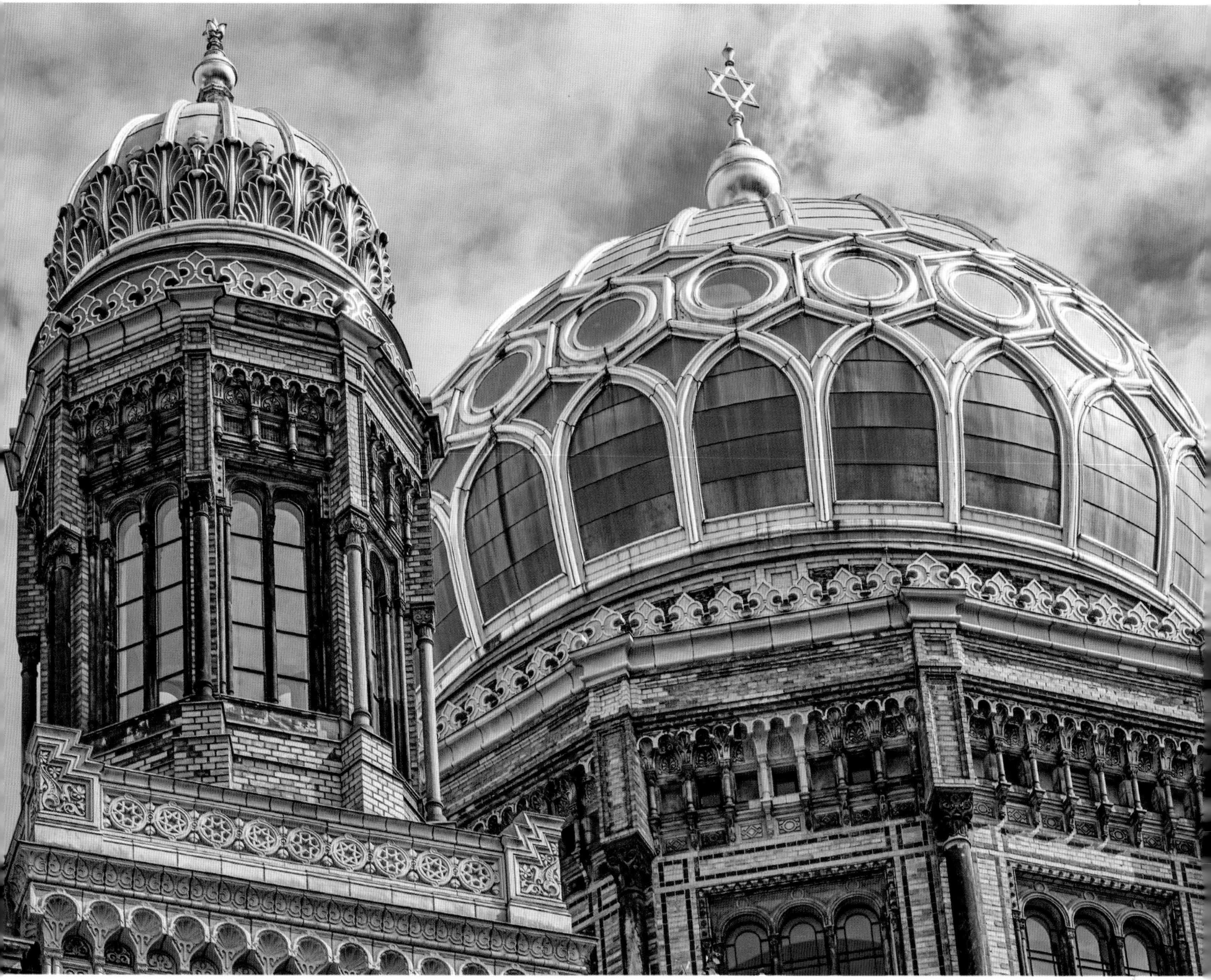

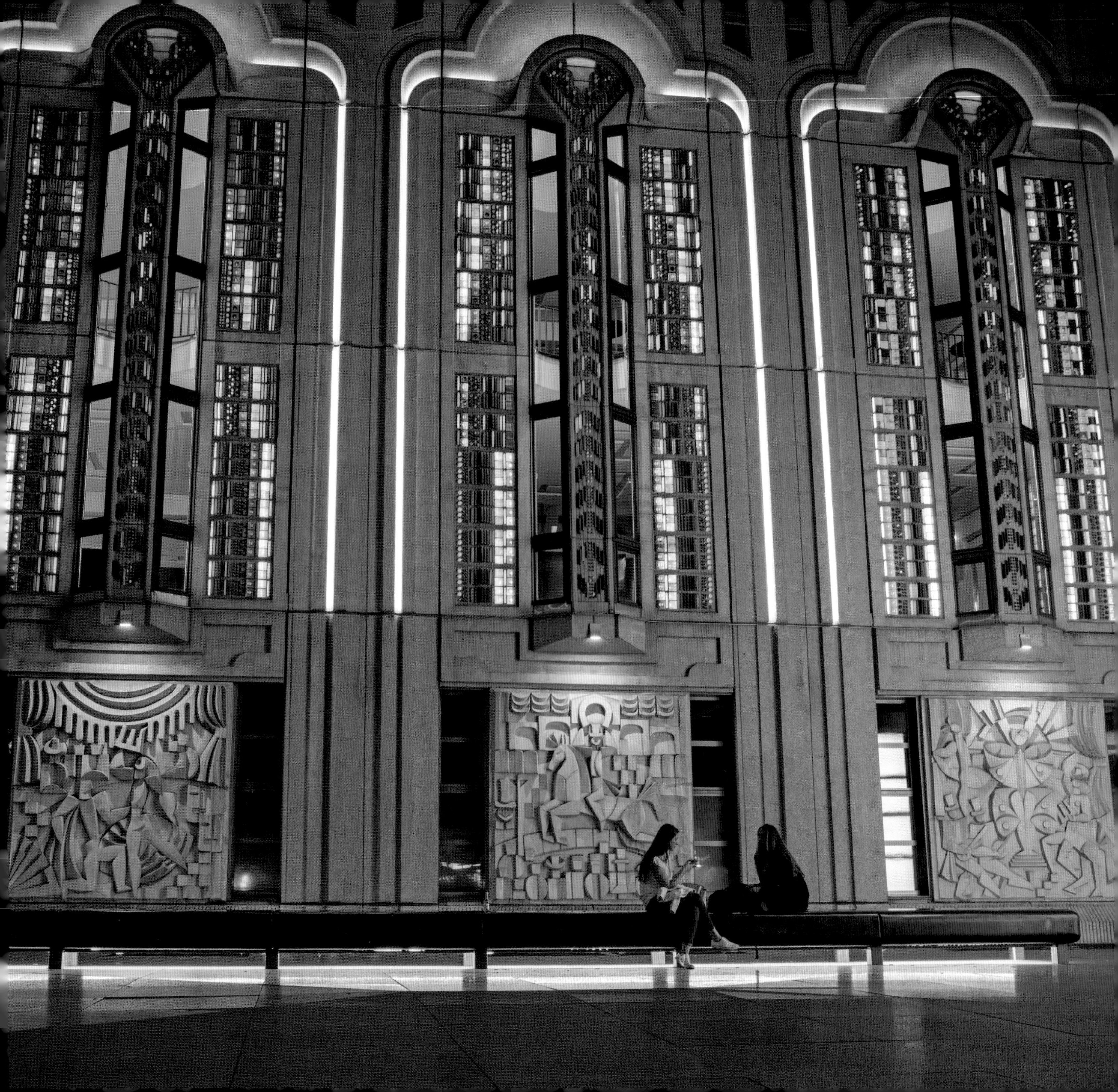

FRIEDRICHSTADT-PALAST

Friedrichstraße, Spandauer Vorstadt

Managing to appear both retro and futuristic at the same time, the Friedrichstadt-Palast show theatre forms a glowing backdrop to the street. This great show theatre, one of the biggest in Europe and with a production ambition that equals Las Vegas, began its life as a theatrically repurposed market hall in the 1870s. Expansion took hold, and by the 1920s the Großes Schauspielhaus (Grand Theatre) was a premier venue in the capital. This old building eventually gave in to ruin, and was demolished, but the new Friedrichstadt-Palast was built in the 1980s, just a stone's throw from the original site.

REICHSBAHNBUNKER

Reinhardtstraße, Mitte

Appearing as a brutalist fortress dropped into the centre of Berlin, the Reichsbahnbunker (Imperial Railway Bunker) illustrates how the Allied strategic bombing campaign of the Second World War came to shape the city. Designed by Karl Bonatz (1882–1951), but under the supervision of Albert Speer (1905–81), one of the Nazi Party's most senior officials, it was an air-raid shelter to house 3,000 travellers on the Reichsbahn. The structure, 18 m (59 ft) high and with walls 3 m (10 ft) thick, could withstand the high-explosive. After the war it became, variously, a warehouse and a fetish club, but from 2007 it has been an art gallery, with penthouse living on the top.

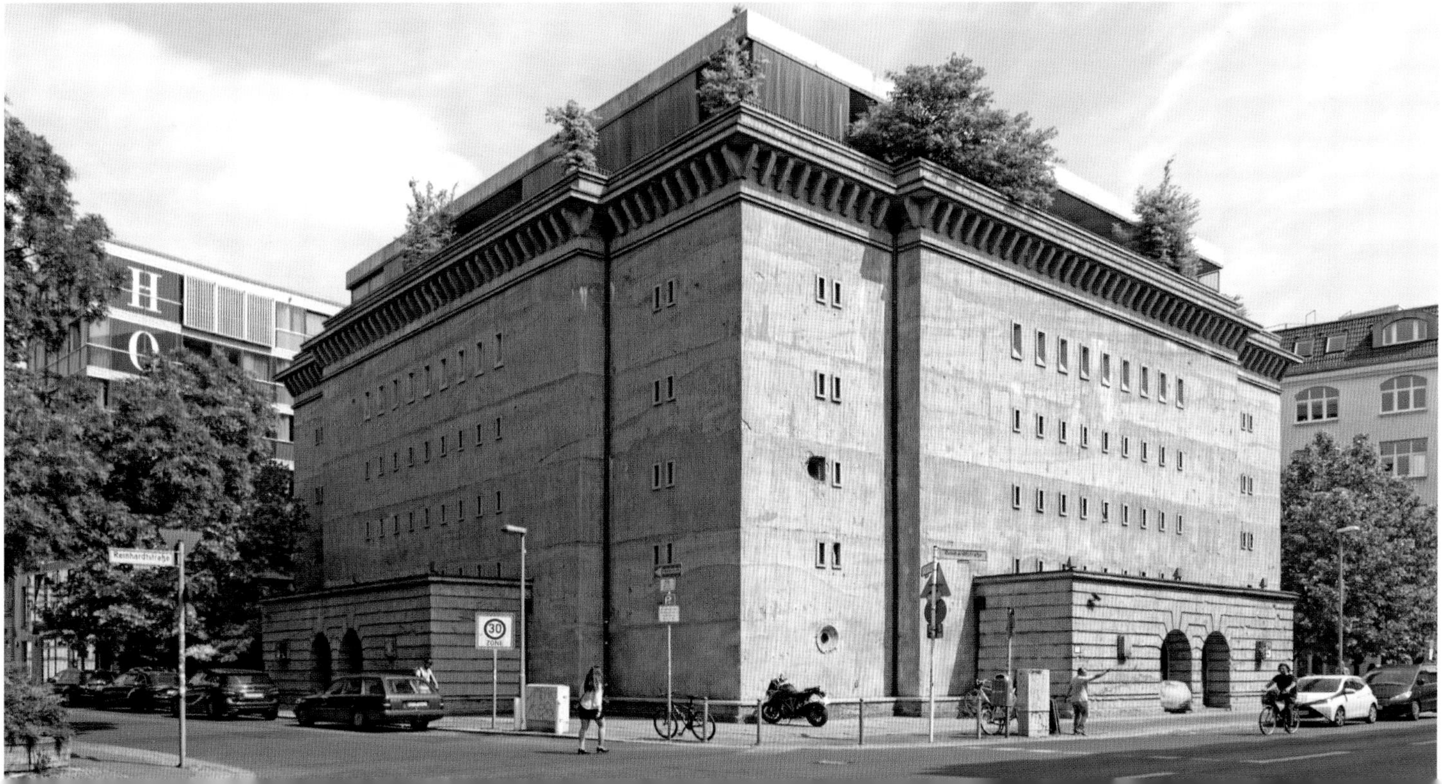

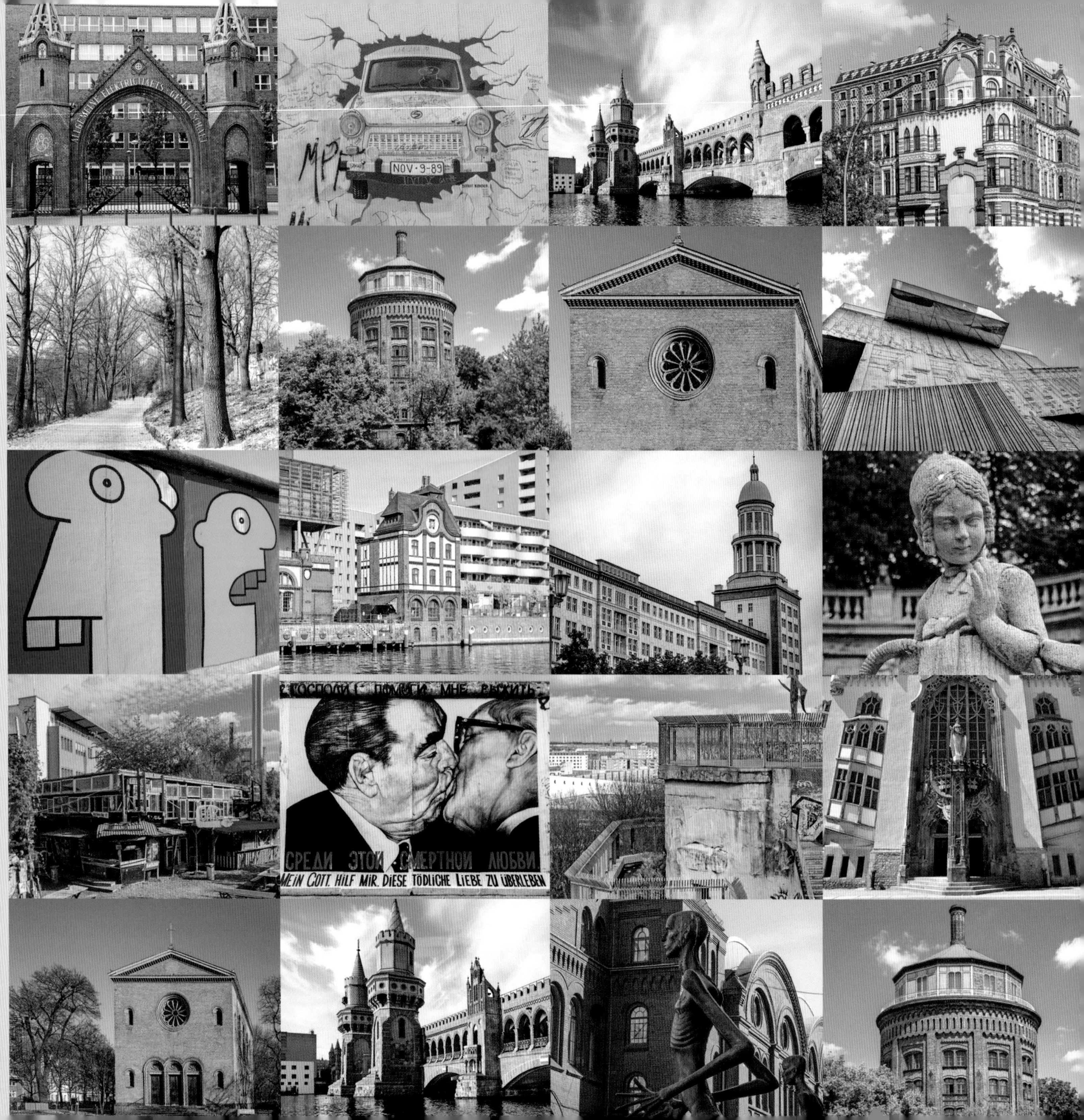
NOV·9-89
СРЕДИ ЭТОЙ СМЕРТНОЙ ЛЮБВИ
MEIN GOTT. HILF MIR. DIESE TÖDLICHE LIEBE ZU ÜBERLEBEN

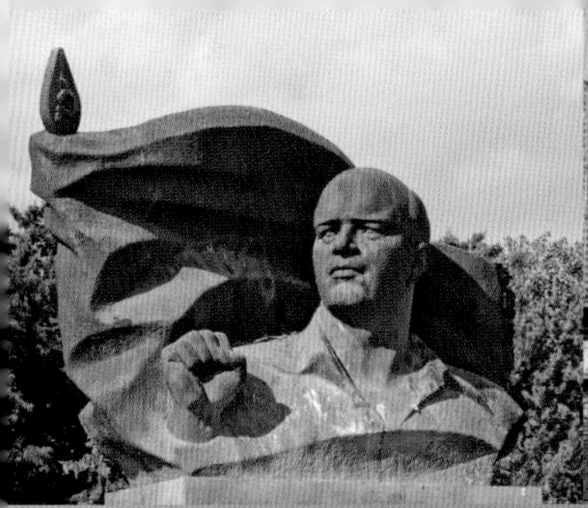
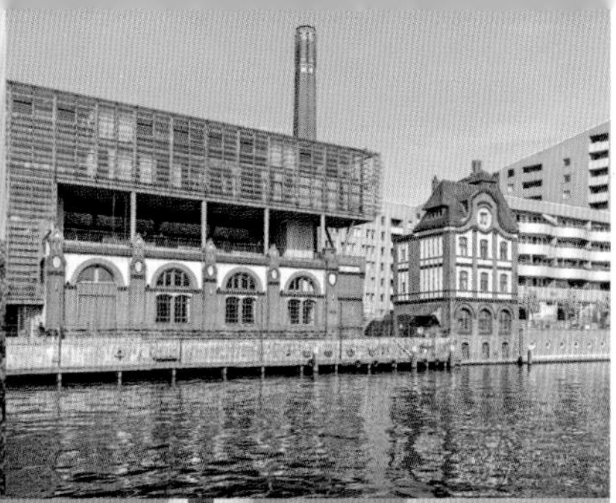
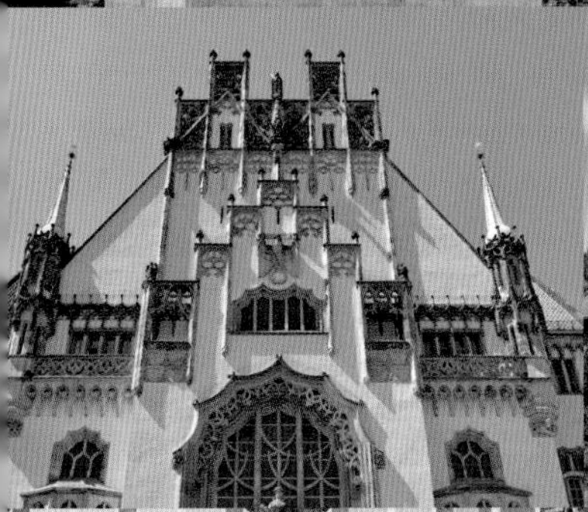
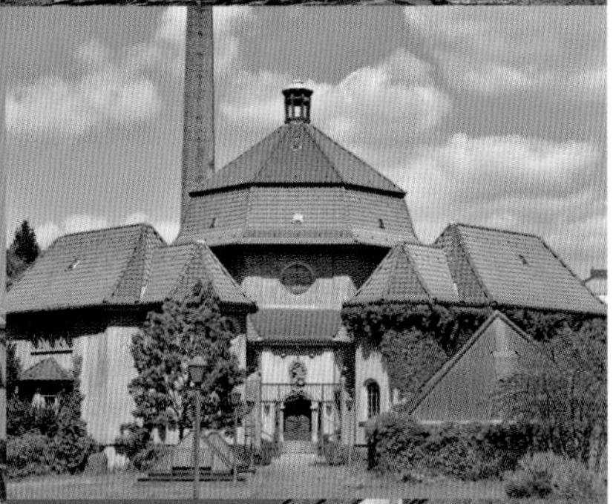
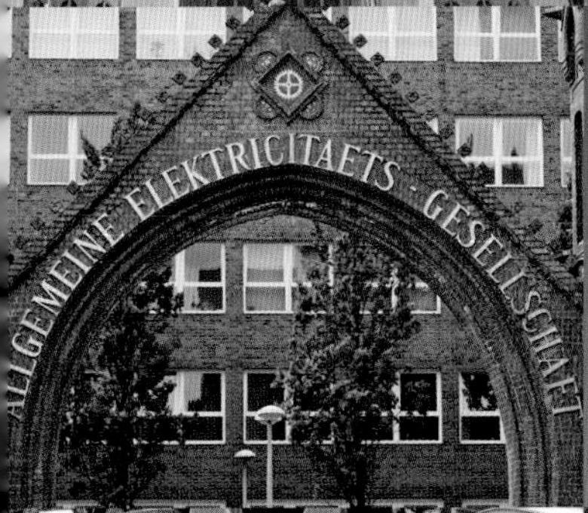

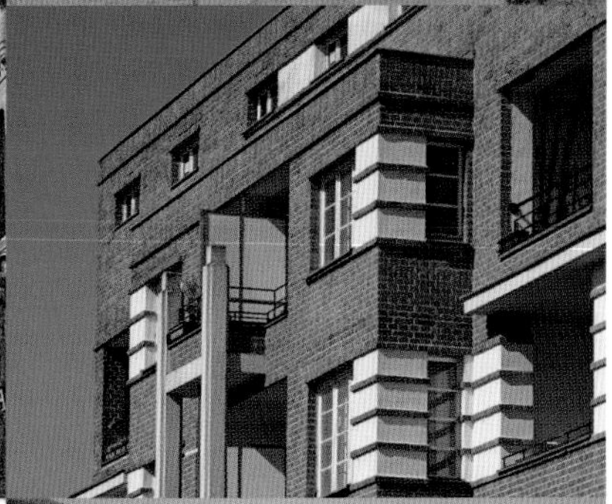
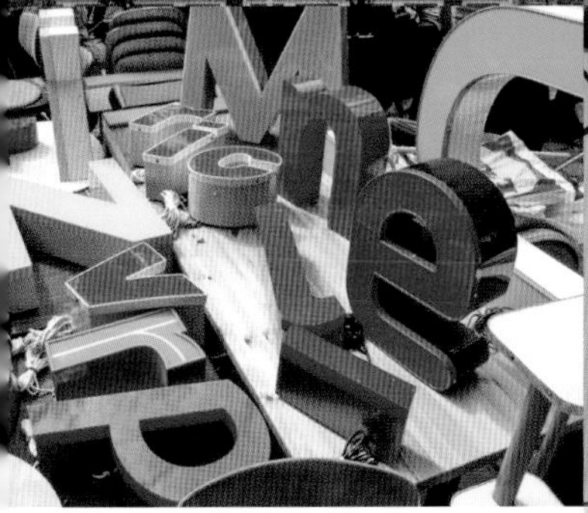
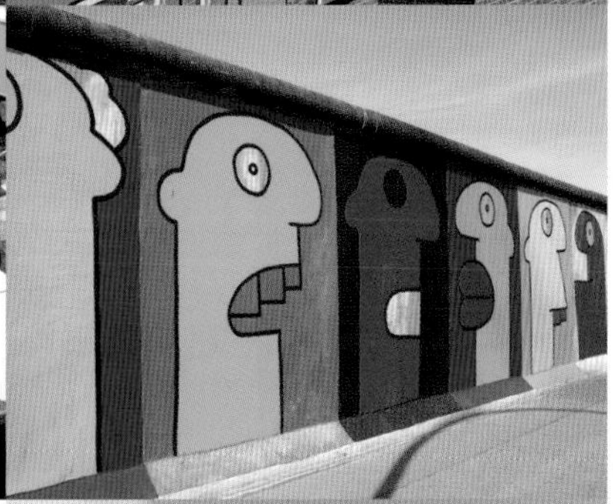
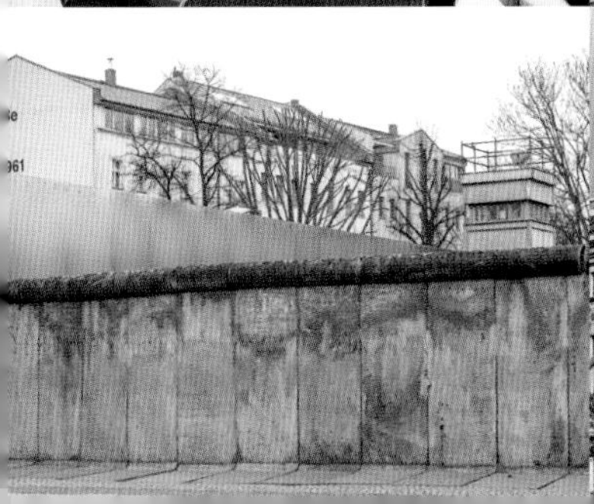
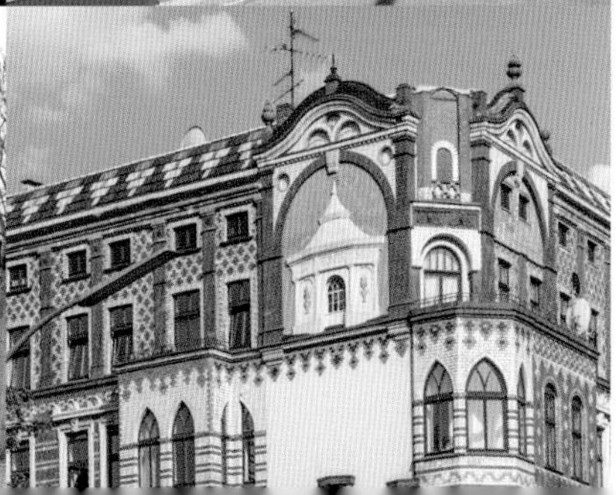

CITY NORTH CENTRAL

There are many parts of Berlin that embody a counter-cultural instinct, but the north-central areas are particularly vibrant in terms of alternative ways of looking at the world.

Boroughs such as Wedding and districts such as Pankow thrive on forging and maintaining their own identities against the relentless throb of commercialism in the centre, this drive assisted by the fact that these districts have more affordable house rentals and thus attract a younger or, conversely, more traditional crowd. There is also the dynamism that comes from putting lots of people in one place; Pankow, for example, is the most populous district in Berlin, with a population of more than 400,000. Quirky art, music and theatre abound. Architecturally, the north-central area ranges from neo-Baroque ornamentation to Modernist simplicity to fairytale pastiche.

But this area of Berlin is also a place of peace and traditionalism. Churches and civic buildings reflect older ways of looking at the world, while park areas offer green spaces for contemplation and escape. There are also further monuments to the city's historical traumas, including massive air-raid shelter 'Flak towers' and border outposts of the Berlin Wall. Above all, north-central Berlin is a place to explore and discover.

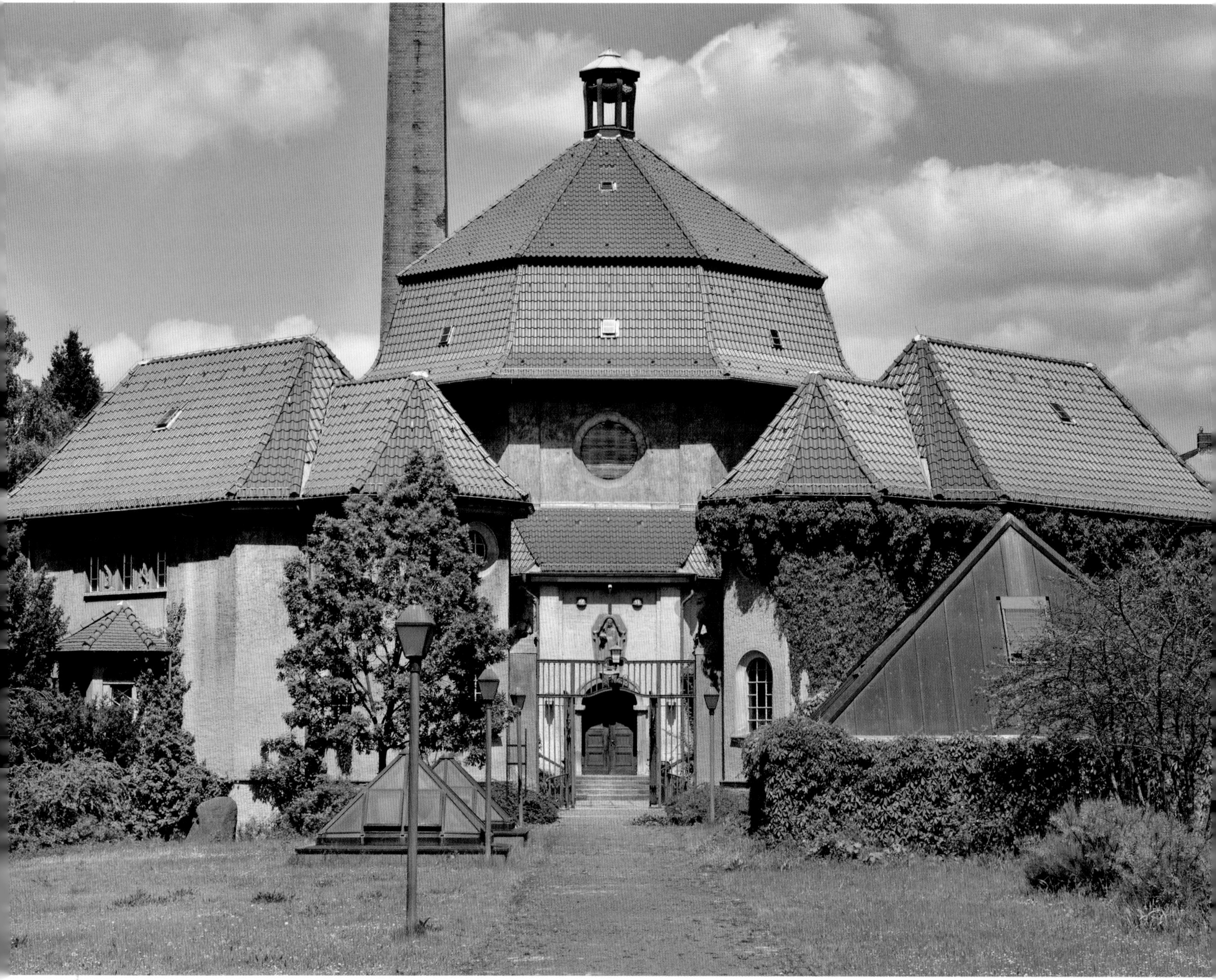

SILENT GREEN KULTURQUARTIER

Gerichtstraße, Wedding

Built in 1911, the rather fairyland appearance of the Silent Green Kulturquartier (Culture Quarter) belies the fact that until 2002 this building functioned as a crematorium. It has some grim historical notes in this regard – the first person killed while trying to cross the Berlin Wall, Ida Siekmann (1902–61), was cremated here. From 2013, however, it was repurposed as a venue for experimental music concerts (it has two performance halls), record-label management and fitness classes.

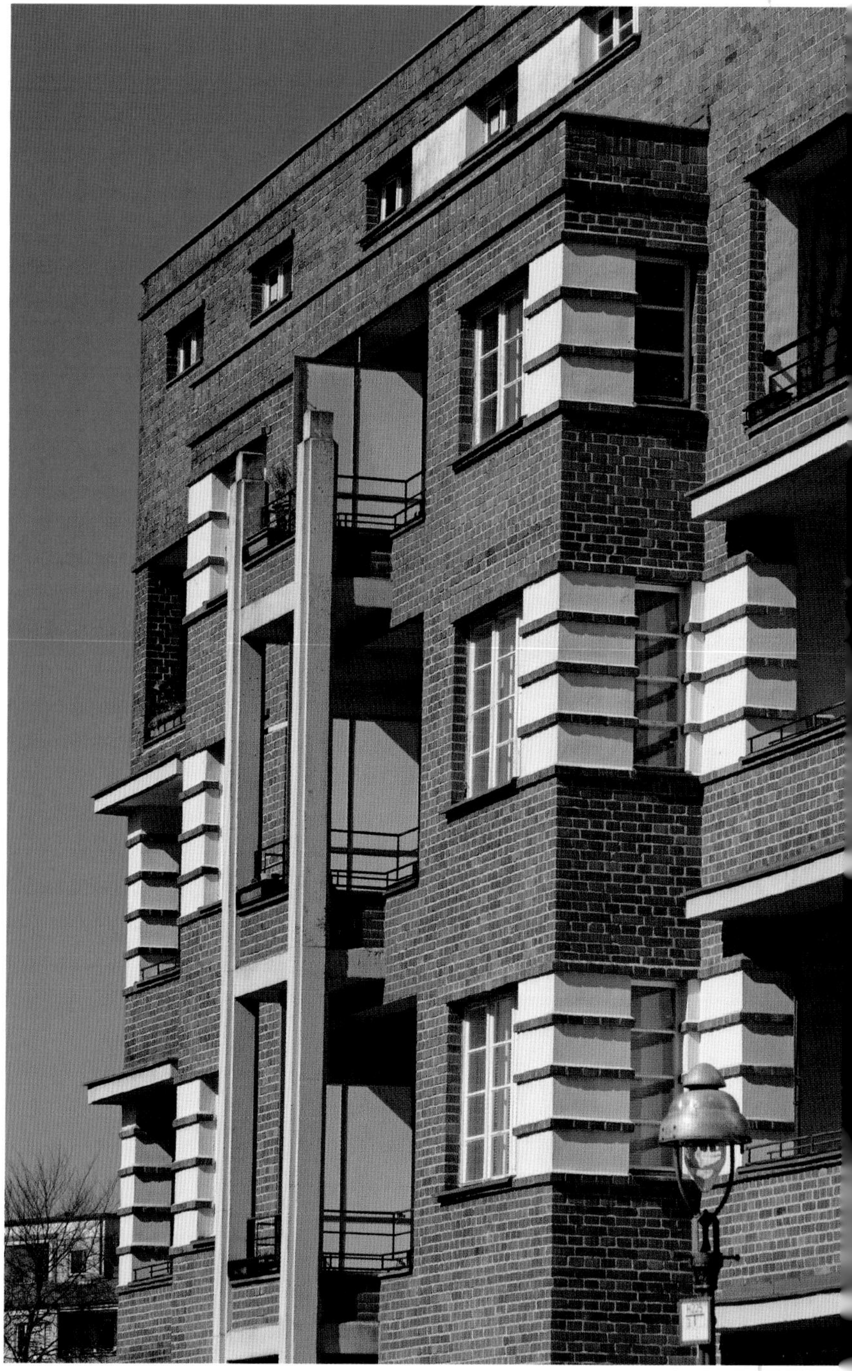

SIEDLUNG SCHILLERPARK

Wedding, Mitte

Weimar-era urban planner and architect Bruno Taut (1880–1938) developed this Modernist housing project as part of a major property development movement in Berlin in the 1920s and 1930s. Inspired by the flat roofs and red-brick structures he saw in the Netherlands, Taut innovated further in form and function, creating urban living that was light and open to the street, the domestic buildings pivoting socially around courtyards, kindergartens and other communal spaces. Despite sustaining damage during the Second World War, the Siedlung Schillerpark has been restored to its former welcoming personality.

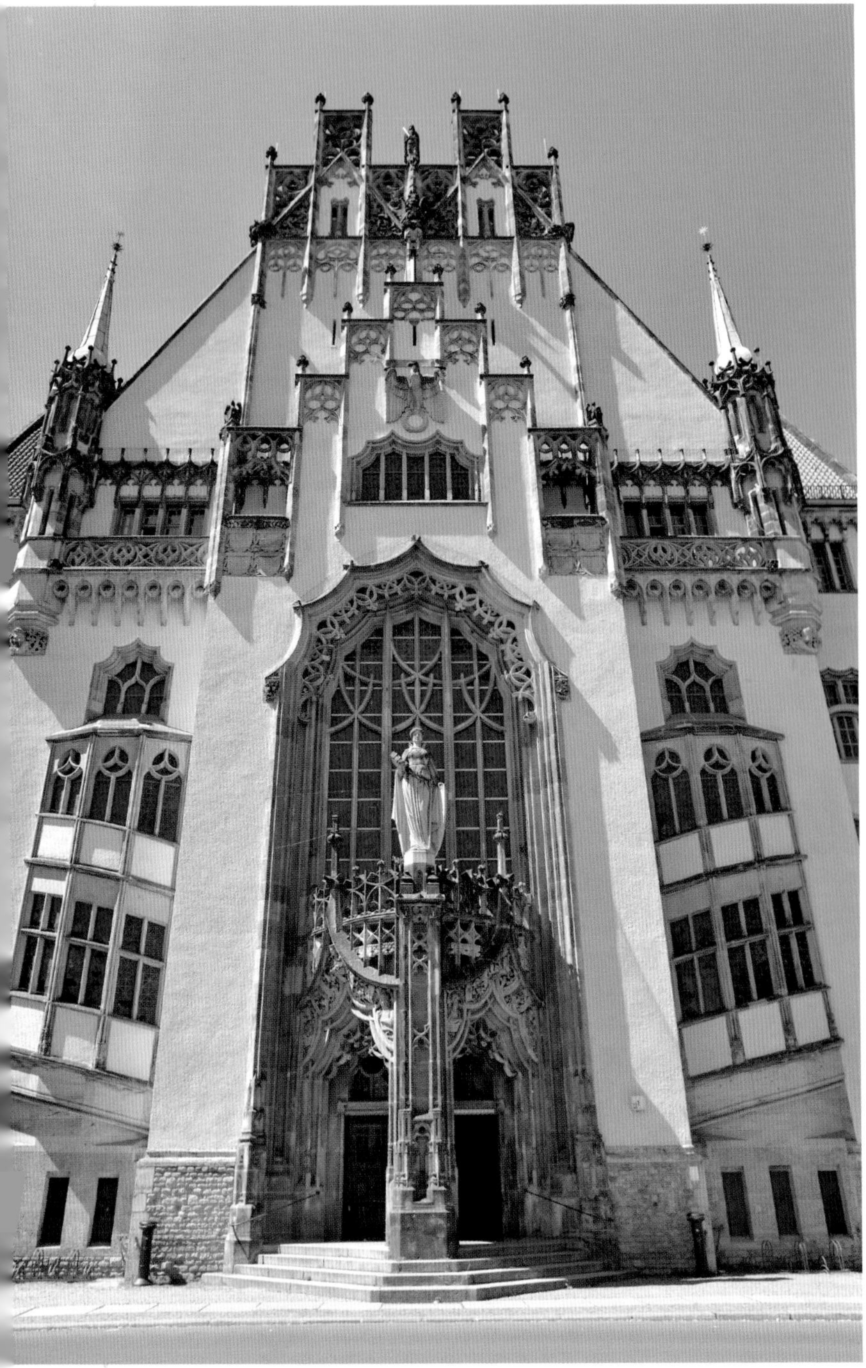

AMTSGERICHT

Brunnenplatz, Wedding

An extraordinary work in the Gothic Revival style, the Amtsgericht (Courthouse) in Wedding leaps out from its more workaday surroundings. It was built between 1901 and 1906, a mixture of opulence and implied threat derived from inspiration by Albrecht Castle in Meissen. During the Nazi era, it dispensed the skewed and merciless legal judgements for which the Third Reich was known; a Nazi-era eagle, its talon-gripped swastika removed, still presides over the entrance. Today, through the Amtsgericht's range of civic roles, it very much works for the people of Berlin, rather than implacably against them.

PLÖTZENSEE

Volkspark Rehberge, Wedding

Plötzensee, in the Volkspark Rehberge, is not entirely what you would expect in a busy capital city. A small glacial lake covering 7.7 hectares (19 acres), it has accrued a man-made beach, public bath and various other attractions. During the summer months it pulls in thousands of sun-seeking visitors, who enjoy a waterside break with a nearly Mediterranean aura. The photo here, however, shows the park and the frozen lake (to the left) in winter, still a crisply refreshing place to visit.

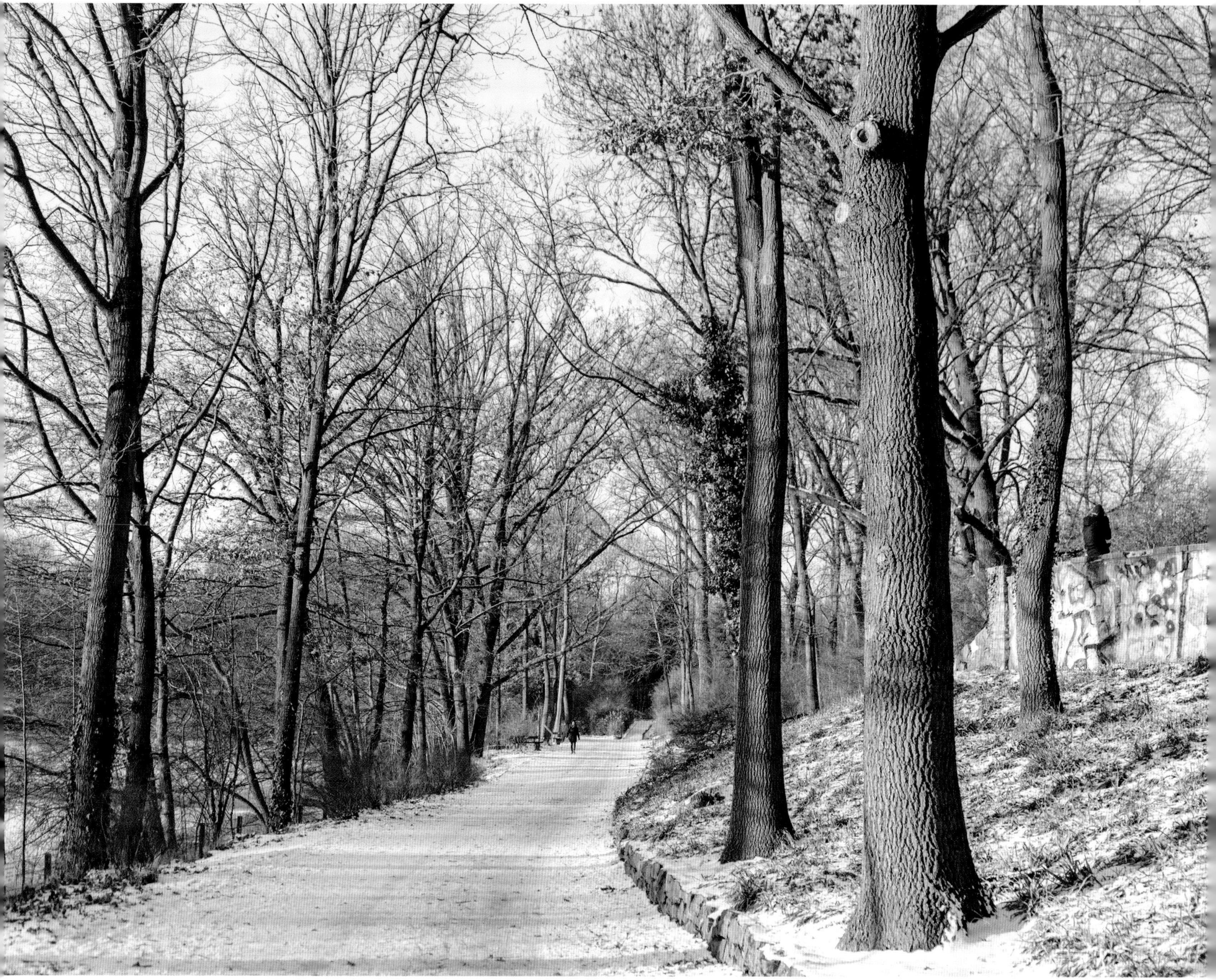

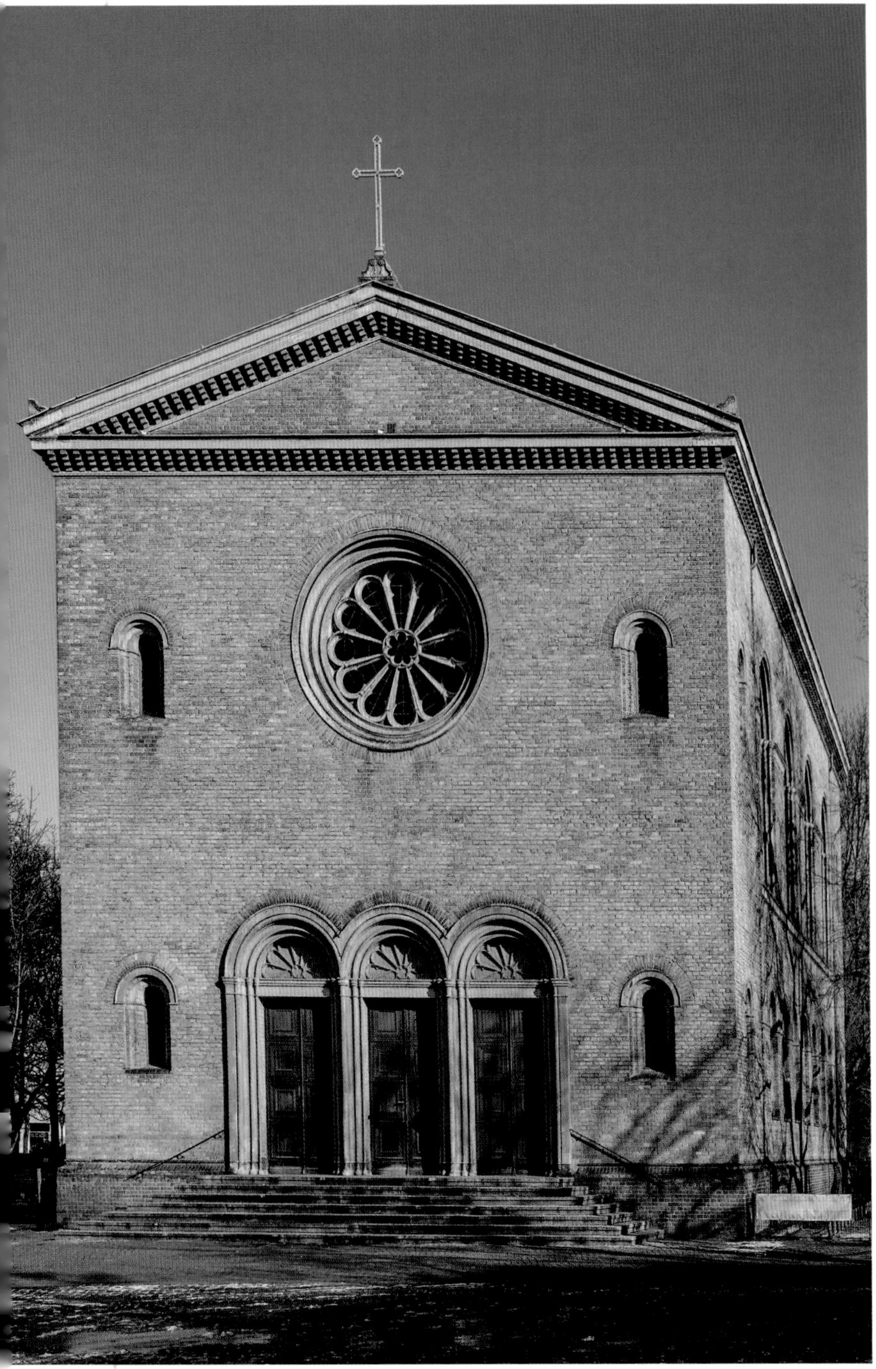

ALTE NAZARETHKIRCHE

Leopoldplatz, Wedding

Berlin is a city of faith, a spirituality that neither fascism nor communism were able to eradicate. The Alte Nazarethkirche (Old Nazareth Church), located in the Wedding subdistrict, is one of many Christian buildings that have endured the centuries. Designed by the renowned Berlin architect Karl Friedrich Schinkel (1781–1841), and built between 1832 and 1835, in an unpretentious yet still lofty style utilizing the red brick often seen in Berlin's religious architecture, the church is currently home to an evangelical community.

LUISENHAUS

Badstraße, Gesundbrunnen

The exquisite decorative features and striking colours of the Luisenhaus arrest the eye in the Gesundbrunnen area of the city. It was designed by the architect Carl Galuschki (1844–1910) between 1892 and 1893, as a six-storey apartment building with commercial space on the ground floor. Ornaments and friezes adorn the exterior; one of the most recognizable elements is the relief of the fountain cottage on the gable end. Sadly, the building did not bring Galuschki good fortune. He found himself deeply in debt and he shot himself on 31 December 1910.

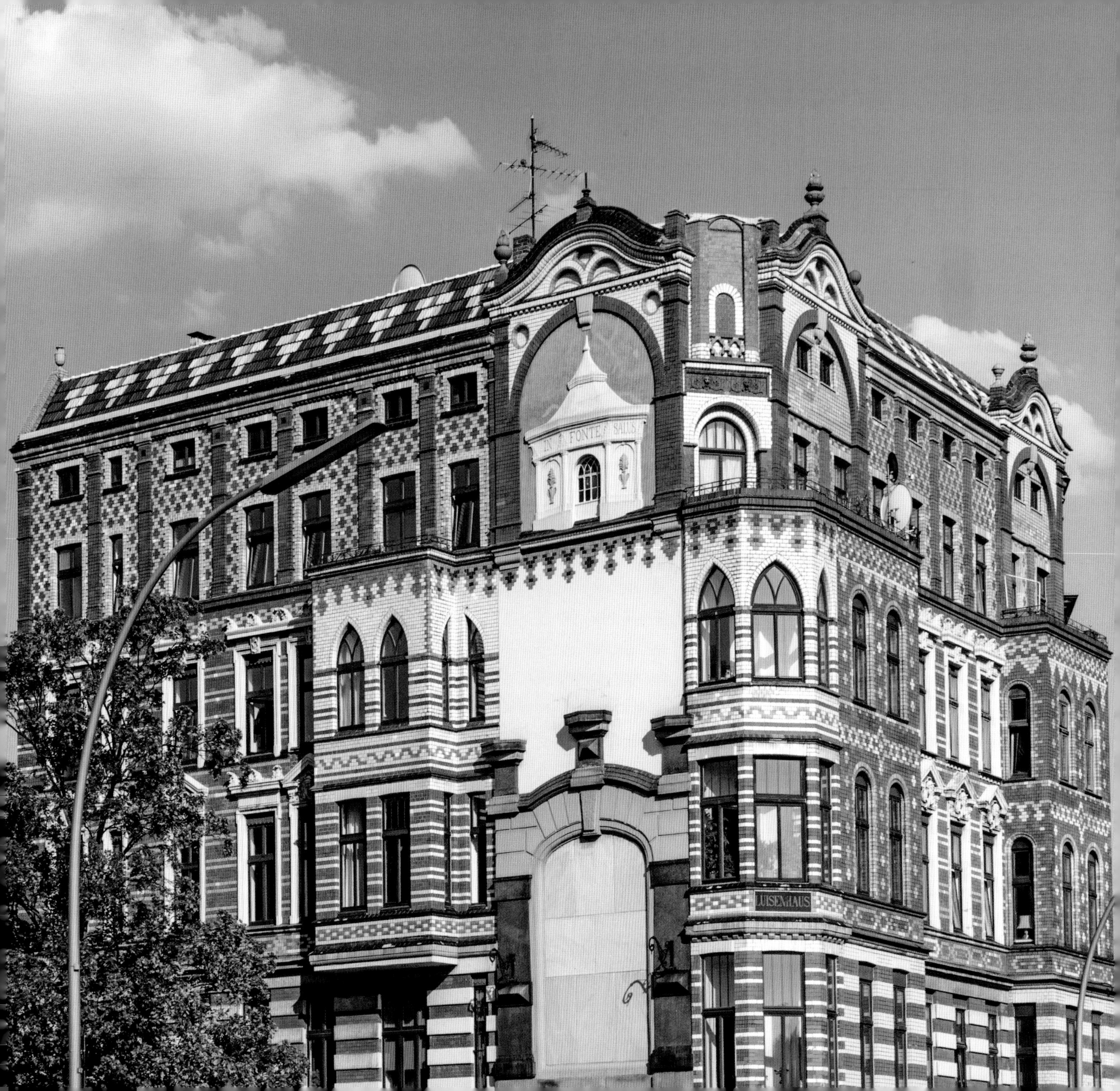
IN FONTE SALUS
LUISENHAUS

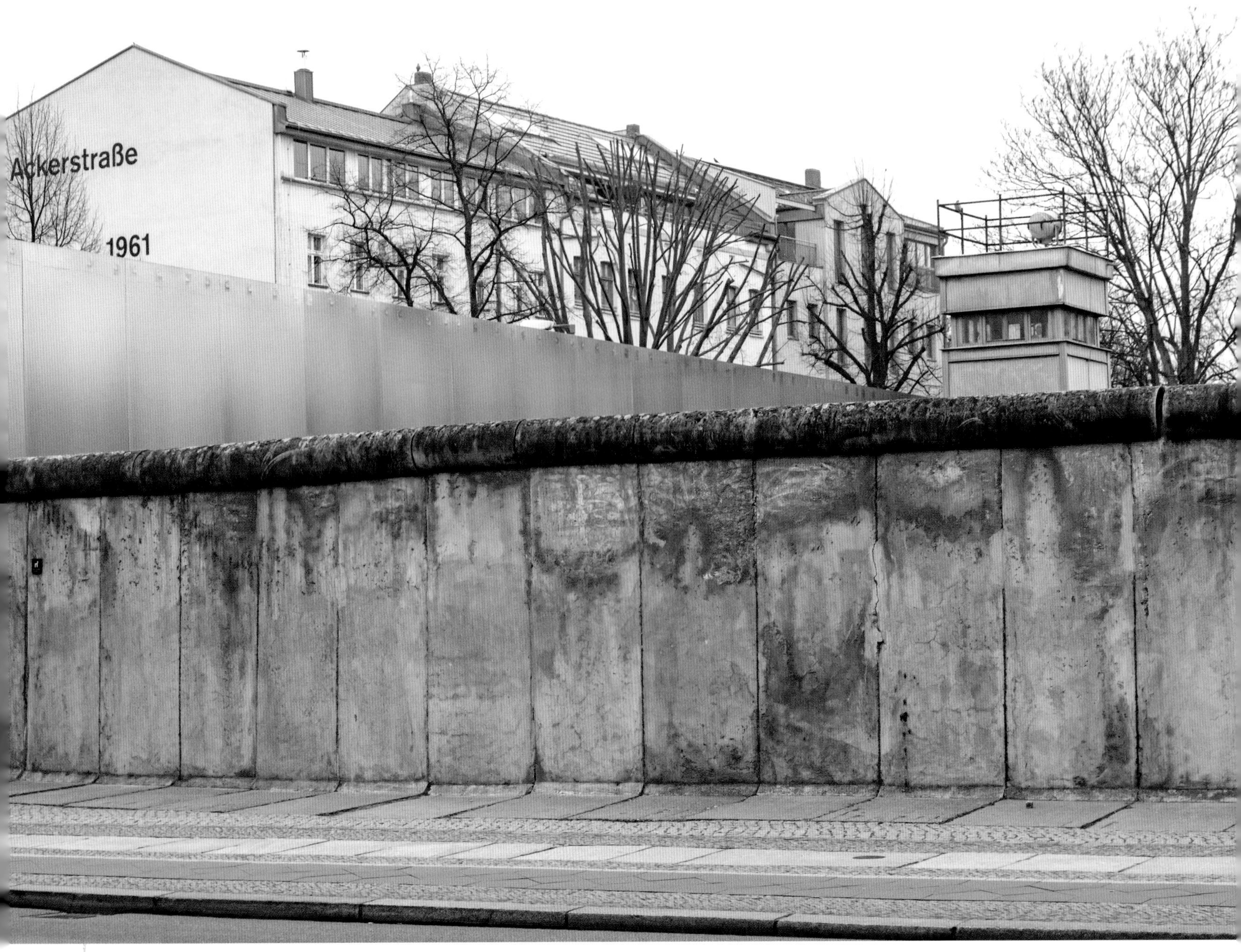
Ackerstraße
1961

GEDENKSTÄTTE BERLINER MAUER

Bernauer Straße, Gesundbrunnen

The Gedenkstätte Berliner Mauer (Berlin Wall Memorial) is an historical act of remembrance to the division of Berlin by the Berlin Wall, a bisection that dominated the lives of Berliners for nearly three decades. The principal focus of the memorial is to reflect upon the 140 lives taken along the border, the majority being East Berliners killed while attempting to flee across the 'death zone' along the wall. The centrepiece of the memorial is a 60-m (200-ft) section of the former border, alongside a five-storey observation tower.

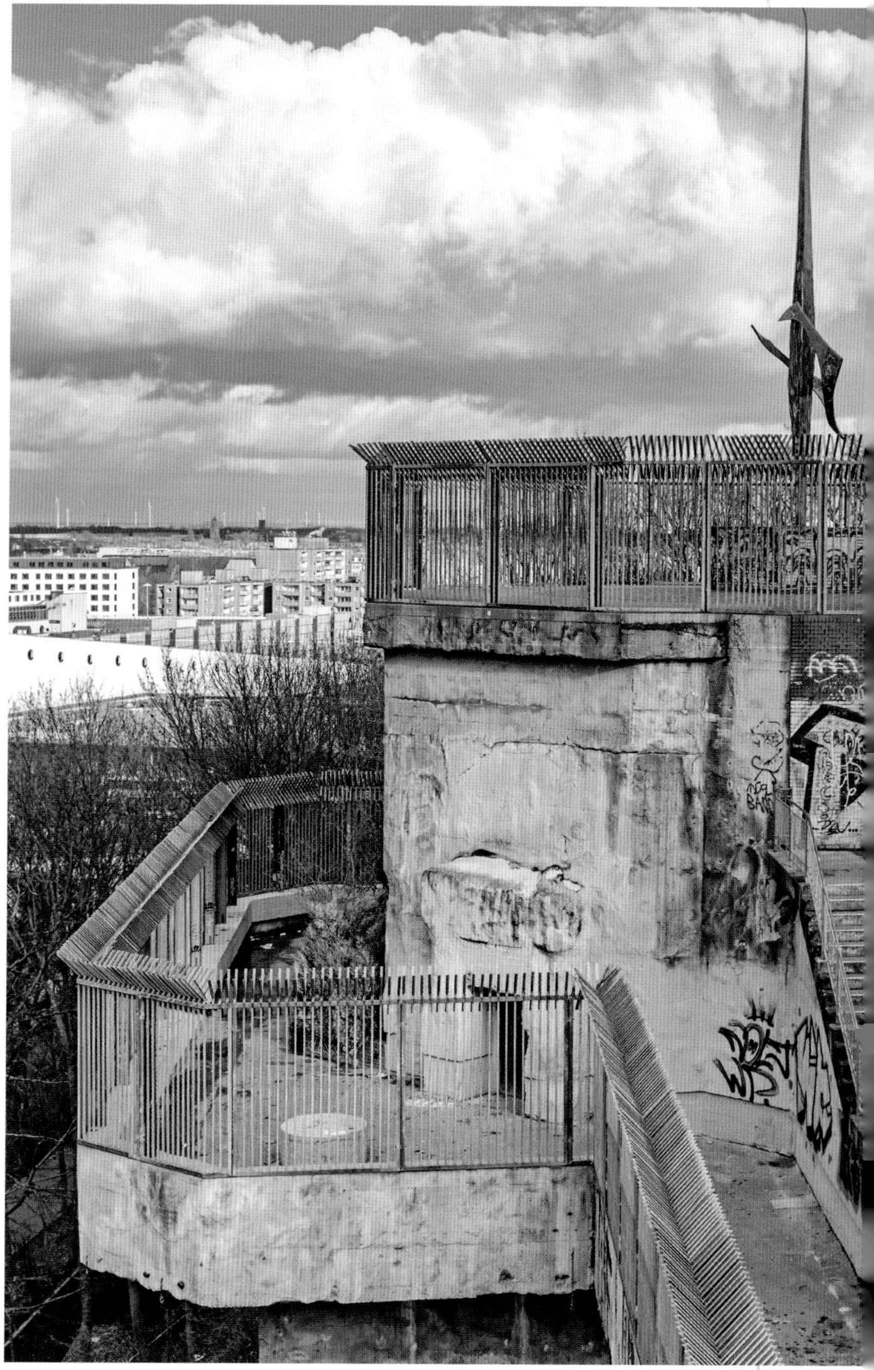

HUMBOLDTHAIN FLAK TOWER

Hochstraße, Gesundbrunnen

Perhaps more than any other landmarks, Berlin's flak towers evoke the apocalyptic days of the Allied strategic bombing campaign, which transformed almost the entire city into an abject ruin. The massive ferro-concrete flak towers were designed to hold thousands of people in relative safety, while the flat roof served as a platform for anti-aircraft guns. The Humboldthain Flak Tower was of the first-generation G-type, and towers to 70.5 m (231 ft) in height. Today it is partially open to historical tours.

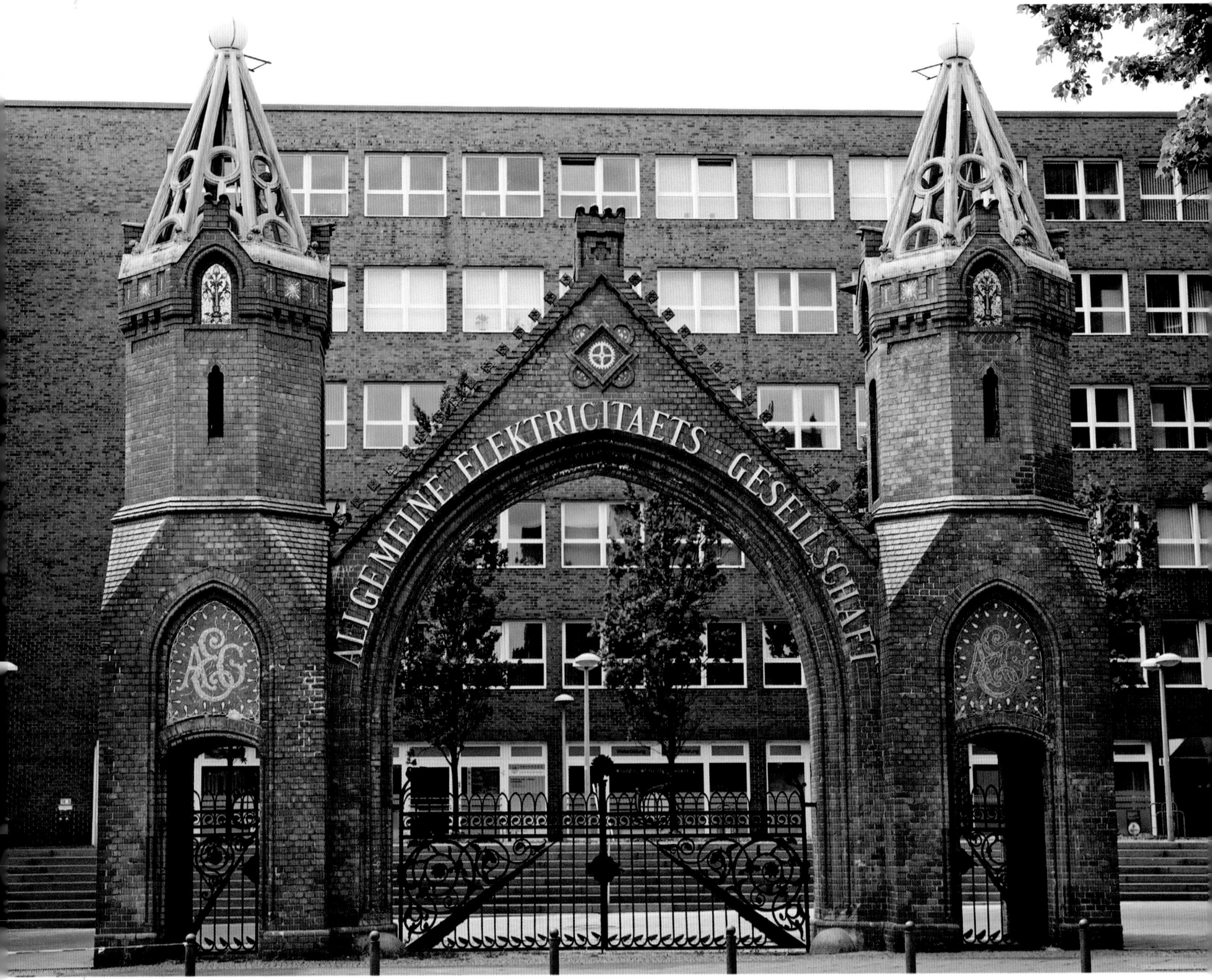
ALLGEMEINE ELEKTRICITAETS - GESELLSCHAFT
AEG
AEG

BEAMTENTOR

Brunnenstraße, Gesundbrunnen

The Beamtentor (Clerk's Gate) is a remnant of the late nineteenth century, part of the original structure of an electrical equipment plant run by the Allgemeine-Electricitäts-Gesellschaft (AEG) company. At this time, Berlin was experiencing the electrical revolution, and architectural developments dedicated to this new industry sprang up thickly in this part of town. The Beamtentor was designed by architect Franz Schwechten (1841–1924) in 1896, the dark red brick suggesting industrial practicality, while the gatehouse design evoked the authority and permanence of ancient civic and fortress designs.

WASSERTURM PRENZLAUER BERG

Prenzlauer Berg, Pankow

The nineteenth century saw even the most utilitarian structures built in grand and authoritarian styles. The Wasserturm (Water Tower) Prenzlauer Berg became operational in 1878, and thus is Berlin's oldest water tower structure. Looking rather like a circular castle bastion, it was actually built by the English Waterworks Company, designed by civil engineer Henry Gill (1824–93), who worked on the city's water infrastructure for some 40 years. Today it is a residential building, having been repurposed in its time as a soup kitchen, storage tank and even, darkly, as an early Nazi concentration camp.

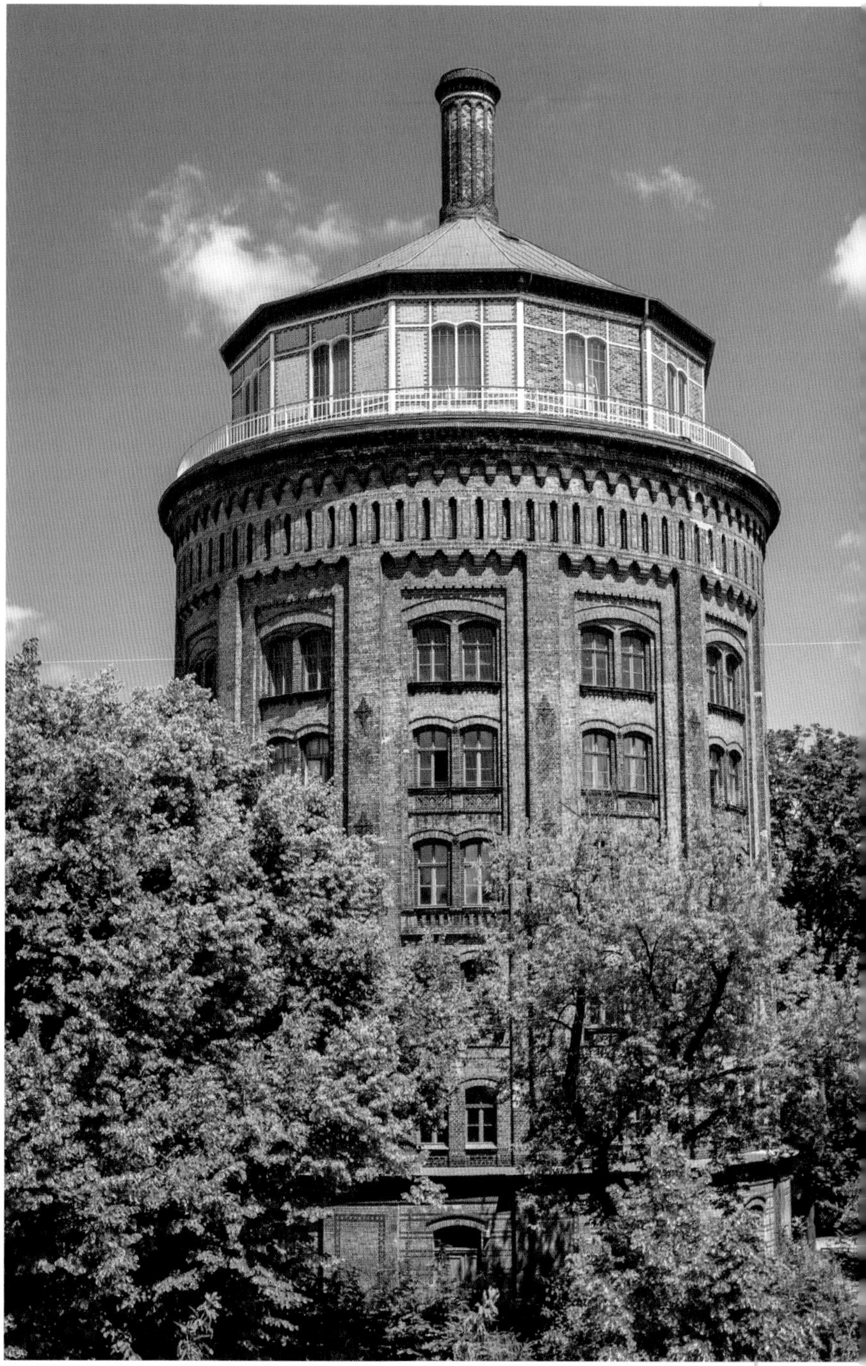

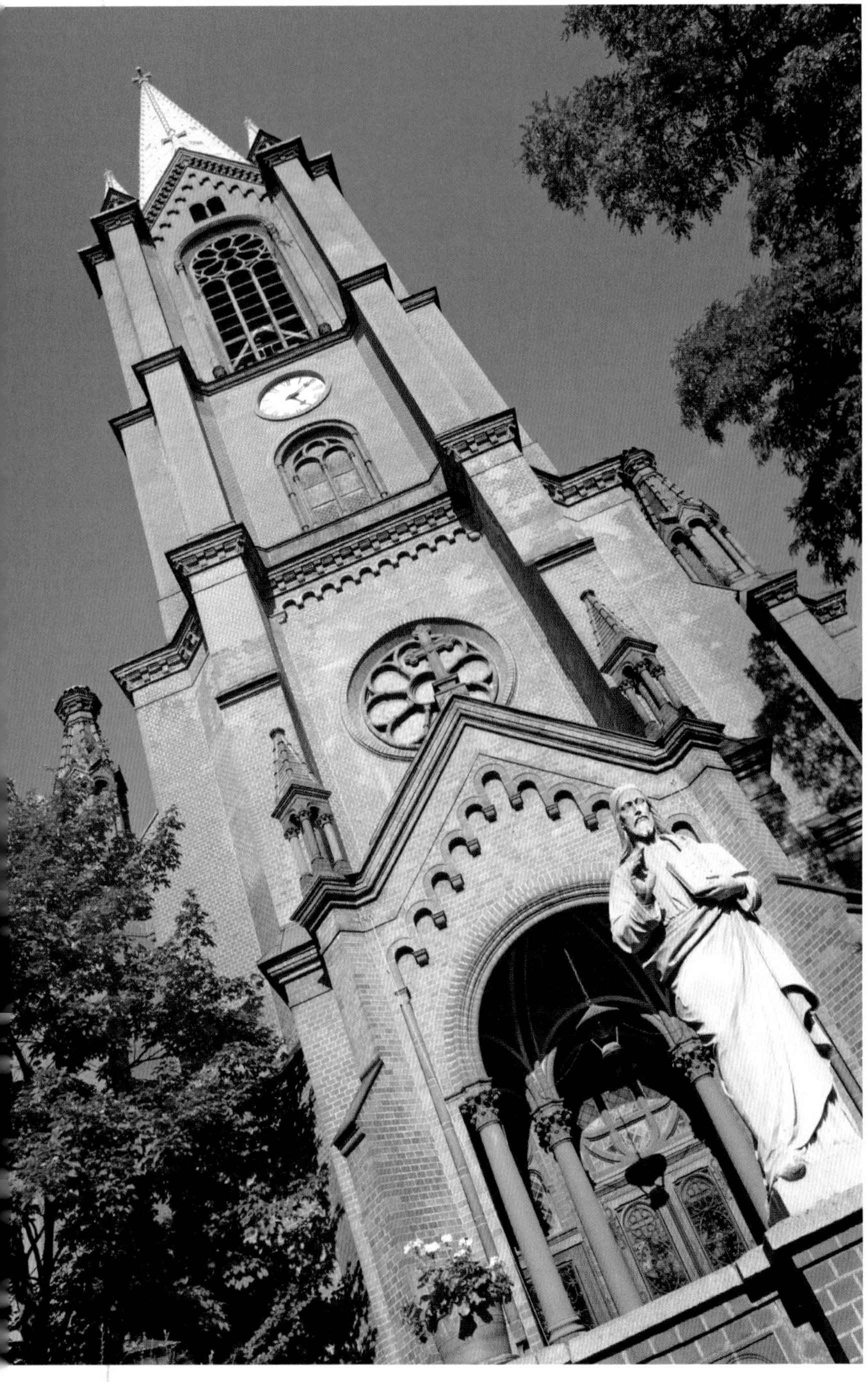

GETHSEMANEKIRCHE

Prenzlauer Berg, Pankow

Despite its orthodox neo-Gothic beauty, the Protestant Gethsemanekirche (Gethsemane Church) actually has a recent history of political protest and subversion. It was built from 1891 to 1893, designed by August Orth (1828–1901), who nodded to industrial realities with the use of steel supports. A century later, in October 1989, protestors gathered in the church to criticize the oppressions of the GDR regime. Then, on 5 November 1989, during an orchestral concert in the church, the senior musical director of the Komische Oper, Rolf Reuter (1926–2007), spoke out that 'The wall must go!', triggering protests that contributed to the breaking of the Berlin Wall four days later.

MAUERPARK FLEA MARKET

Prenzlauer Berg, Pankow

For those hunting for bargains or curiosities, the flea market at Mauerpark (Park of the Wall) in the Prenzlauer Berg subdistrict of Pankow is the place to go on a Sunday between 9am and 6pm. The range of purchases there are eclectic – musical instruments, vinyl records, clothes and shoes, vintage hats, toys, bicycles and bits and pieces from across Berlin's history. The event also features karaoke in the amphitheatre in the park. Needless to say, the flea market gets very busy within an hour or so of opening.

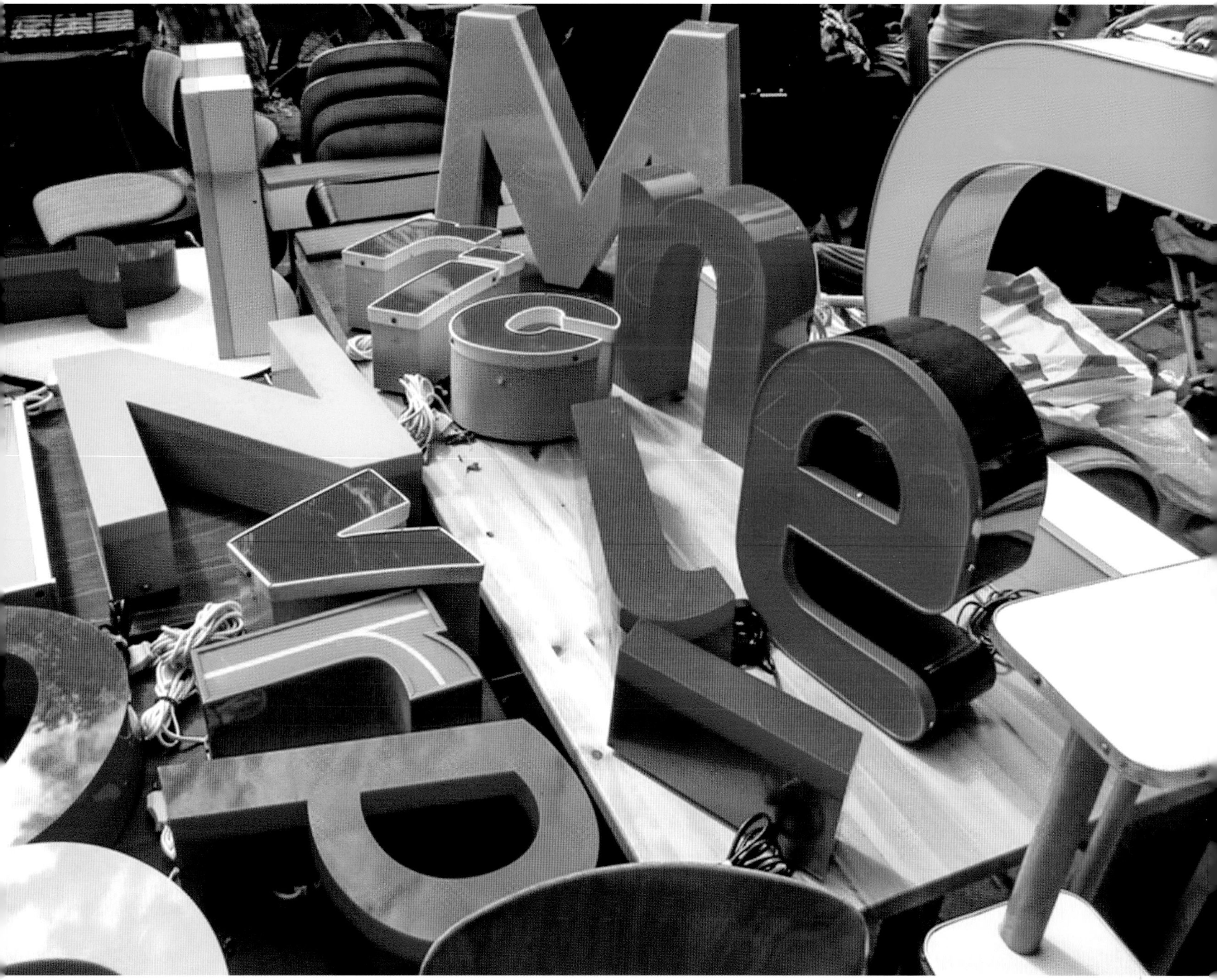

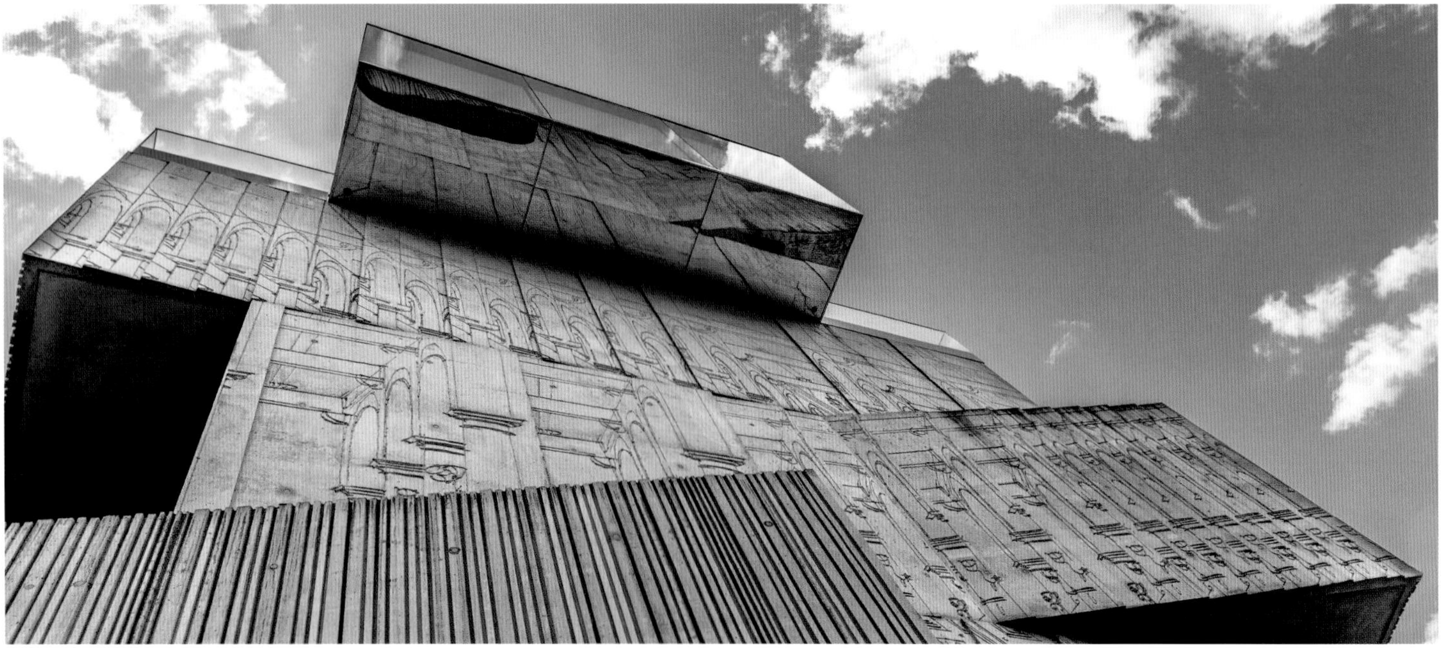

MUSEUM FÜR ARCHITEKTURZEICHNUNG

Prenzlauer Berg, Pankow

The Museum für Architekturzeichnung (Museum for Architectural Drawing), run by the Tchoban Foundation, was completed in 2013. Sophisticated, but with a hint towards the childlike propensity to stack blocks – arguably the moment when architectural thought begins – the building structure features four 'solid' cast concrete floors topped by a light glass-enclosed area at the top. The Tchoban Foudation promotes the skill of architectural drawing, and the general lack of windows helps preserve valuable documents.

ERNST-THÄLMANN PARK

Prenzlauer Berg, Pankow

Although much of this park consists of concrete austerity (prior to the park it was the site of a coal gas plant), it is nevertheless worth the trip to be confronted by the 14-m (46-ft) high memorial bust of former Communist Party leader Ernst Thälmann (1886–1944), executed by the Nazis in 1944 (his death was actually blamed on an air raid). The statue was created by Soviet sculptor Lev Kerbel (1917–2003), and is in a classic revolutionary style. The park itself was developed with housing, sports facilities, a planetarium and various other civic buildings, and today it has various art galleries, public houses and a small theatre.

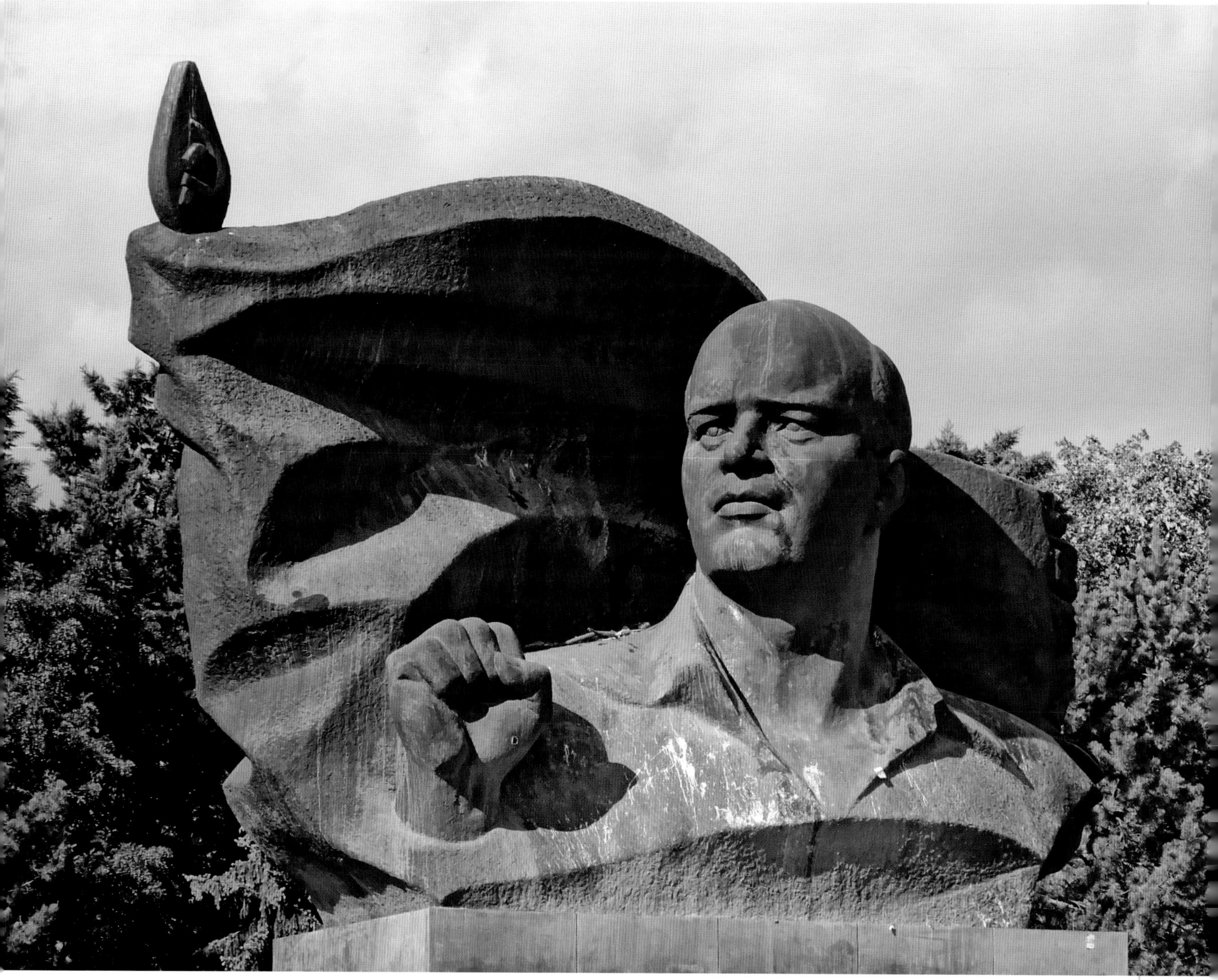

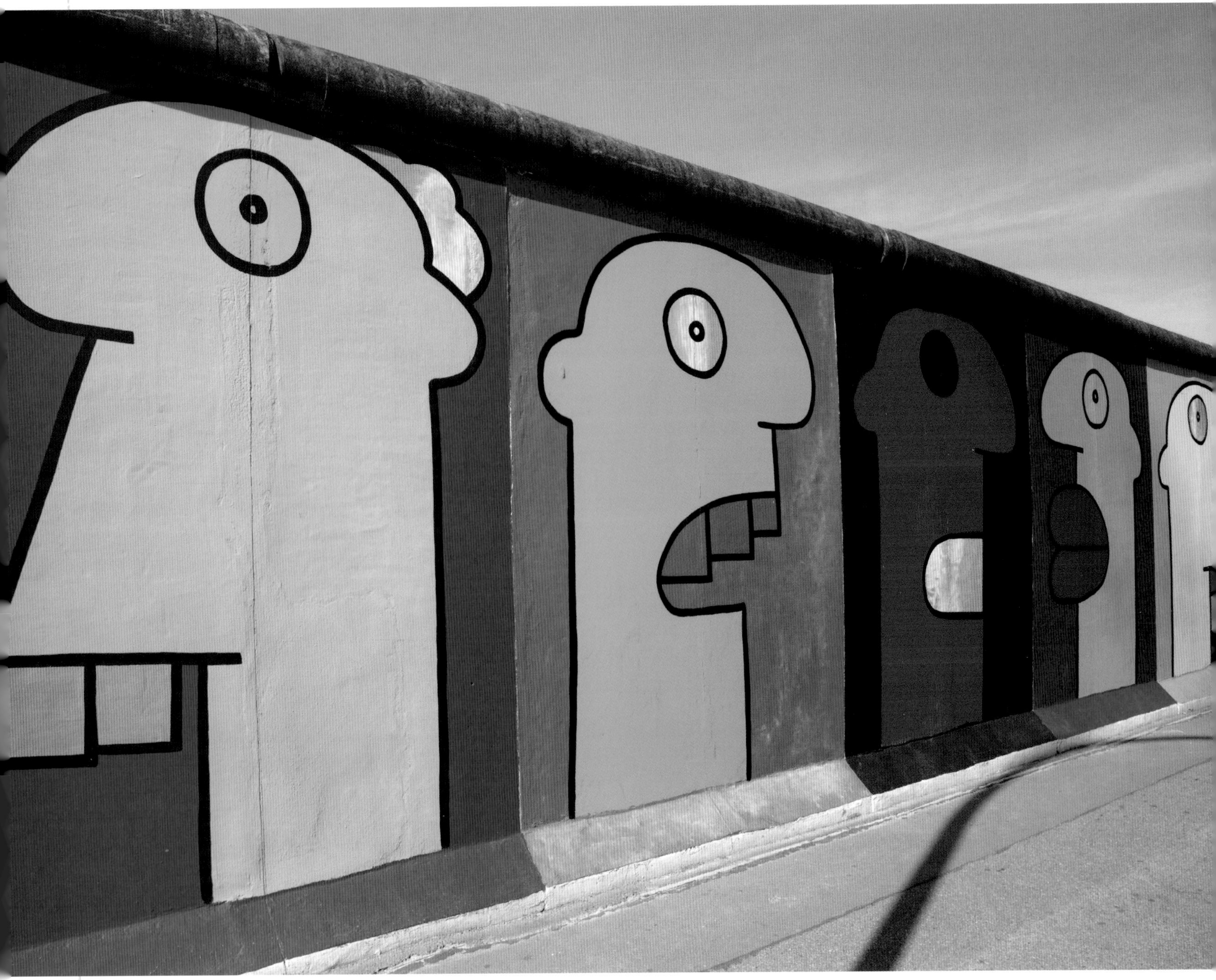

EAST SIDE GALLERY

Mühlenstraße, Friedrichshain

The East Side Gallery is a remarkable social and political record of the seismic events of 1989 and 1990. Its fabric is 1.3 km (0.8 miles) of extant Berlin Wall, running along the banks of the Spree in Friedrichshain. The fall of the Wall unleashed tremendous creative energy, and 118 artists from 21 countries painted this section (such as the bold, colourful heads by Thierry Noir, b. 1958, here), making it a vast, colourful canvas of cultural change. Including such iconic art as Dmitri Vrubel's (b. 1960) *Fraternal Kiss* (*see* page 9) and Birgit Kinder's (b. 1962) *Trabant breaking through the wall* (*see* page 3), the wall has been preserved as a gallery and monument since 1996.

KULTURBRAUEREI

Prenzlauer Berg, Pankow

The Kulturbrauerei (Culture Brewery) speaks of both the past purpose and present activities of this site in the Prenzlauer Berg. Formerly, the complex of distinctive red and yellow clinker buildings was the location for the Schultheiss brewery, which began producing beer back in 1842. Today the Kulturbrauerei, which evolved from the early 1990s, offers various forms of cultural entertainment and expression, including an eight-screen cinema, several theatres, dance clubs, a museum of life in the GDR, publishing houses and more. Outside stand unsettlingly gaunt bronze sculptures of Adam and Eve, by Rolf Biebl (b. 1951).

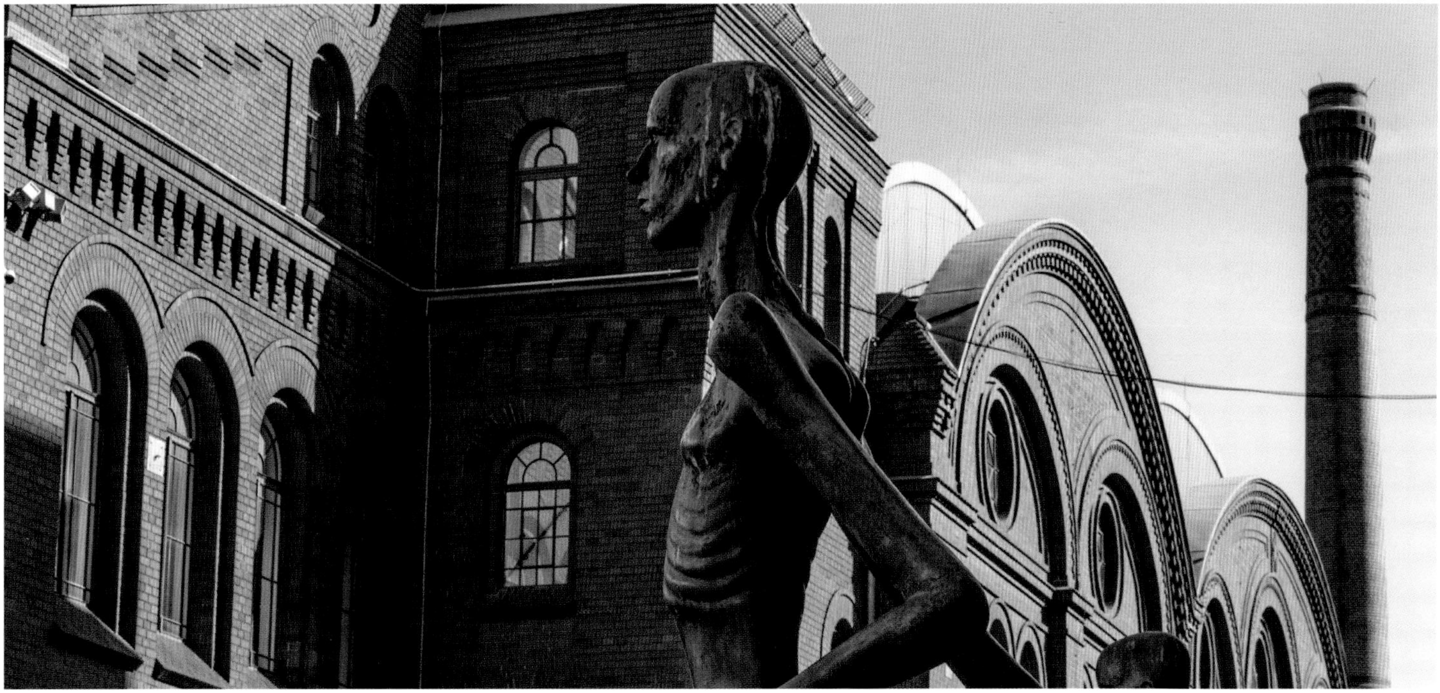

OBERBAUMBRÜCKE

River Spree, Kreuzberg and Friedrichshain

Linking the Berlin subdistricts of Kreuzberg and Friedrichshain over the River Spree, the seven-arched Oberbaumbrücke (Oberbaum Bridge) looks like something emerging from a Harry Potter novel, courtesy of the medieval-style turrets that punctuate its length. It was constructed in 1895 using concrete faced with a granite and brickwork façade and has two levels, the lower level for vehicular traffic and the upper level for U-Bahn trains. During the Cold War era, the bridge was a crossover point between east and west, and hence was sternly policed.

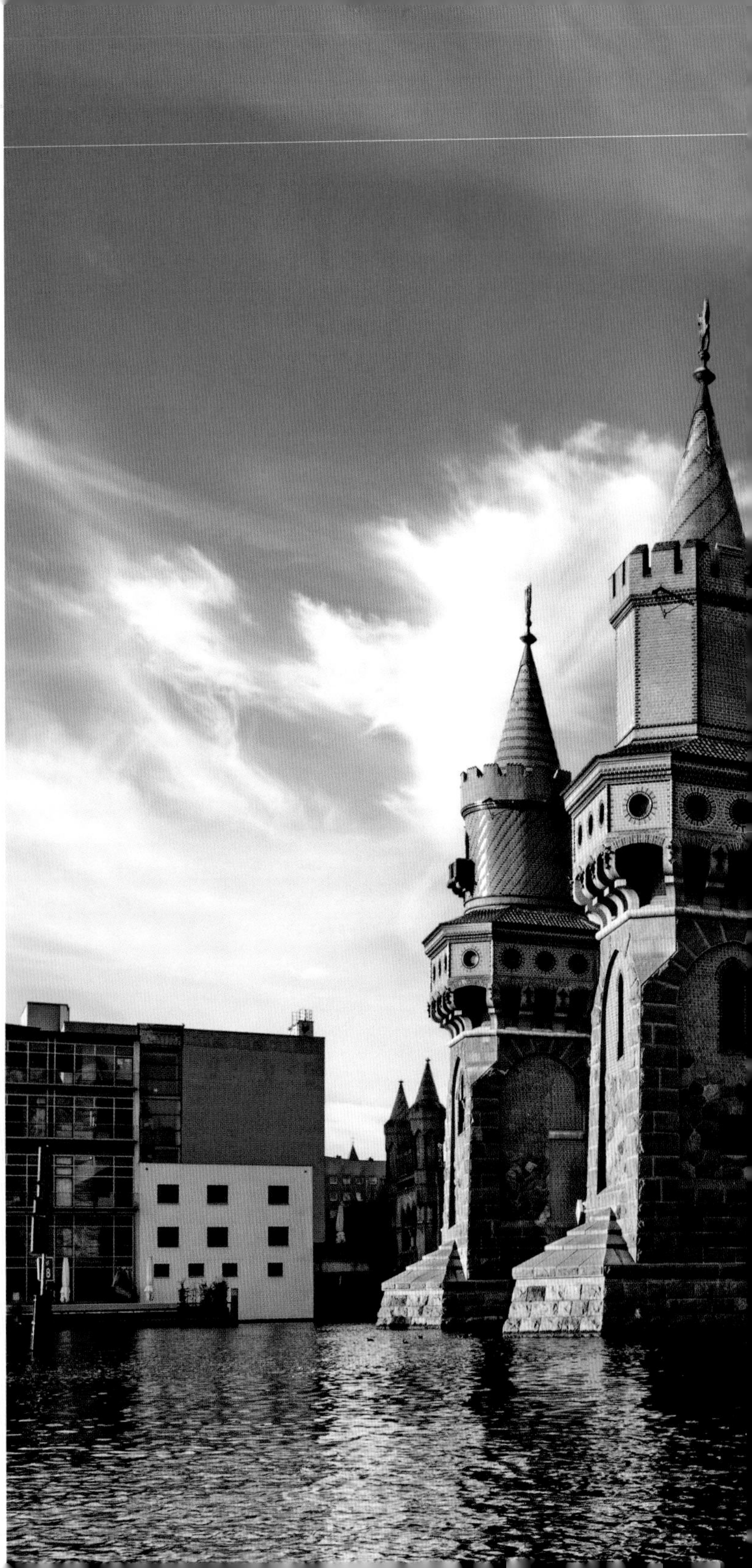

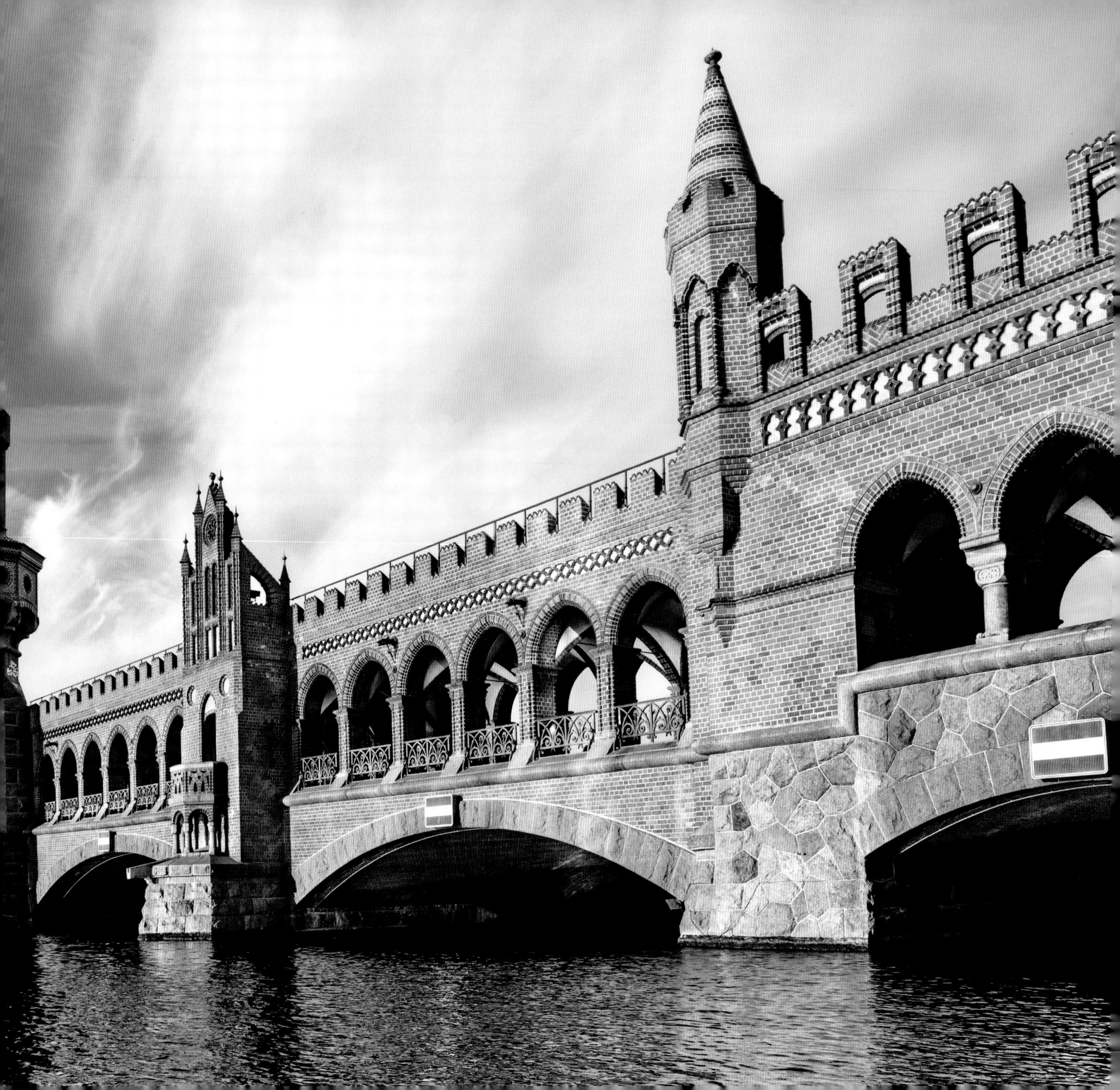

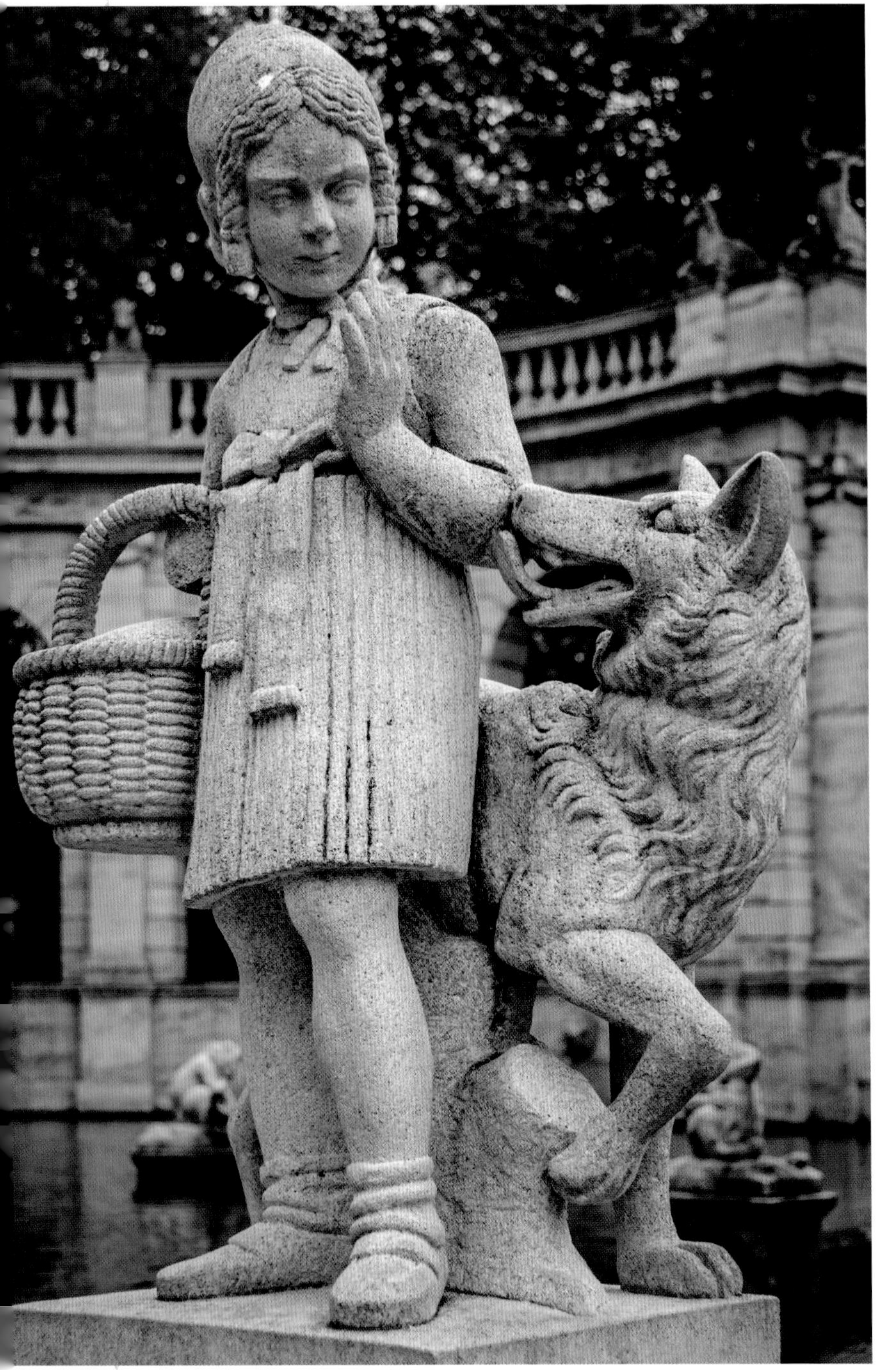

MÄRCHENBRUNNEN

Volkspark Friedrichshain, Friedrichshain

Opened on 15 June 1913, the Märchenbrunnen (Fountain of Fairy Tales) is a magical space conceived by architect Ludwig Hoffmann (1852–1932). A neo-Baroque masterpiece, the Märchenbrunnen consists of four cascading waterfalls surrounded by the most exquisite sculptures of figures from folklore and fairy tales. Many of these sculptures, created by artists such as Ignatius Taschner, Georg Wrba, and Josef Rauch, disappeared at the end of the Second World War, but were subsequently rediscovered in a garden in 1950 and the fountain complex was restored from the 1950s onwards.

RADIALSYSTEM V

River Spree, Friedrichshain

The Radialsystem V building, at least the parts that visibly belong to the nineteenth-century trend for brick neo-Gothic design, was designed by the architect Richard Tettenborn (1857–1923) as a pumping station for Berlin's sewer system, opened in 1881 and subsequently extended in 1905. The bombing of the Second World War meant that much of the building was destroyed, but the surviving parts eventually took listed status. Since 2006, these spaces, and new developments around them, became the home of Radialsystem V, which hosts musical, dance and theatrical events.

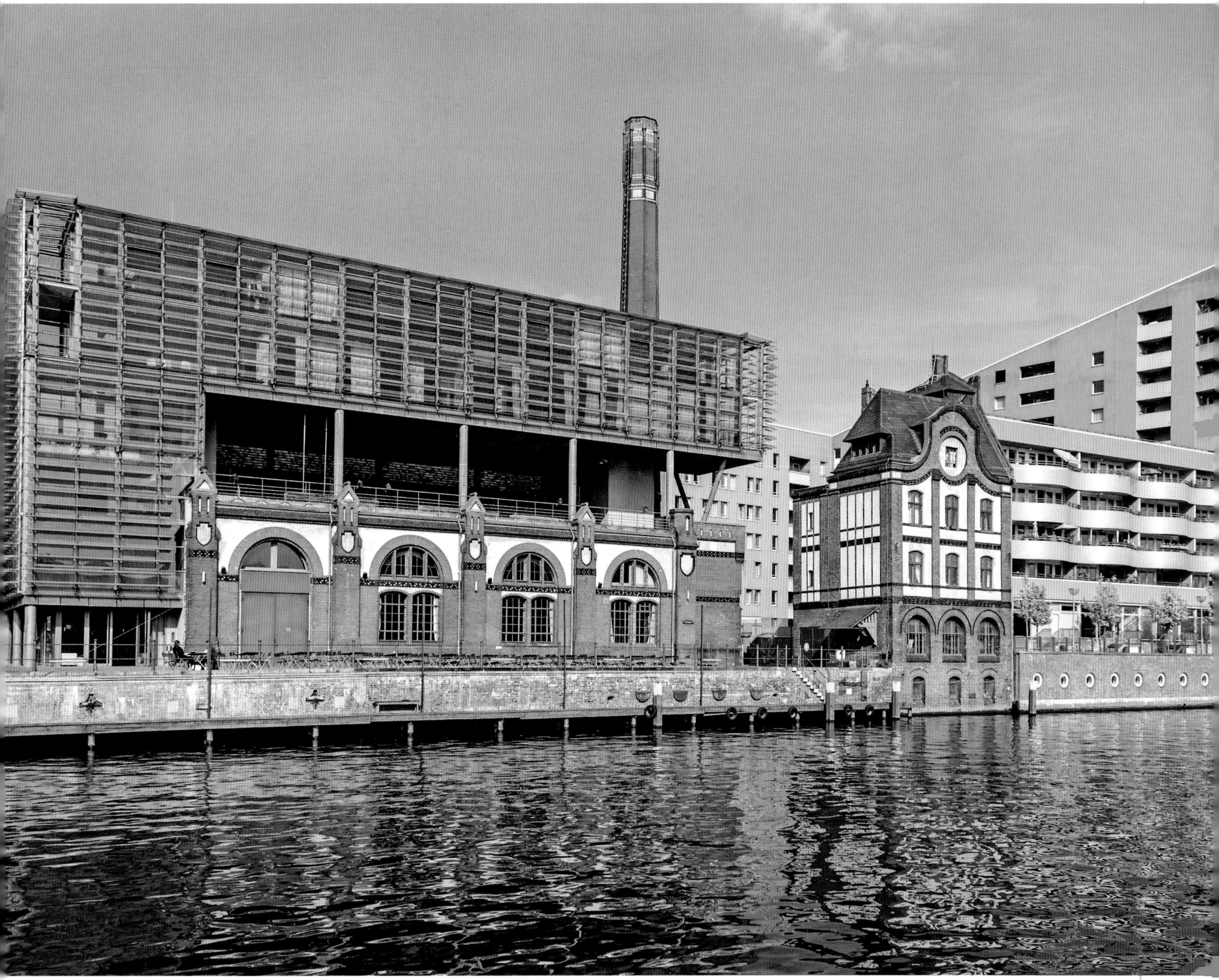

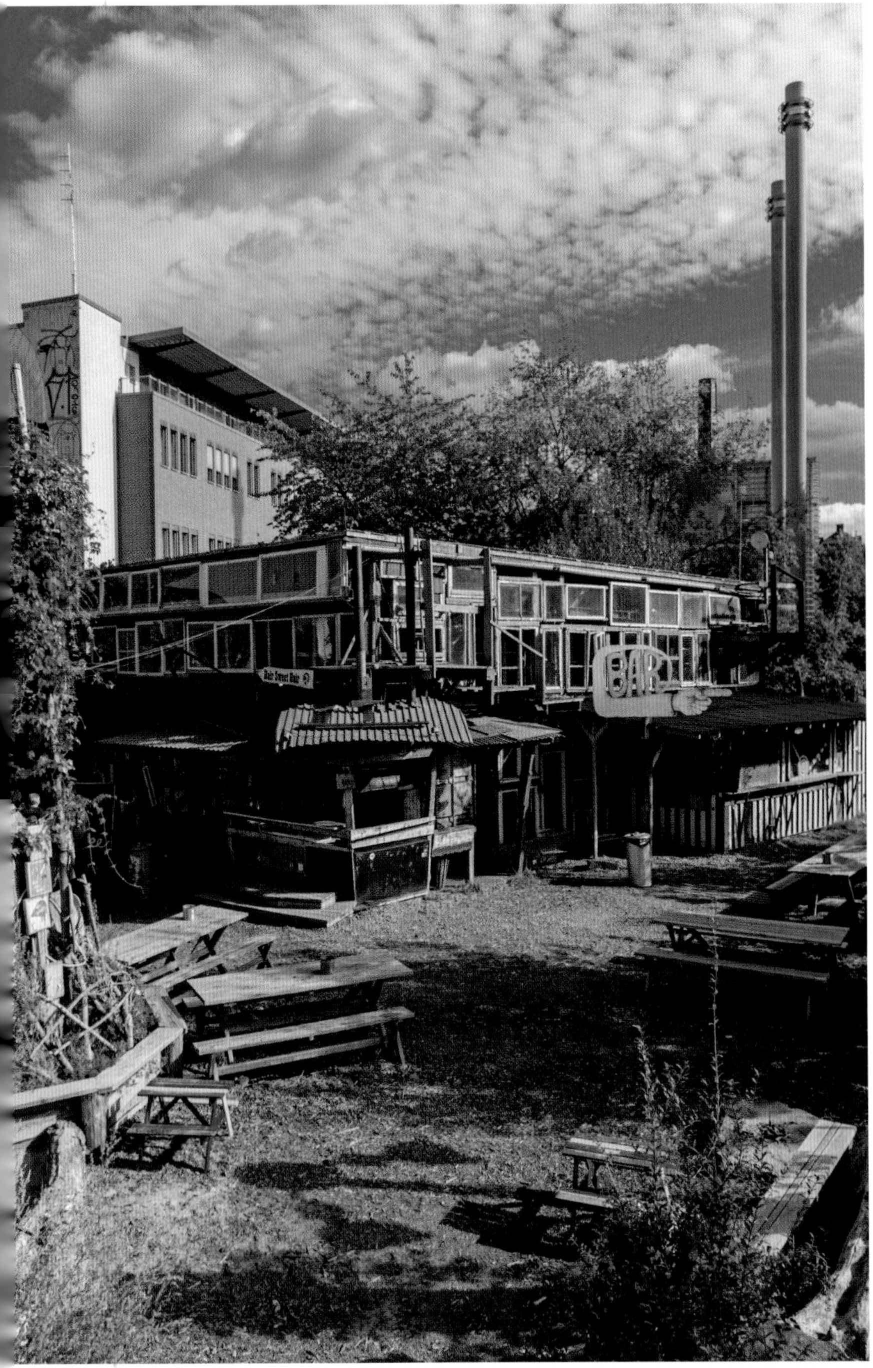

HOLZMARKT

River Spree, Friedrichshain

The Holzmarkt has been heralded as a zone for 'creative placemaking', the transformation of an urban wasteland into a collective of cultural and social expression. Bar owners Juval Dieziger and Christoph Klenzendorf led what was in effect a resistance movement against developing the area along familiar lines of big business and commercialism, creating instead a space for the Holzmarkt 25 Cooperative and Cooperative for Urban Creativity. Today the site includes a theatre, dance club, bar, restaurant, music club and kindergarten, all run with a sense of free expression.

FRANKFURTER TOR

Friedrichshain

Flanked by two grand Italianate towers, the Frankfurter Tor (Frankfurter Gate) square was an expression of socialist confidence, a location around which the more influential and important members of East German society would live. The towers themselves were built between 1953 and 1956, and they act as sentinels over this important intersection of major roads in Berlin. Beneath the square is also the Frankfurter Tor U-Bahn station. Today the buildings, square and street intersection all have listed status.

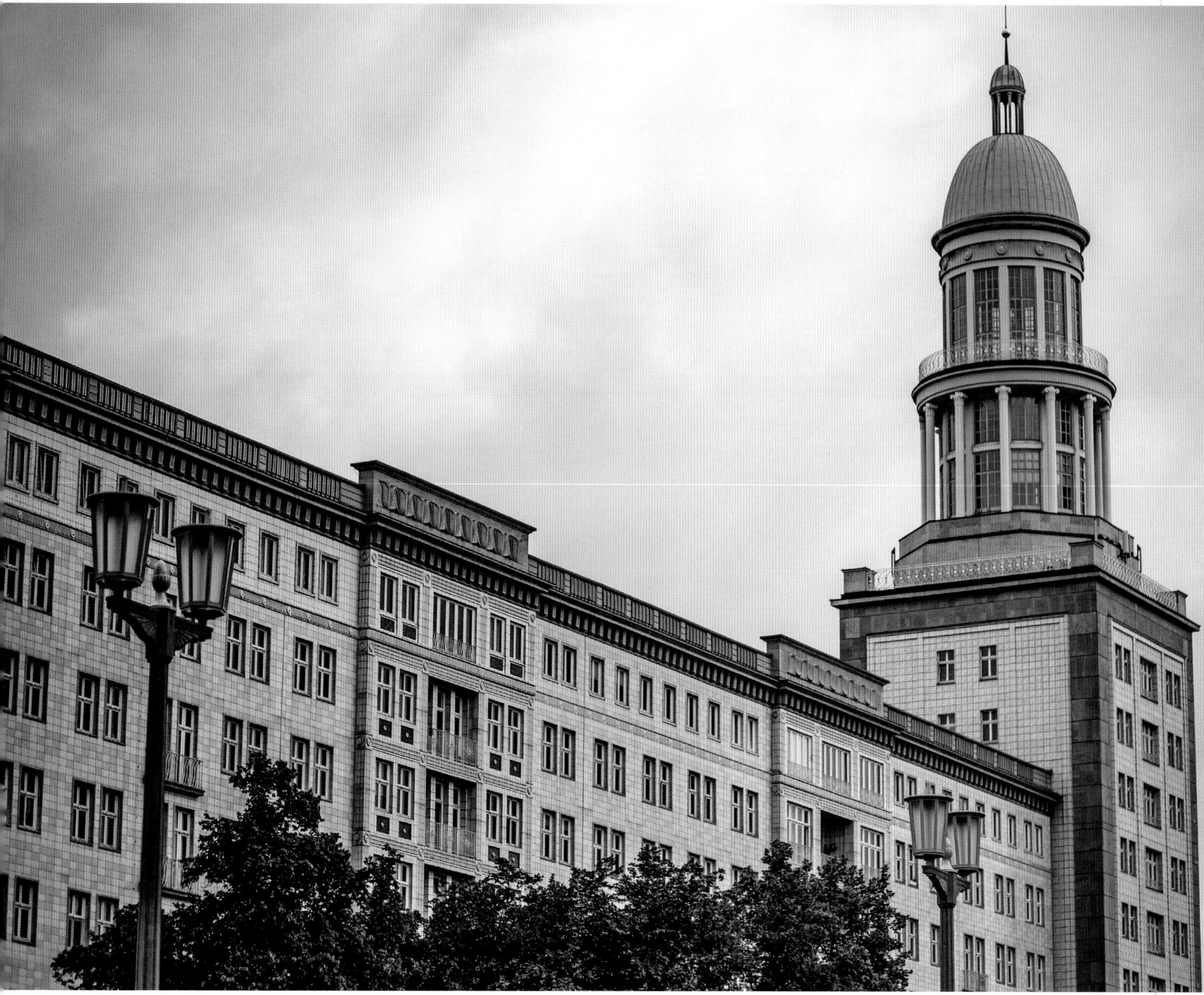

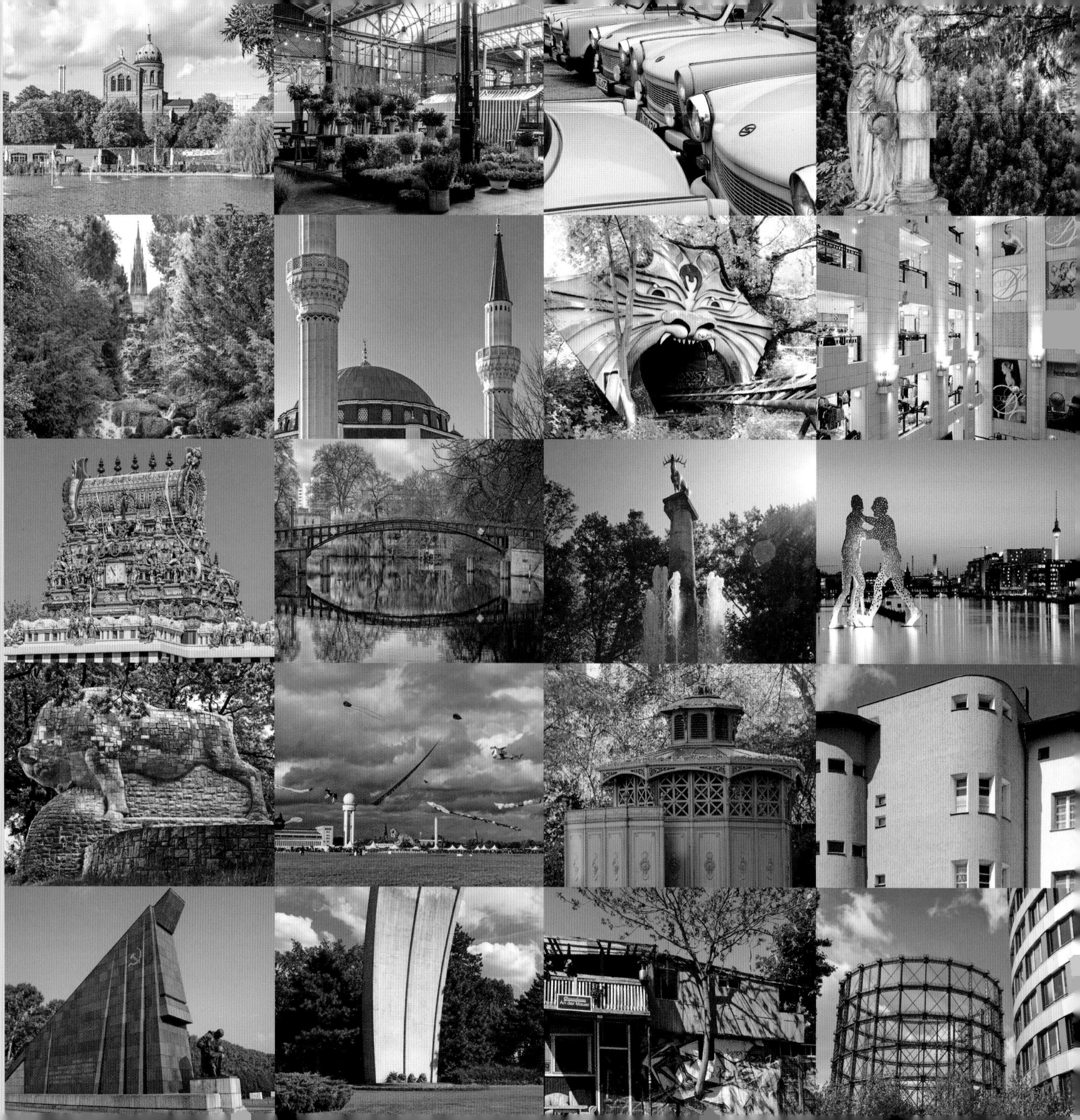
An der Mauer

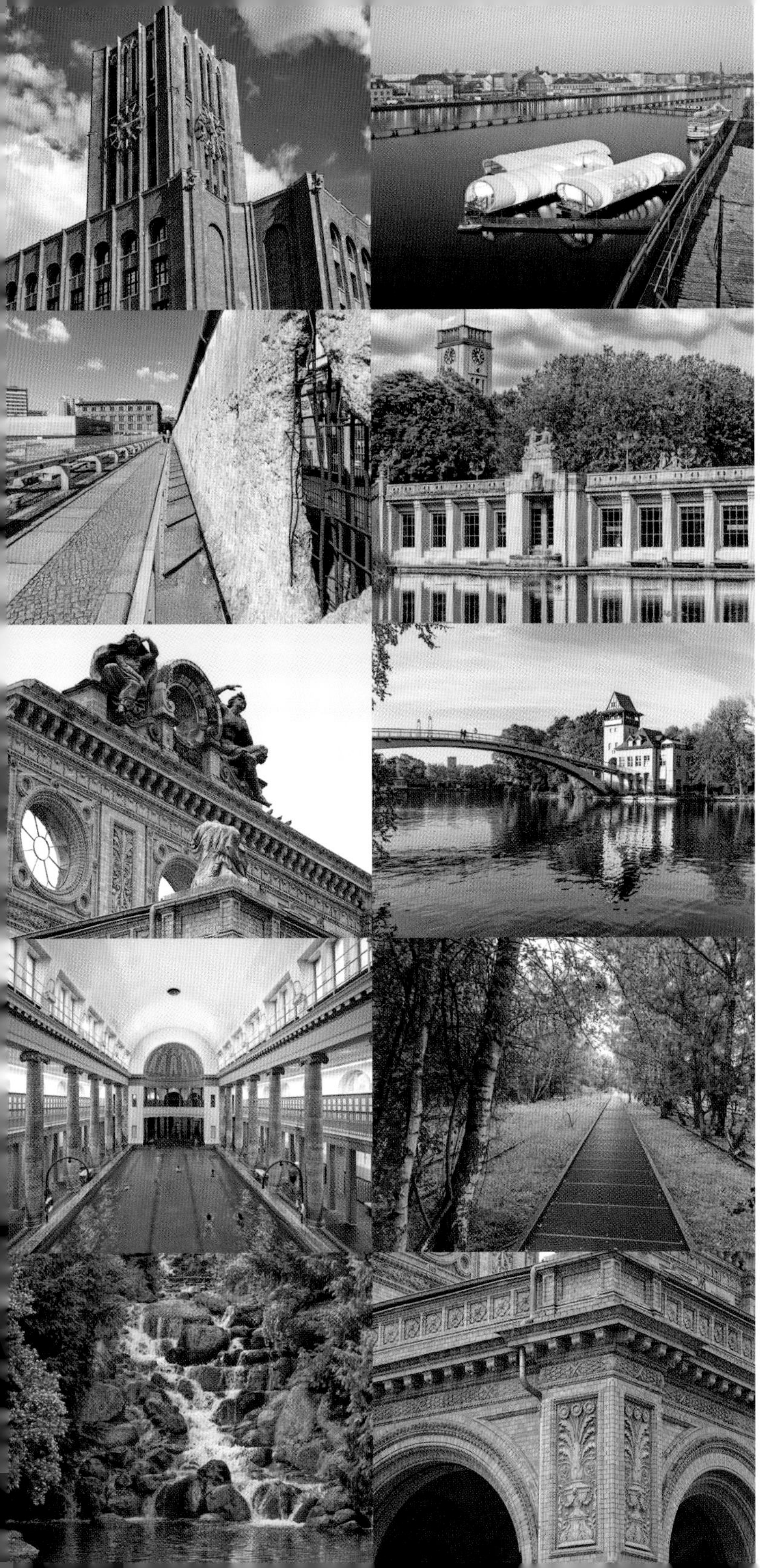

CITY SOUTH CENTRAL

Looking south of the centre of Berlin on a map, we spot a different patchwork of colours compared to many other regions of the city. Large green areas signify open land, especially parks such as Viktoriapark, Tempelhofer Field, Treptower Park and Britzer Garden. Some of these spaces have had a profound relationship with Berlin's modern history, not least the former Flughafen Tempelhof (Tempelhof Airport), to which, during the Berlin Blockade of 1948–49, the Allies established their aerial lifeline.

As the selection of entries in this chapter will show, the south-central parts of Berlin often wear their history close to the surface, in their canals, railway stations and palaces, numerous venerable and overgrown cemeteries, and their sections of the Berlin Wall. Indeed, for those who want to capture the ghosts of Berlin's past, this area has many shadowy corners to explore. Yet south-central Berlin is not ossifying. Districts like Tempelhof-Schöneberg and Neukölln are amongst the most populated districts in the city, having more than 645,000 people between them. Both districts have very high levels of immigration, with about 30 per cent of the populations being non-German; the result is a highly multicultural atmosphere.

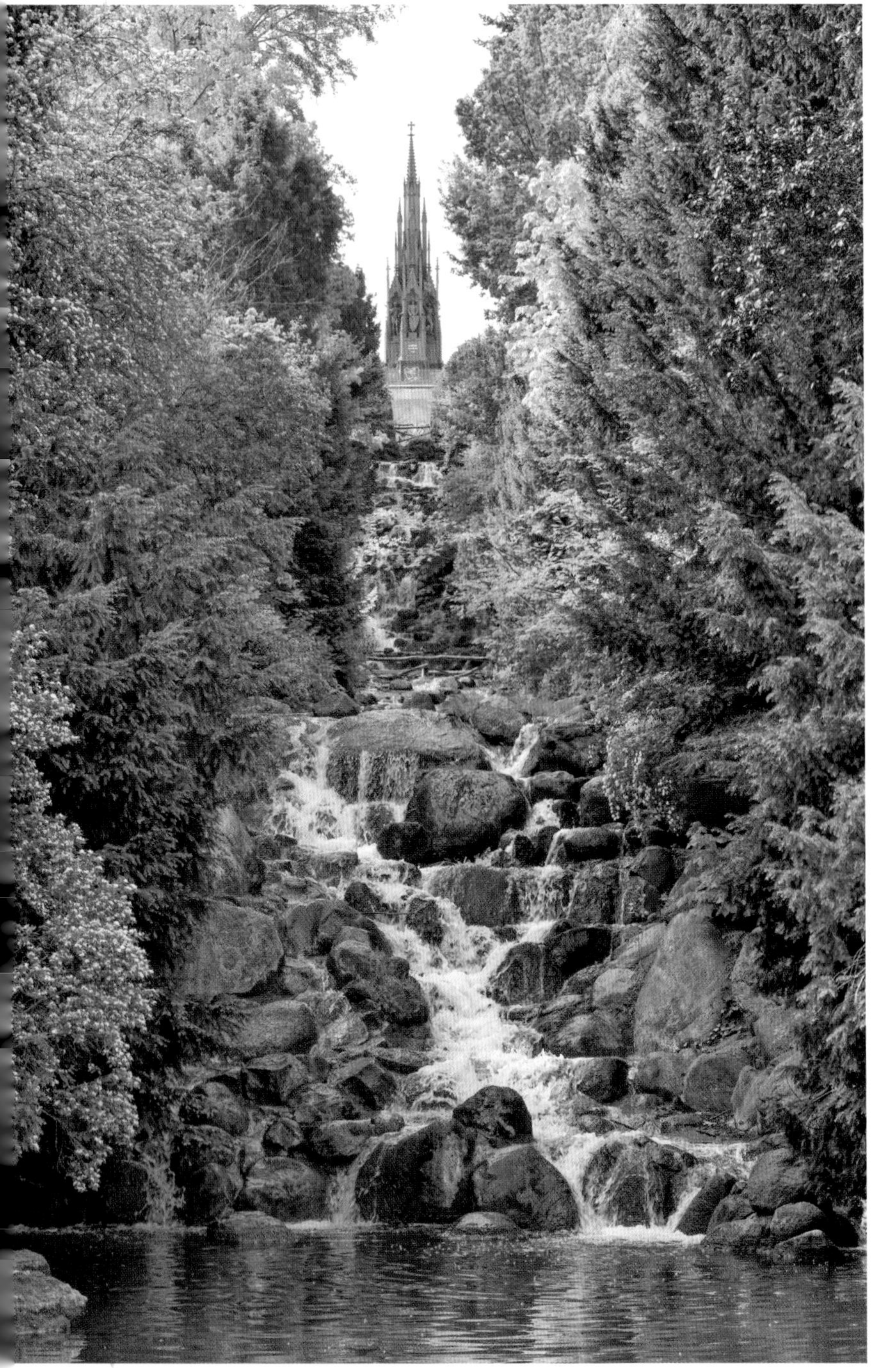

VIKTORIAPARK

Kreuzberg

The Viktoriapark is a striking oasis. The park's name is that given by Frederick III (1831–88), in honour of his beloved English wife Victoria, in 1888, but the first stage in the park's creation was the construction of a neo-Gothic national memorial atop the 66-m (217-ft) hill in the Kreuzberg, the memorial by Karl Friedrich Schinkel dedicated to those who fell and fought in the war against Napoleon Bonaparte. The 24-m (79-ft) waterfall subsequently cut into the hillside is a highly precise scaled-down version of a waterfall found in the Riesengebirge mountains on the border between Poland and the Czech Republic.

LANDWEHRKANAL

Kreuzberg

Forming a border between Kreuzberg and Neukölln, the Landwehrkanal waterway splits out from the Spree in Friedrichshain and takes a parallel course to the major river for 10.7 km (6.6 miles). It winds a picturesque route, through leafy woodlands and suburbs (it passes through the Tiergarten), beneath railway lines, the canal interspersed with locks and bordered by many places to stop, eat and ponder. There are some darker parts to the canal's history; it was here the body of the socialist Rosa Luxemburg (1871–19) was dumped following her murder by the Freikorps in January 1919.

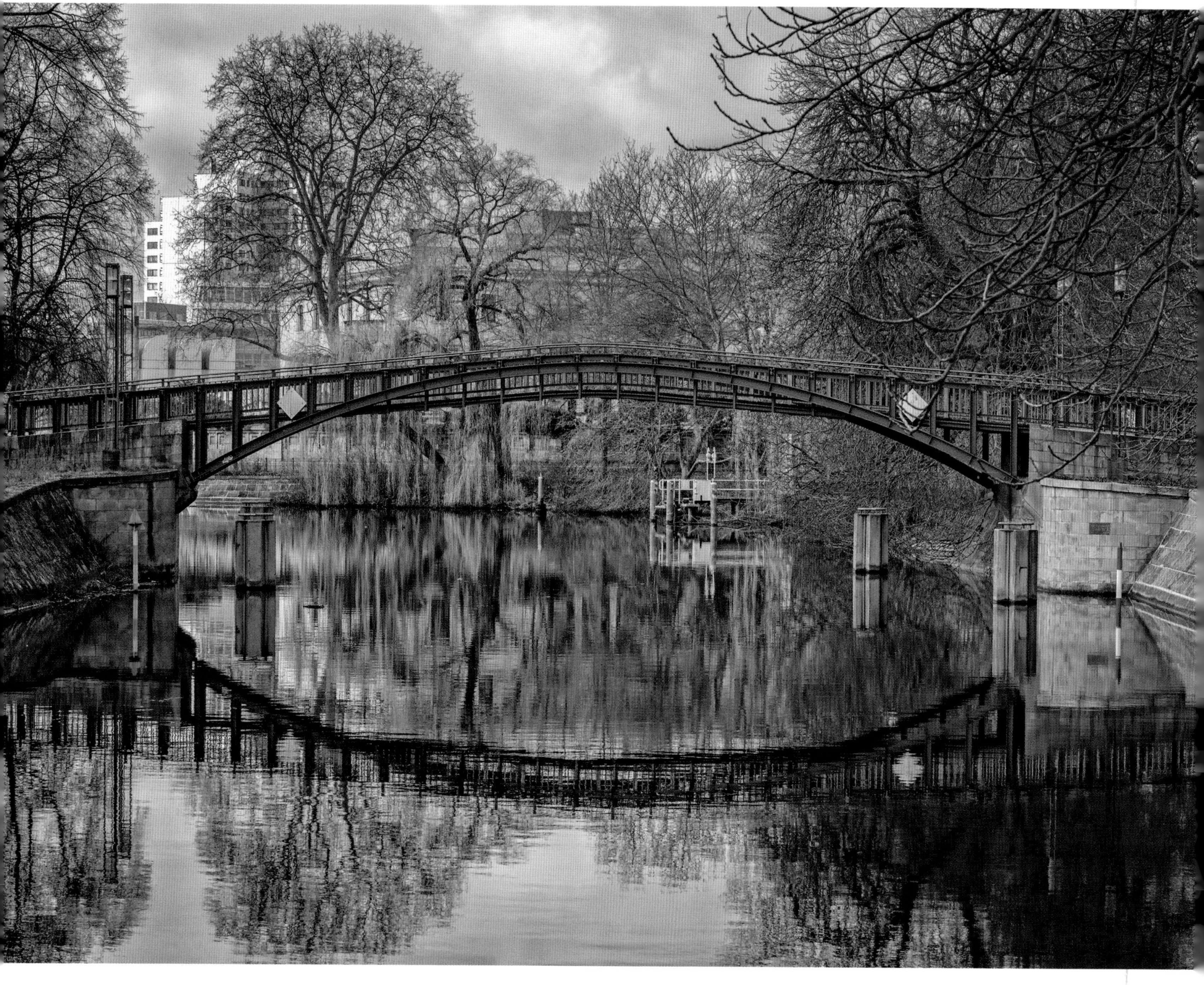

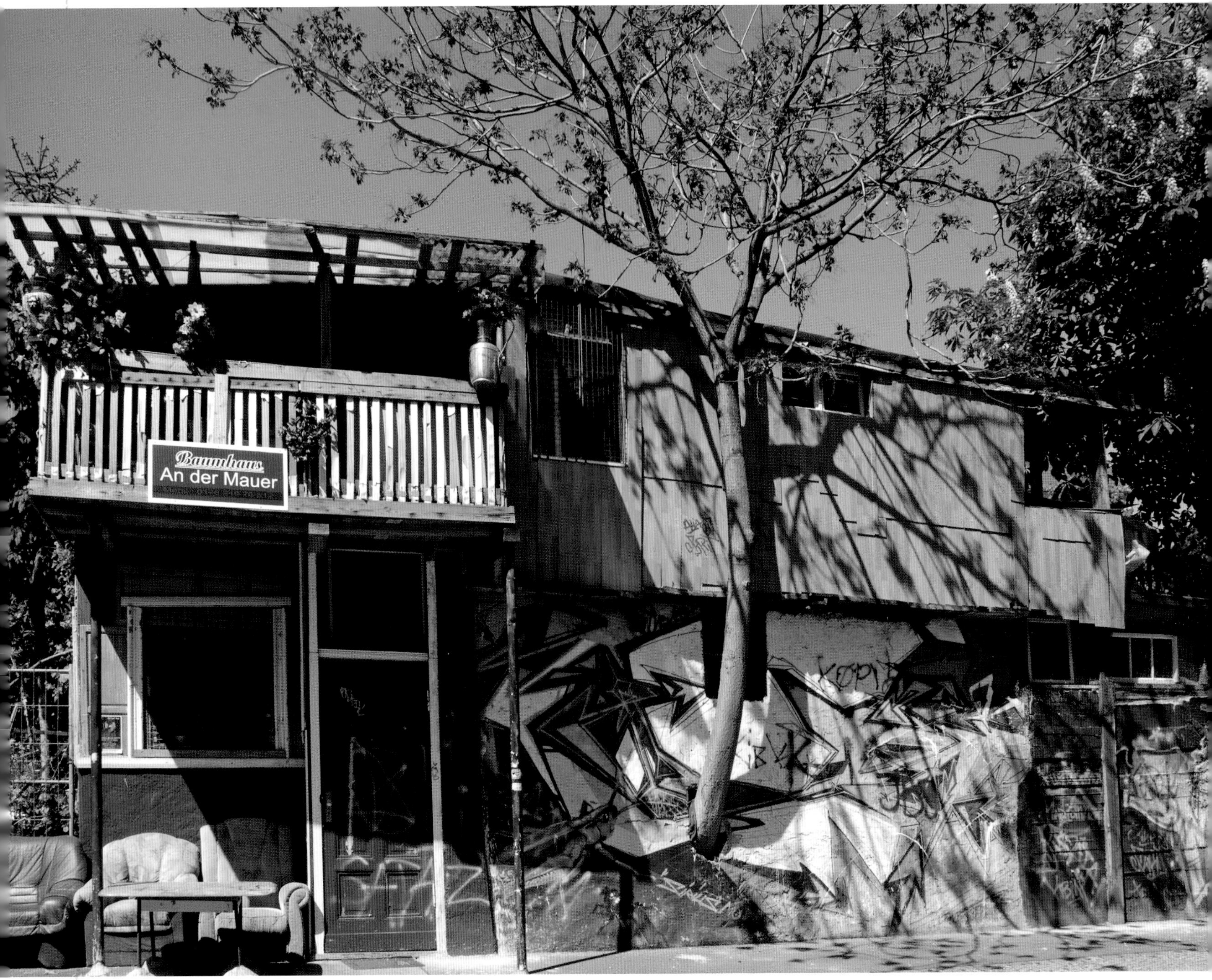
Baumhaus
An der Mauer

BAUMHAUS AN DER MAUER

Mariannenplatz, Kreuzberg

What appears rather like an improvised shack is actually something of an historical landmark in Berlin's Cold War history. In 1983, Turkish immigrant Osman Kalin built a two-storey hut around two trees, located between the districts of Mitte and Kreuzberg, and positioned ambiguously in the no-man's-land between East and West Germany. Constructed largely from scrap materials, the building became known as the Baumhaus an der Mauer (Treehouse on the Wall), and after unification popular support prevented it from being pulled down.

ANHALTER BAHNHOF

Askanischer Platz, Kreuzberg

For a time during the later decades of the nineteenth century, the Anhalter Bahnhof (Anhalter Station) was the biggest train station in both Germany and continental Europe, with a cathedral-like iron and glass roof that measured 171 m (561 ft), 62 m (203 ft) wide and, at the centreline, 34 m (112 ft) in height. By the 1930s, some 44,000 people a day used the station, travelling out to destinations such as Leipzig, Frankfurt am Main and Munich, and, via Dresden, Rome, Naples and Athens. It was also, tragically, used to deport 55,000 of the city's Jews during the Holocaust. Devastated by bombing during the war, the station remains today in haunting fragments.

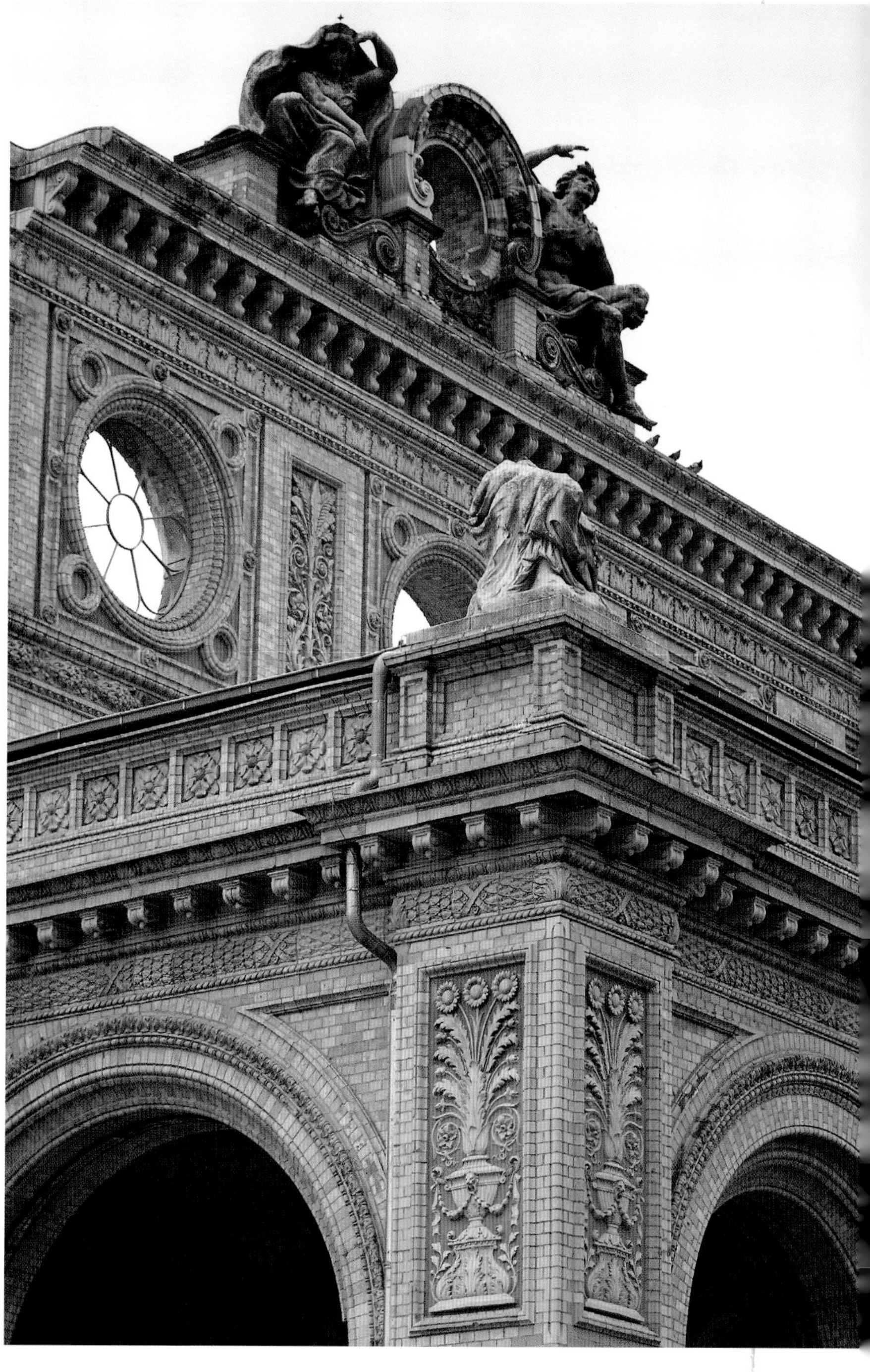

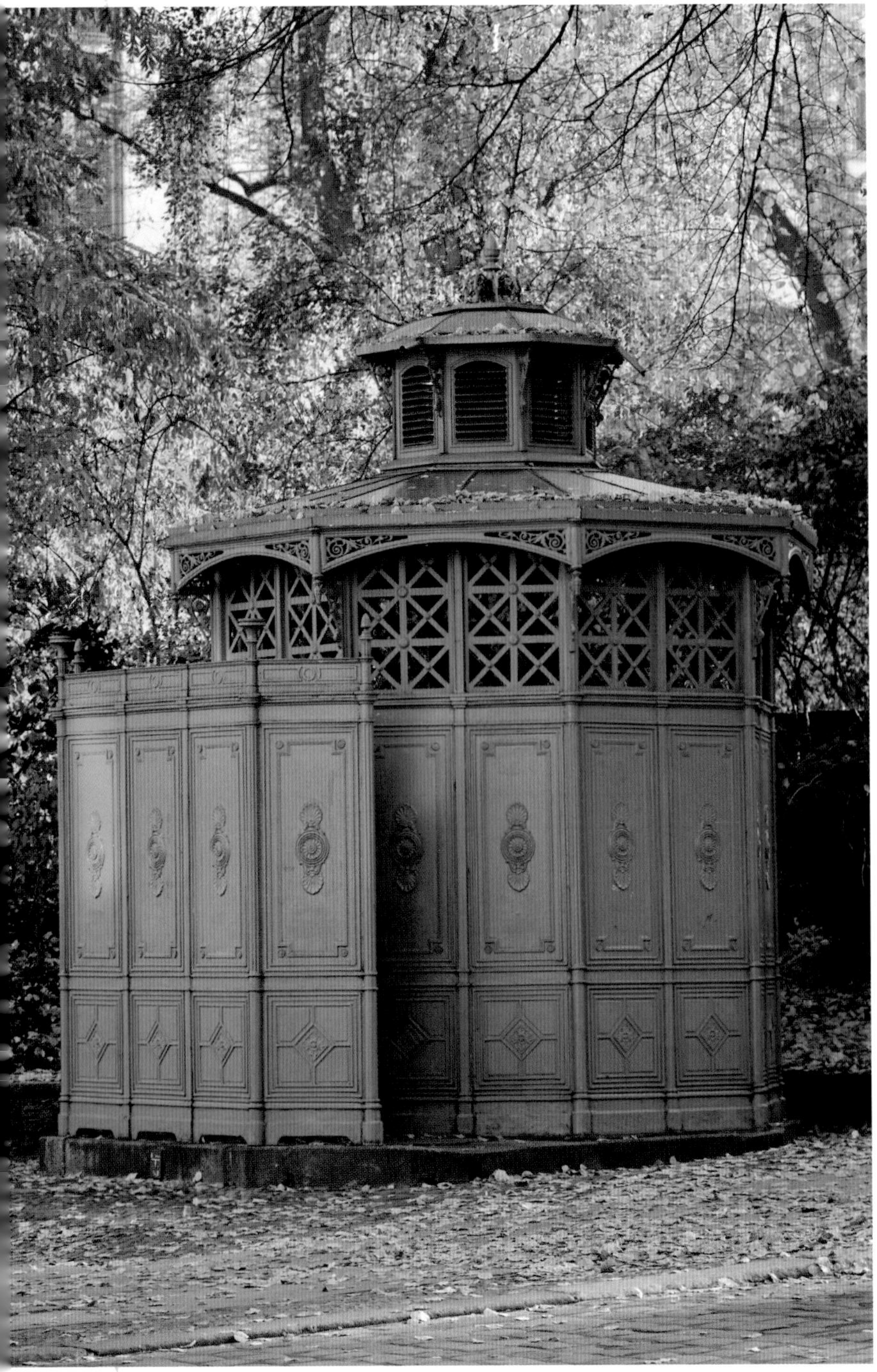

CHAMISSOPLATZ

Bergmannkiez, Kreuzberg

Chamissoplatz (Chamisso Place) is a prime destination for those wanting something of a time-warp experience, seeing Berlin as it looked at the turn of the twentieth century. In its imperial heyday, the area was home to many middle-class professionals, such as teachers, civil servants and professional craftsmen, each house packed with 15–20 families (today it attracts wealthier members of German society). With its cobbled streets, courtyards and preserved gas lanterns, the area has been used as the backdrop for several period film and TV productions.

CEMETERY

Bergmannstraße, Kreuzberg

Berlin is dotted with venerable cemeteries, many of them rather forlorn and haunting spaces from the eighteenth and nineteenth centuries, with granite angels and paupers' graves treated equally by the weather and encroaching vegetation. There are actually five cemeteries along Bergmannstraße, although the visitor can often move seamlessly between them via holes in the border walls. Famous burials in these cemeteries include members of the Mendelssohn musical family and scholars/educators such as Karl Lachmann (1793–1851) and Theodor Mommsen (1817–1903).

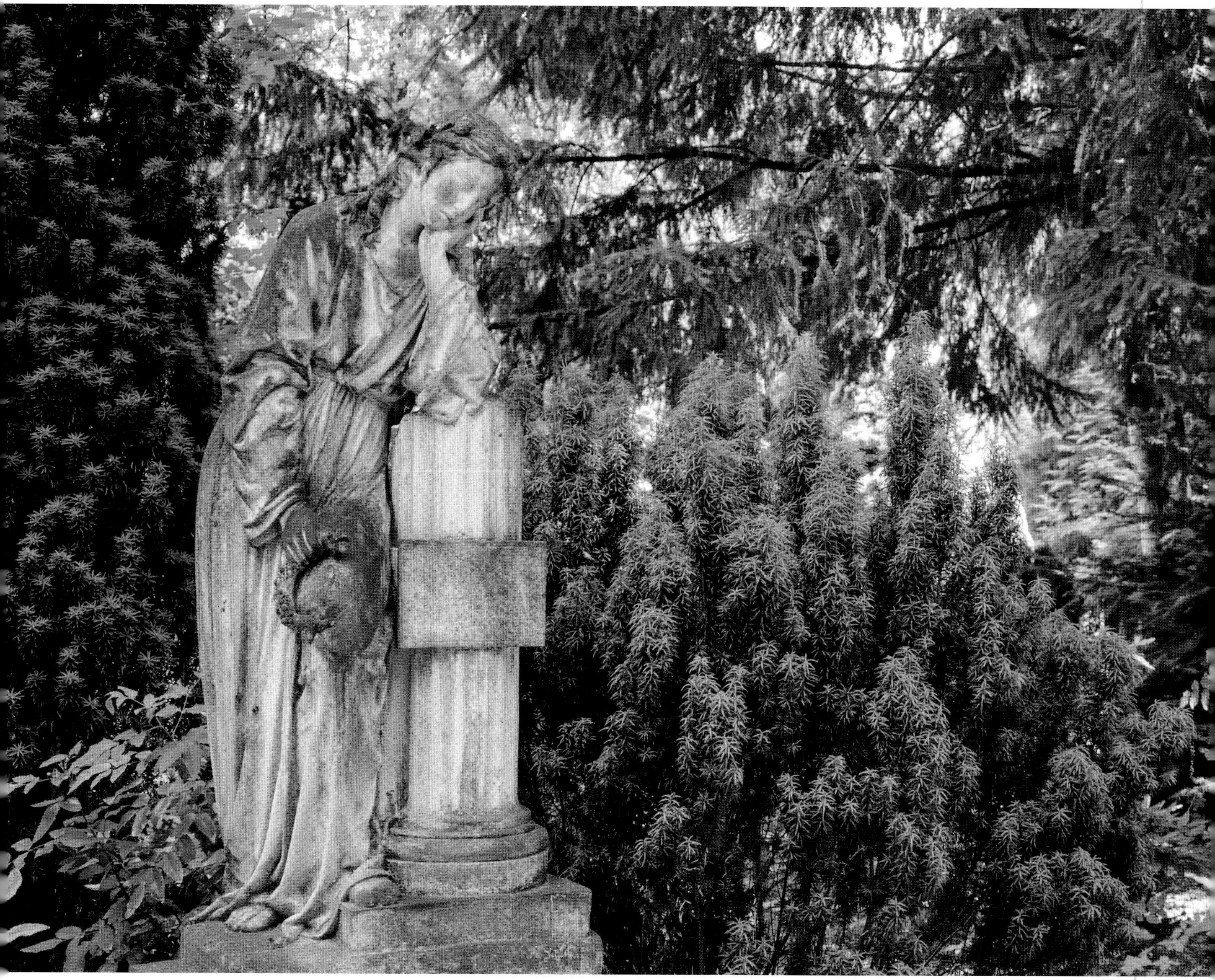

SANKT-MICHAEL-KIRCHE

Michaelkirchplatz, Kreuzberg

Seen here from the south, the Sankt-Michael-Kirche (St Michael's Church) is located on the Michaelkirchplatz in Engelbecken (Angel's Pool), the water in the foreground being the remnants of the old Luisenstadt Canal. A Roman Catholic church, it was designed by the architect August Soller (1805–53) in 1845, with definite Gothic leanings, but construction ran from 1851 until 1861, during which Soller died (he is buried inside). Almost destroyed during the Second World War, the church went through several iterations of post-war restoration, and today stands as an historical monument, capped by the statue of Archangel Michael by August Kiss.

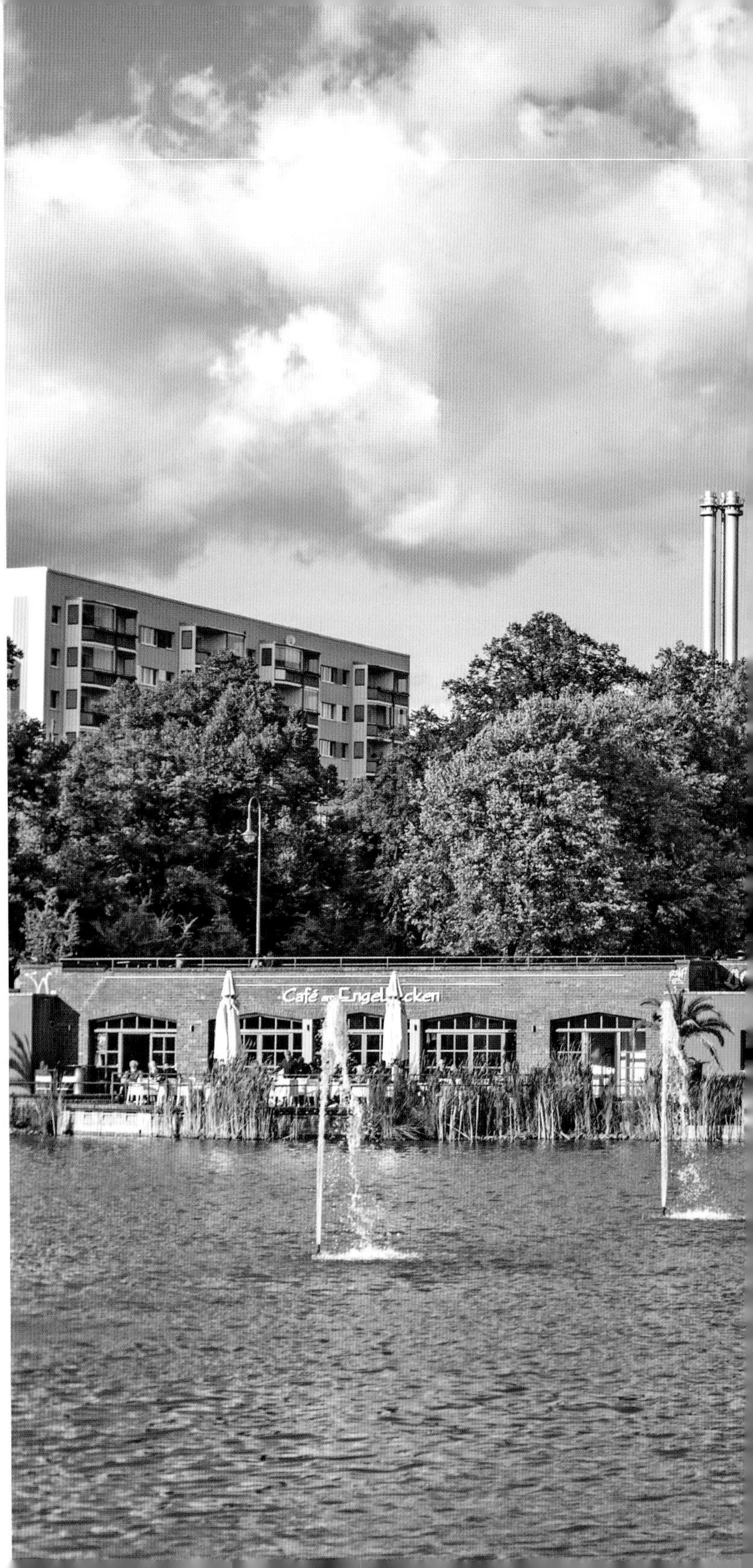

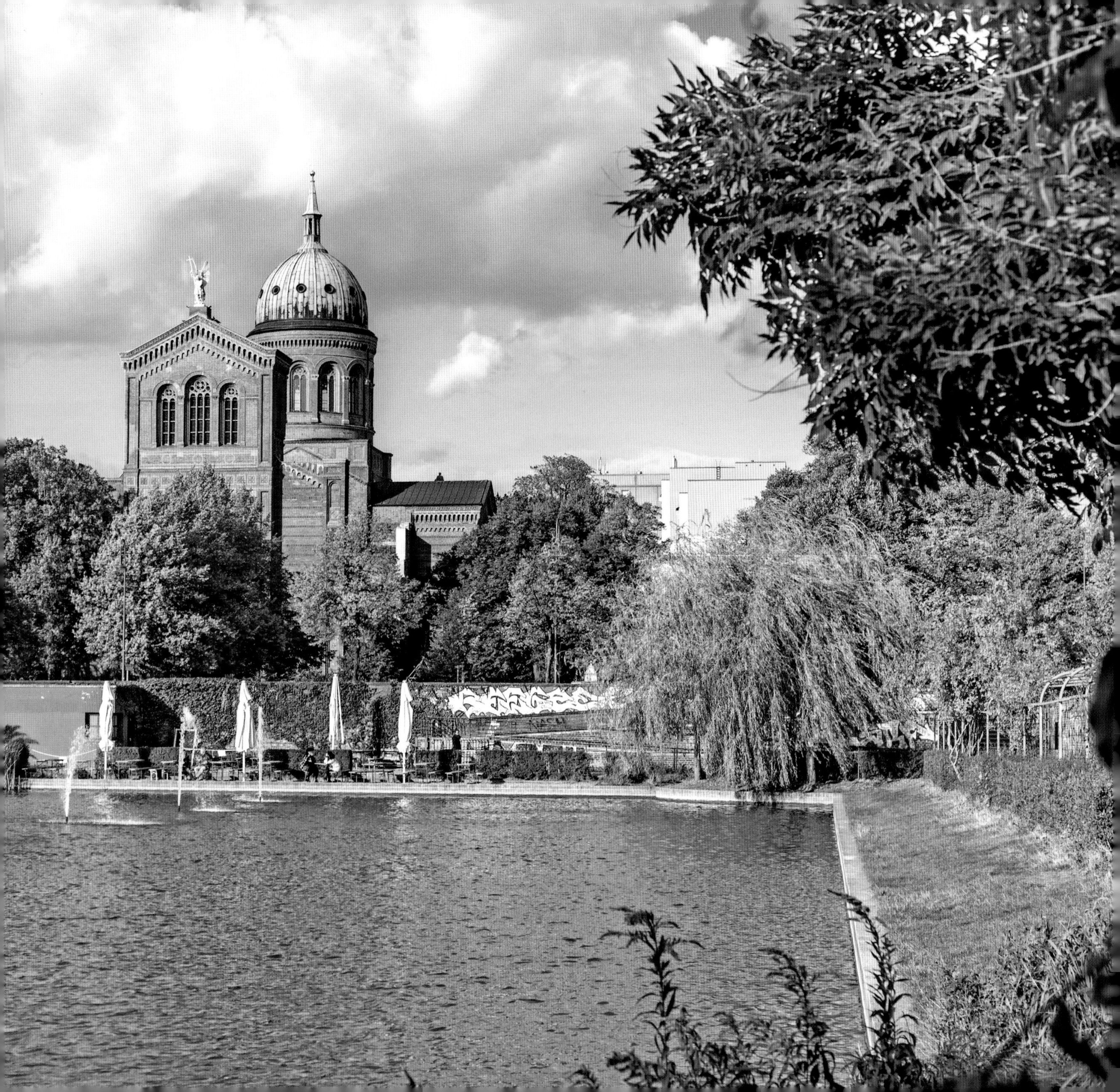

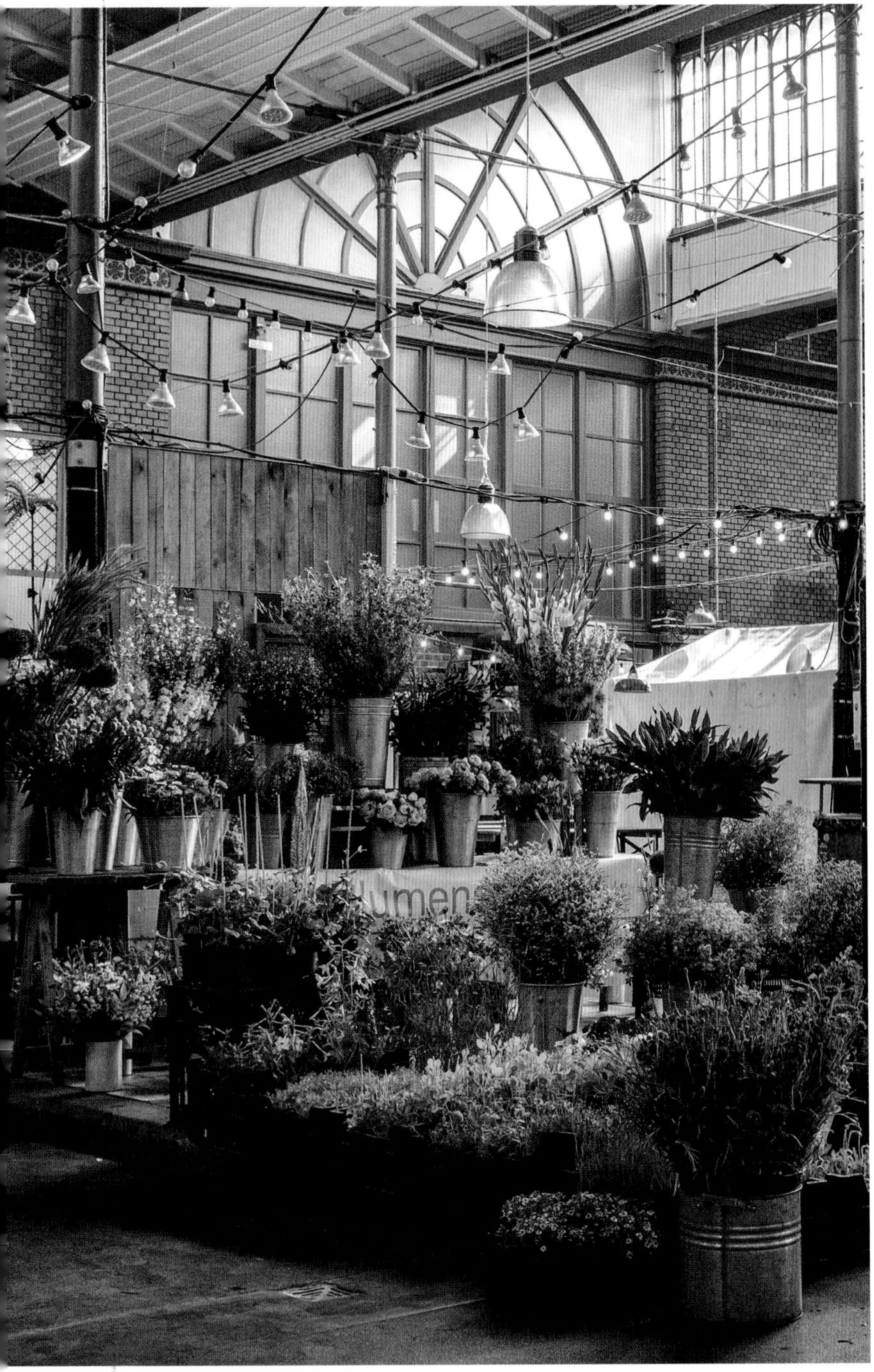

MARKTHALLE NEUN

Eisenbahnstraße, Kreuzberg

A destination for the hungry, Markthalle Neun (Market Hall Nine) is a gastronomic delight, an airy nineteenth-century space packed with every conceivable type of food and drink, either for take-away purchase or for consumption in one of the many cafés, bars and restaurants. The market has a history dating back to its opening in 1891, when it was simply 'number IX'. Remarkably, it largely survived the bombing of the Second World War, and passionate representatives also kept it out of the hands of large-scale urban developers.

BERLIN WALL

Niederkirchnerstraße, Friedrichshain

Although modern history now refers to the 'fall of the Berlin Wall', much of the fabric of this structure still lies dotted around the city at various locations. This is unsurprising, given that the wall at its most extensive ran for 155 km (96 miles) around Berlin and 43 km (27 miles) in the separation of East Berlin from West Berlin. In its most advanced state of improvement, the wall was built from 45,000 separate sections of reinforced concrete, each of these 3.6 m (12 ft) high and 1.2 m (4 ft) wide. This section of the wall is on the site of the former Gestapo HQ, now the Topography of Terror museum. Also pictured (in centre) is the restored nineteenth-century Gropius-Bau building, a renowned art museum and exhibition venue.

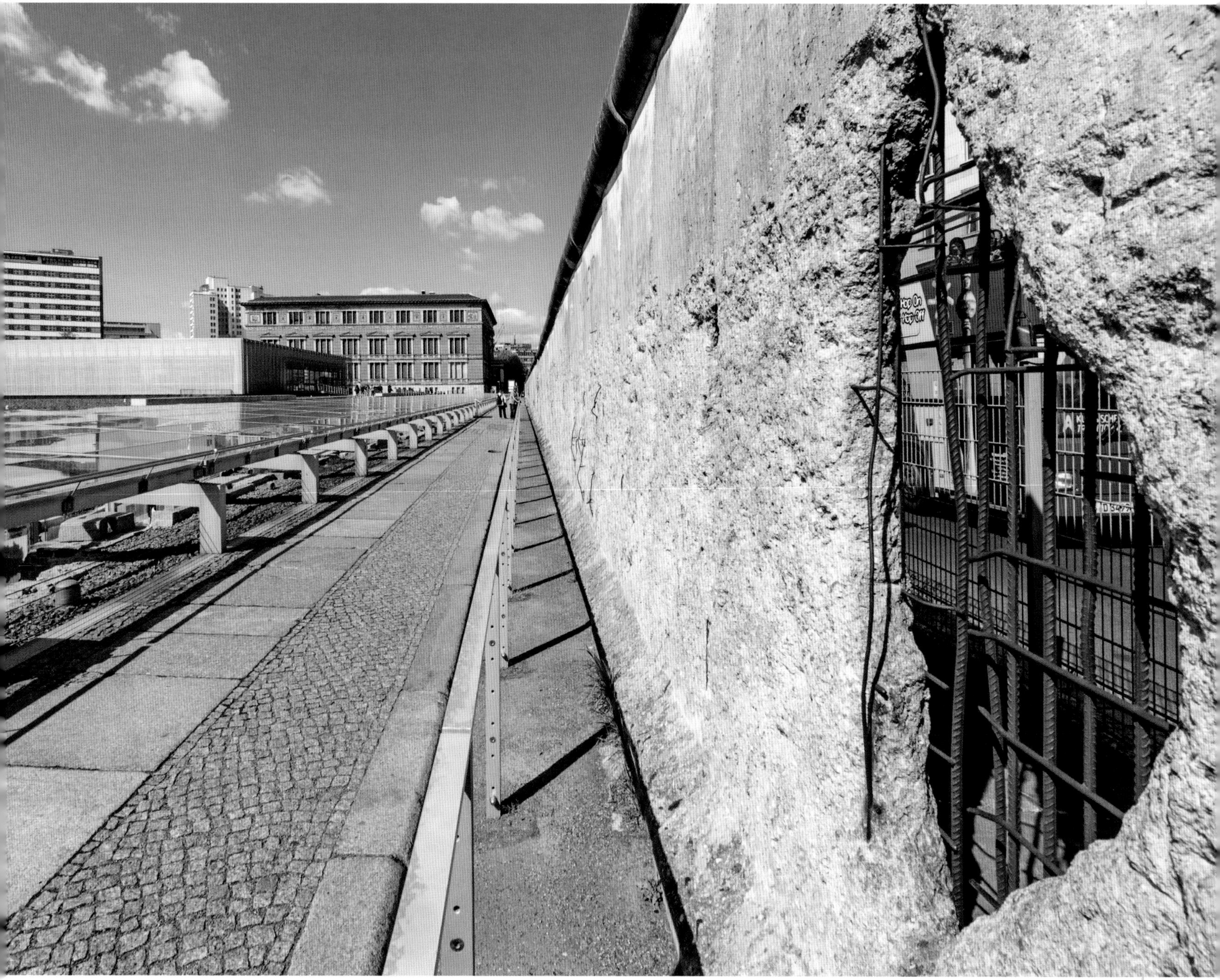

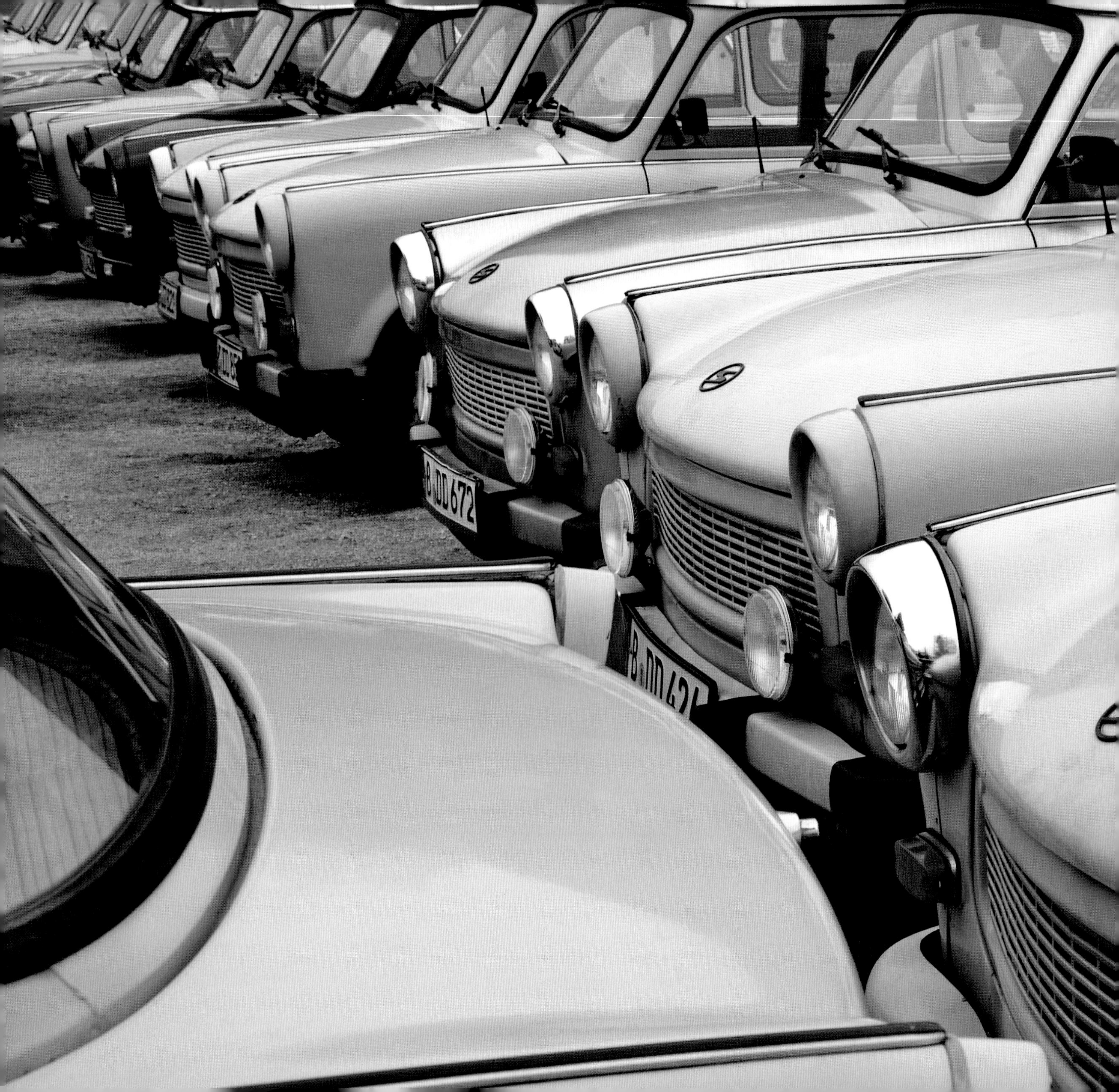
B DD 672

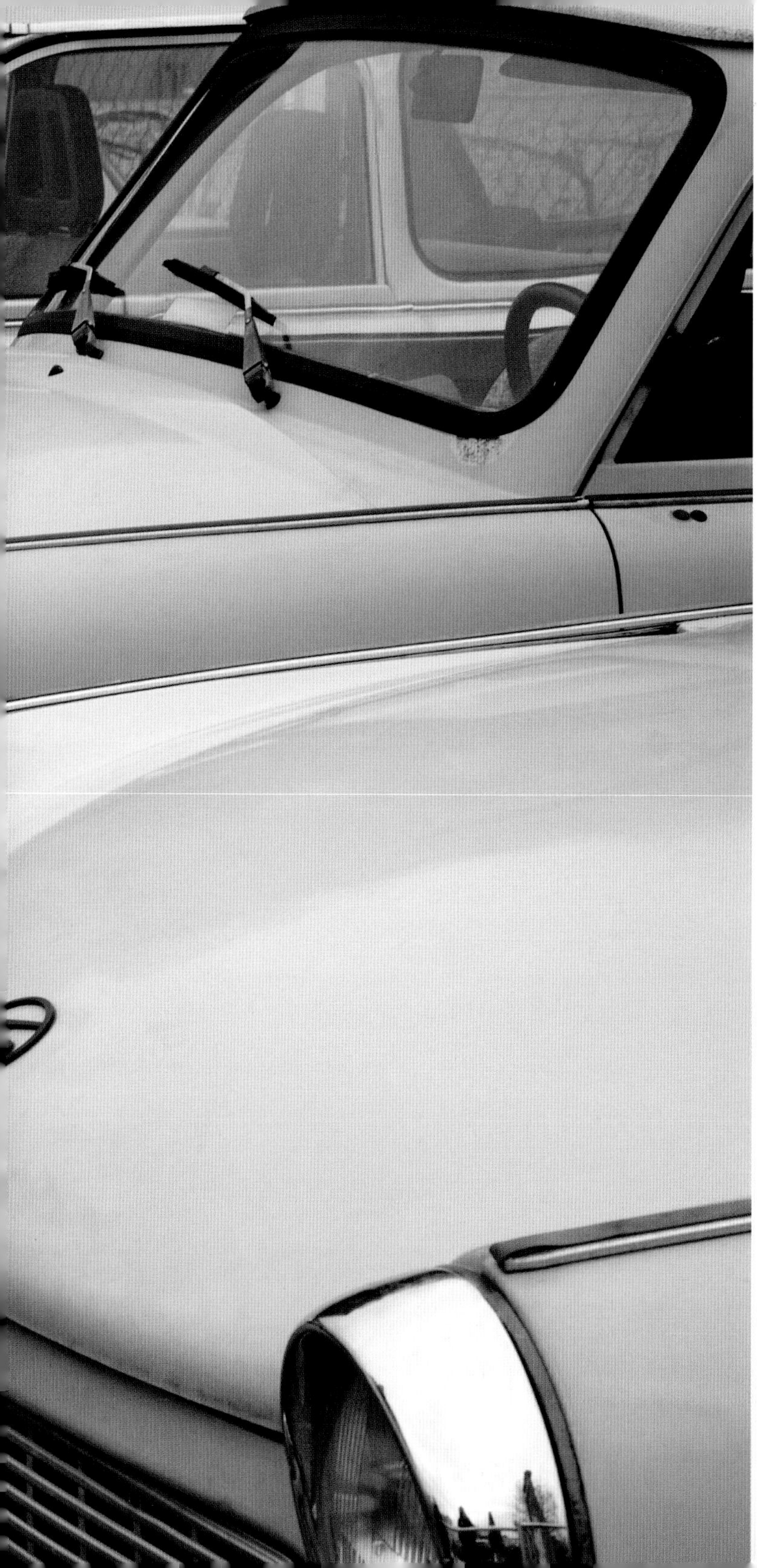

TRABANT CARS

Zimmerstraße, Kreuzberg

Trabant cars, more than three million of them, were the principal form of transport for East Germans between 1957 and 1990, the production years of the monopolist state manufacturer VEB Sachsenring Automobilwerke Zwickau. Trabants are known for their crudity, unreliability and complete lack of design flair – they have been referred to as a 'spark plug with a roof'. Ironically, it is these very qualities that have given the Trabants a chic collectability. In 2013, near Checkpoint Charlie, the Trabi-Museum Berlin opened, some of whose collection is seen here.

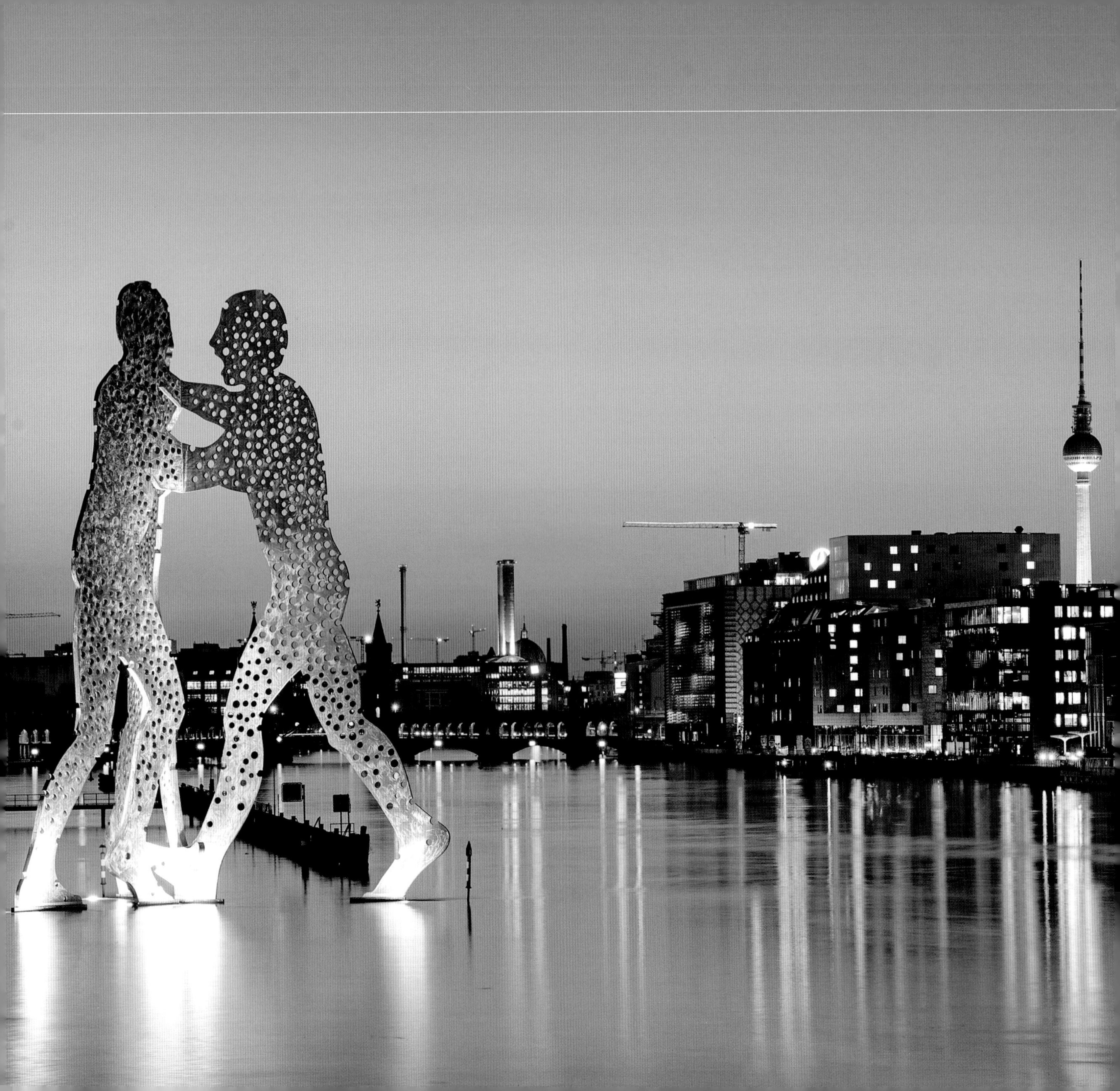

MOLECULE MEN

River Spree, Alt-Treptow

Molecule Men by American sculptor Jonathan Borofsky (b. 1942) is emphatic in demanding our contemplation. It stands 30 m (98 ft) in the middle of the River Spree, exactly as the intersection between three districts: Treptow, Kreuzberg and Friedrichshain. The interaction between the three figures, cut from aluminium, demonstrates unification, while the holes that pierce their bodies illustrate what Borofsky saw as the 'molecules of human beings coming together to create an existence'. There are similar Molecule Man sculptures in California and Utah.

SPREEPARK BERLIN

Treptow-Köpenick

Also known as Kulturpark Plänterwald Berlin (its earlier name), Spreepark has a creepy horror-film vibe that is now at the core of its attraction. The Kulturpark Plänterwald entertainment park opened in the GDR in 1969, and it became the Spreepark Berlin after reunification in 1991. By 2002, however, the park plunged into insolvency, and has been abandoned ever since. The rides and stalls remain, slowly rusting and being strangled by vegetation; many were destroyed in a fire in August 2014, likely arson. What the future of the park will be is unclear, although it has appeared in both films and music videos.

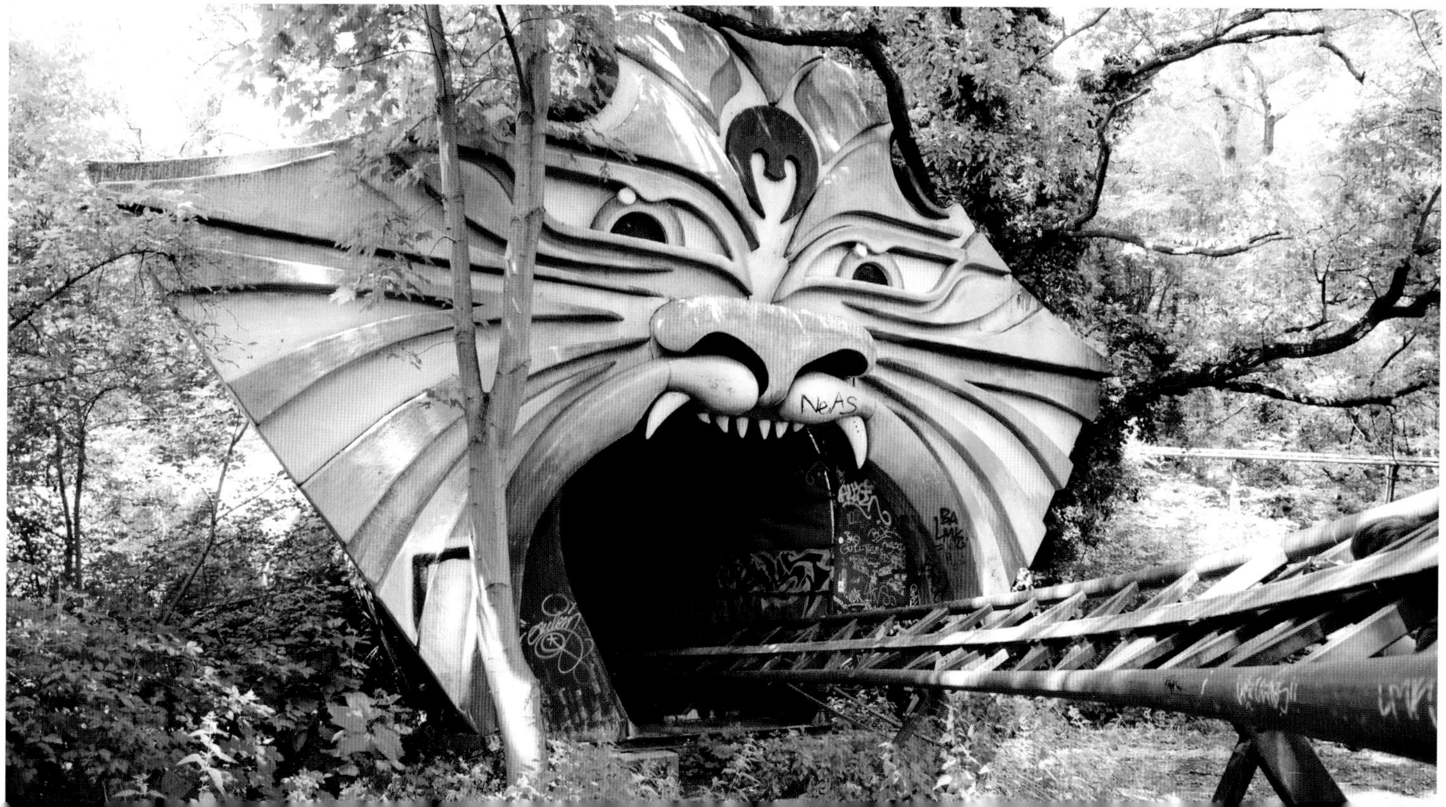

INSEL DER JUGEND

River Spree, Alt-Treptow

Berlin offers numerous opportunities and locations for leisurely escapism, and the Insel der Jugend (Island of Youth) between Treptow Park and Forst Plänterwald (Plänterwald Forest) is representative. The island is accessed via the quaint Abteibrücke (Abbey Bridge), and there the visitor will find not only sunlit patches of park for picnics and relaxation, but also art, music and cultural events in the Kulturhaus on the island. There is also an open-air cinema and boat rental.

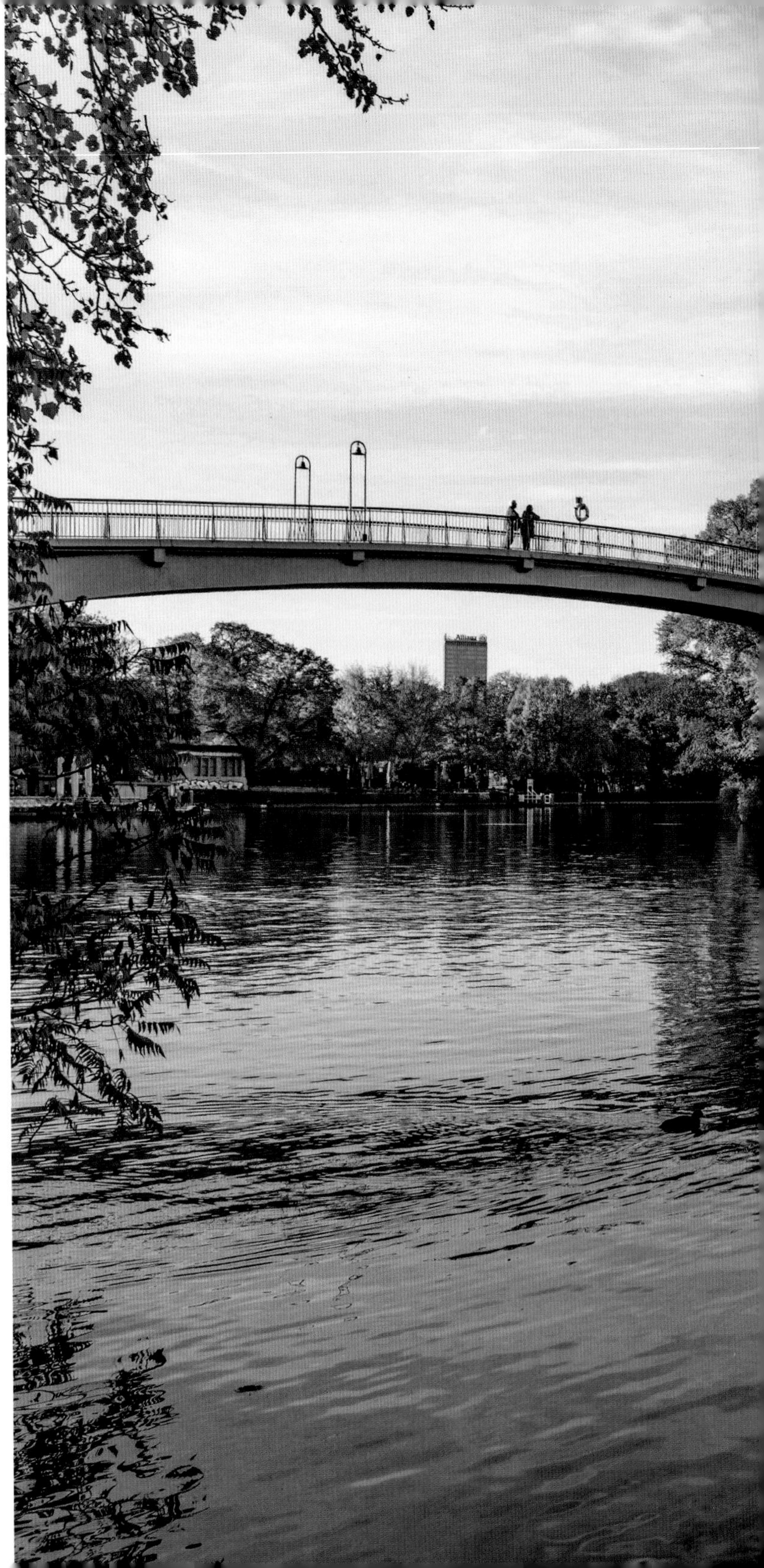

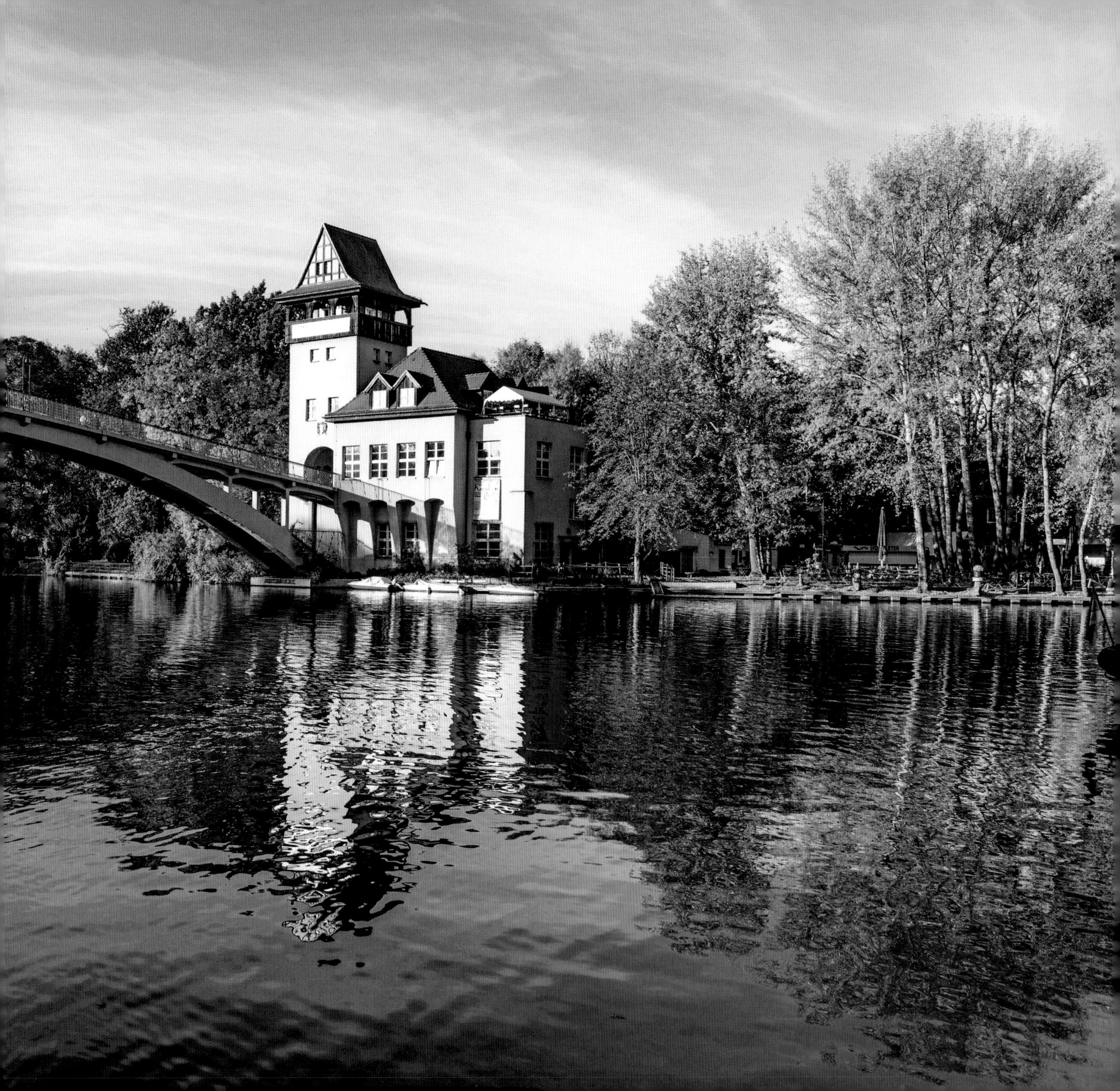

BADESCHIFF

East Harbour, River Spree, Alt-Treptow

Although the River Spree itself is not safe for bathers, the Badeschiff (Bathing Ship), set in the East Harbour of the river, delivers a notable riverside experience. The Badeschiff is actually a floating swimming pool within the Spree, created using a harboured barge, and with dimensions of 32 by 8 m (104 by 26 ft). In addition to the pool itself, the site provides lots of surrounding space for sunbathing, parties, festivals and music, making the Badeschiff a popular and youthful attraction for those looking to escape urban life.

SOVIET WAR MEMORIAL

Treptower Park, Alt-Treptow

Some 80,000 Soviet soldiers died in the battle for Berlin in April 1945, and following the war Berlin was graced with three powerful Soviet war memorials to remember the dead. The one in Treptower Park was built between 1946 and 1949 by a collective of artists, engineers and sculptors. Here we see two of the enormous red granite stylized Soviet flags, beyond which are various sculptures of ineffable grief and nobility, tinged with the stoic patriotism of the era.

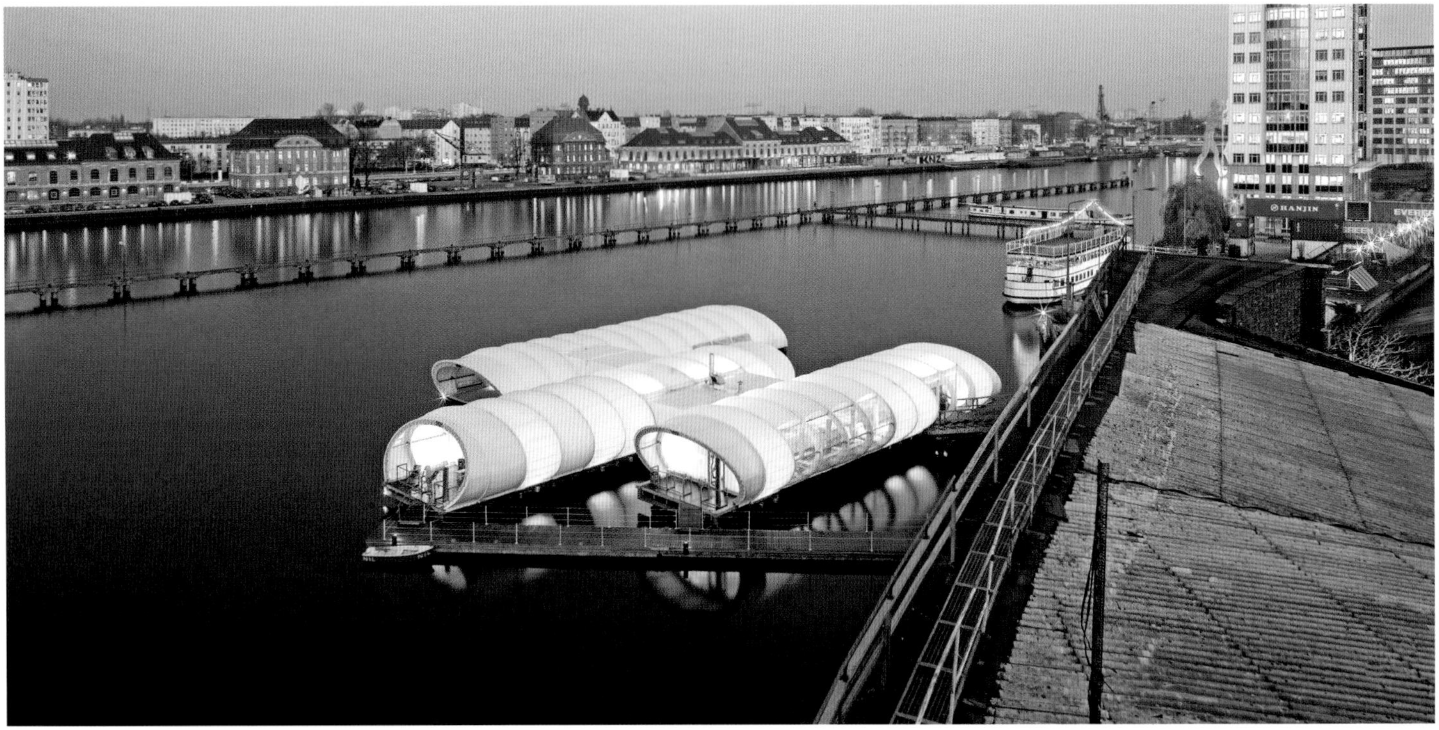

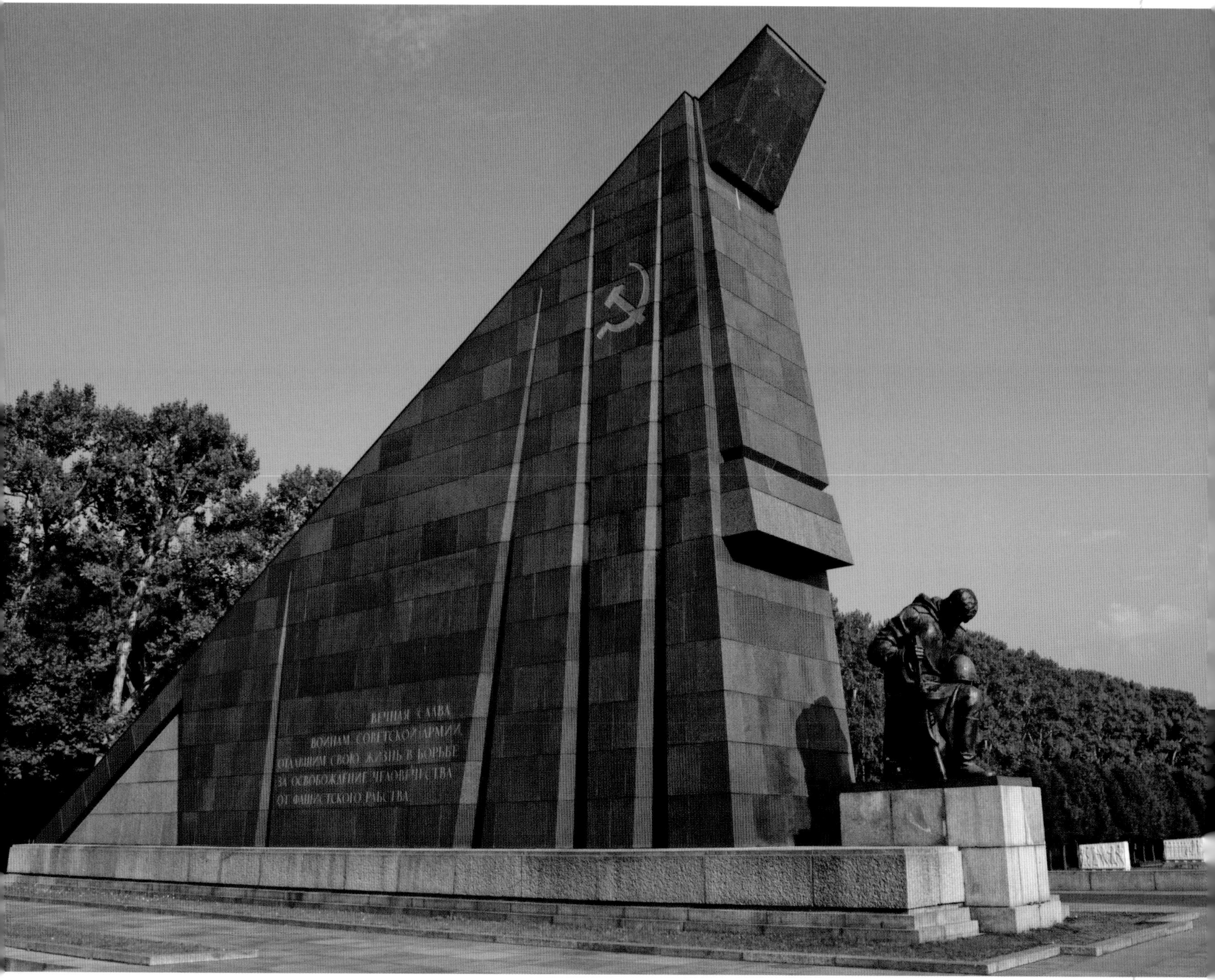
ВЕЧНАЯ СЛАВА
ВОИНАМ СОВЕТСКОЙ АРМИИ
ОТДАВШИМ СВОЮ ЖИЗНЬ В БОРЬБЕ
ЗА ОСВОБОЖДЕНИЕ ЧЕЛОВЕЧЕСТВА
ОТ ФАШИСТСКОГО РАБСТВА

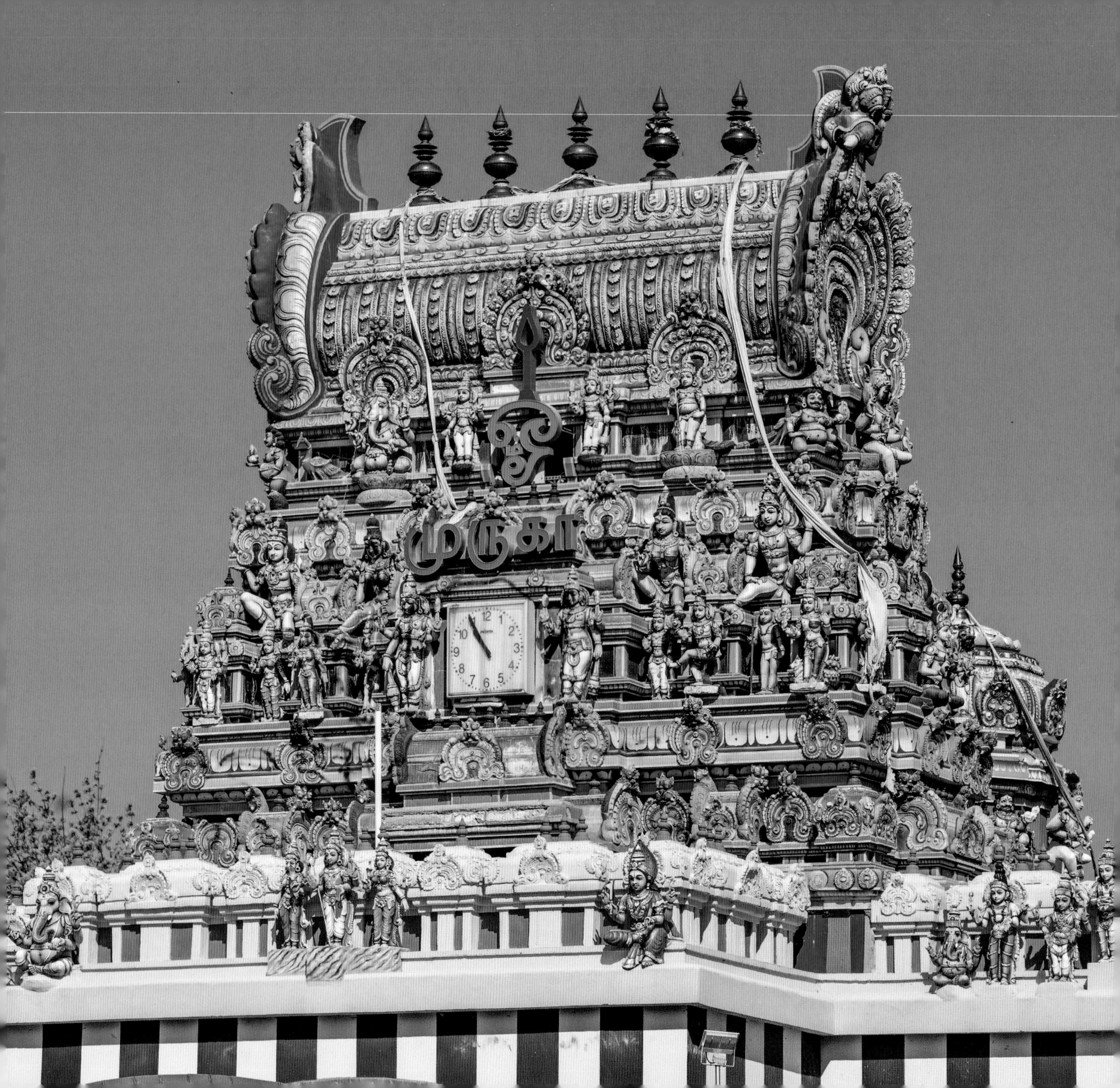
முருகா

SRI MAYURAPATHY MURUGAN TEMPLE

Blaschkoallee, Neukölln

Berlin is a multicultural city but, even giving this full consideration, the Sri Mayurapathy Murugan Hindu temple is an astonishing vision within a European capital. Replete with wooden carvings of Hindu deities and architectural features of the most ornate and colourful style, the temple was constructed in 1991, capped by a 12-m (39-ft) tower. The overall design is indebted to that the thirteenth-century Nallur Murugan Kovil temple in Sri Lanka, but the temple is welcoming to visitors of any religious persuasion.

HUFEISENSIEDLUNG

Neukölln

It is sometimes difficult for us to understand the heated politics behind seemingly innocuous architectural choices. The flat roofs and functional simplicity of architect Bruno Taut's Hufeisensiedlung (Horseshoe Estate) – so-called because of its overall horseshoe layout – created between 1925 and 1933, later attracted the antipathy of the Nazis, who regarded Taut's architectural Modernism as somehow 'degenerate' and separated from the nationalistic folk style. Taut actually fled Germany for the Soviet Union in 1933, but his pleasing estate remains, much of it now a World Heritage Site.

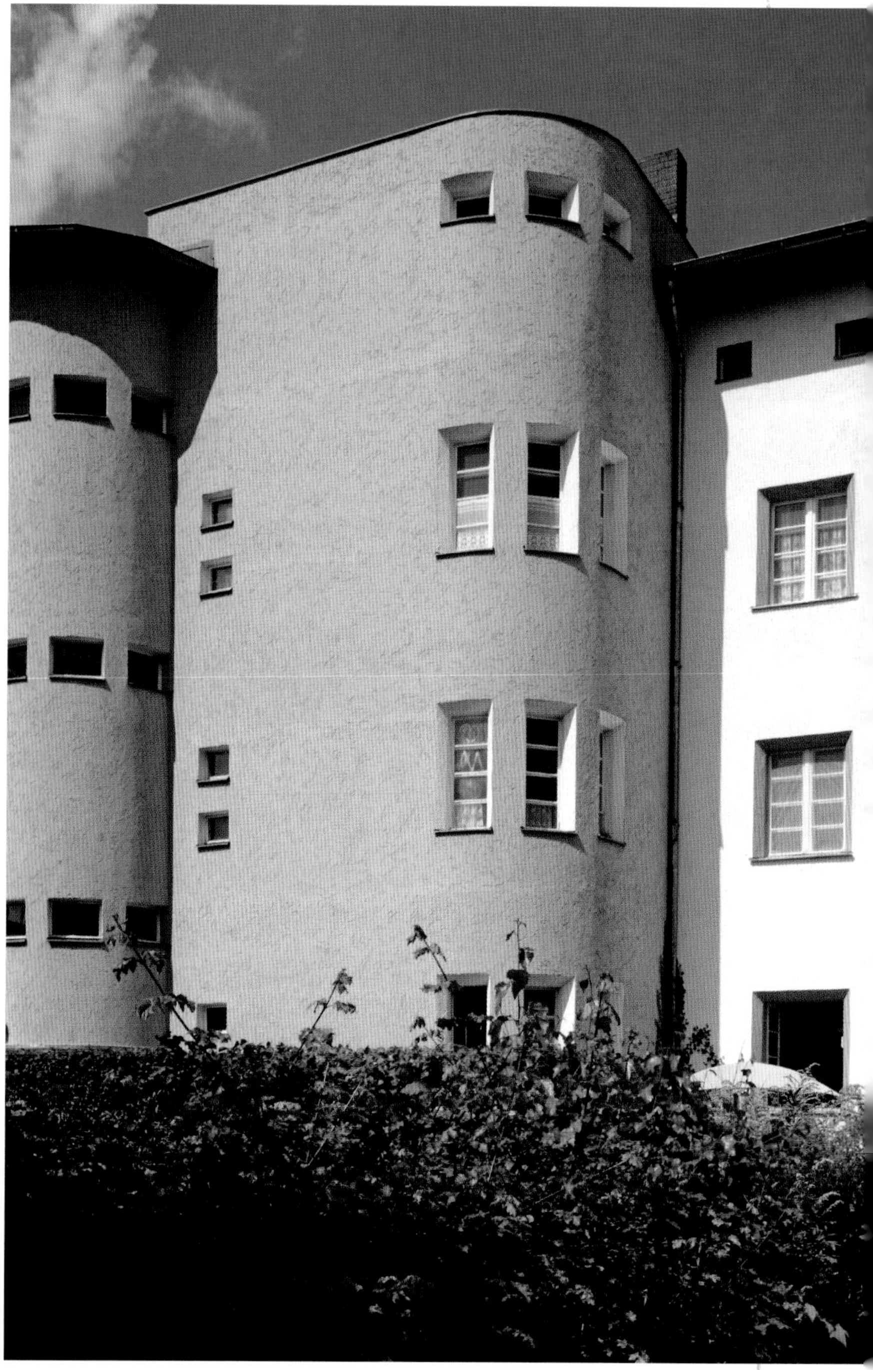

STADTBAD NEUKÖLLN

Ganghoferstraße, Neukölln

The Stadtbad Neukölln (Neukölln City Baths), inaugurated in 1914 and designed by architect Reinhold Kiehl (1874–1913), is a public bath offering opulent escapism. Towering pillars, exquisite marble, ornate mosaics – the aesthetics of the place evoke ancient temples and Roman baths, plus a sense of Eastern European heritage. The facility is popular with both locals and foreign travellers, attracting some 10,000 people every day, either to swim in the lofty main hall or to steam out their stresses in the sauna rooms.

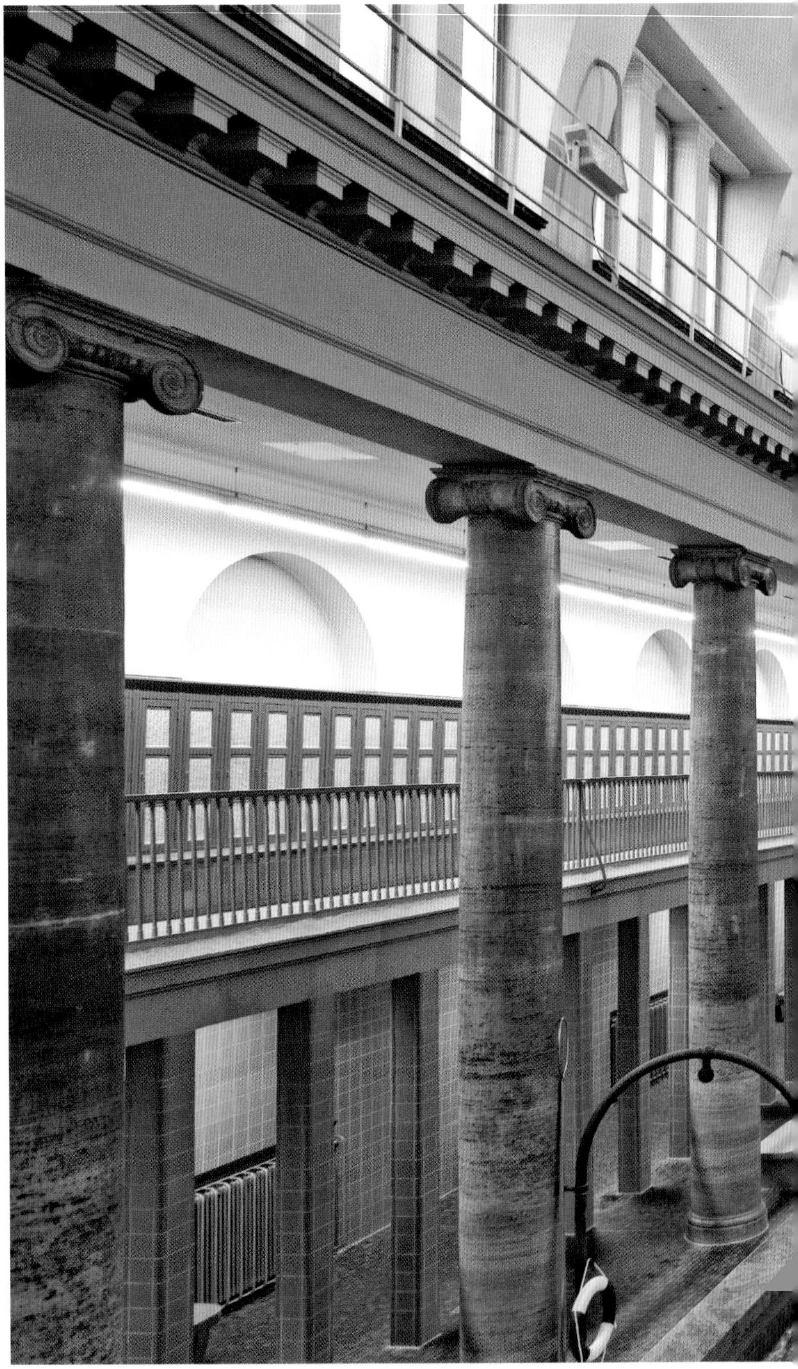

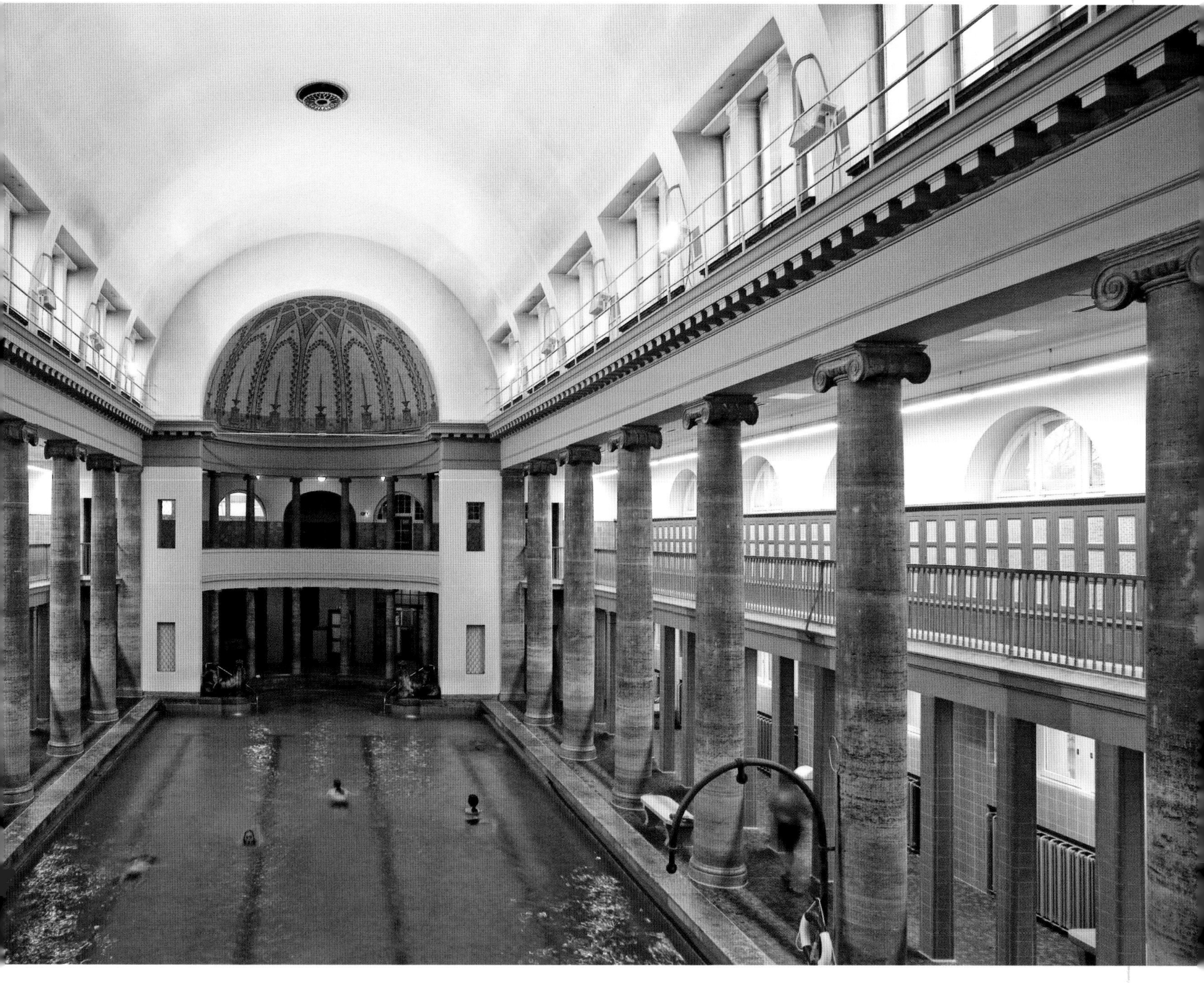

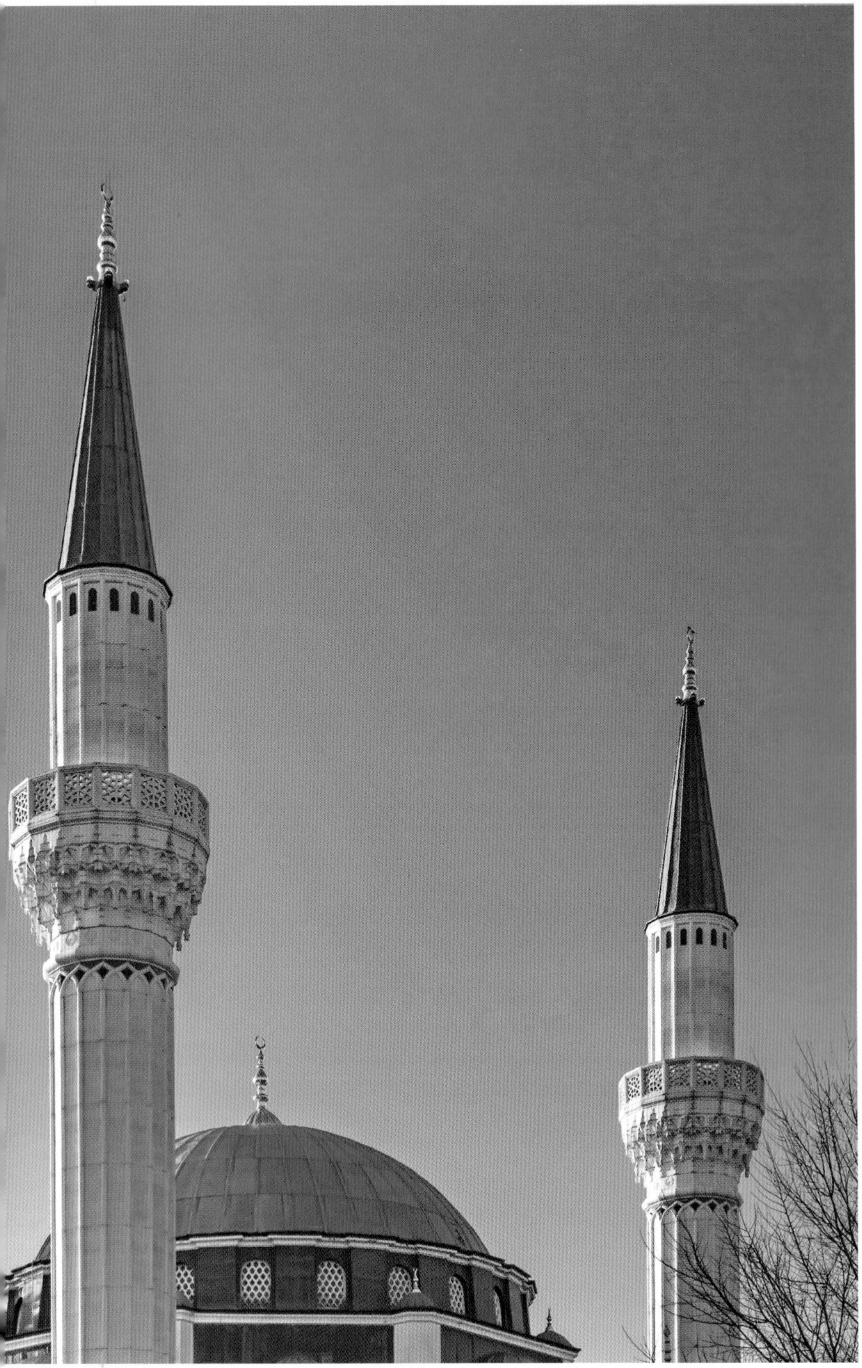

ŞEHITLIK MOSQUE

Columbiadamm, Tempelhof

With an architectural grace connecting back to the Ottoman architecture of the sixteenth and seventeenth centuries, the Şehitlik Mosque is an ineffably beautiful place of worship for Berlin's Muslim community. The mosque opened in 2005 after six years of construction, built on land actually granted to the Ottoman Empire by German Emperor William I (1797–1888) for use as a Muslim cemetery. An elegant dome, illuminated on the inside with calligraphy and abstract patterns, on the outside is flanked by two minarets, from which the muezzin calls some 1,500 worshippers to prayer.

FLUGHAFEN TEMPELHOF

Tempelhof

The Flughafen Tempelhof (Tempelhof Airport) was former parade ground that became a flying field in the early years of the twentieth century, and an expanding airport in the 1920s and 30s, eventually becoming one of Berlin's greatest transport hubs. Over its nearly nine-decade history (the airport was closed in 2008), it witnessed epic moments in aviation, some great, some ignominious. They include Orville Wright's altitude record of 160 m (525 ft) in 1909; the use of the airport as a major combat base during the Second World War; and being the destination for blockade-busting flights between June 1948 and May 1949. Today, its former runways silent, it is an international event location.

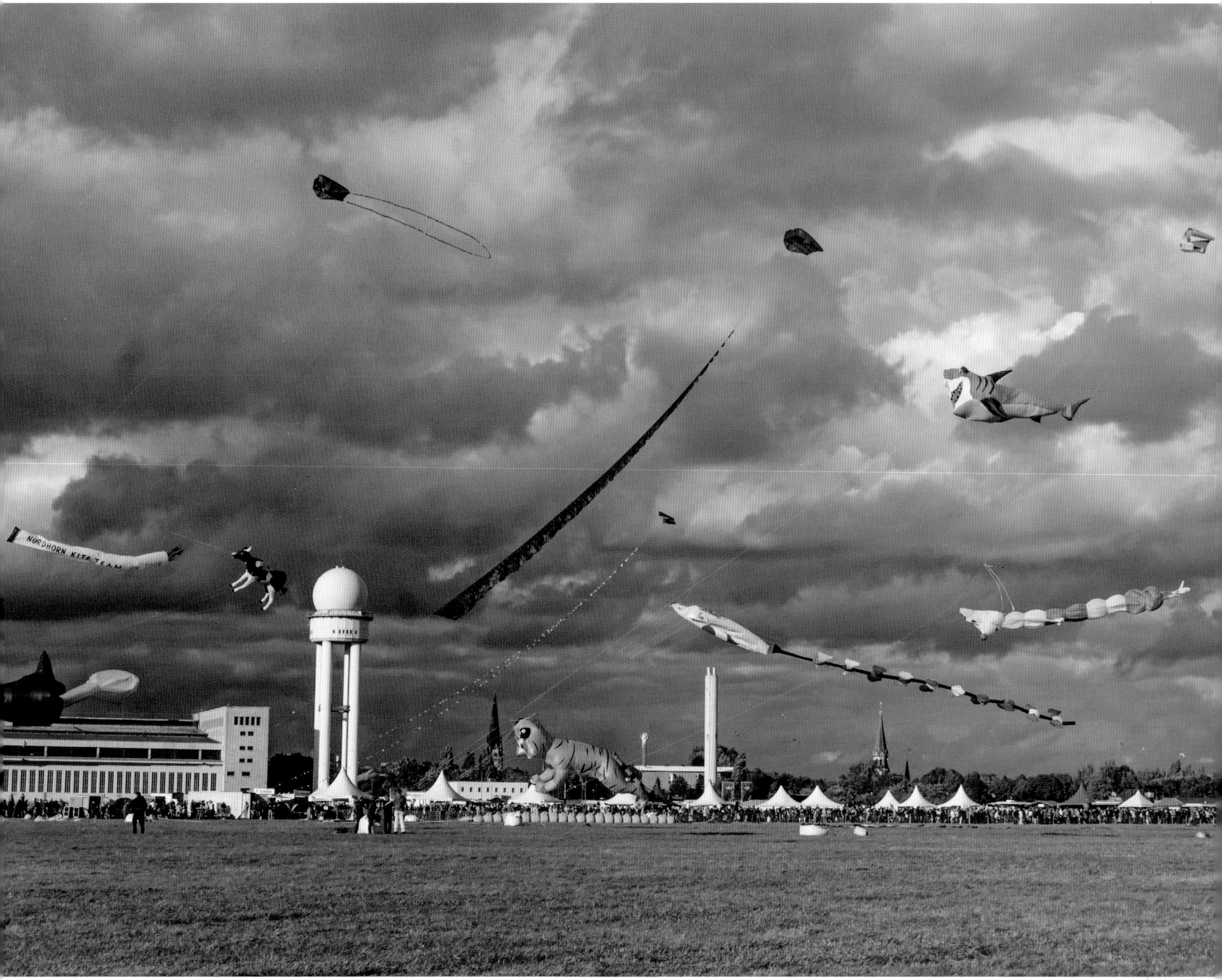
NORDHORN KITE TEAM

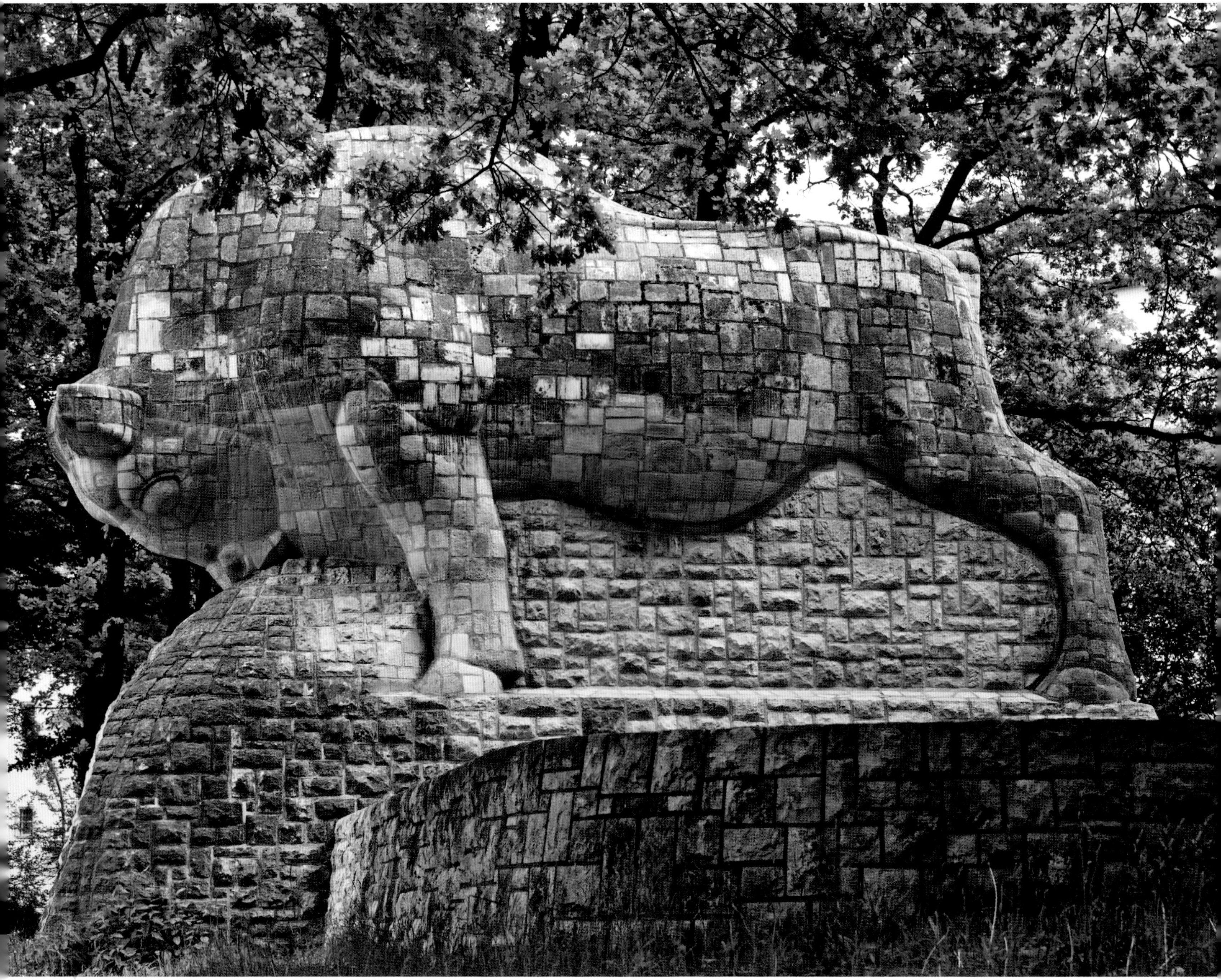

BULL STATUE

Alboinplatz, Tempelhof

Sculptor Paul Mersmann (1929–2017) created this 7-m (23-ft) high and 9-m (29-ft 6-in) long bull in the Alboinplatz monumental garden in 1934. It was a work of extraordinary labour, formed from 3,000 small limestone blocks from the Rüdersdorf limestone quarry. Some have seen in the Mersmann's bull an endorsement of contemporary Nazi ideology, in the power of its statement, but analysis indicates that Mersmann was more focused on mythological representation, and the Nazi authorities actually rejected an official endorsement of the work.

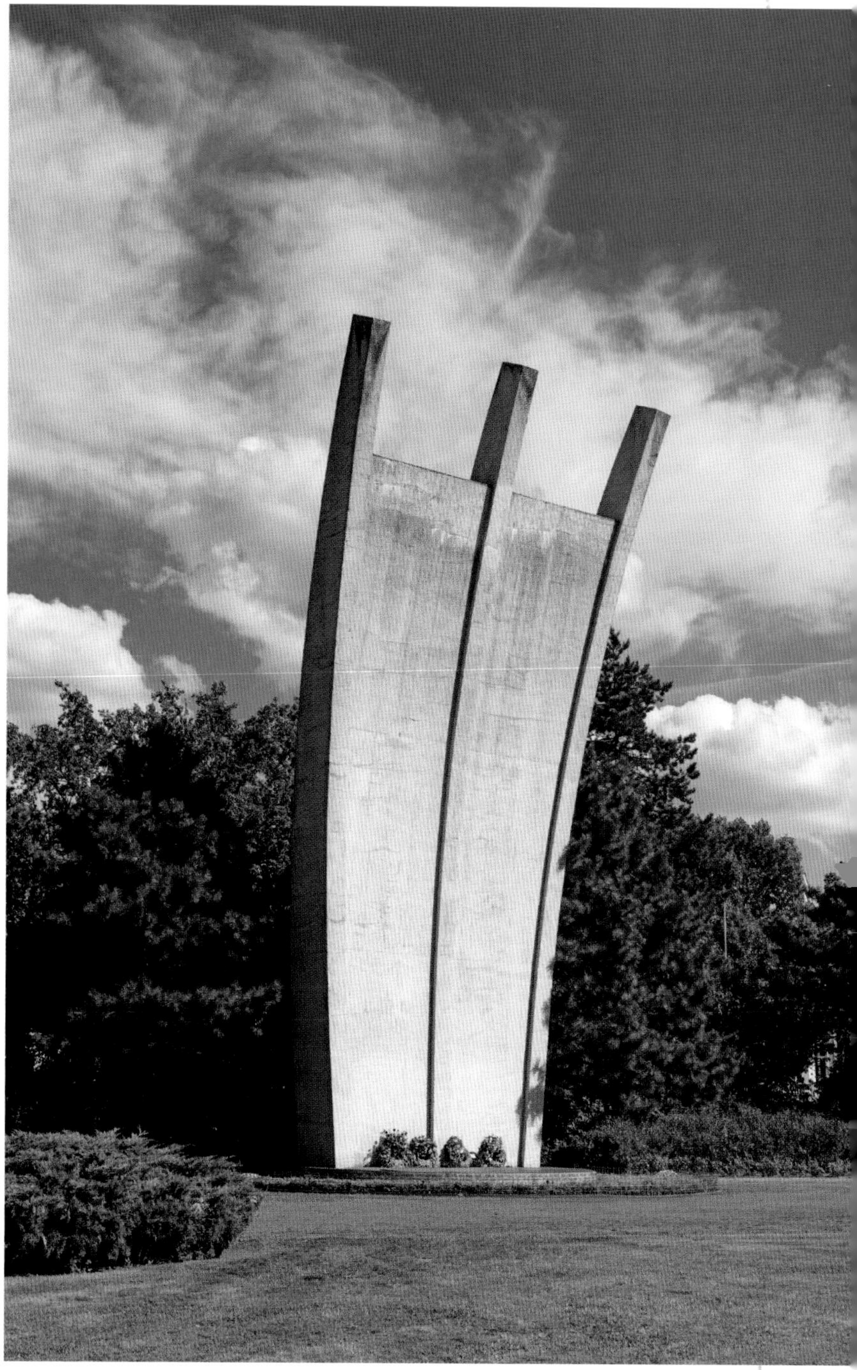

LUFTBRÜCKENDENKMAL

Tempelhof

On 24 June 1948, the Soviets severed the physical road, rail and river links between West Berlin and the outside world, threatening the 2.2 million residents of West Berlin with severe deprivations. The solution was what is now known as the Berlin Airlift, round-the-clock supply flights by the Western Allies that lasted for 323 days, landing at Berlin Tempelhof airport. The breaking of the blockade is commemorated in the concrete Luftbrückendenkmal (Airlift Memorial) by Eduard Ludwig, the three claws representing the three air corridors and the three Allied occupying forces (American, British, French).

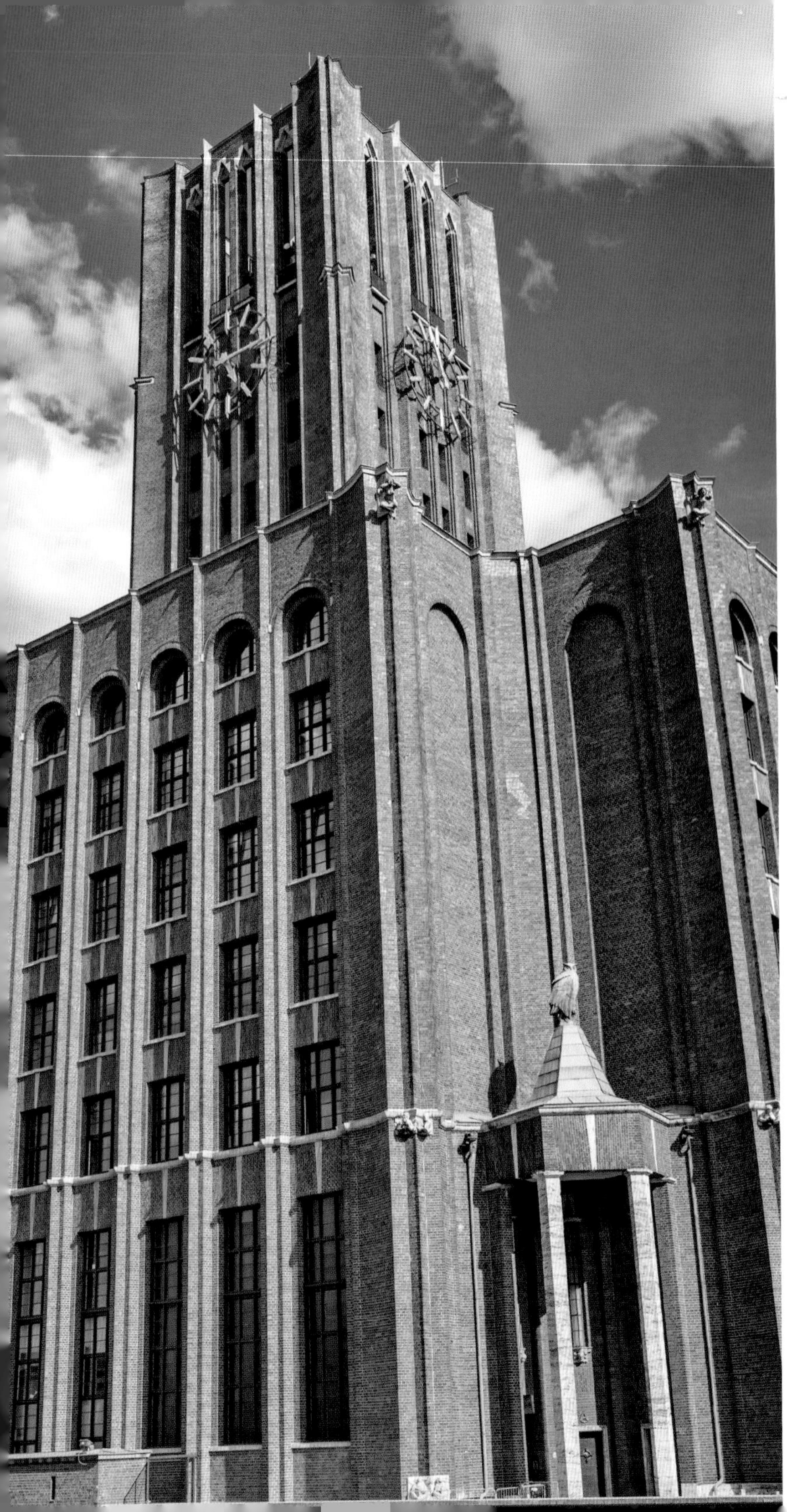

ULLSTEINHAUS

Ullsteinstraße, Tempelhof

Brick, that most utilitarian of building materials, is applied in its full creative possibilities in Berlin, not least in the Ullsteinhaus, home of the Ullstein Verlag publishing company. A towering and monolithic example of what has been called 'Brick Expressionism', the building was constructed between 1925 and 1927 specifically for Ullstein Verlag, as a printing house. The central tower reaches up to 76 m (249 ft) and the building features the bronze Ullstein Owl sculpture by Fritz Klimsch (1870–1960).

KAUFHAUS DES WESTENS

Tauentzienstraße, Schöneberg

The Kaufhaus des Westens (Department Store of the West), abbreviated to KaDeWe, is known nationally throughout Germany as a famous department store, one offering the ultimate in consumer luxury and breadth of service. The building was built in 1907 at Wittenbergplatz on Tauentzienstraße, principally selling high-value luxury goods. Today it has a total of 60,000 sq m (655,000 sq ft) of shopping floor space, and employs about 2,000 people. Of particular note is the gourmet department on the sixth floor, which offers fine dining as well as excellent views over the city.

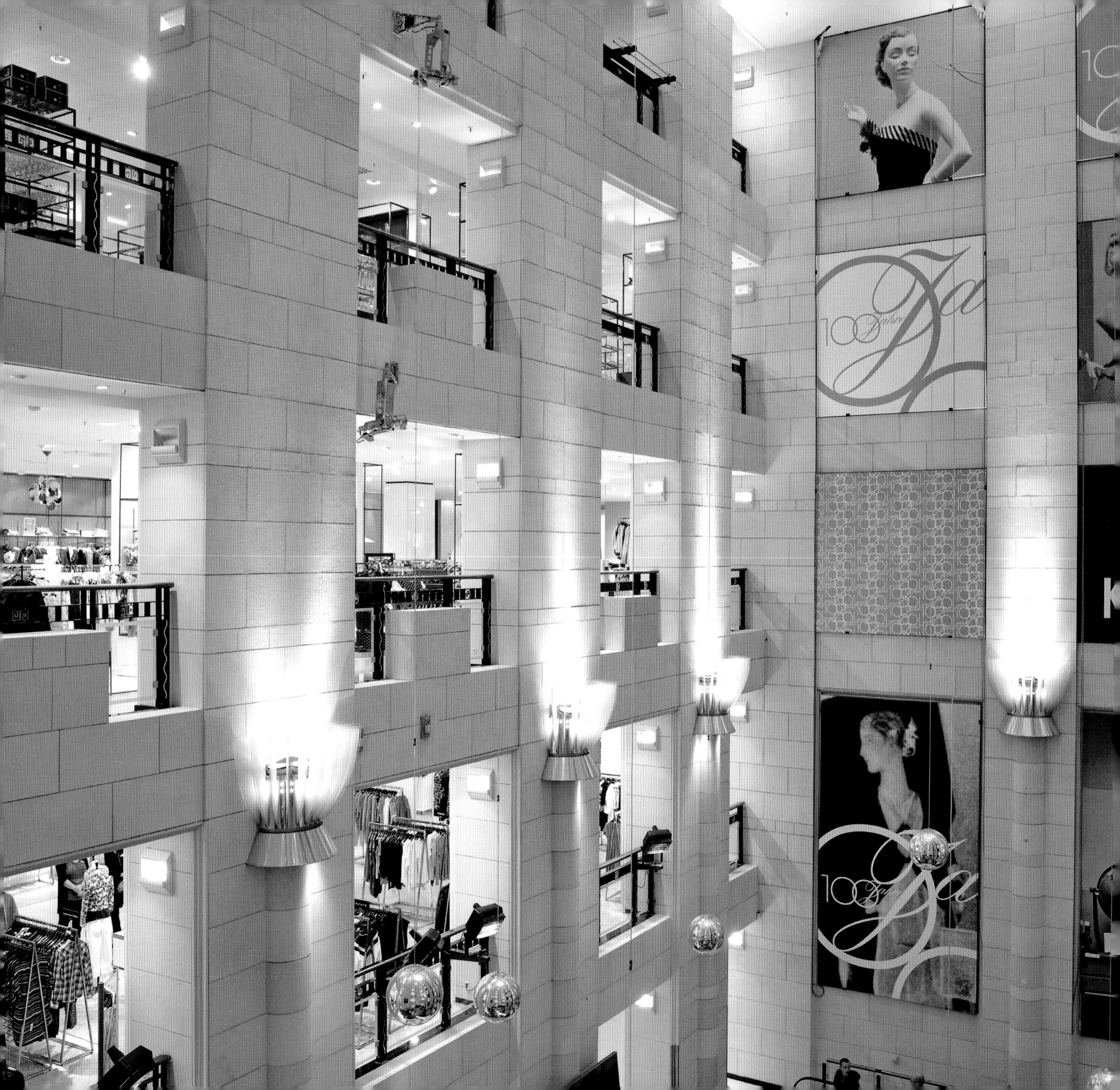
100 Jahre
100 Jahre

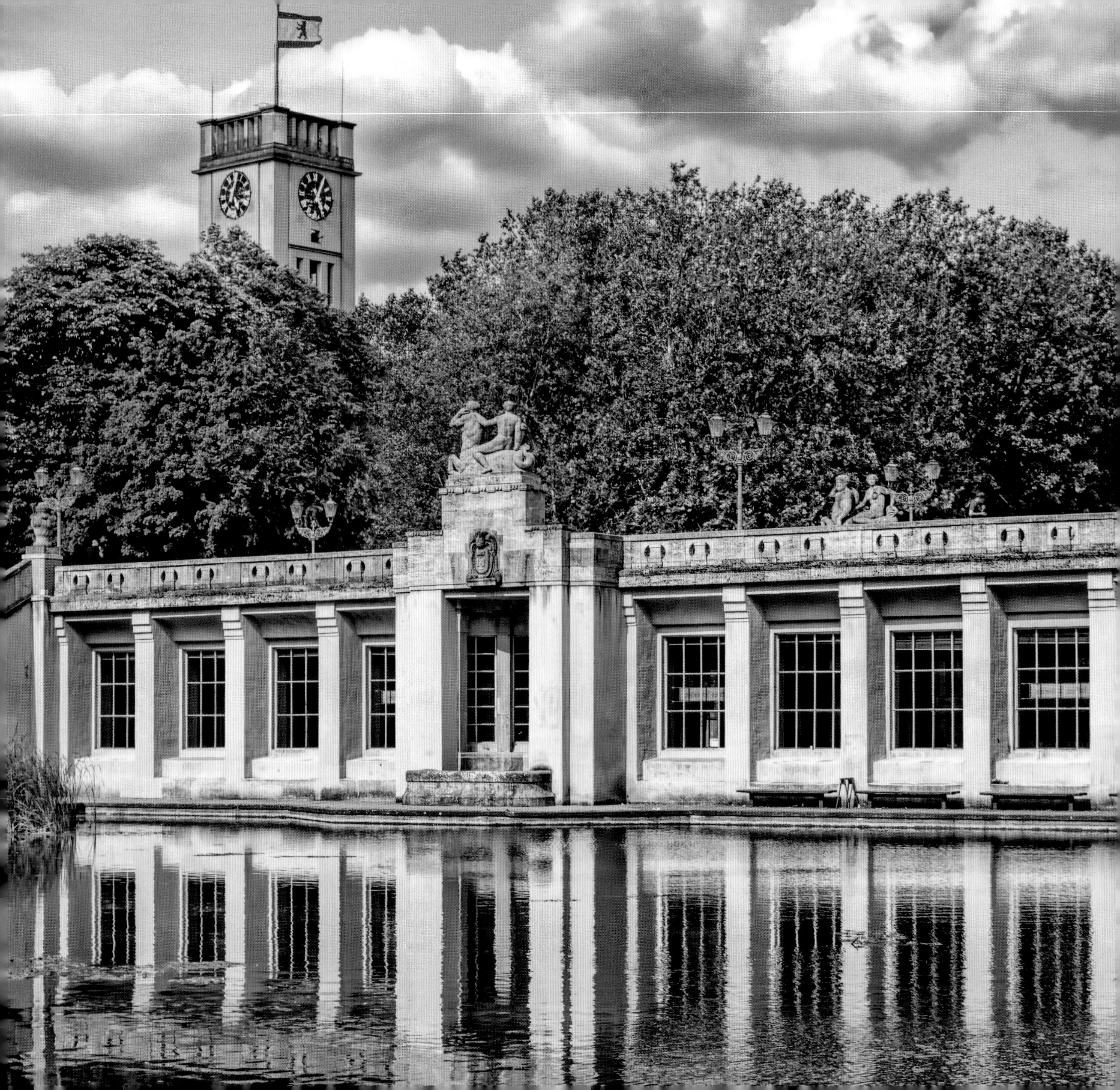

RATHAUS SCHÖNEBERG

Schöneberg, Tempelhof-Schöneberg

Although the Rathaus Schöneberg, the city hall for the borough of Tempelhof-Schöneberg, might not be well known outside the locale, it has had its moments of historical significance. It was in front of this building on 26 June 1963 that the US President John F. Kennedy delivered his famous 'Ich bin ein Berliner' ('I am a Berliner') speech, reaffirming the United States' commitment to defy communism and support West Germany. Today the building still serves in a civic role and celebrated the centennial of its construction in 2014.

GOLDENER HIRSCH

Rudolph-Wilde-Park, Schöneberg

The German sculptor and Expressionist artist August Gaul (1869–1921) was most active during the later decades of the nineteenth century and up to his death. He was a founding member of the Berlin Secession, a group of modernist artists who sought ways to defy convention. Yet there is something poetically traditional about his Goldener Hirsch (Golden Stag) statue that stands on a column in Rudolph-Wilde-Park, the centrepiece of the Hirschbrunnen (Stag Fountain), which was built in 1912. The stag is the motif of the Berlin district of Schöneberg.

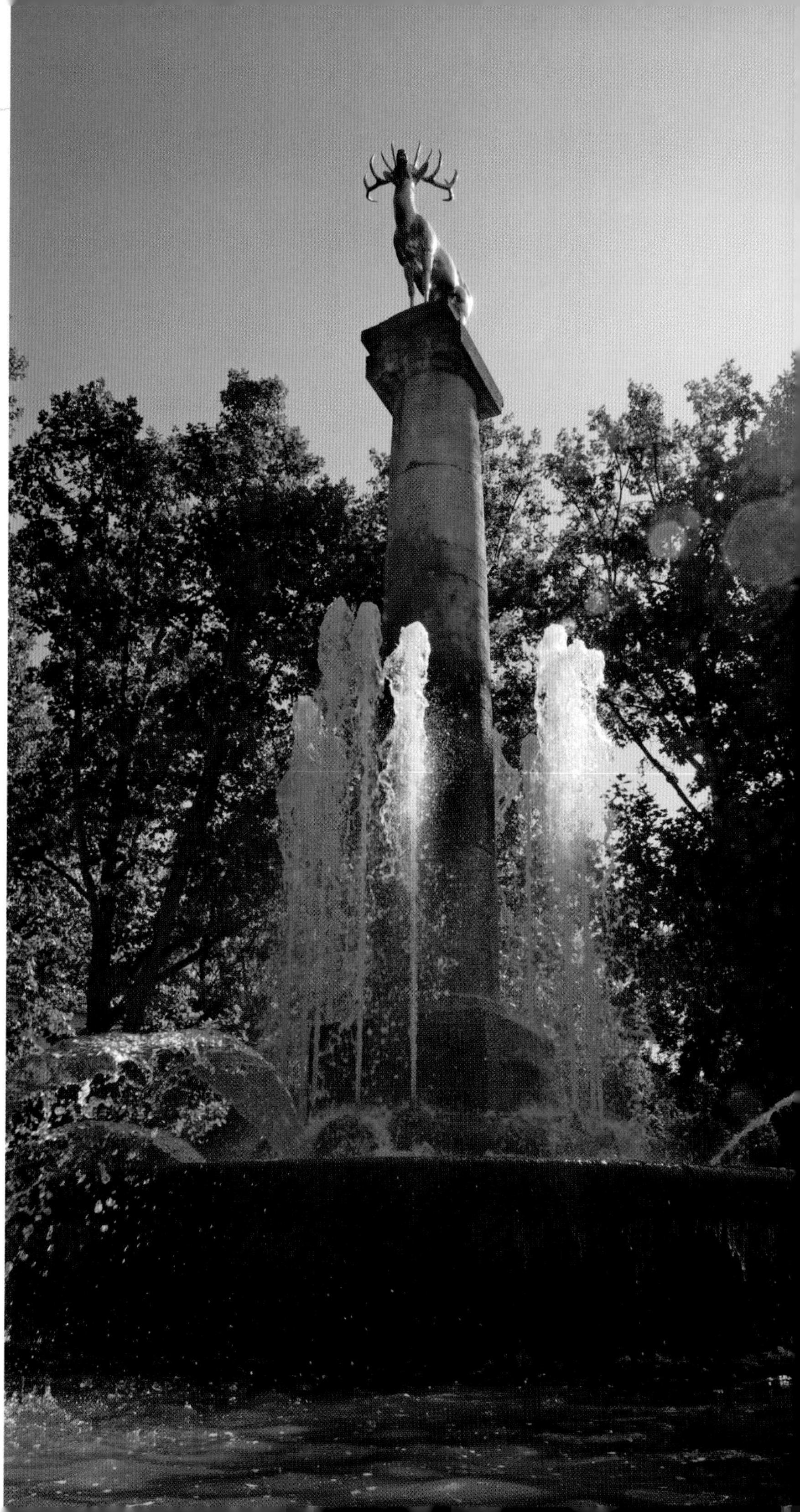

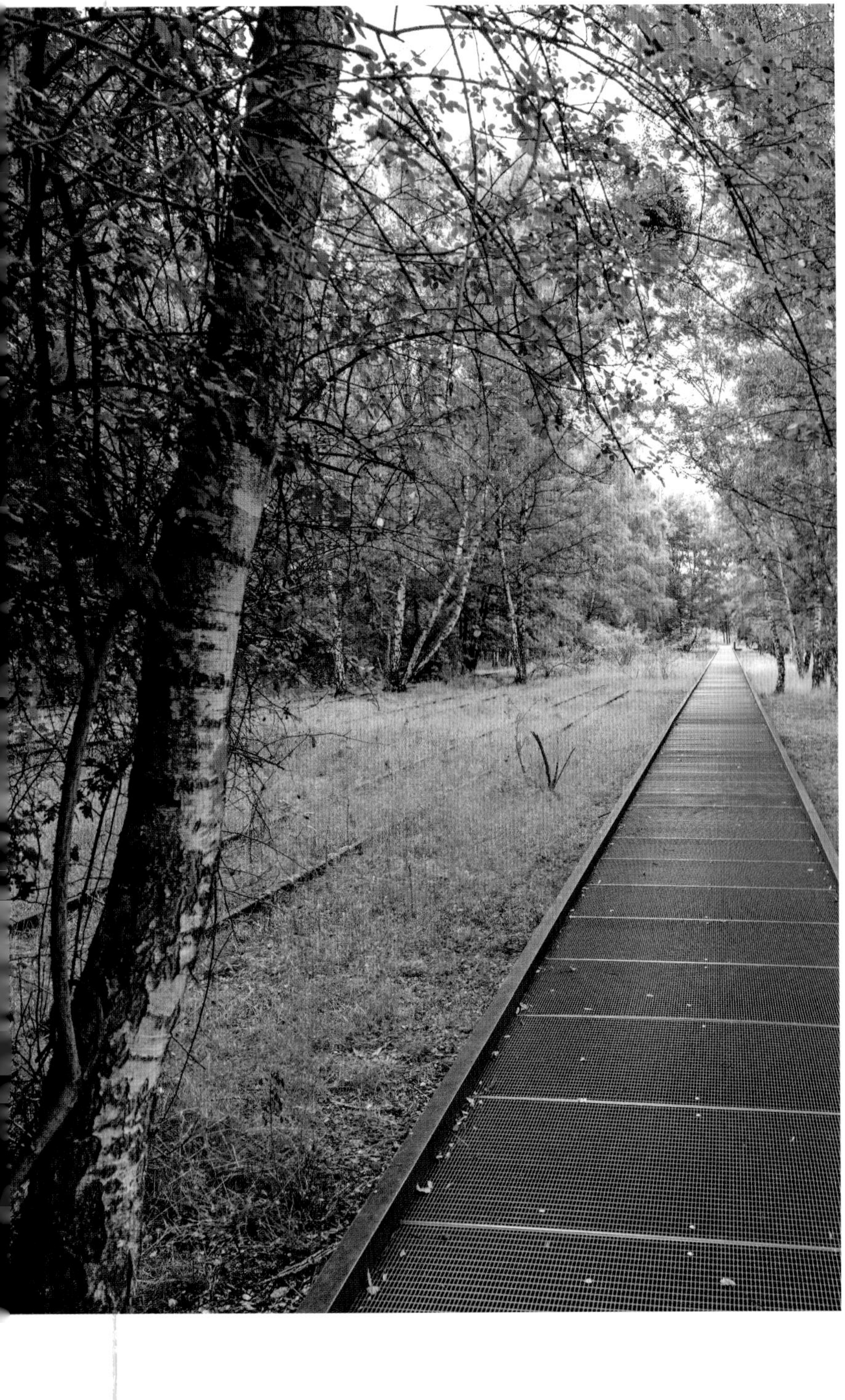

NATUR-PARK SCHÖNEBERGER SÜDGELÄND

Schöneberg

Since 2002, the Natur-Park Schöneberger Südgelände has been a curious place for the public to explore, an intermingling of art, nature and defunct technology. Much of the equipment and infrastructure of Tempelhof shunting railyard, which closed in 1952, remains on the site, including steam locomotives and a water tower, but wrapped in the trees and plants that are reclaiming the site, in the process generating impressive biodiversity. The park also provides a space for sculpture, music, painting, photography and other visual arts. Interleaved with walkways, the park is a fascinating location for the mind as well as the body to wander.

GASOMETER SCHÖNEBERG

EUREF-Campus, Schöneberg

The Gasometer Schöneberg is just one of the now defunct low-pressure gas storage containers common throughout Germany. But now open to the public to ascend, it has become something of an adventure experience. Originally built in 1913, and classed as a listed building, the skeleton steel framework of the container towers 80 m (262 ft) into the air. Weather and season depending (it is only open in the summer), the tower can be climbed as part of an organized tour, providing some vertiginous views from the top.

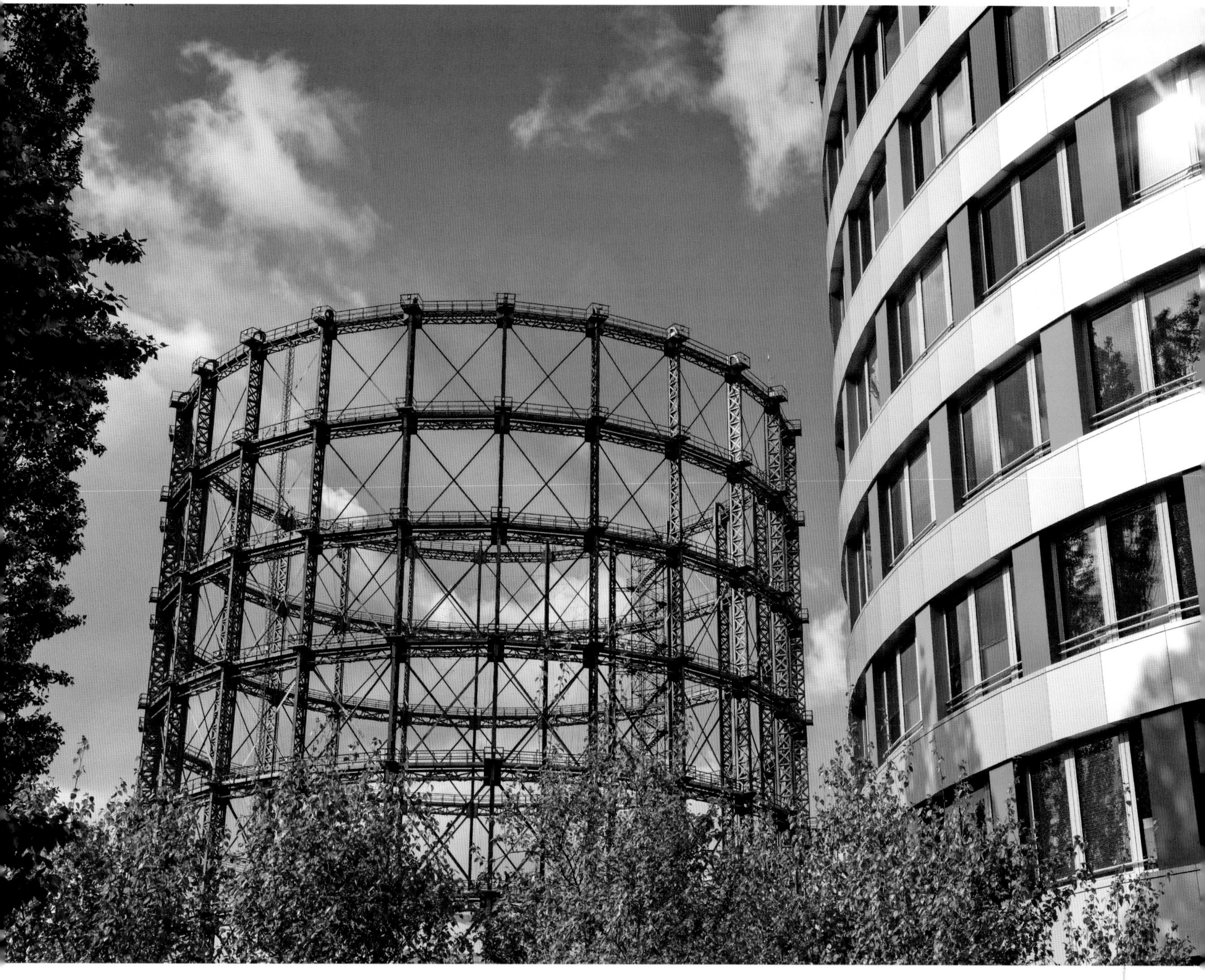

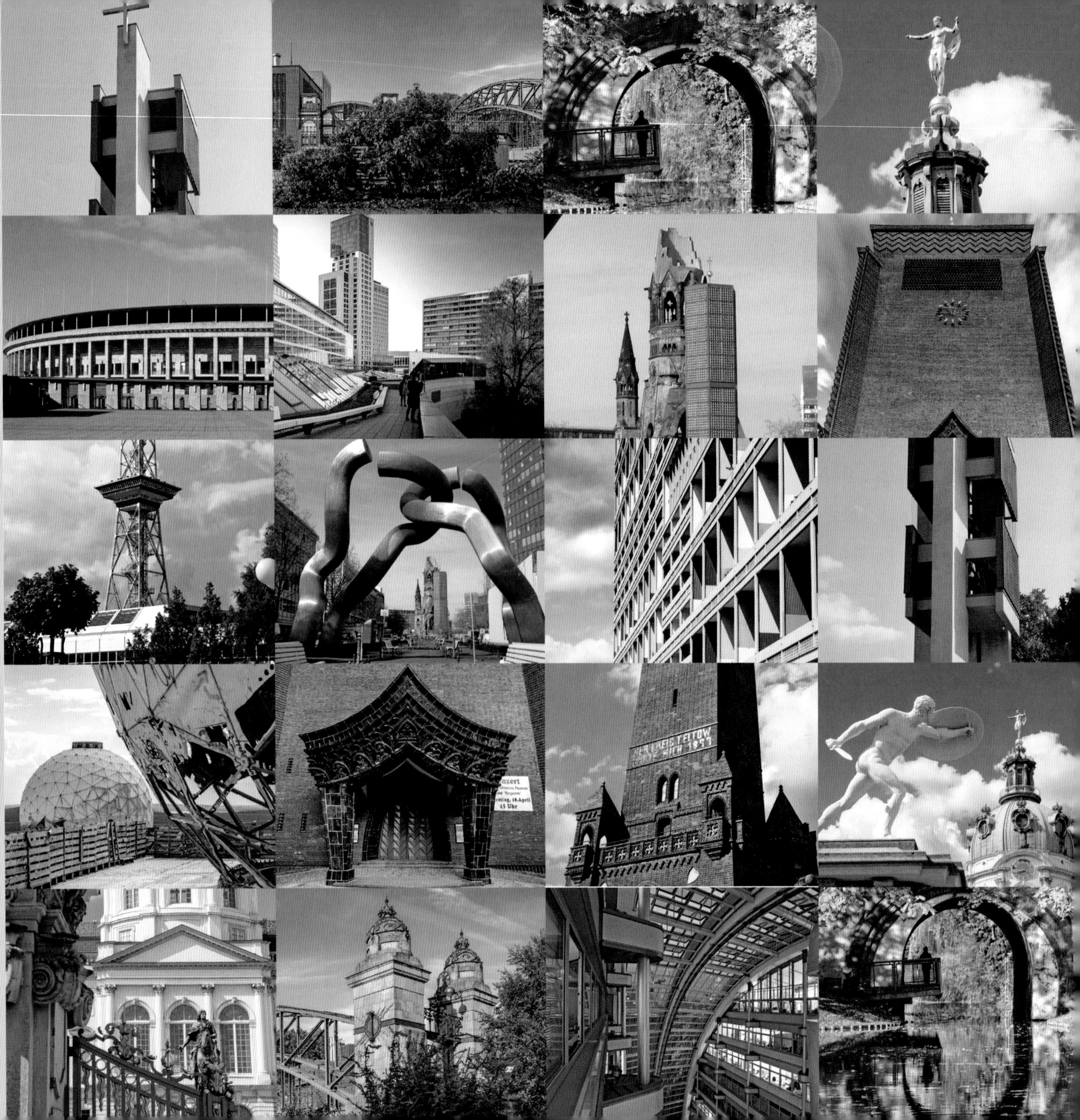
nzert
"Requiem"
15 Uhr
TELTOW
MICH

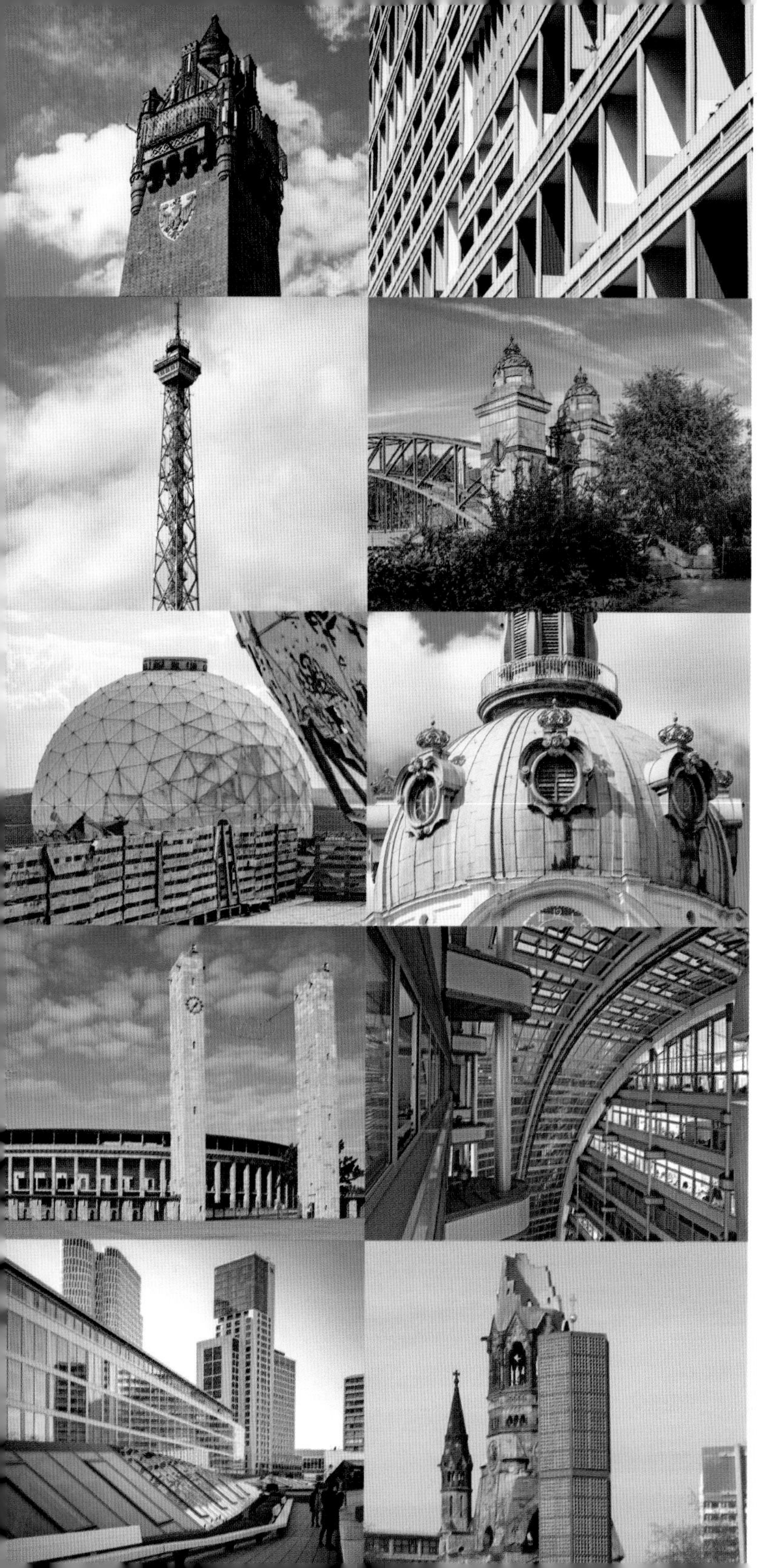

CITY WEST

The major district of what we can call 'City West' is Charlottenburg-Wilmersdorf, located directly to the west of the Tiergarten. The district is popularly known for what is described as its 'laid-back vibe', the pace of life here being considerably more sedate than that of inner districts such as Mitte and Friedrichshain-Kreuzberg. There is also a certain level of affluence out here, suggested in the many expensive-looking houses, which nestle amongst leafy streets and boulevards.

The district certainly offers much for the keen shopper, whether that person wants the brand-aware sophistication of the Kurfürstendamm (Electors' Boulevard) or the 'concept mall' experience offered by Bikini Berlin. It is also home to the Olympiastadion (Olympic Stadium), so on a regular basis the peace of the area is broken by the roar of more than 74,000 sporting fans.

City West is not purely a place for conventional pursuits, however. It also contains some of Berlin's most curious historical attractions, such as the now derelict Teufelsberg US Cold War listening station. The station's broken radomes sit atop a hill created from the rubble of Berlin at the end of the war, and it is hard to think of other geological features that have a back story as tragic as this.

BIKINI BERLIN

Budapester Straße, Charlottenburg

Bikini Berlin is self-labelled a 'concept shopping mall'. It was born in the Zentrum am Zoo (Centre at the Zoo) buildings, erected in the 1950s by architects Paul Schwebes (1902–78) and Hans Schoszberger (1907–97), which by the 1960s had become a major hub for shopping and eating. Renovation and rebuilding in the 2000s produced Bikini Berlin, so-called because its 200-m (656-ft) long 'Bikinihaus' building is said to resemble the bare midriff of a bather in a bikini (the rooftop terrace is seen here).

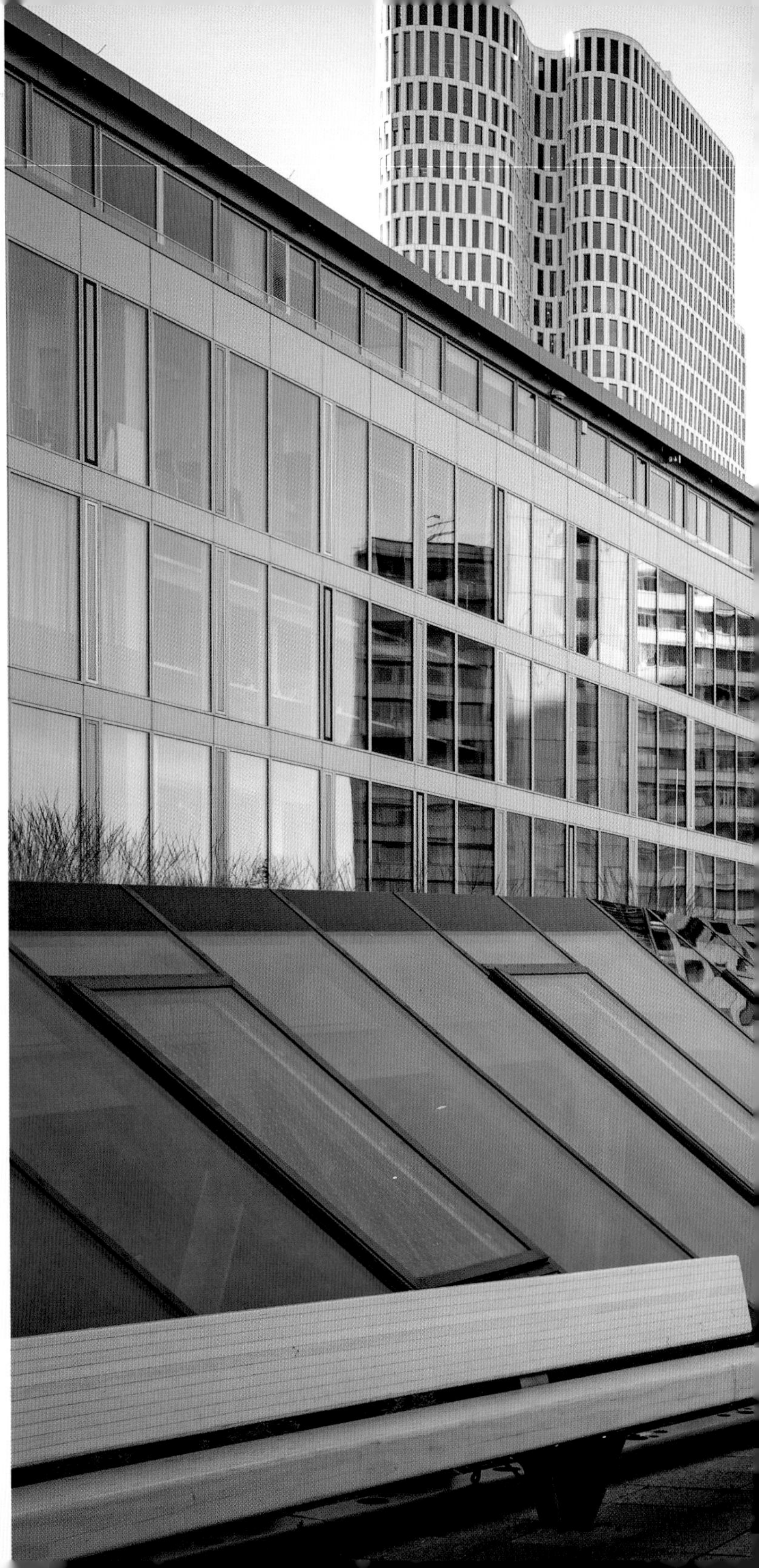

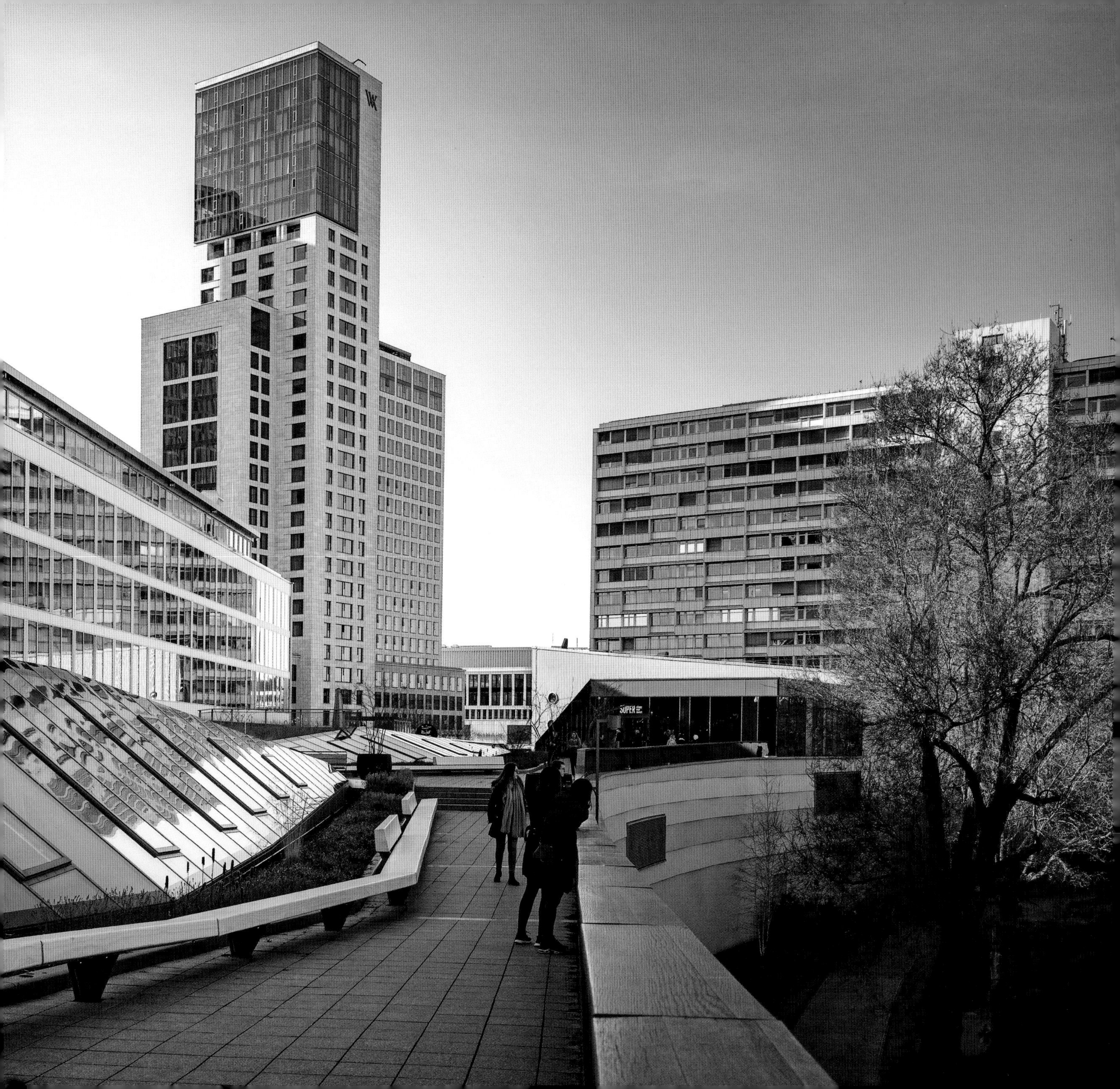
SUPER

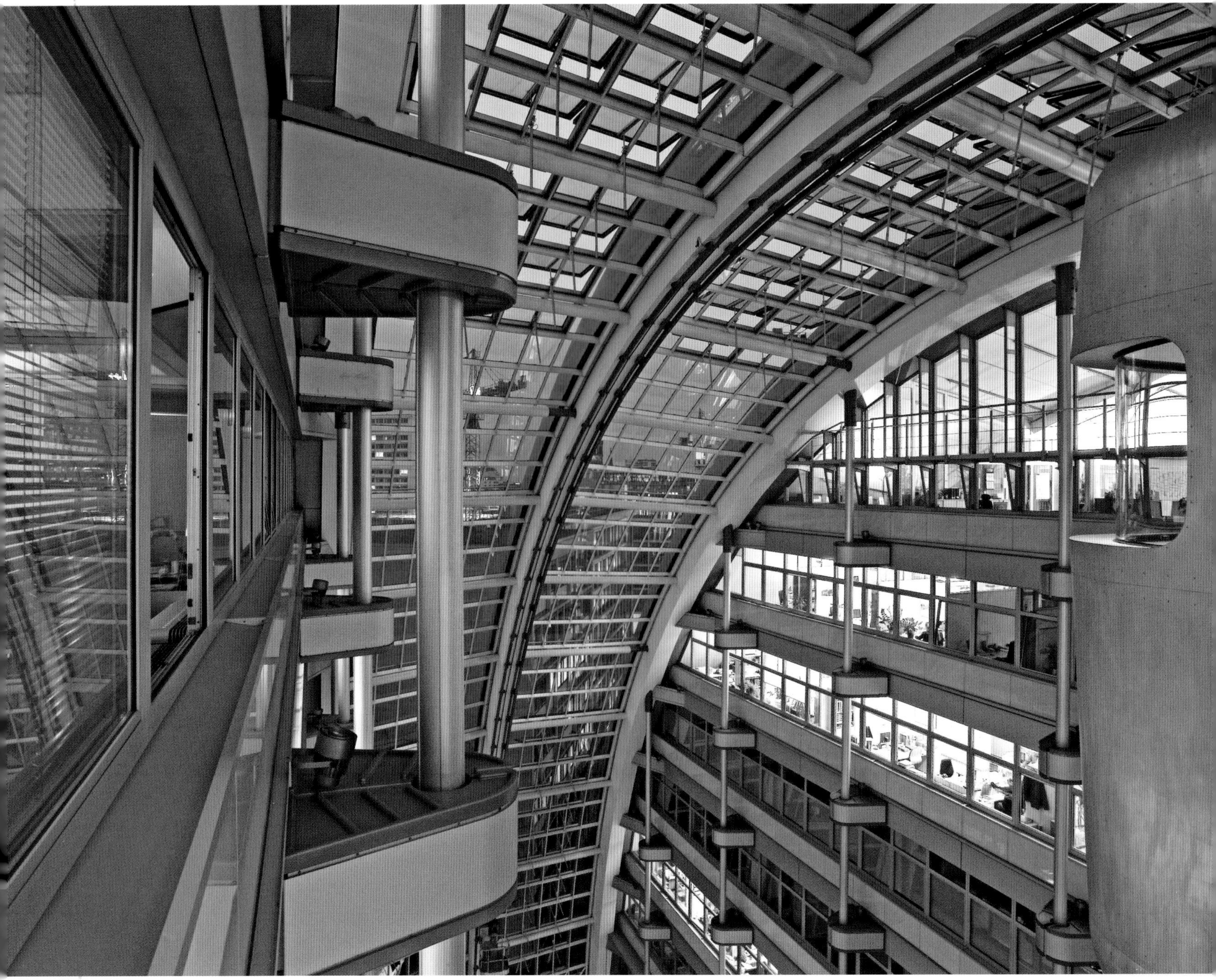

LUDWIG ERHARD HAUS

Fasanenstraße, Charlottenburg

Appearing as a giant ribcage of steel and glass, the Ludwig Erhard Haus (LEH) was designed and built in the second half of the 1990s, and is widely regarded as an architectural masterpiece of the late twentieth century. The building is formed from 15 elliptical arches of variable size, which tower to 38.6 m (127 ft) high and stretch 61.2 m (200 ft) wide at their maximum, the expansiveness of the structure emphasized by copious glasswork. The building features an open public boulevard at ground level.

SCHLOSS CHARLOTTENBURG

Charlottenburg

A building of unbounded imperial splendour, the Schloss Charlottenburg (Charlottenburg Palace) was built as an act of love, by Frederick III, Elector of Brandenburg (1657–1713) in 1699 as a summer palace for his wife, Sophia Charlotte (1668–1705). The palace has experienced expansion and renovation since its creation, and there is much to regale visitors architecturally and artistically, including major collections of eighteenth-century French art, exquisite Chinese and Japanese porcelain, orangeries and endless exquisite stately rooms. The domed tower centrepiece of the palace features a statue of Fortuna, the goddess of luck and fortune, that turns as the wind blows.

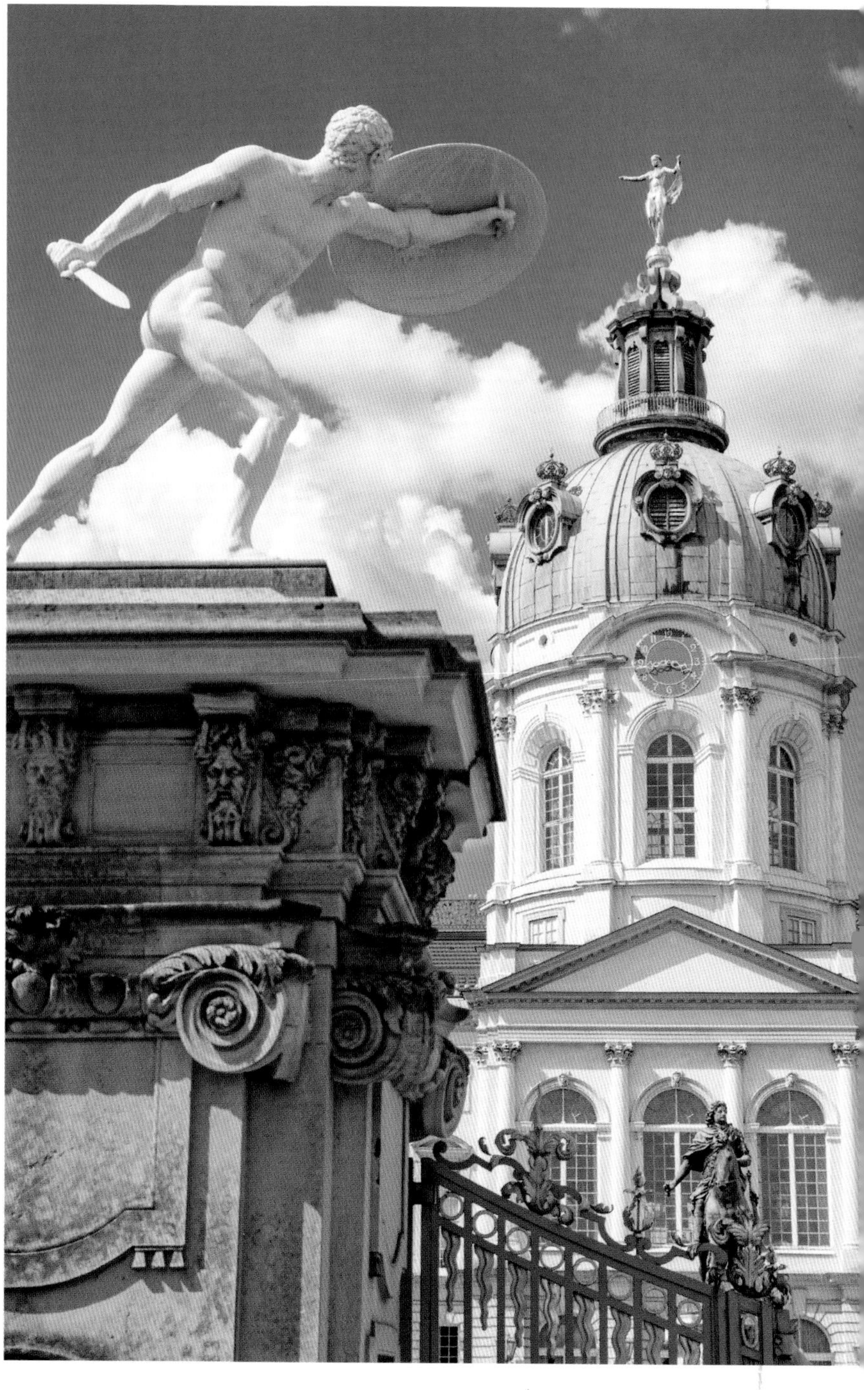

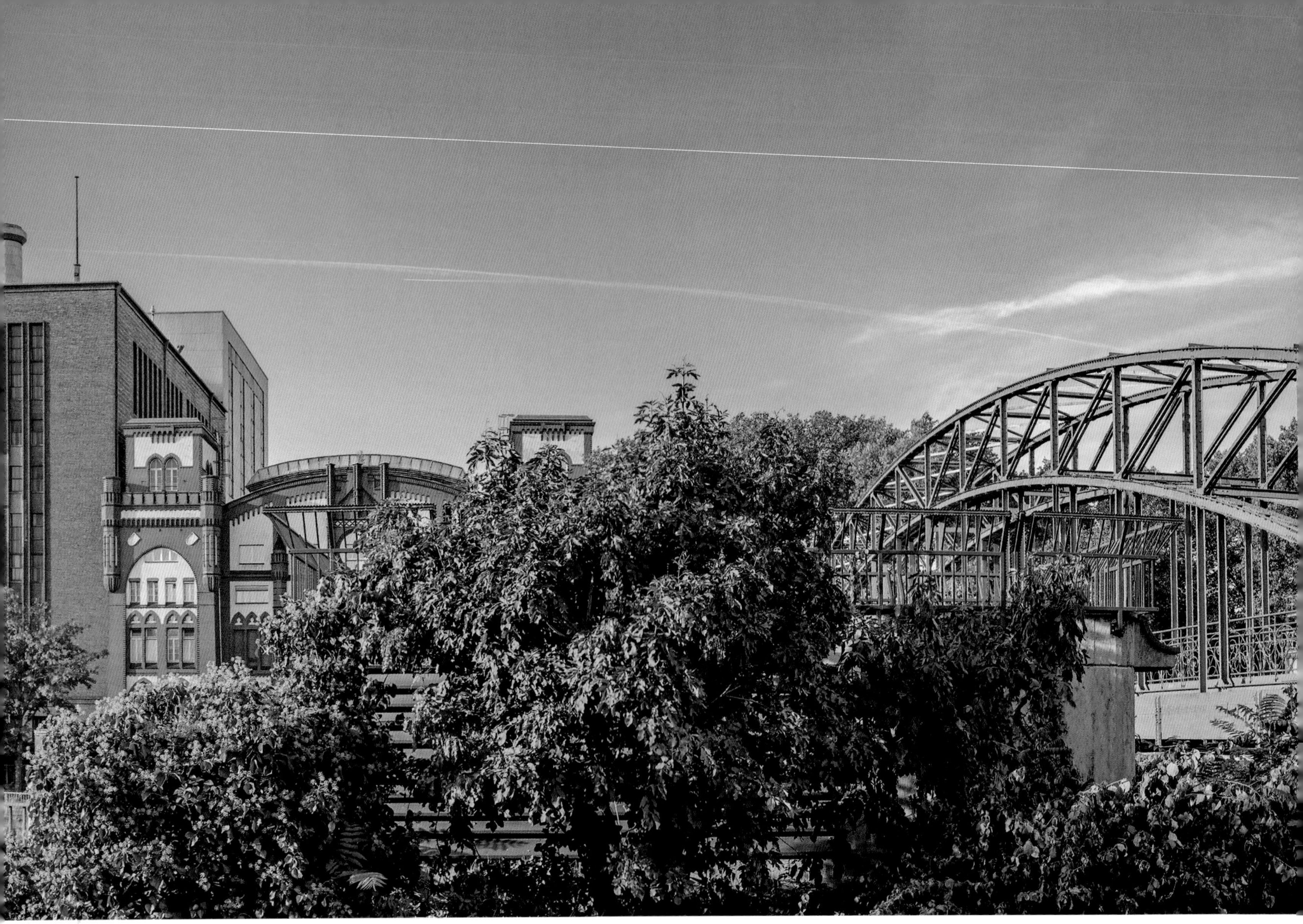

SIEMENSSTEG

River Spree, Charlottenburg

Pre-war bridges are something to be treasured in Berlin, as so many were destroyed during the final months of 1945.

The Siemenssteg (Siemens Bridge) was built in 1900, partly as a footbridge and partly as a structure to direct electrical power lines from the nearby power station, hence the cable and lightning motifs on the bridge's sandstone pillars.

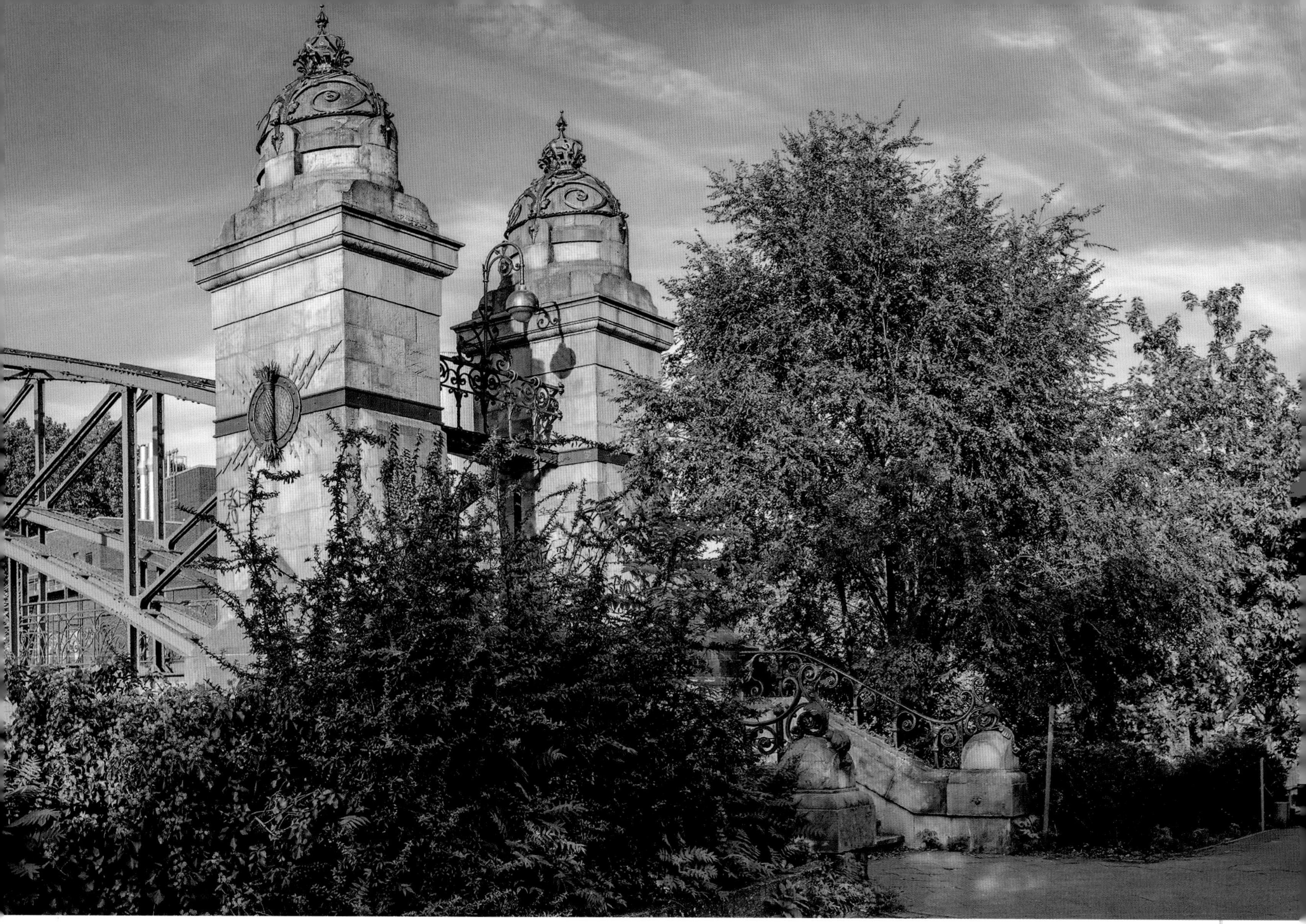

In 1902 the bridge was named after Werner von Siemens (1816–92), the prominent industrialist, who lived nearby. Its lack of tactical importance saved it from destruction in 1945, and during the 1960s it was extensively restored. With the colourful Art-Deco-influenced brickwork of the power station in the background, this bridge provides a picturesque way to cross the Spree.

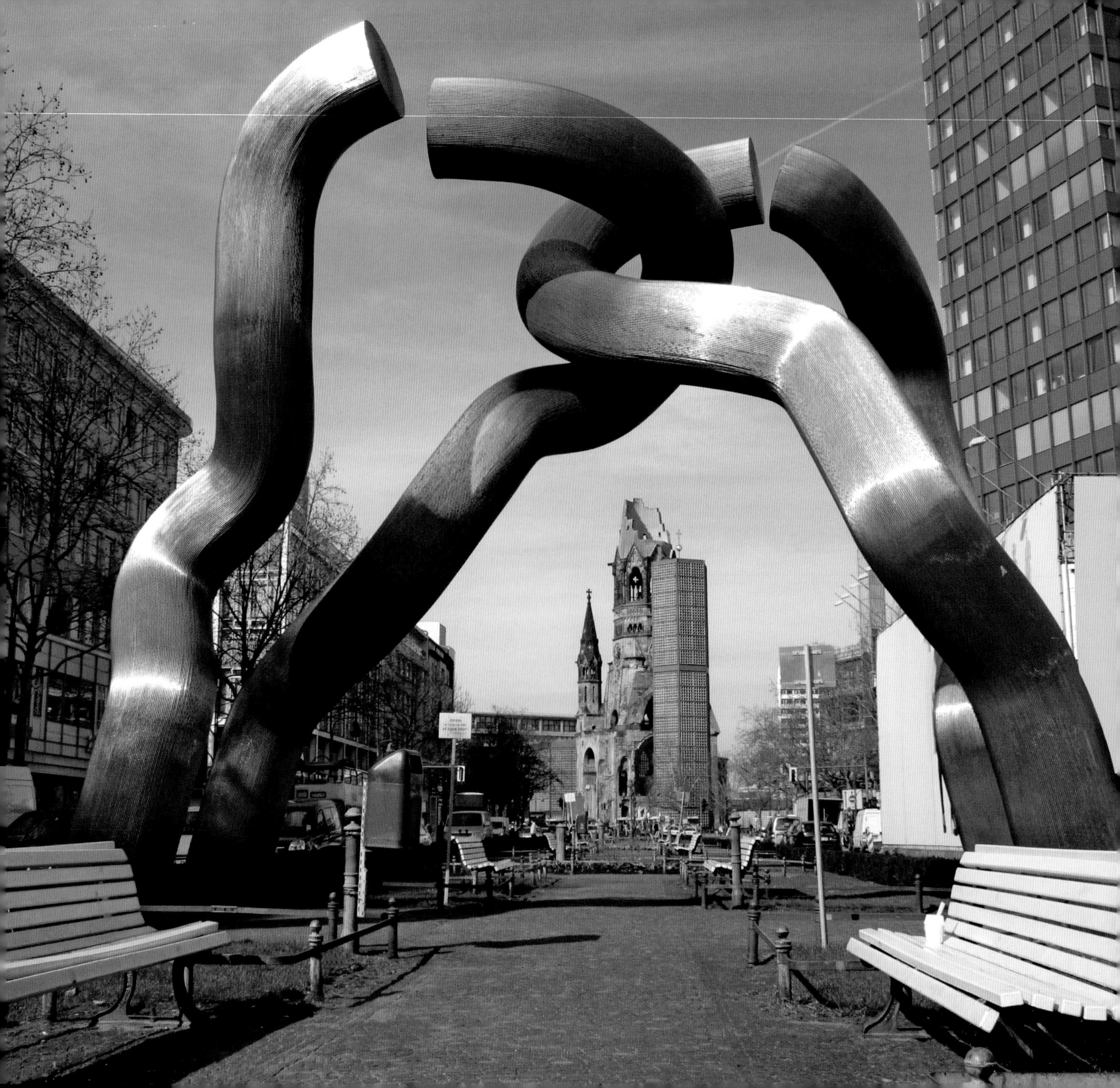

KURFÜRSTENDAMM

Charlottenburg

The Kurfürstendamm (Electors' Boulevard), abbreviated by locals to Ku'damm, is a 3.5-km (2-mile) long boulevard packed with high-end shops, theatres and cinemas, plus numerous cafés, restaurants and bars. But there are other things to see and do on the street. This street sculpture, entitled Berlin, was created by Brigitte Matschinsky-Denninghoff and Martin Matschinsky, the broken links of a huge chain representing the division between east and west Berlin (this statue was unveiled in 1987, prior to reunification); see also Hercules (page 37). Just visible through the sculpture is the remains of Gedächtniskirche (Kaiser Wilhelm Memorial Church), also known as the 'hollow tooth'. It was the only building in the area not be totally destroyed during Allied bombing raids during the Second World War, and has been deliberately left as an anti-war memorial to peace and reconciliation.

CURRYWURST

Kaiser-Friedrich-Straße, Charlottenburg

This plaque (seen below left), appearing on the corner of Kant and Kaiser-Friedrich streets, celebrates the life and culinary contribution of Herta Charlotte Heuwer (1913–99). According to tradition, in 1949 Heuwer, a food kiosk owner, invented currywurst, a steamed and fried pork sausage coated with a curried tomato ketchup (see below). The perfect fast food, it appealed to the tired workers rebuilding the war-devastated city, and by 1974 she was selling 10,000 servings a week. Although the origin story is contested by some, the fact that some 800 million currywurst are eaten in Germany every year, shows that Heuwer was on to something.

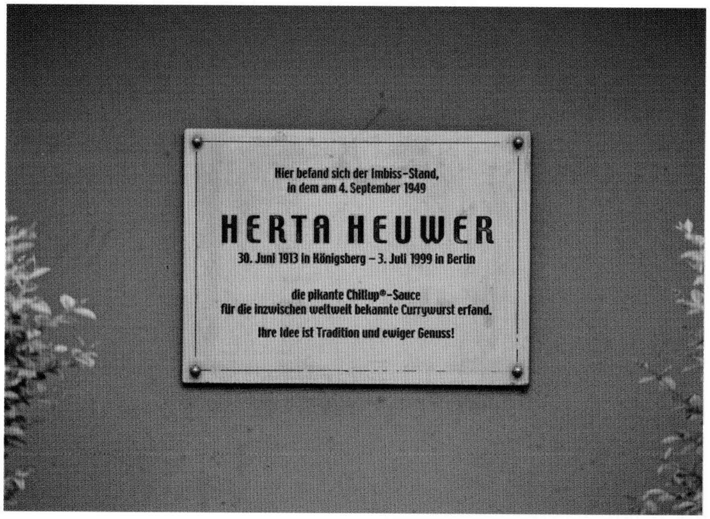

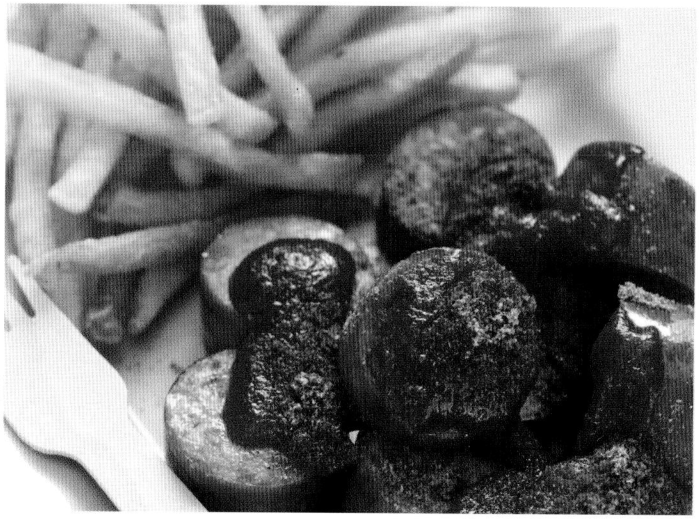

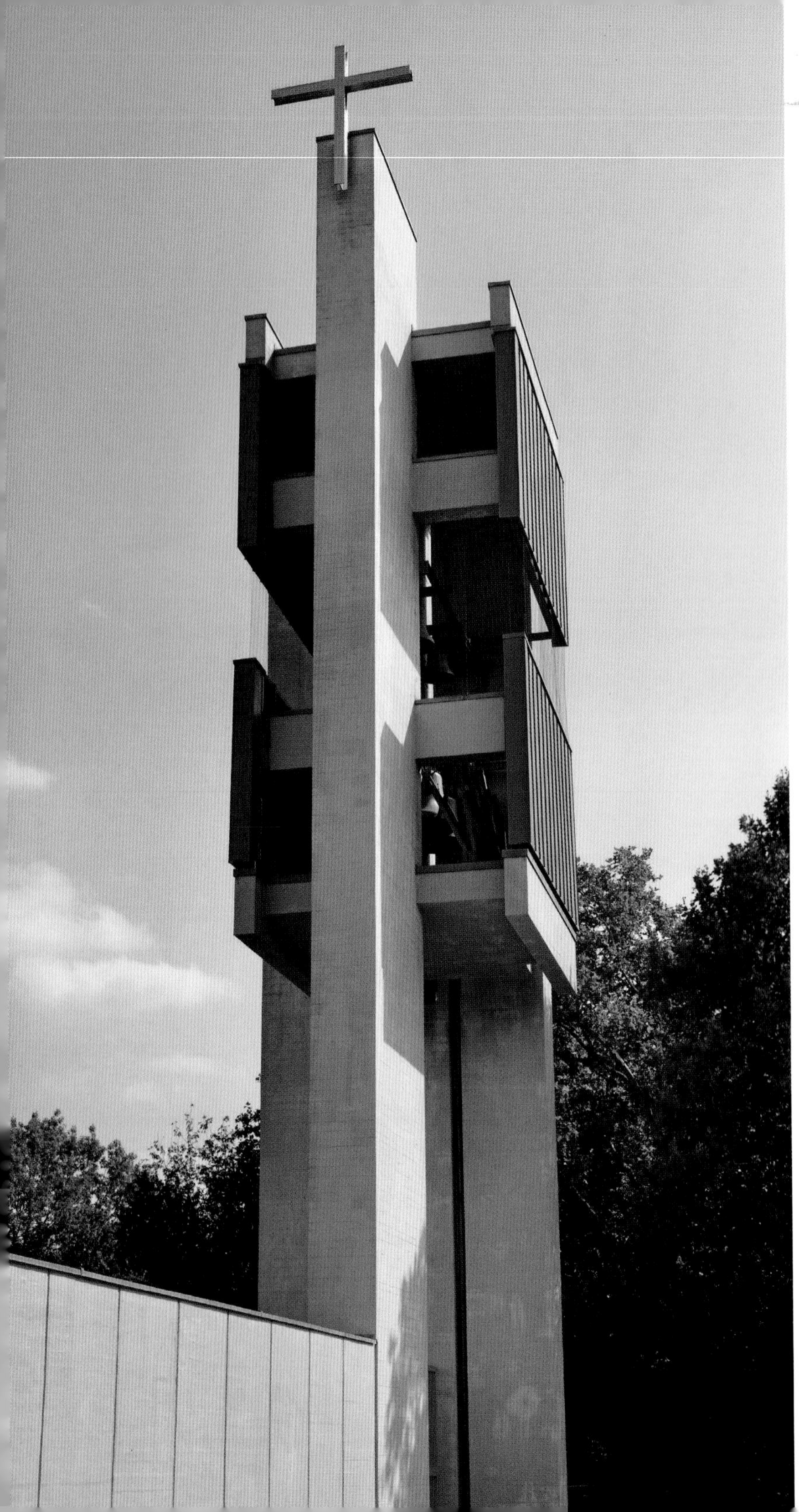

GEDENKKIRCHE MARIA REGINA MARTYRUM

Heckerdamm, Charlottenburg

The campanile of the Gedenkkirche Maria Regina Martyrum (Commemorative Church of Mary Queen of Martyrs), seen here, is a soaring Modernist marker of this Roman Catholic church in the Charlottenburg-Wilmersdorf area. The church was built during the 1960s, its name referring to German Catholics martyred during the Nazi era (1933–45). Inside the church, there are poignant memorials, sculptures and frescos, including the tripartite sculpture Apocalyptic Woman by Fritz Koenig (1924–2017), a bronze Pietà by the same artist, and an open-air altar by Otto Herbert Hajek (1927–2005).

LIETZENSEEPARK

Charlottenburg

The Lietzenseepark (Lietzensee Park) has been a refuge from the noise and pace of the city for more than two centuries now, its two lakes, towering trees and meandering paths providing a stillness and quietness away from the surging traffic in the distance. The park's origins date back to 1823, when it was commissioned by Lieutenant-General Job von Witzleben (1783–1837) as a summer residence for his wife and children. The park was opened to the public in the early years of the twentieth century, and has remained a place for public rest and recuperation ever since.

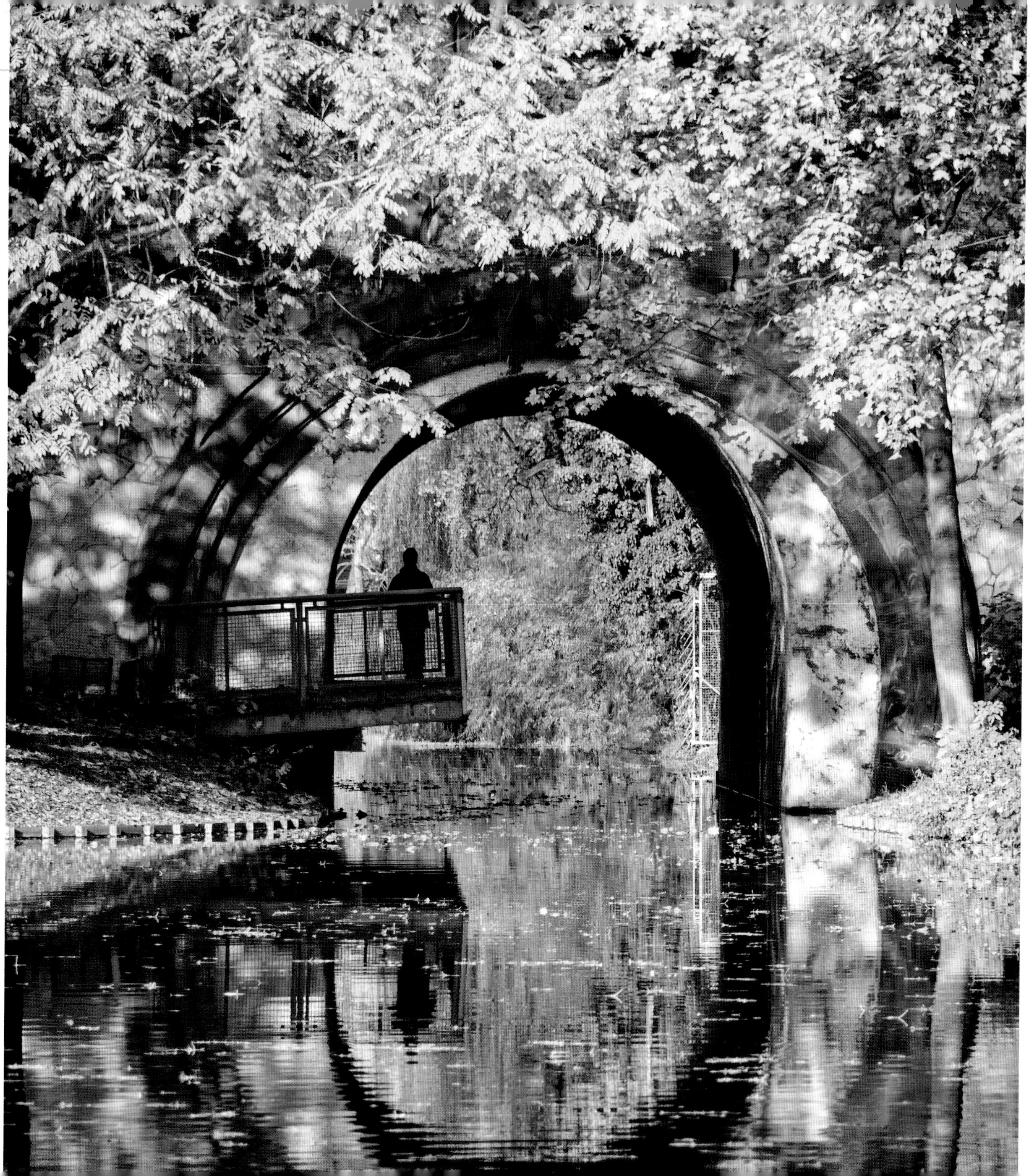

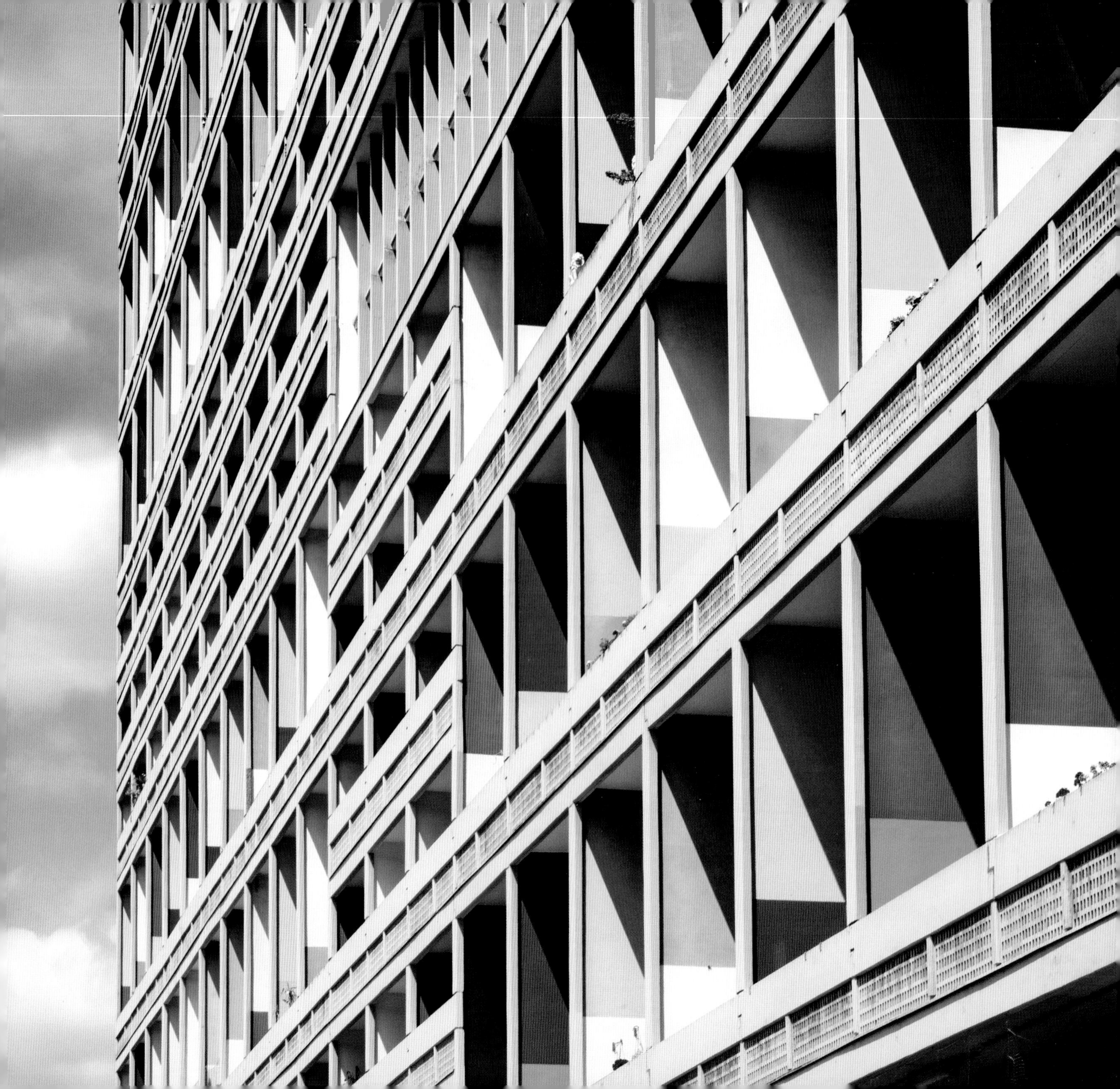

CORBUSIERHAUS

Westend, Charlottenburg-Wilmersdorf

In utter contrast to the organic shapes of the nearby Grunewald Forest, the Corbusierhaus (Corbusier's House) is a bold example of Brutalist architecture by one of its leading proponents, the Swiss-French architect Le Corbusier (Charles-Édouard Jeanneret, 1887–1965).The building was erected between 1956 and 1958, using slabs of prefabricated rough-cast concrete to create a uniform structure 52.94 m (174 ft) in height, 141.2 m (463 ft) in length and 22.96 m (75 ft) in width. In total, the building has 530 apartments, but its ground floor also has a store and cinema/exhibition area.

FUNKTURM

Westend, Charlottenburg-Wilmersdorf

With an inspiration clearly derived from Paris's Eiffel Tower, the Funkturm (Radio Tower) by Heinrich Straumer (1876–1937) stretches up 150 m (492 ft) from ground level, although visitors can enjoy spectacular views out over the city from the observation deck at 126 m (413 ft). This great landmark was opened in 1926 and was used for early radio and TV transmissions; today it is still used as a communications platform for police radio and mobile phone networks. An interesting fact is that, with every new coat of paint, 9 kg (20 lb) is added to the structure's 600-tonne (590.5-long-ton) weight.

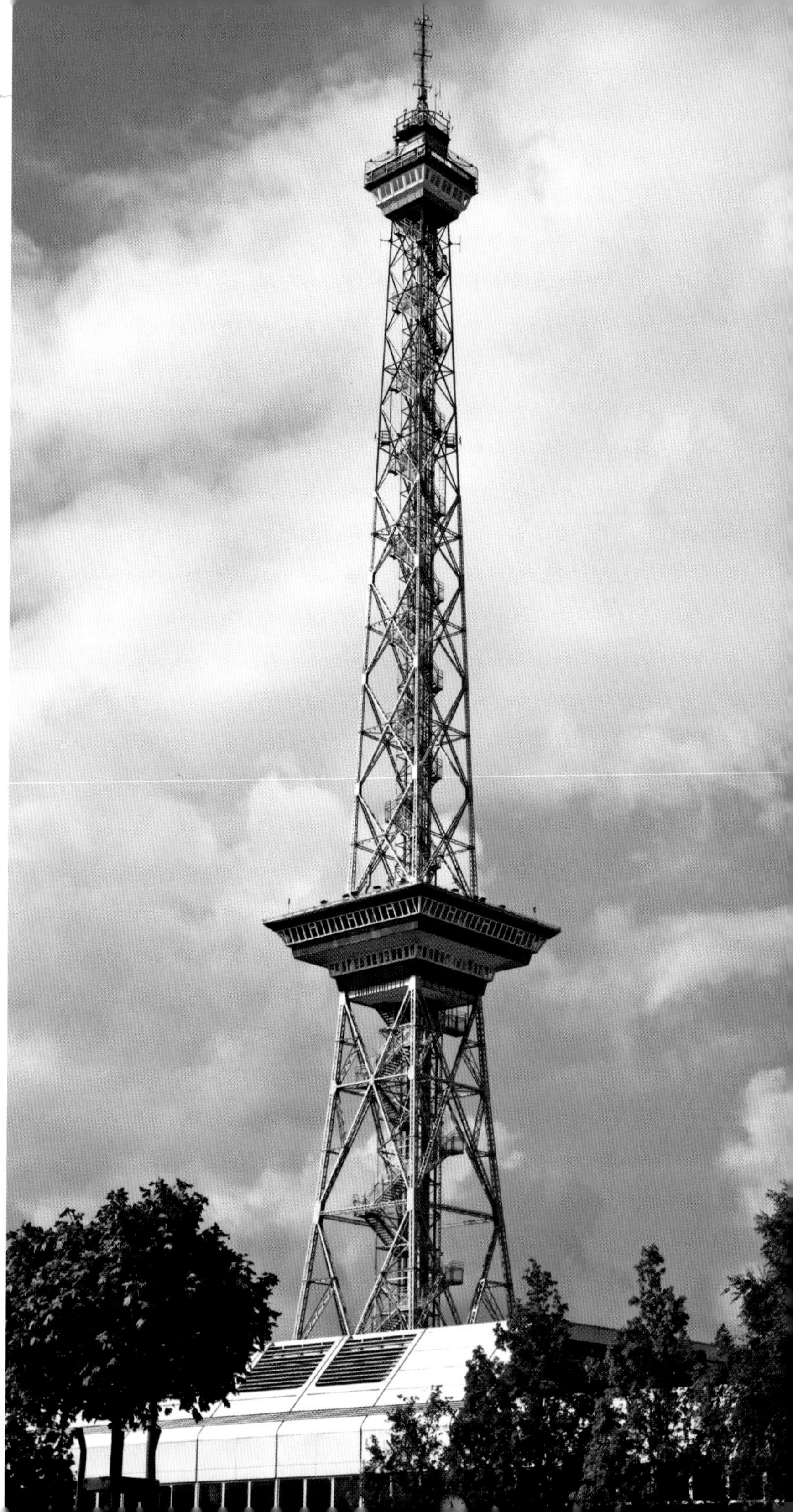

OLYMPIASTADION

Westend, Charlottenburg-Wilmersdorf

With a capacity for 74,475 spectators, Berlin's Olympiastadion (Olympic Stadium) is a major European sporting venue. Recently hosted events include the 2006 World Cup Final, the 2009 World Championships in Athletics, and the 2018 European Athletics Championships. The first stadium on the site functioned between 1916 and 1934, before the Nazi regime created the new Olympiastadion for the 1936 Olympic Games, with 110,000 spectators. While elements of that structure still stand, a massive renovation between 1990 and 2004 transformed the stadium into the state-of-the-art facility we see today.

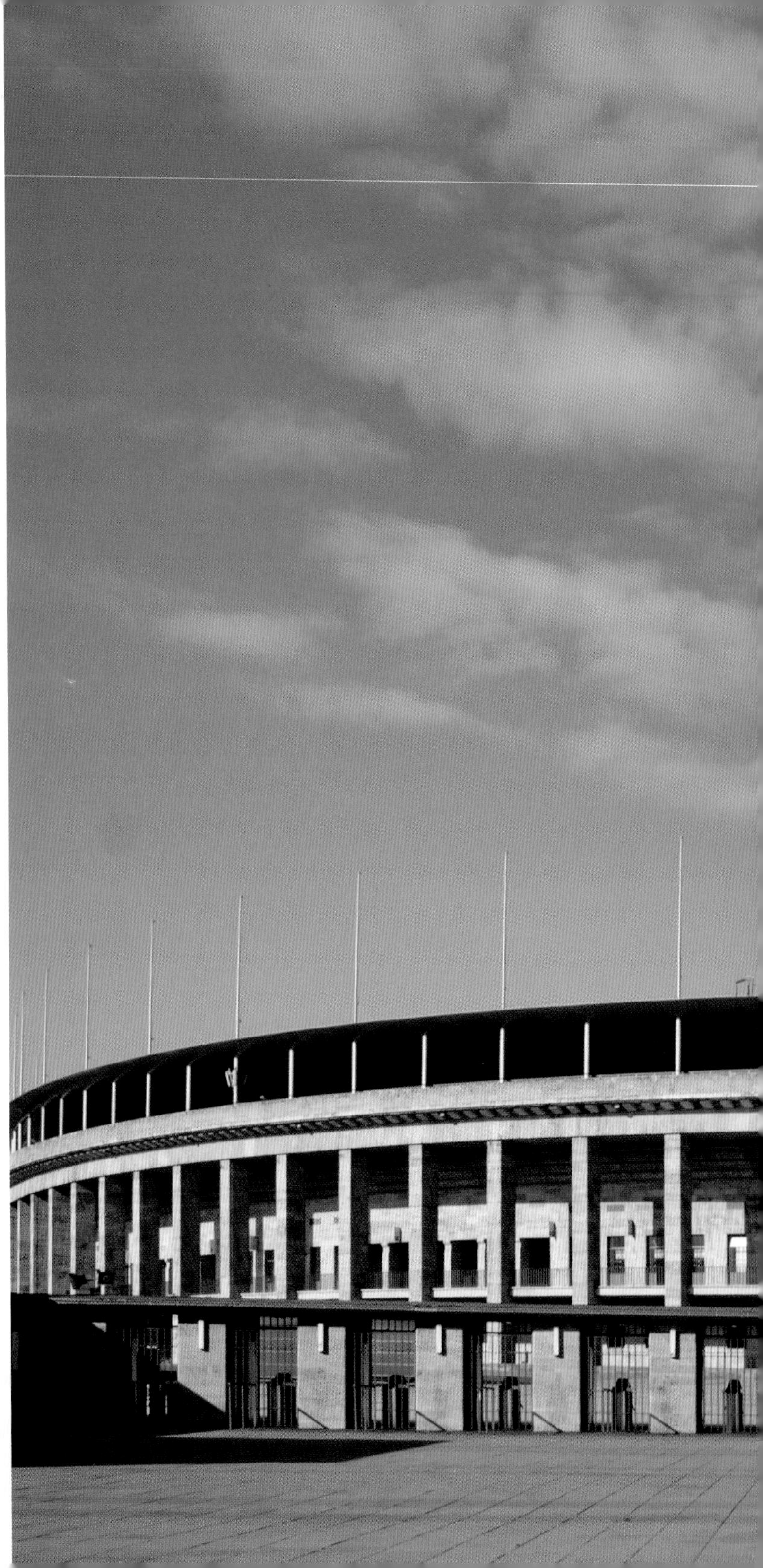

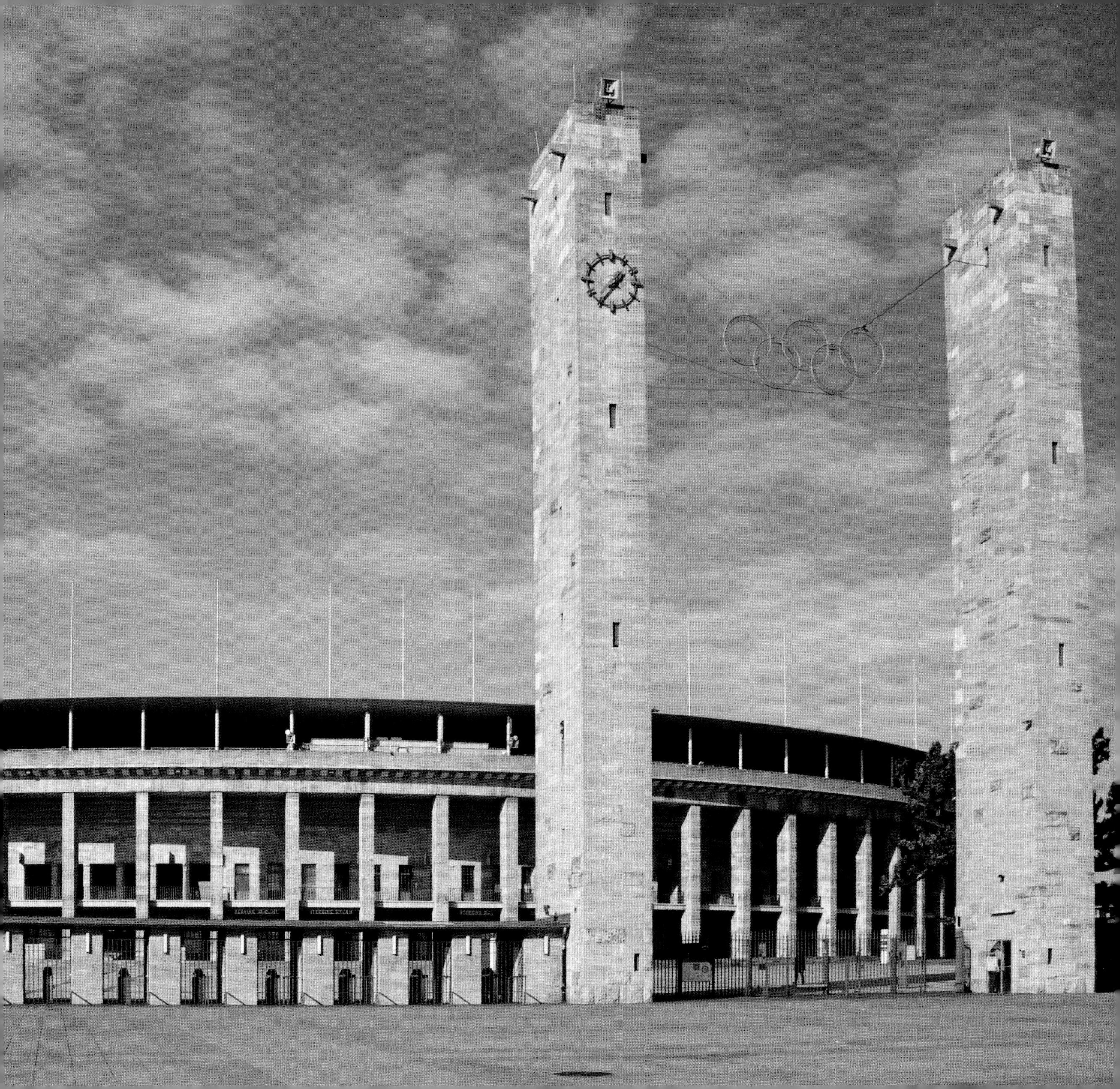

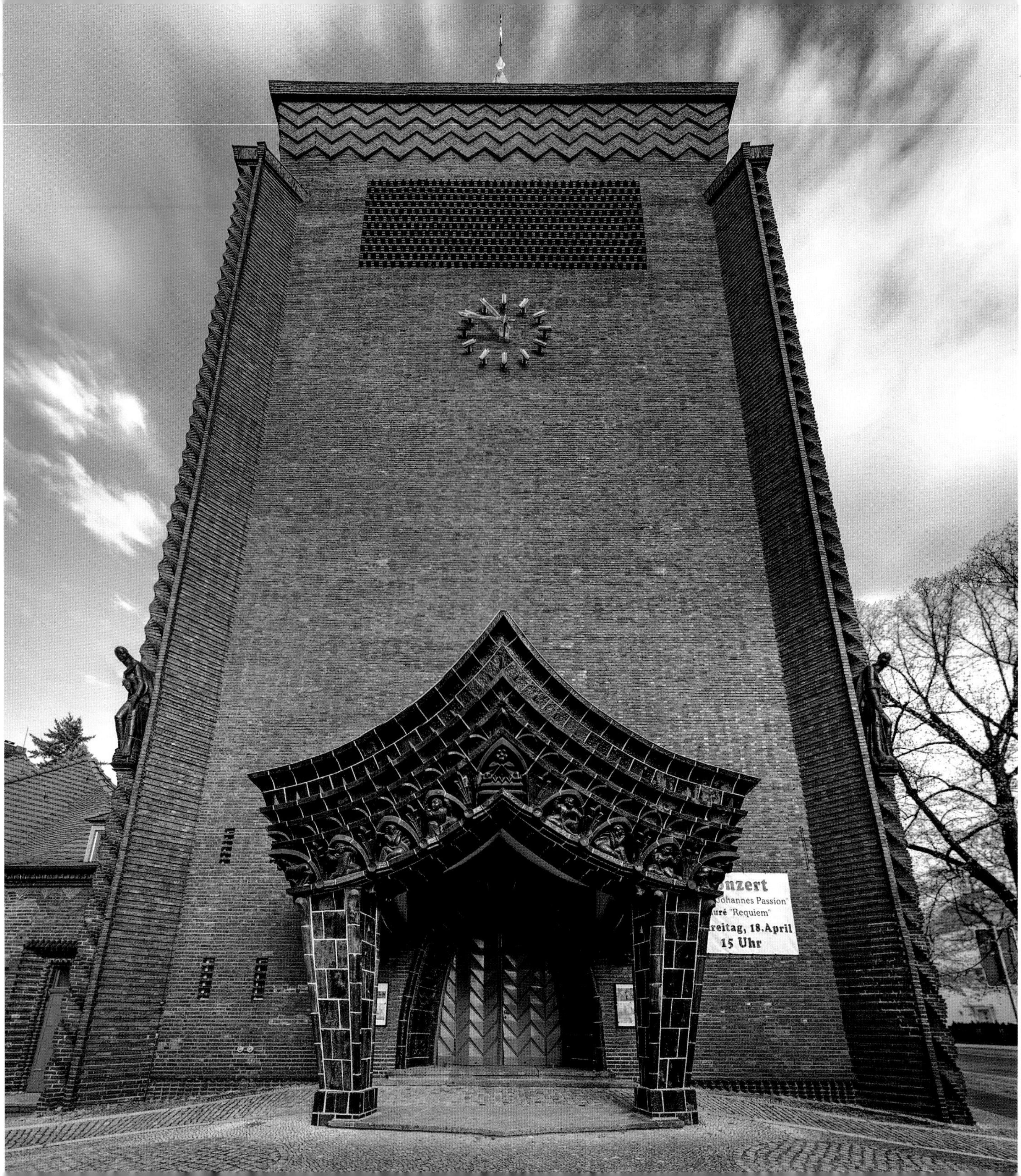
onzert
Johannes Passion
uré "Requiem"
reitag, 18.April
15 Uhr

KREUZKIRCHE

Hohenzollerndamm, Schmargendorf

Architecturally bold, the Kreuzkirche (Cross Church) on Hohenzollerndamm has many idiosyncratic elements in its design, leaning as much towards Asiatic influences as European ones. Designed by architects Ernst Paulus (1868–1935) and his son Günther Paulus (1898–1976), and built between 1927 and 1929, the church has an Expressionist sensibility with its three green spires and the pagoda-like porch of blue glazed pottery. Inside there is equal experimentation, with an octagonal church hall and bright colours, but the effect is still peaceful and contemplative.

GRUNEWALDTURM

Havelchaussee, Grunewald

The Grunewaldturm (Grunewald Tower) is another of Berlin's great Brick Gothic Revival monuments, this one built in 1897–99 to mark the 100th birthday of the King of Prussia and German Emperor William I. Originally called the König-Wilhelm-Turm, the tower stood 55 m (180 ft) tall, its elevation enhanced by the 79-m (259-ft) high Karlsberg hill on which it stands. As well as a marble statue of William I by sculptor Ludwig Manzel (1858–1936), standing in the memorial hall, the tower has a viewing platform with long views out over the Havel, Wannsee and Grunewald.

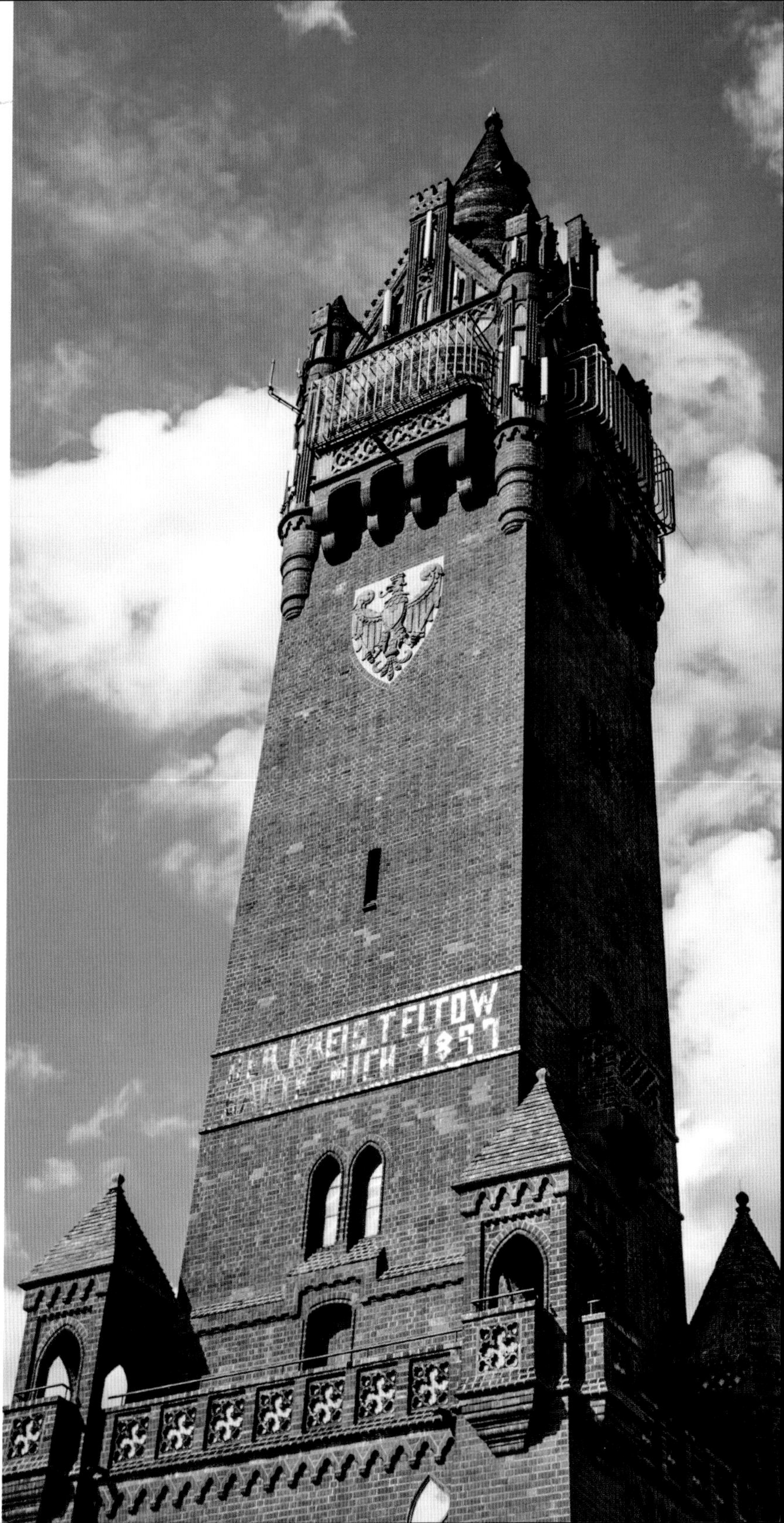

TEUFELSBERG

Grunewald

The Cold War was a time of suspicion and surveillance, and the Teufelsberg (Devil's Mountain) US listening station captures the tension of that era. The Teufelsberg – a 120-m (394-ft) high hill in the Grunewald, created from Berlin's wartime rubble – provided a practical site for surveillance technology and electronic warfare, with monitoring antennae installed in huge radomes during the 1960–80s. With the end of the Cold War, the American personnel left and, after a period in which the site was used for air traffic control, the giant radomes and towers slowly descended into an atmospheric decrepitude.

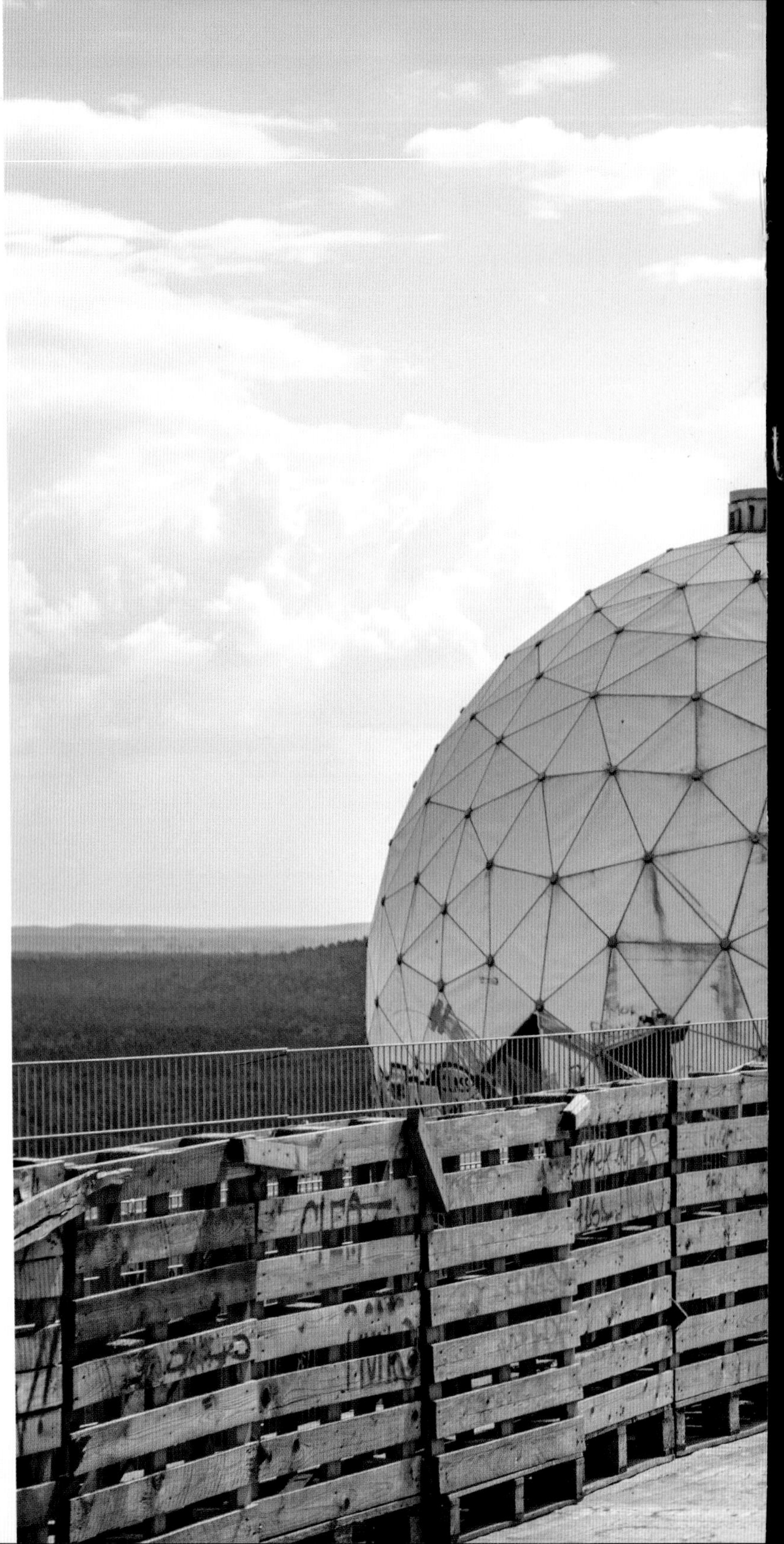

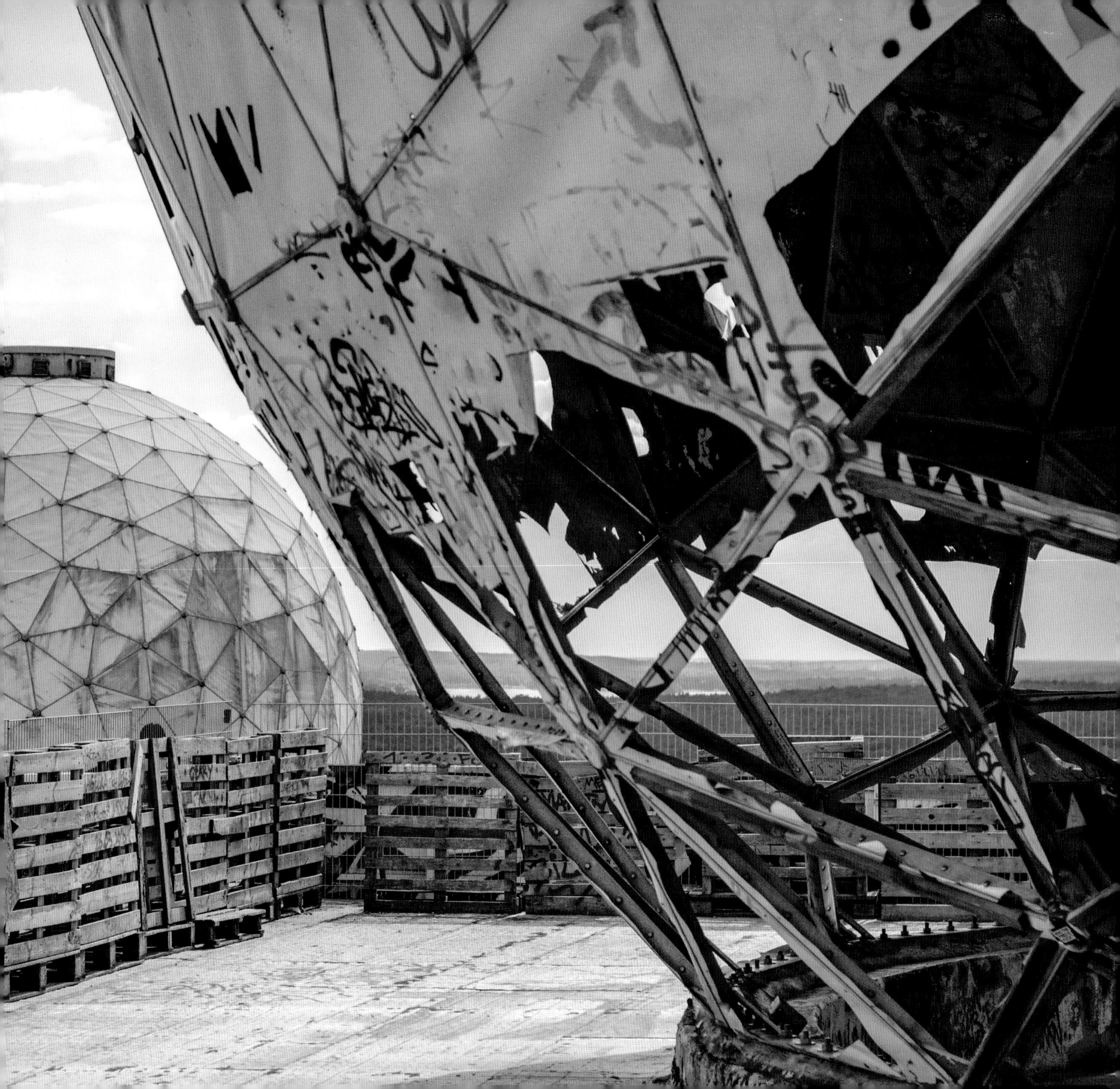

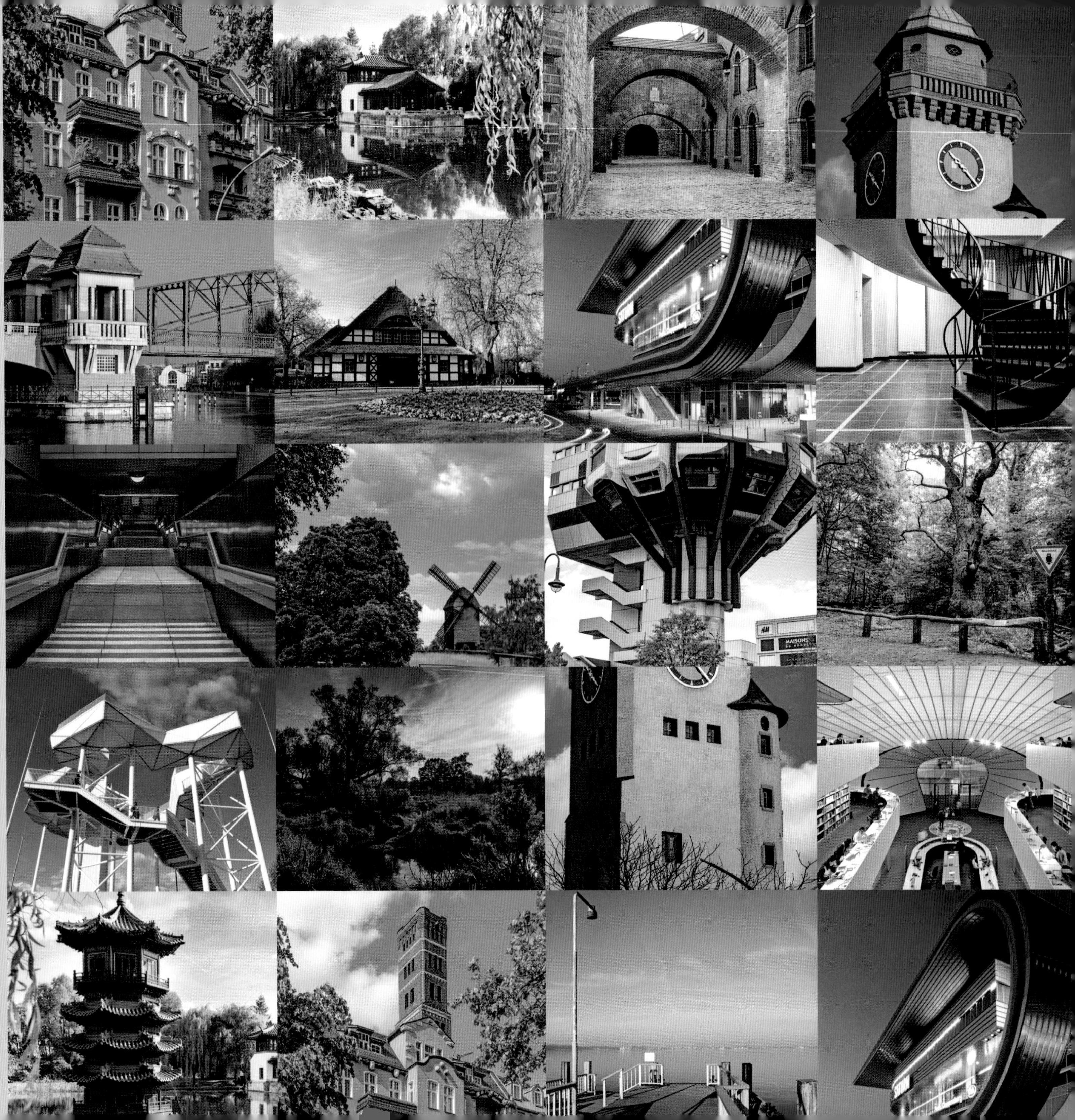
MAISONS

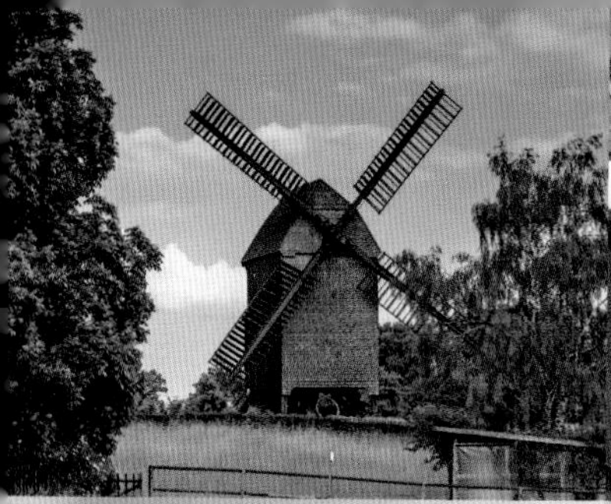
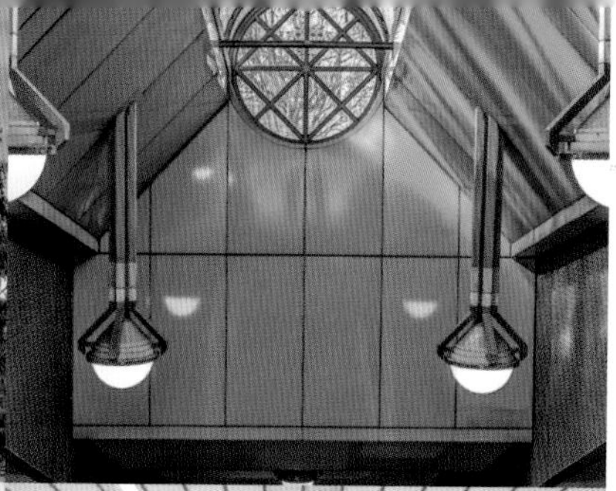
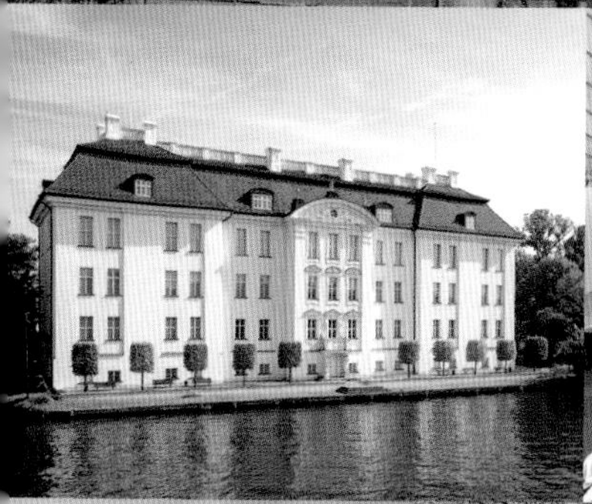
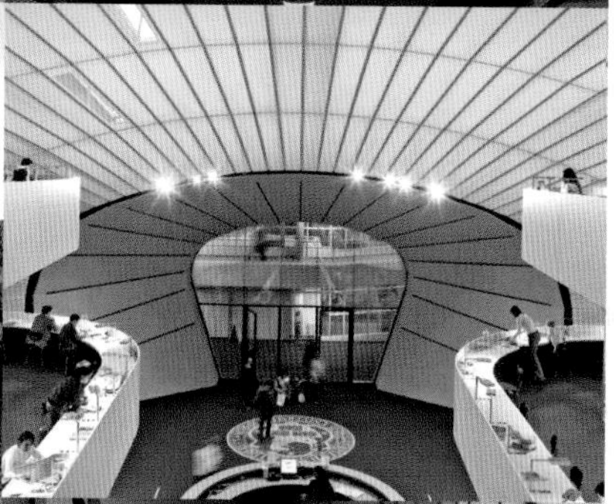
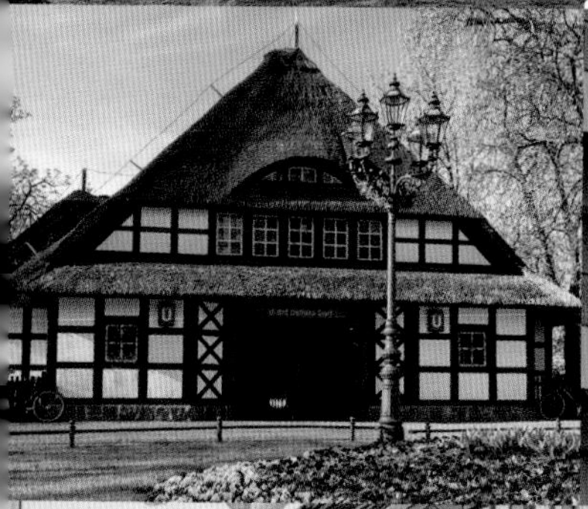
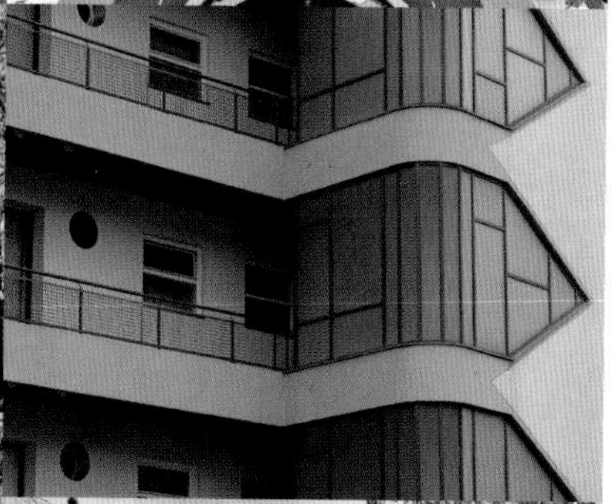
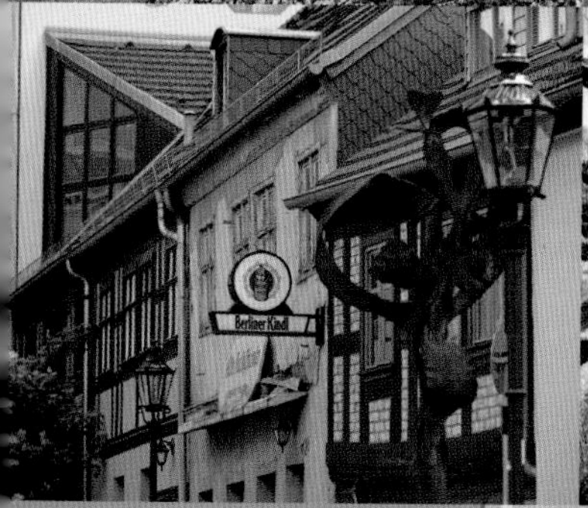

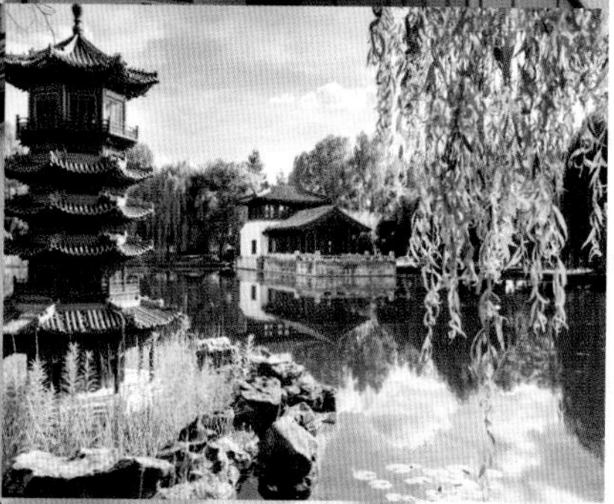
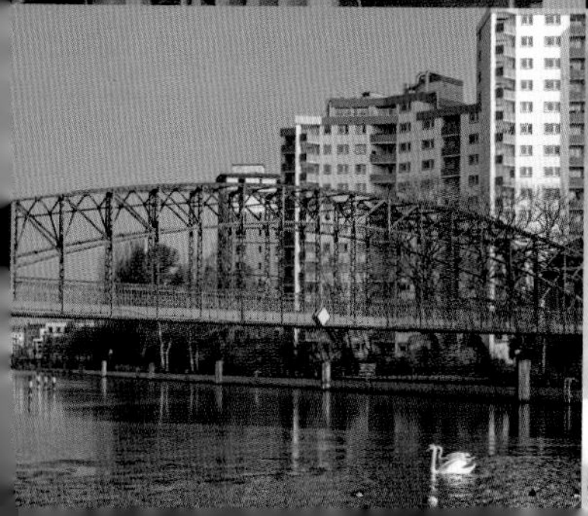
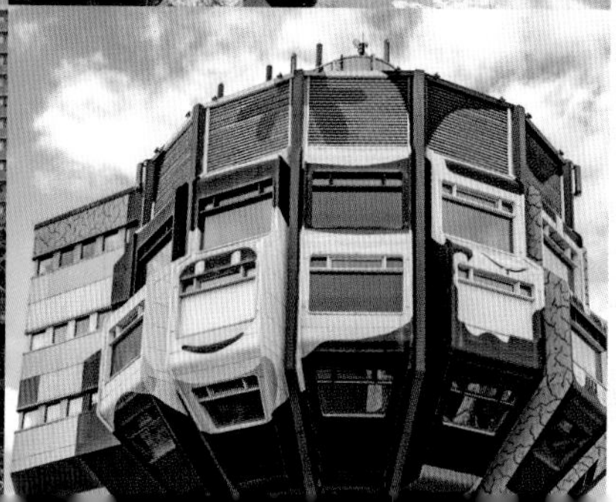

CITY SUBURBS

Life is very different for Berliners out in the suburbs of the city. We get a sense of this from population density figures. Friedrichshain-Kreuzberg, the inner-city borough, has a population density of 13,187 people per square kilometre. In the relatively rural Spandau, by contrast, that figure drops to 2,441 people, and in Treptow-Köpenick just 1,406 people, figures that suggest the citizens of the suburbs have considerably more space on their hands.

Nature also starts to take over more dramatically as we head out from the centre. The western borders of Berlin, for example, edge on to large areas of either agricultural land, rolling hills or forest, with the mighty River Havel making the outer western borders of Steglitz-Zehlendorf and Charlottenburg-Wilmersdorf, while Spandau goes even further beyond.

As our final chapter will show, however, there are many good reasons to leave Berlin's centre and travel out to the more distant parts of this city-state. The architecture remains diverse and important, not least in terms of village-like places that give you a flavour of Berlin as it was 100 years ago and more, although there remains plenty of 1960s and 1970s experimentalism as well. There is even a great oak tree, as old as – or perhaps even older than – the city of Berlin itself.

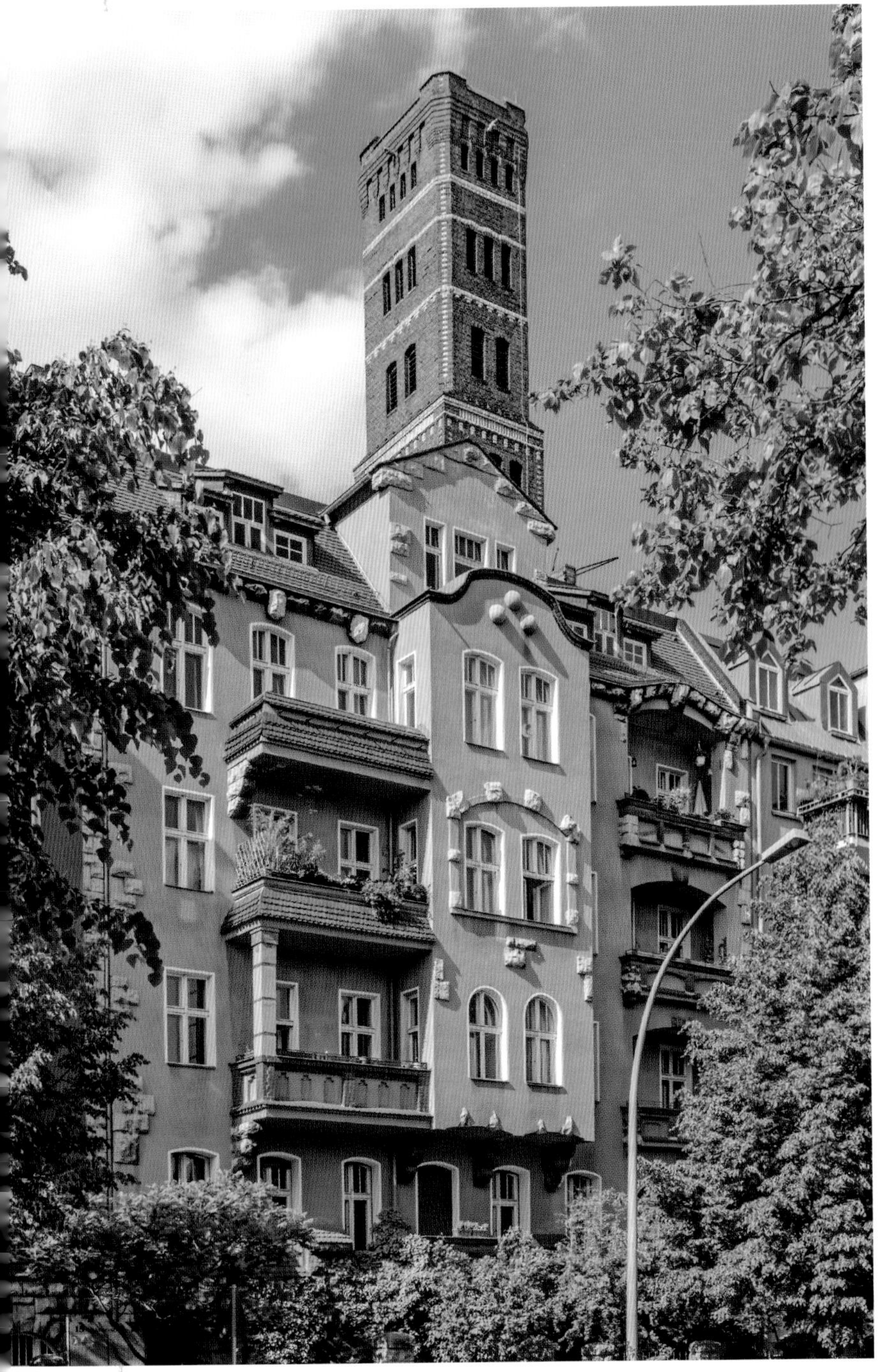

SCHROTKUGELTURM

Nöldnerstraße, Lichtenberg

Schrotkugelturm means 'shot ball tower', and from 1908 the tower was used by Bleigießerei und Maschinenfabrik Juhl & Söhne (Lead Foundry and Machine Factory Juhl & Sons) in the production of lead shot for use in shotguns. The tower is 38 m (125 ft) high, the top reached by 197 steps. Lead was melted at the top, and the drops, freefalling down the tower via a drop tube, formed the perfect spheres required for the smooth flight of the pellets; by the time they reached the bottom they had also cooled and solidified. A listed building today, the Schrotkugelturm can be visited as part of a guided tour.

STASI MUSEUM

Normannenstraße, Lichtenberg

The Ministerium für Staatssicherheit (Ministry for State Security), more commonly known as the Stasi, locked the population of East Germany under repressive scrutiny from 1950 until the collapse of communism. The Stasi Museum in Normannenstraße is located in the former Stasi headquarters, with much of the museum consisting of rooms and features (such as this spiral staircase) left virtually untouched since the Stasi left quickly in 1990. The building even has the office of Erich Mielke (1907–2000), Minister of State Security and head of the Stasi from 1957 to the fall of the Berlin Wall in 1989. It is an unsettling museum, with memories still fresh in the minds of many Berliners.

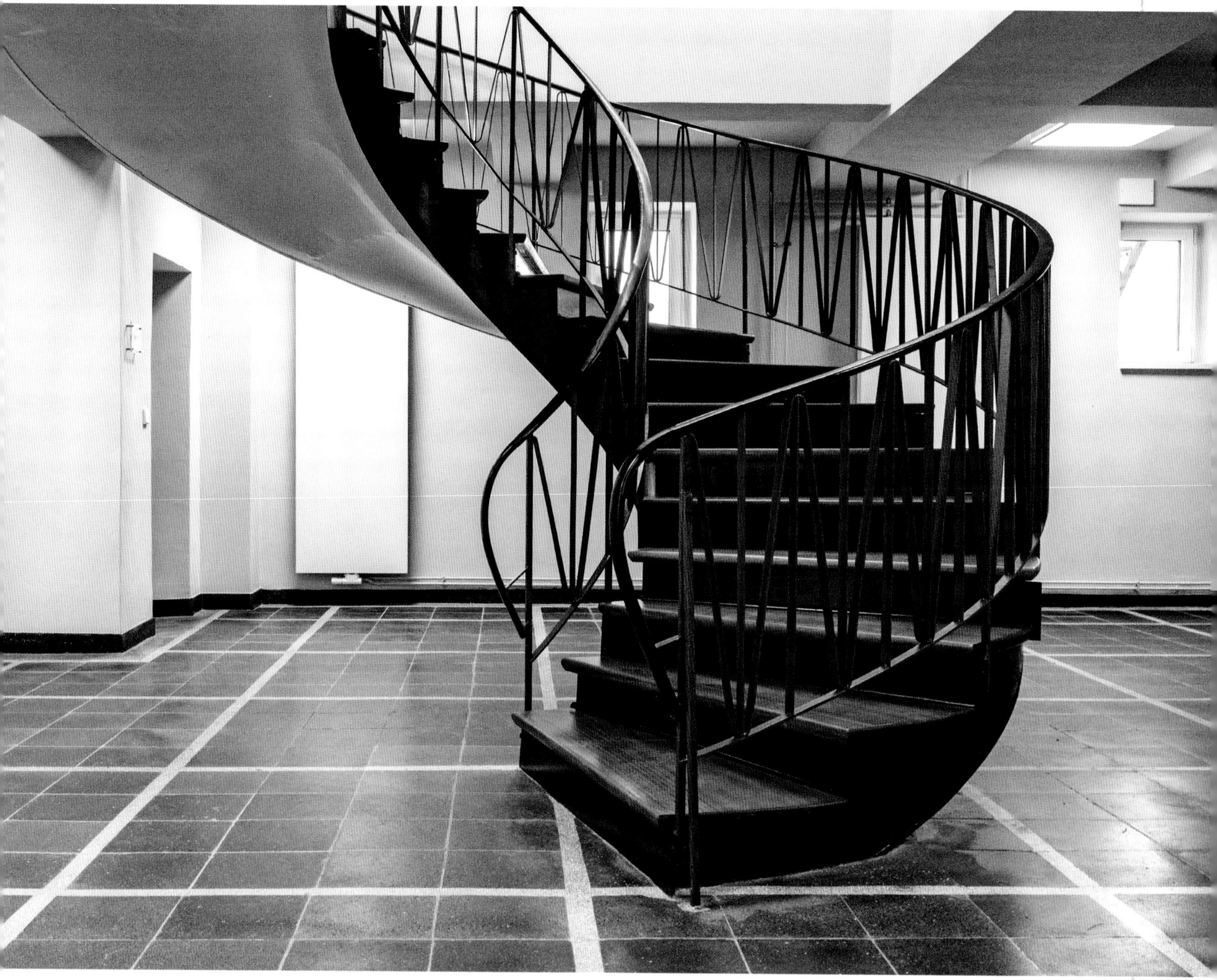

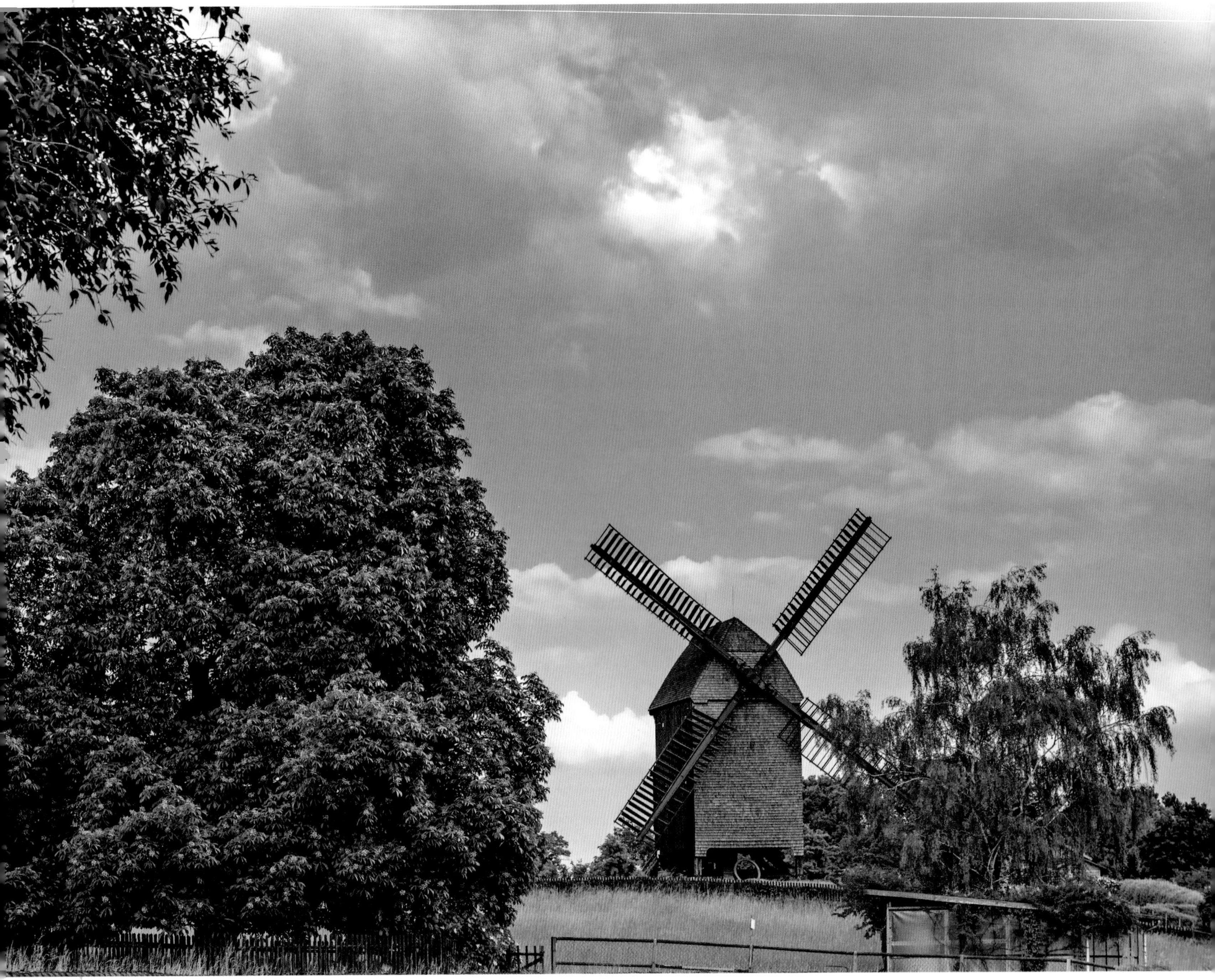

BOCKWINDMÜHLE MARZAHN

Landsberger Allee, Marzahn

The Bockwindmühle Marzahn (Marzahn Windmill) is a memory of a time when wind played a central role in food production. The first incarnation of the windmill was back in 1815, but the current iteration of the structure was unveiled on 12 May 1994, a replica of that first windmill. The windmill is fully functioning, grinding grains and producing flour used to make the local 'Marzahner Mühlenkruste' bread. In an acceptance of modernity, however, the windmill also includes a hi-tech wind-monitoring station.

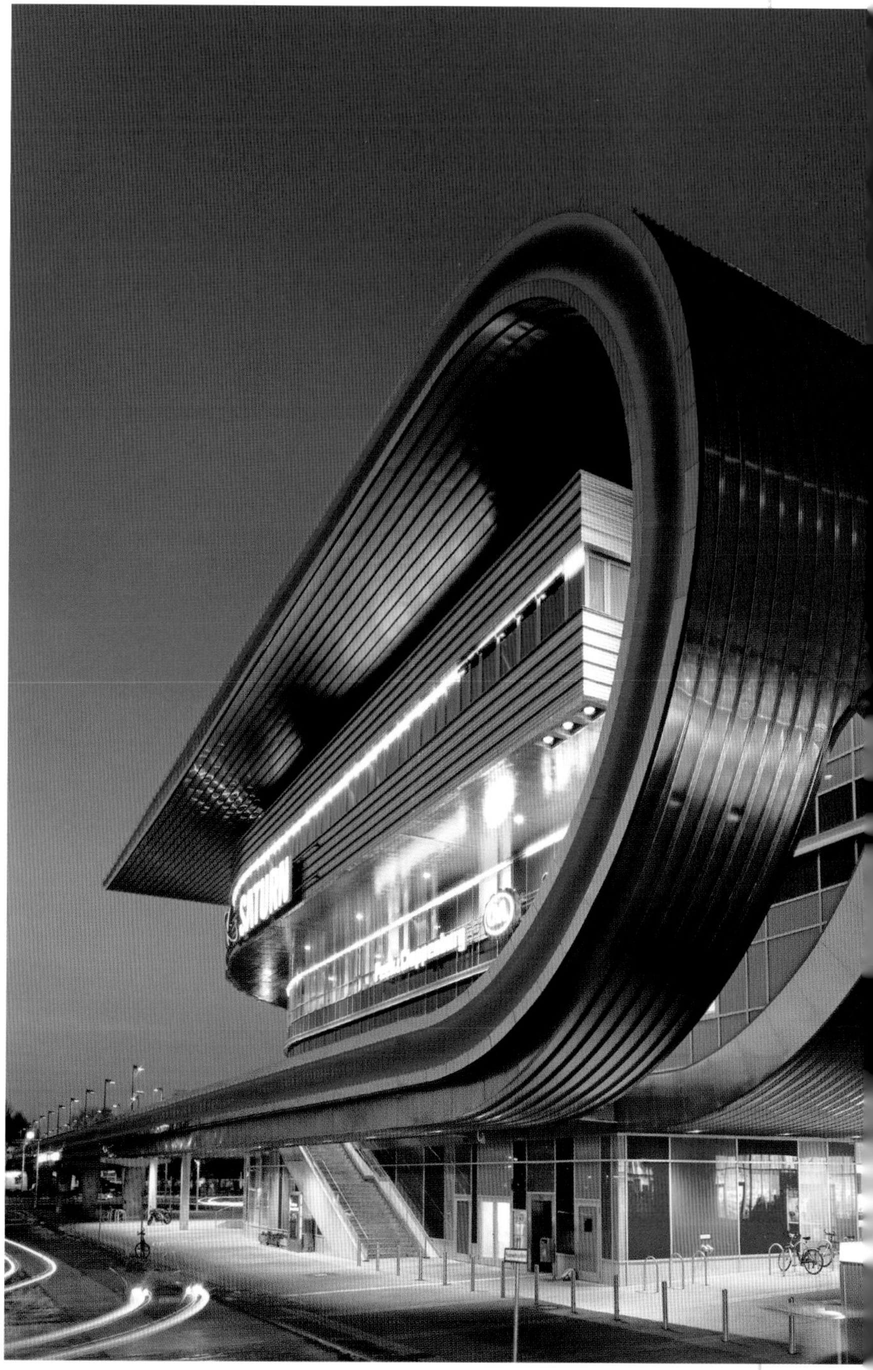

EASTGATE

Marzahner Promenade, Marzahn

The architecture of Eastgate shopping centre conveys both nostalgia and futurism in the same breath. It opened in 2005, having taken two years to build, the building plugging into the public transport network via a pedestrian bridge connecting it to the S-Bahn station Marzahn (car parking is also integrated into its roof). Inside the brightly lit space are some 150 shops, of every description, located across two sales floors, plus numerous cafés and restaurants. Large, well-lit rotundas also provide spaces to meet and relax.

GÄRTEN DER WELT

Marzhan Park, Marzahn

The Gärten der Welt (Gardens of the World) at Marzahn Park are aptly named. The 40-hectare (99-acre) site is home to 10 individual gardens, each of them styled authentically after their country of origin. The gardens include Japanese (seen here), Chinese, Italian, Balinese, Middle Eastern, Korean and other arboreal worlds, planted authentically and featuring peaceful water features and wandering paths. The park also hosts major gardening and cultural festivals every year, such as the spring Cherry Blossom Festival, and has a 5,000-seat open-air stage.

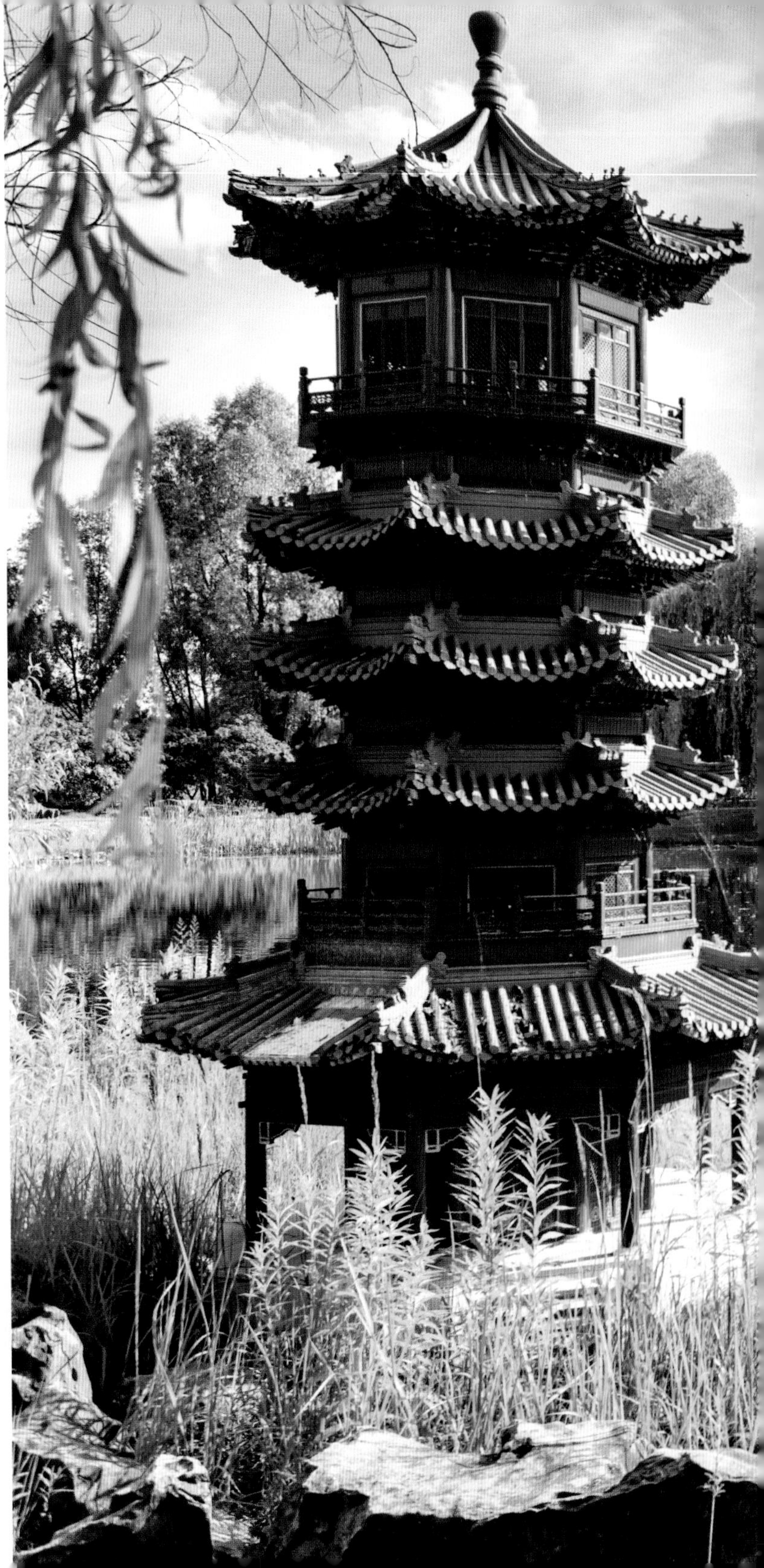

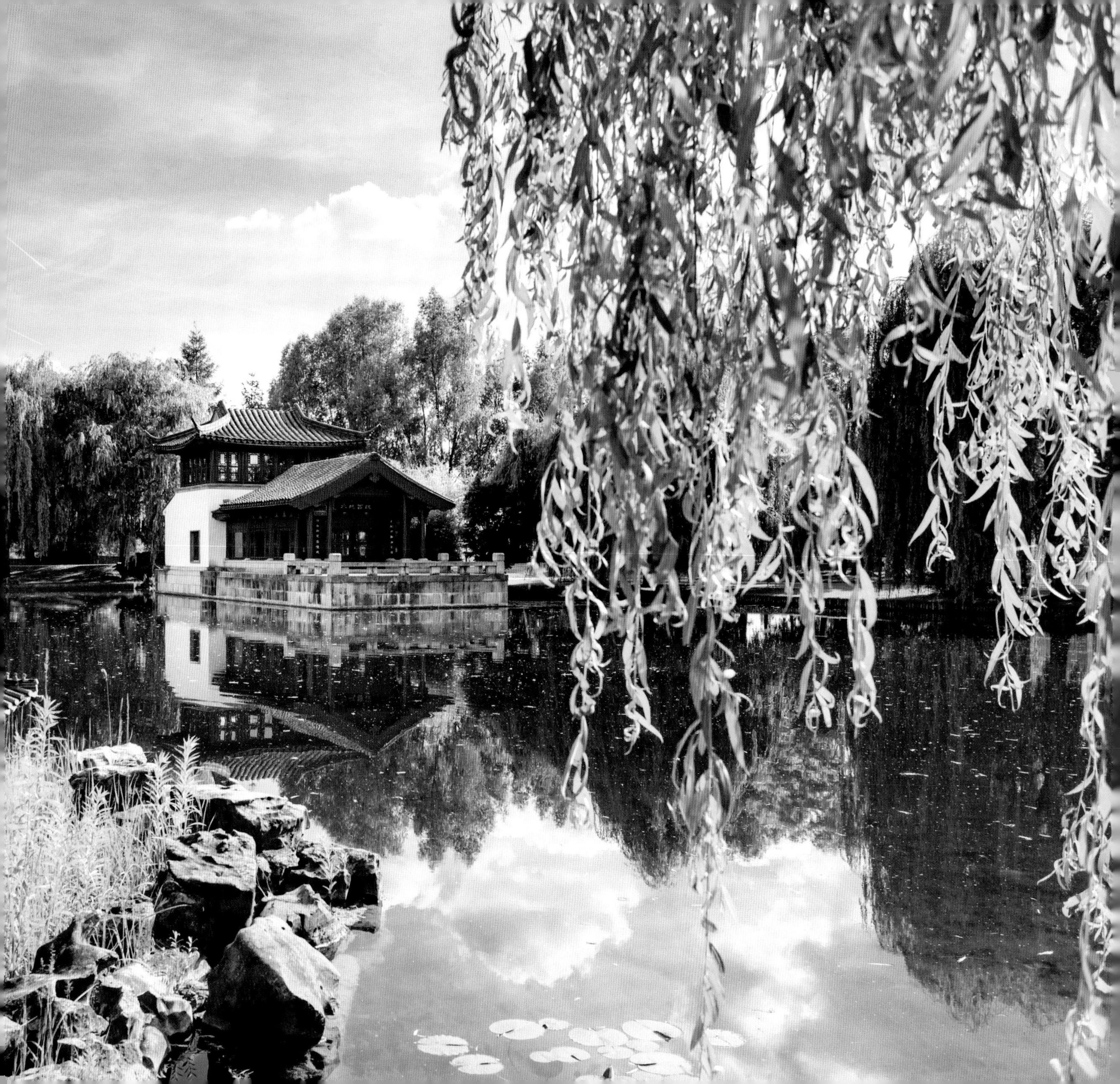

WOLKENHAIN

Kienberg Park, Marzahn

The Wolkenhain is a marvel of engineering, an observation tower in a 'cloud' of translucent textile membranes that reach up to 120 m (394 ft) above sea level. At night these membranes are illuminated spectacularly, glowing with multiple colours on the Berlin skyline. Braced high above the ground by a steel framework, the Wolkenhain provides perfect views out over the Gärten der Welt (see page 170) and across to central Berlin. It also features an integrated panoramic restaurant, so you can eat while viewing.

MÜGGELSEE

Treptow-Köpenick

The Müggelsee in south-eastern Berlin is the German capital's largest lake, 4.5 km (3 miles) long and 2.5 km (1.5 miles) across. This expanse of water naturally lends itself to a variety of water sports for both professionals and sauntering amateurs; boat rental stations are found around the perimeter of the lake. The edge of the lake features many other attractions, such as restaurants and cafés, the historical fishermen's town of Rahnsdorf to the south-east, and the Museum im Alten Wasserwerk (Waterworks Museum) on the northern bank, telling the gritty but always fascinating history of water treatment and sanitation in Berlin.

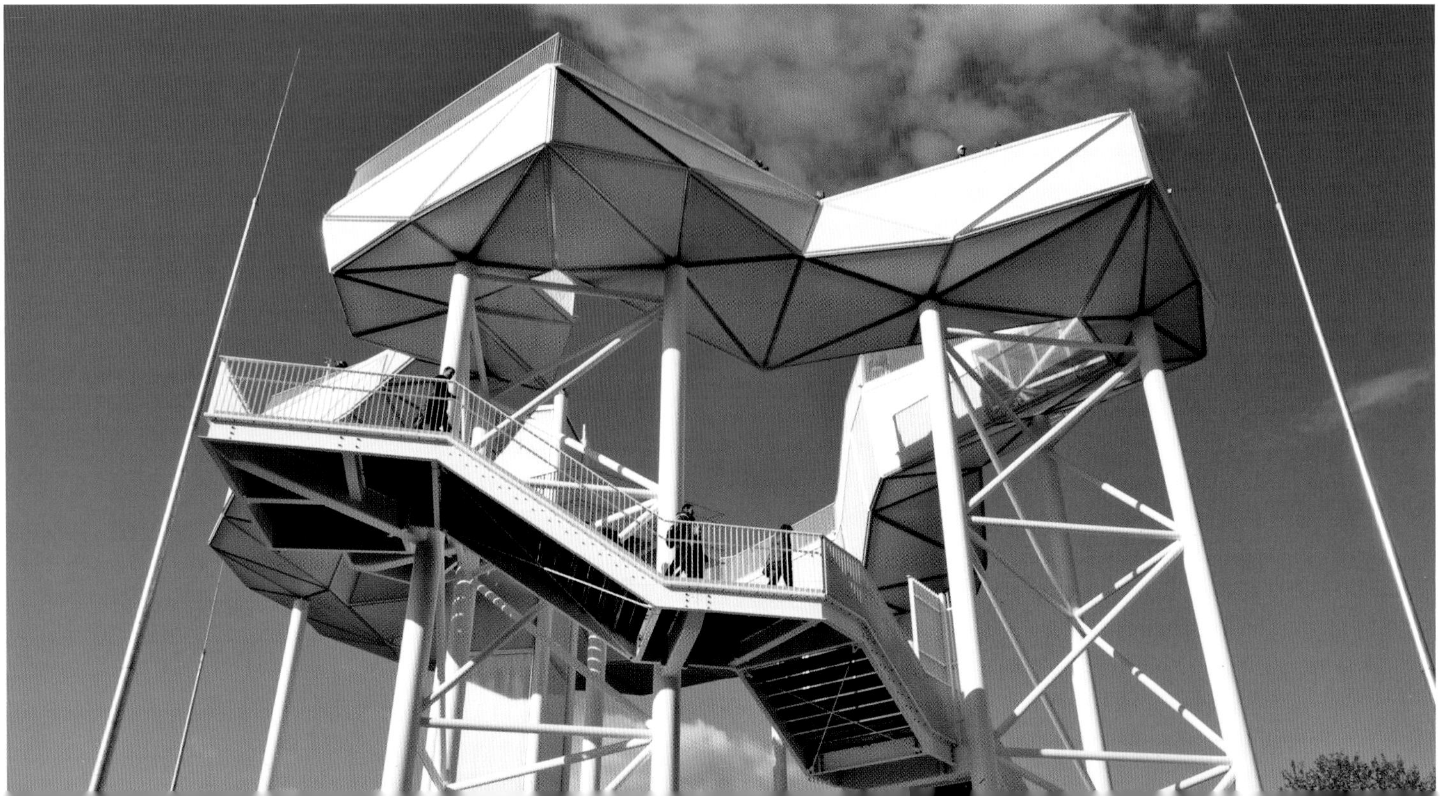

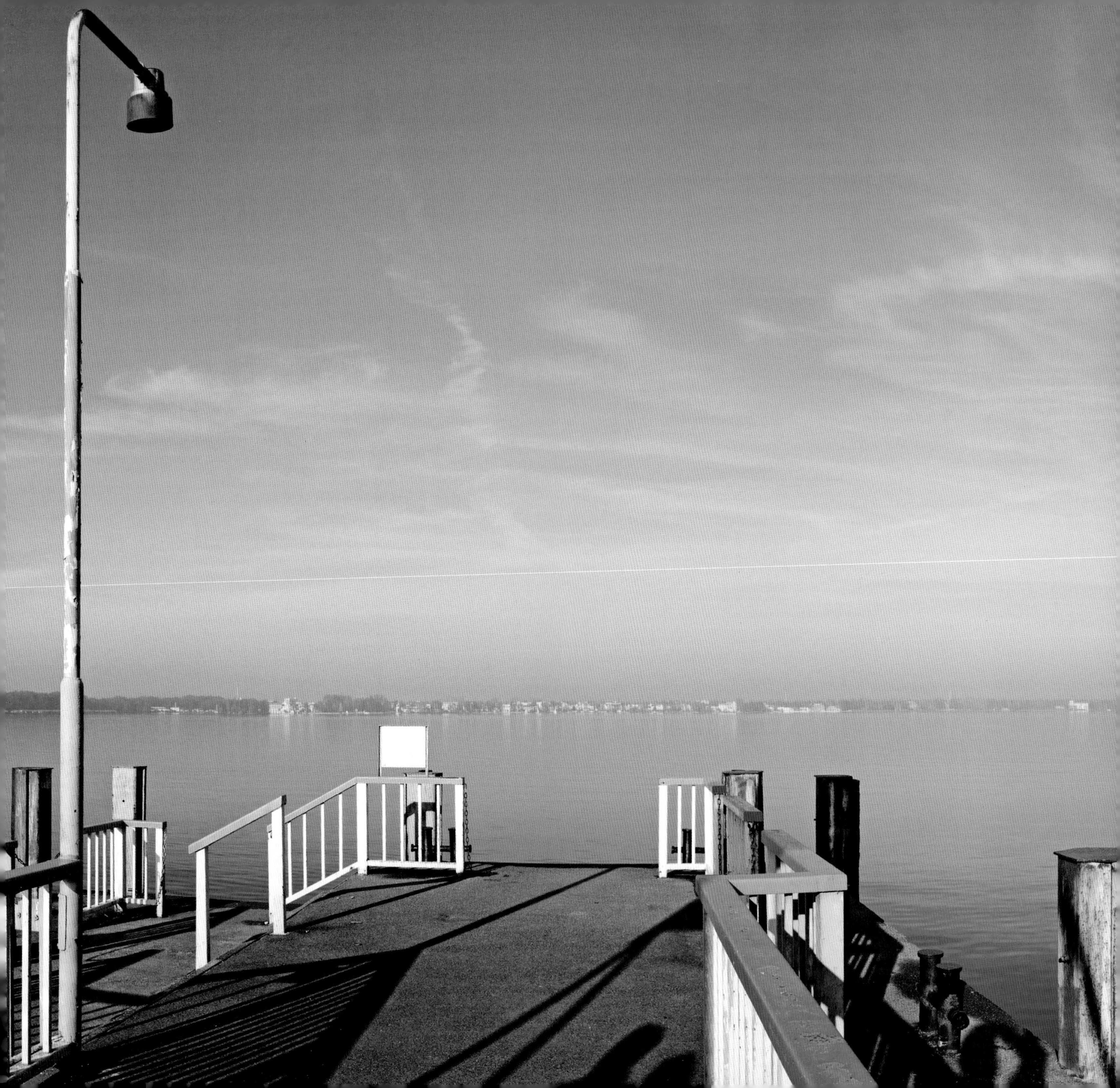

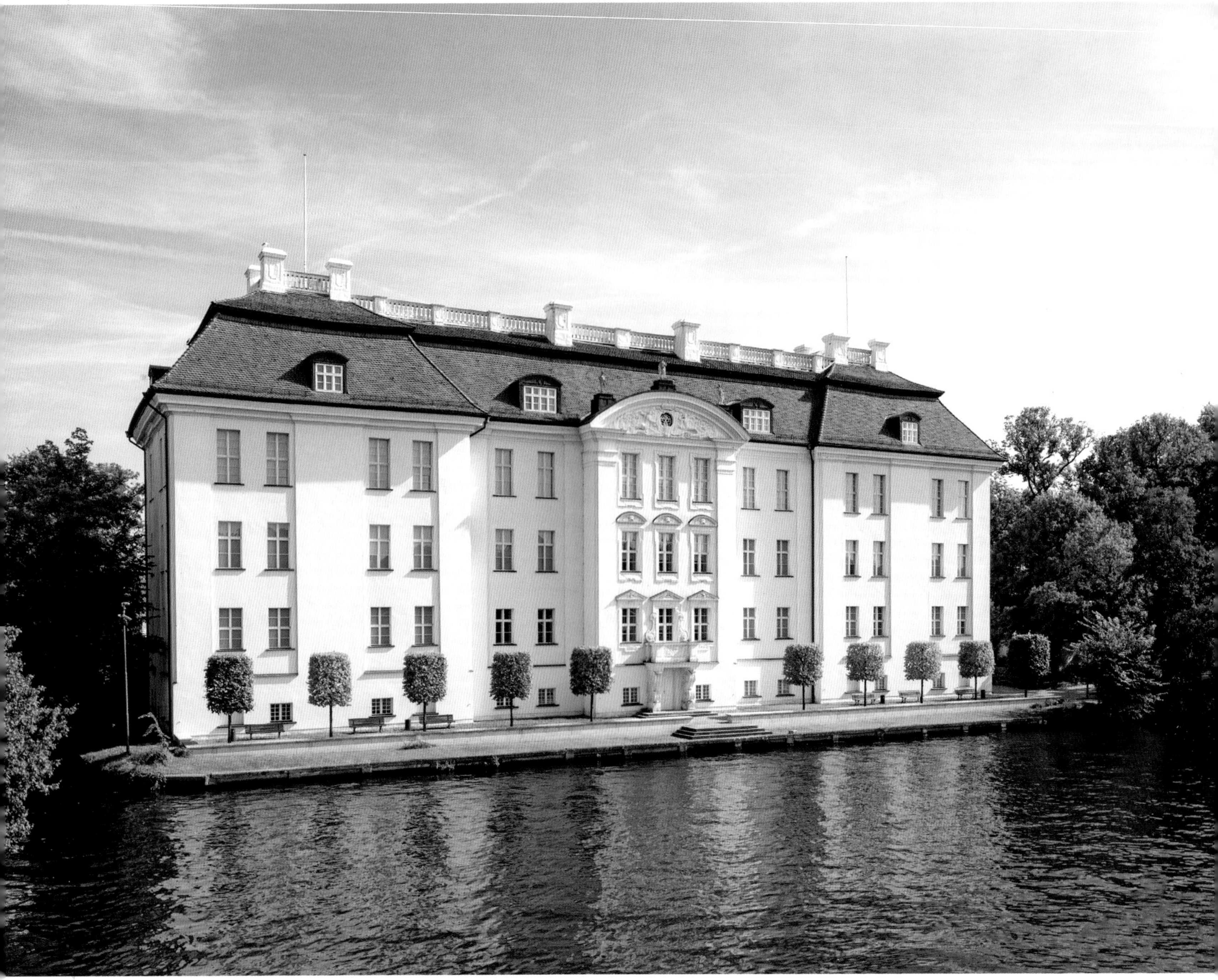

SCHLOSS KÖPENICK

Dahme River, Köpenick

Built on an island in the Dahme River, the Schloss Köpenick (Köpenick Palace) is a seventeenth-century Baroque palace, designed by architects Rutger van Langervelt (1635–95) and Johann Arnold Nering (1659–95) on the site of a former Renaissance-style hunting lodge for Joachim II, Elector of Brandenburg (1505–71). It was commissioned by Frederick I of Prussia (1657–1713), and in 1730 a young future Frederick II (1712–86), better known as Frederick the Great, was court-martialled by his father for attempting to run away to England. Frederick's friend was beheaded for the same crime as a most emphatic warning not to try it again.

BIERPINSEL

Schloßstraße, Steglitz

Towering over the Steglitz neighbourhood of South Berlin, like an alien spaceship making a visitation, the Bierpinsel (Beer Brush) was designed and built in the 1970s by architect couple Ursula and Ralph Schuler. It is recognized as an extreme expression of experimental Brutalism, the structure appearing somewhere between a tree and an observation tower, an overdose of angles and colours. (The exterior was painted by graffiti artists.) Inside there are three floors, featuring a restaurant and a nightclub.

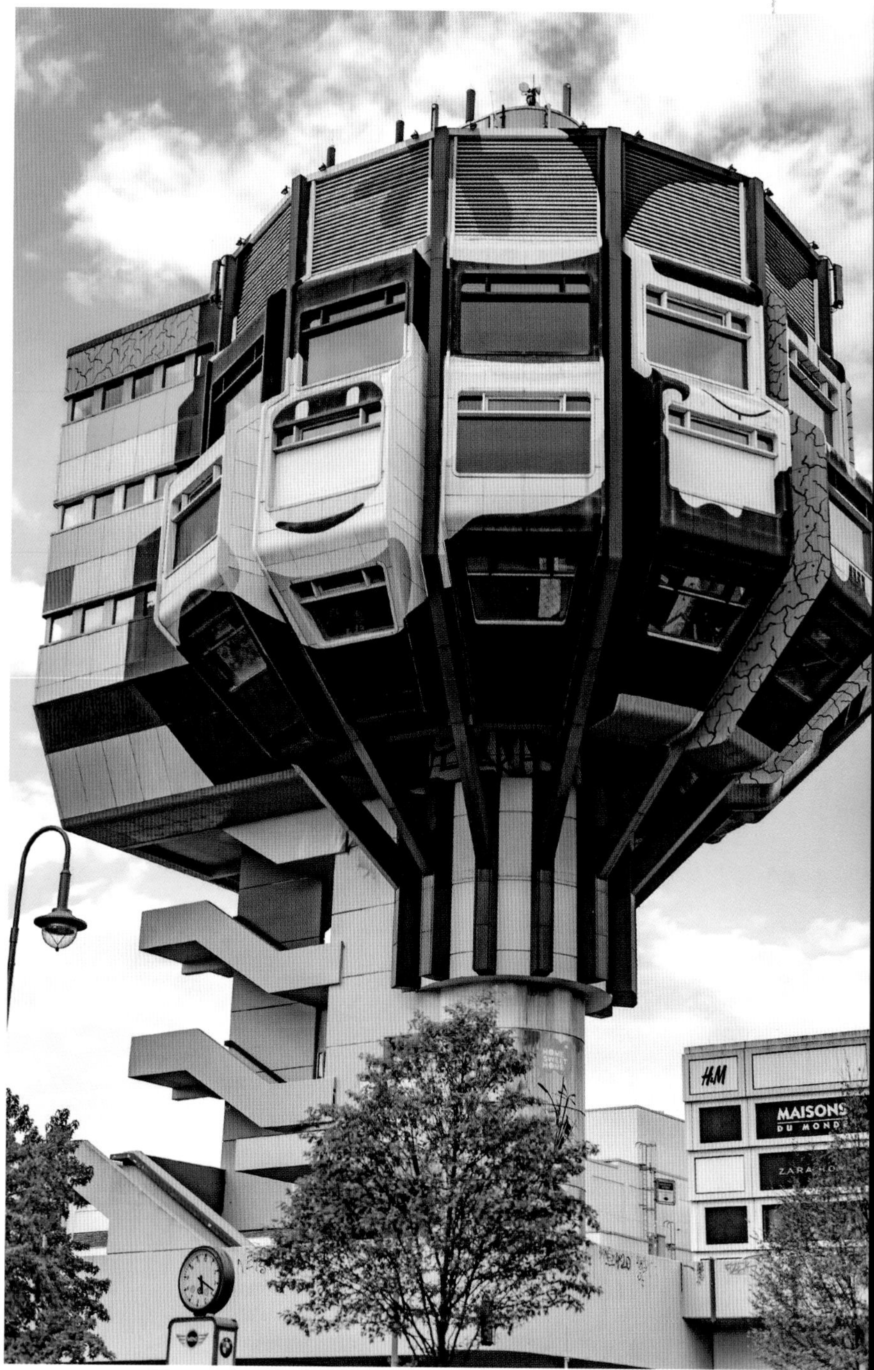

DAHLEM-DORF

Dahlem

Despite its pastoral quaintness on the outside, the Dahlem-Dorf is actually a U-Bahn rail station. The building was designed by Friedrich and Wilhelm Hennings and built in 1913, the architects striving (and succeeding) in creating a building that evoked a traditional German farmhouse, including a thatched roof. The war years were hard on the building, it being destroyed and later rebuilt, and the post-war station has suffered two catastrophic fires. Yet it stands today, and has been labelled by some as Europe's most beautiful station.

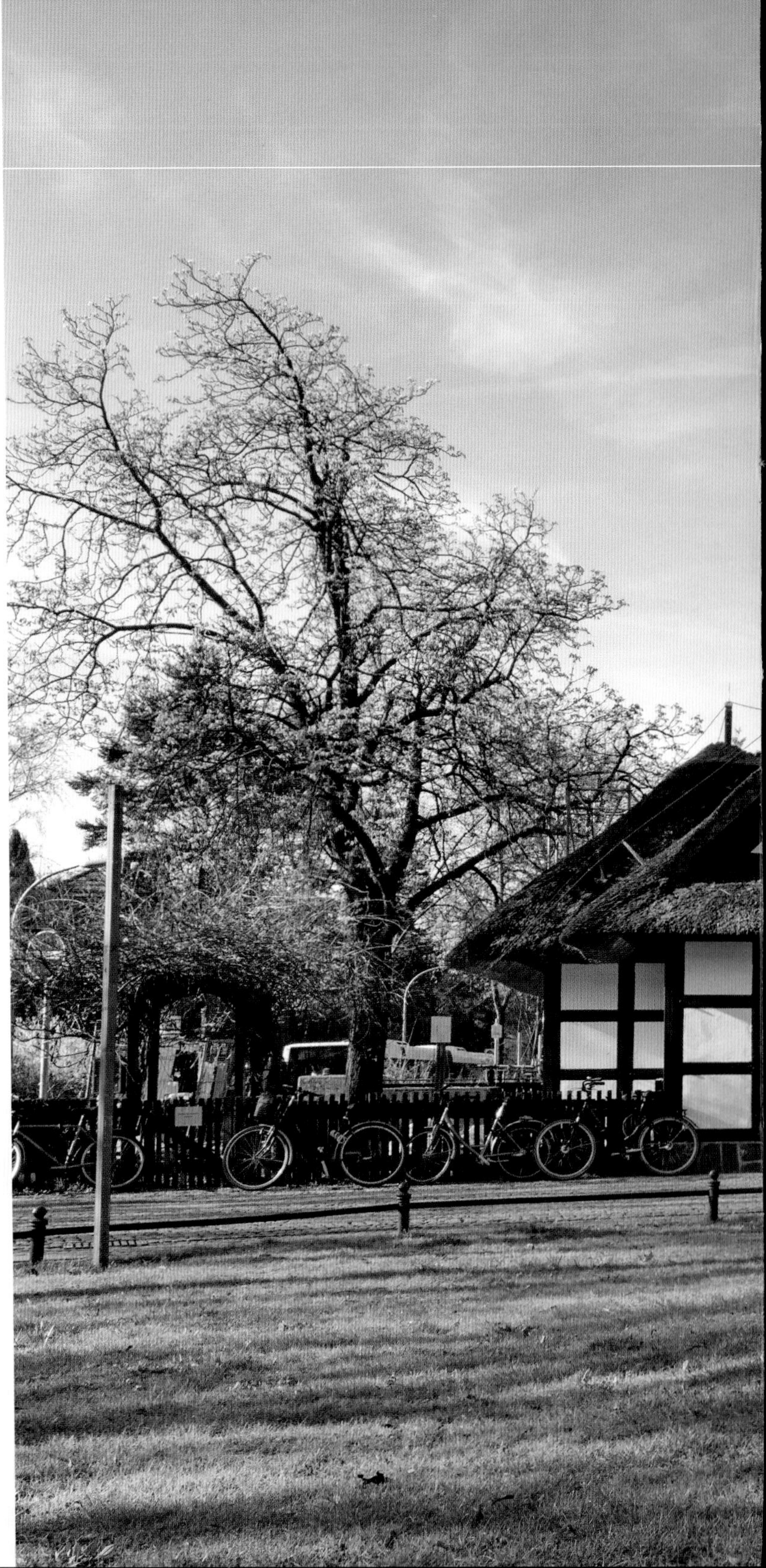

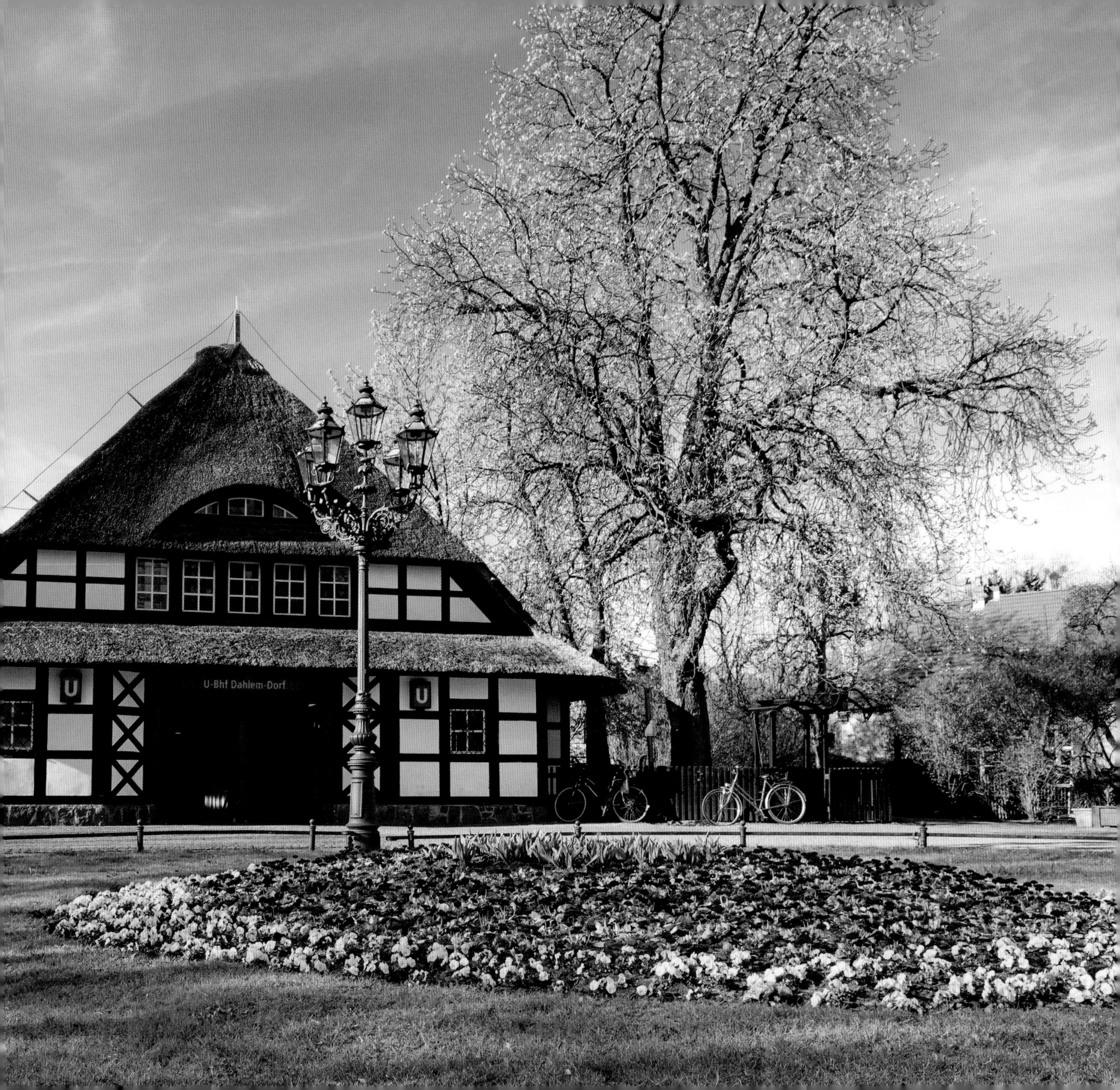
U
U-Bhf Dahlem-Dorf
U

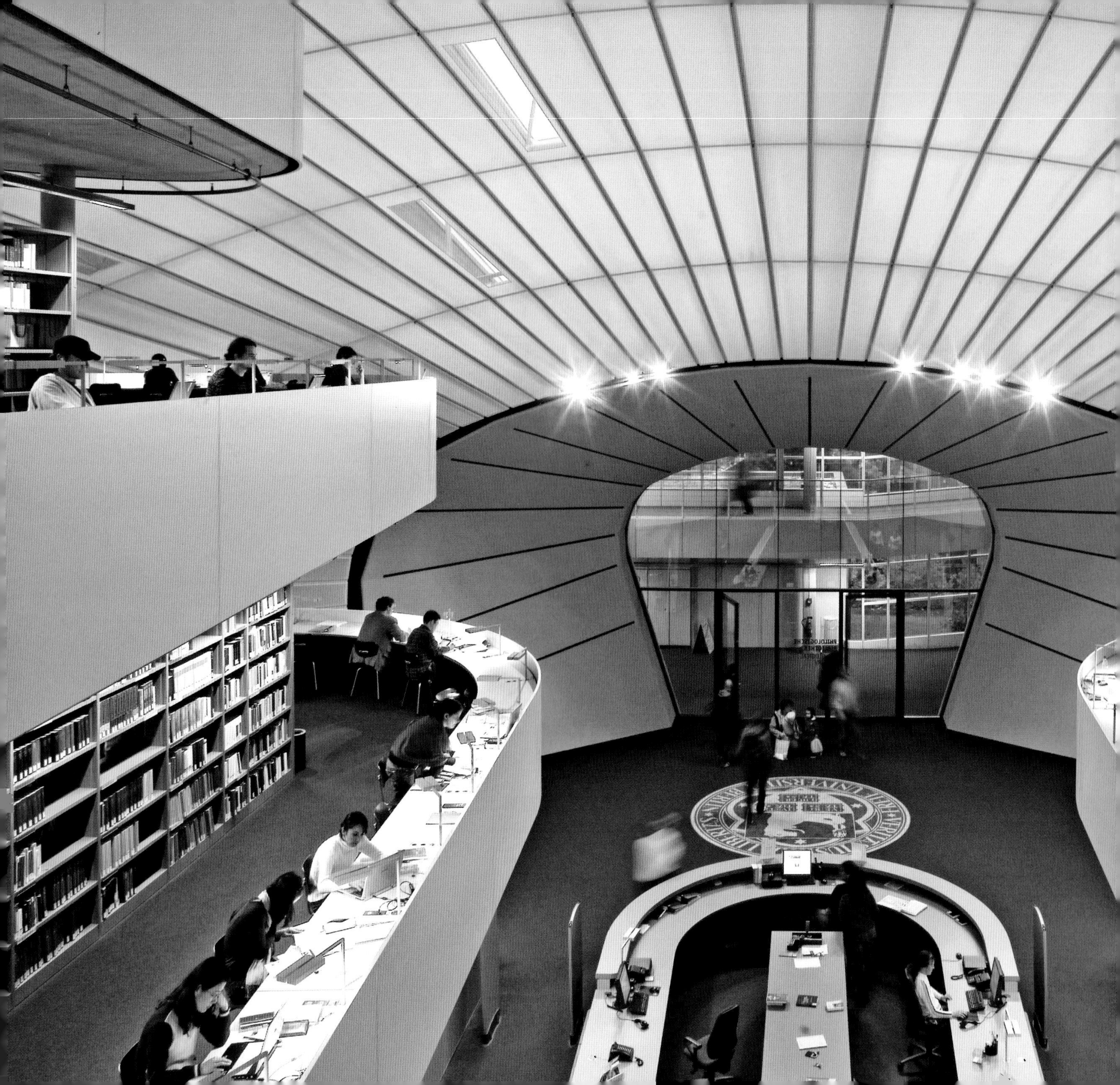

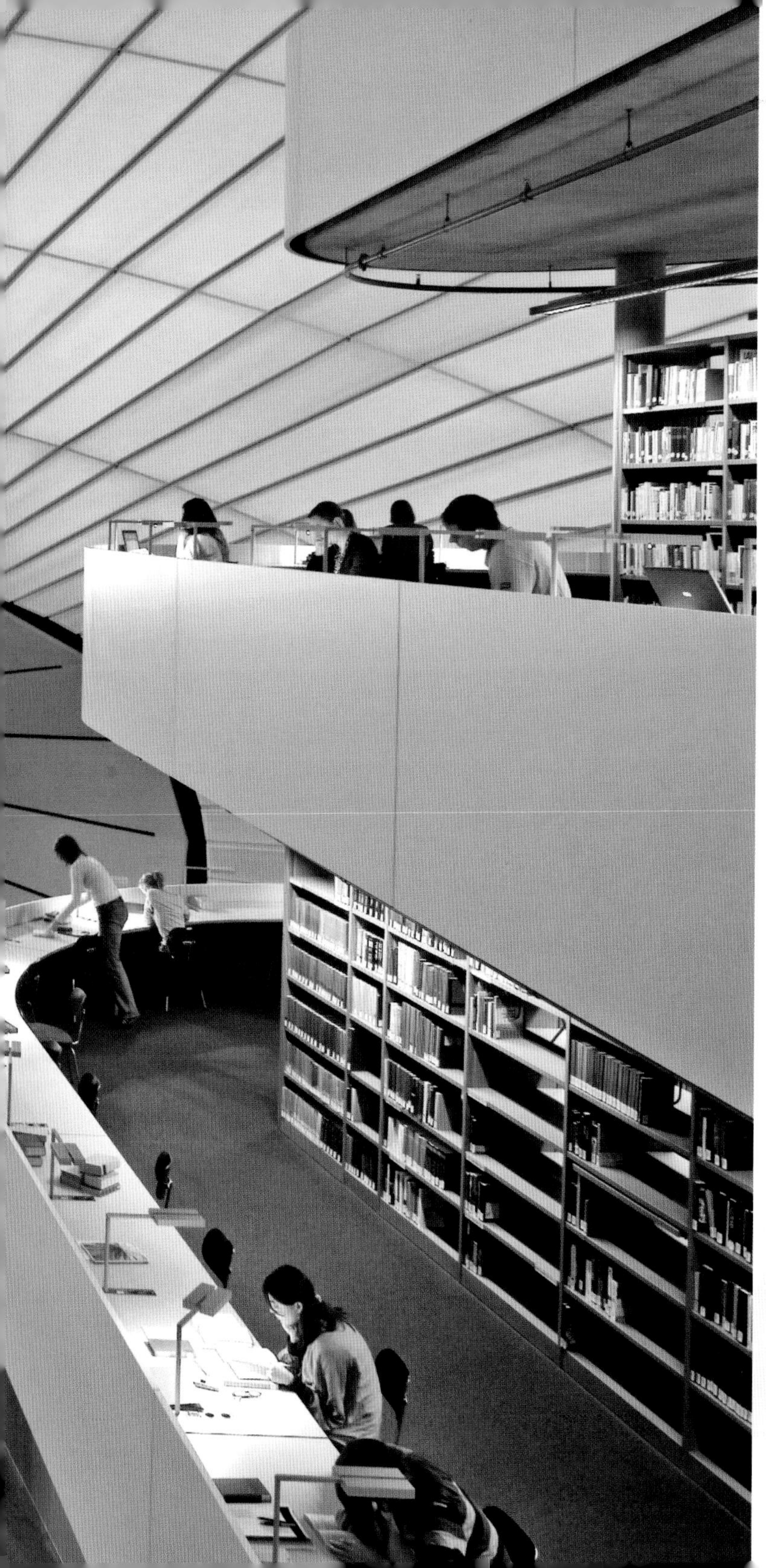

PHILOLOGISCHE BIBLIOTHEK

Freie Universität Berlin, Dahlem

The Philologische Bibliothek (Philological Library) in the Freie Universität Berlin (Free University of Berlin) is a modern architectural masterpiece by the British architect Lord Norman Foster (b. 1935). Light and expansive, but also intimate, the design of the building is brain-like in form and structure, with an interior harmony of white, grey and red free from elements that might distract thought and concentration. It is also designed to maintain the free flow of fresh air and to maintain a steady temperature for the students and academics at the research tables.

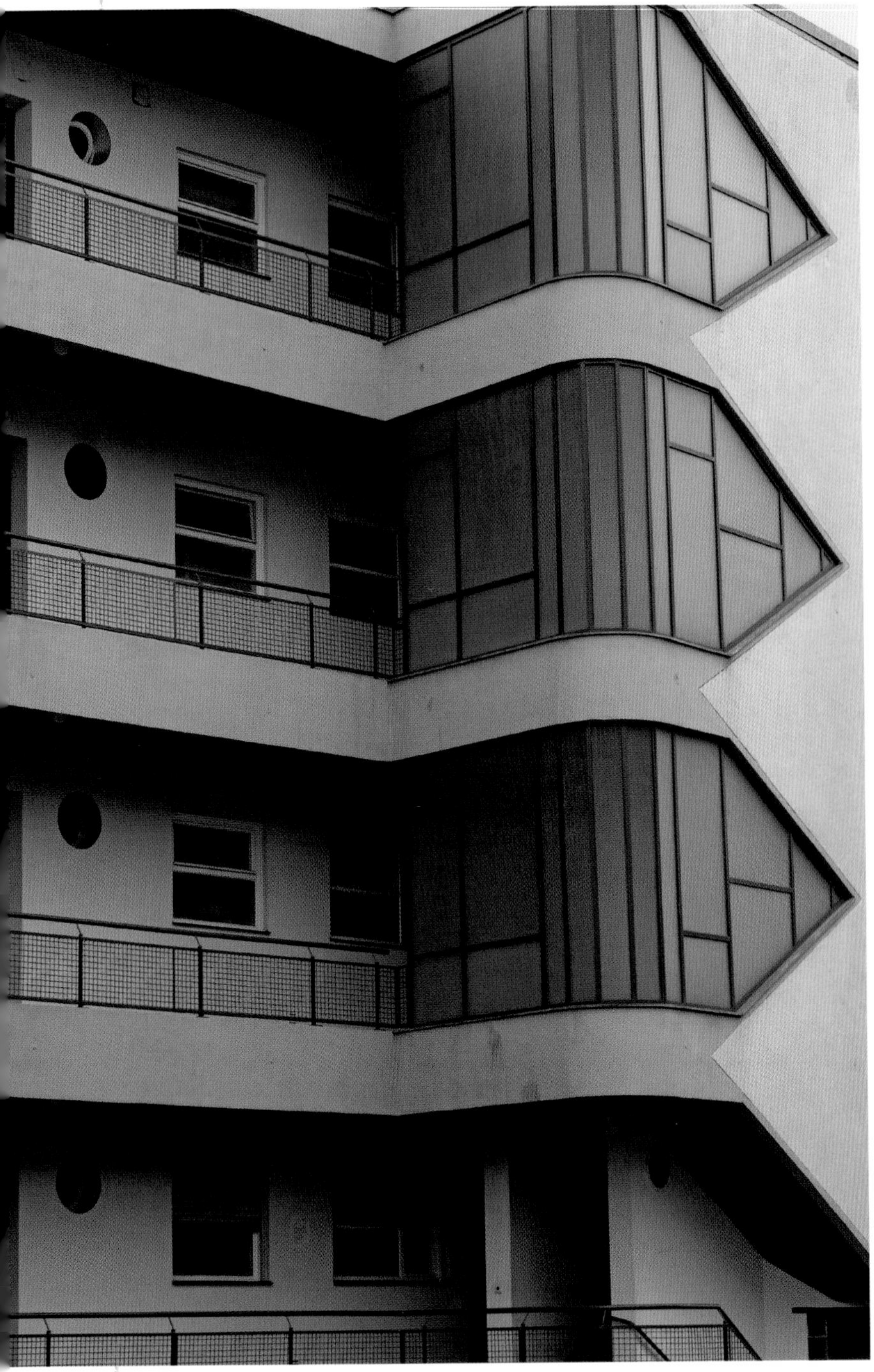

SIEMENSSTADT

Siemensstadt, Spandau

The name of the Siemensttadt (Siemens City) housing estate refers to its original purpose, being developed between 1929 and 1934 for the employees of a nearby Siemens manufacturing plant. What makes the estate fascinating, and which has since 2008 given it UNESCO World Heritage Site status, is the way that the 1,379 apartment buildings were designed by six great modern German architects: Walter Gropius, Hans Scharoun, Otto Bartning, Hugo Häring, Fred Forbát and Paul Rudolf Henning. Built with a mind to sanitary and light living conditions, the estate thus forms a microcosm of modern domestic architecture.

ZITADELLE SPANDAU

Spandau

This muscular Renaissance fortress, mainly built during the sixteenth century, sits protected by the waters of the Havel, with few physical connections to surrounding Spandau. Parts of the fortress complex are even older; the Julius Tower dates back to the thirteenth century, making it the oldest building in Berlin. The visitor can climb its 153 steps to the top, for impressive views out over the river. Structurally, the fortress is dominated by its four bastions, each given a regal title, joined by the curtain walls in a symmetrical arrangement, with no hiding spaces for attackers.

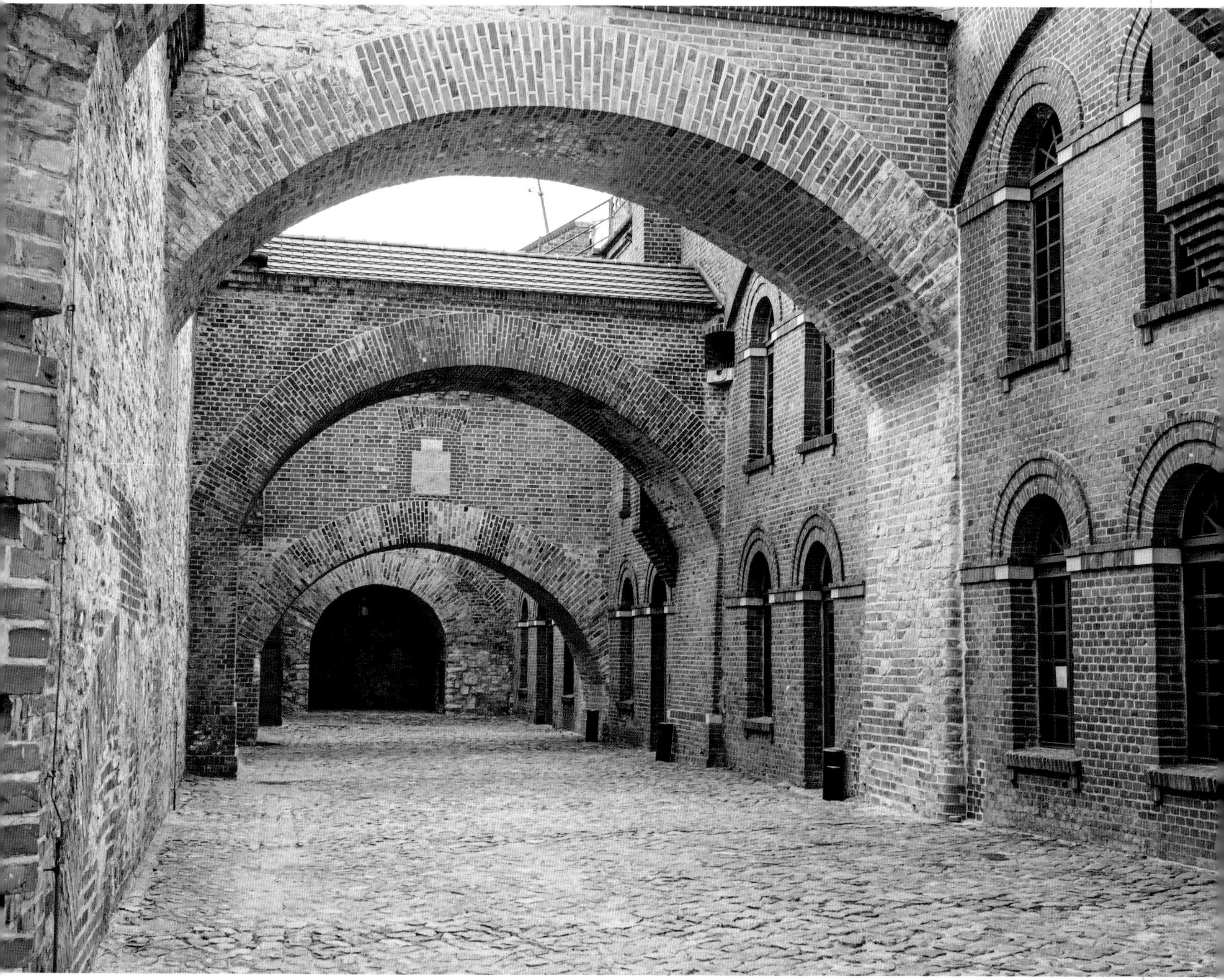

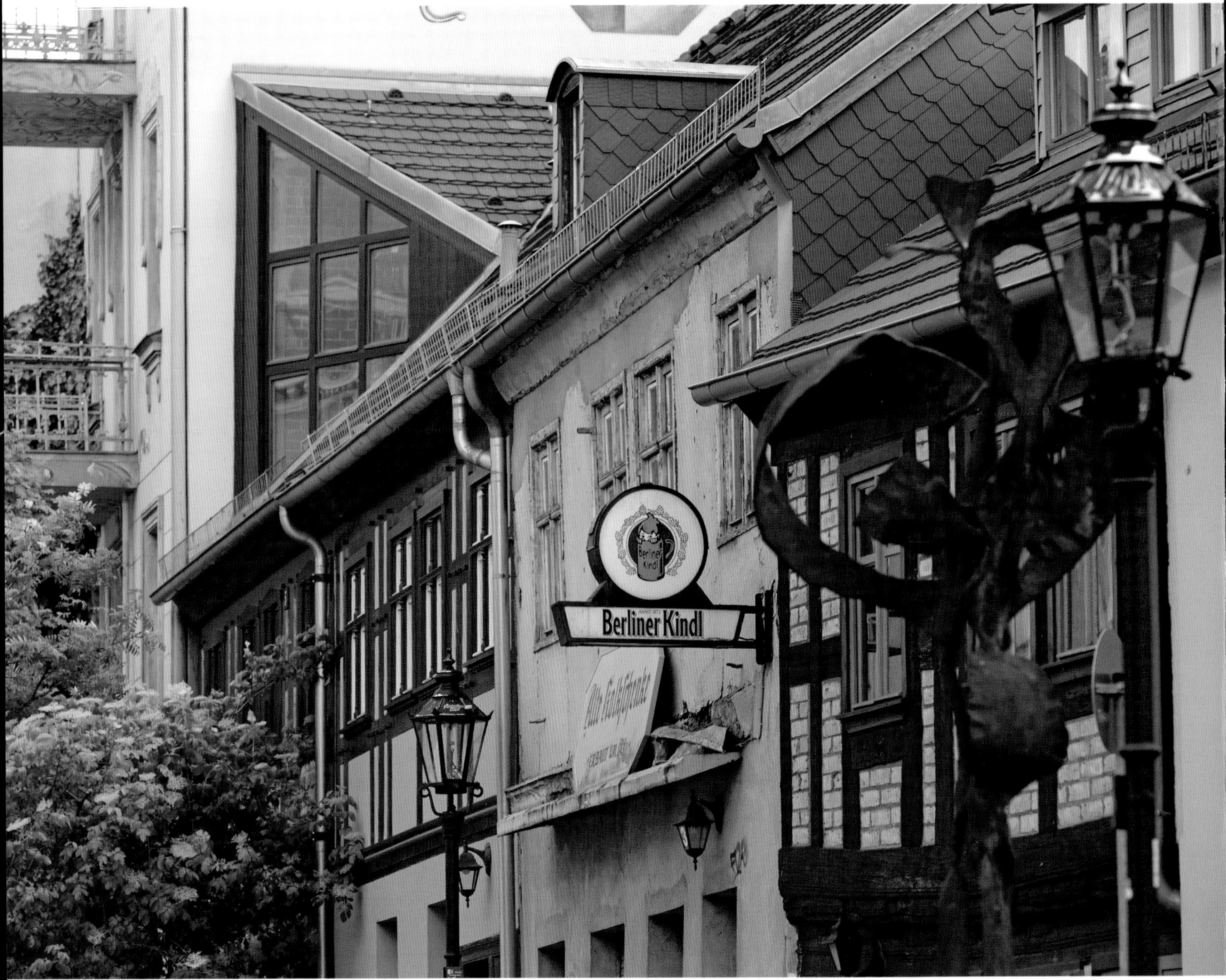
Berliner Kindl
Berliner Kindl

KOLKVIERTEL

Old Spandau, Spandau

The Kolkviertel (Kolk Quarter) transports the visitor back in time, the narrow streets and timber-framed houses dating back mainly to the eighteenth and nineteenth centuries, but including some features of the medieval era. A notable feature is the Alte Kolkschänke (here seen in the centre, with the bar signs outside), a building that used to be the standard haunt of soldiers stationed in Berlin's Zitadelle. Add in the cobbled streets and peaceful atmosphere, and it is easy to forget that one is in a modern capital city.

KASINOTURM

Frohnau, Reinickendorf

Located in Berlin-Frohnau, Reinickendorf, in the far north, the Kasinoturm (Clock Tower) is another elevated time piece that provides Berliners with temporal orientation as they go about their business. The structure has a rather militaristic quality to it, suggesting a castle bastion, complete with fake machicolations, and was built in the first decade of the twentieth century, being completed on 1 May 1910.

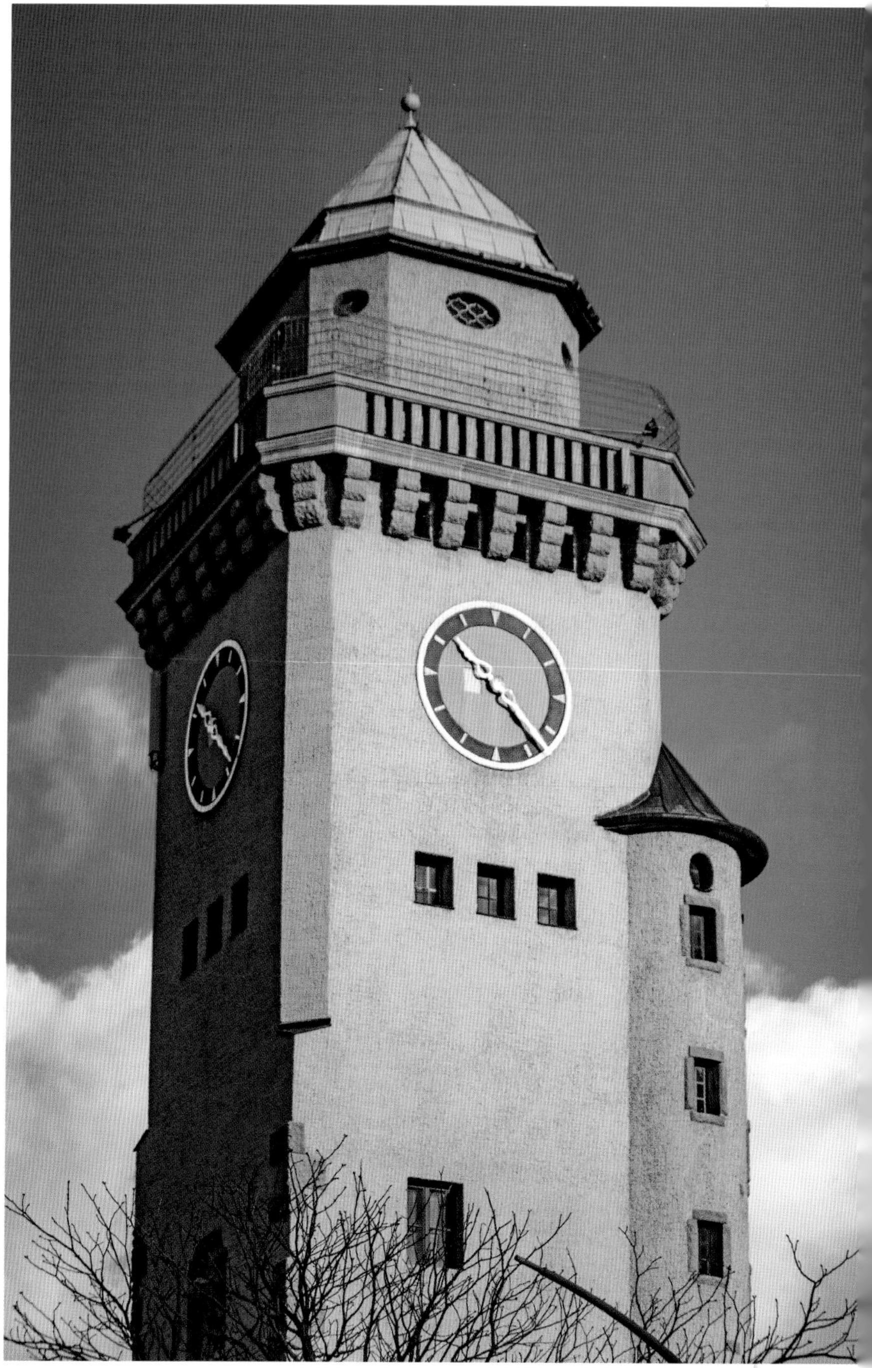

LÜBARS

Reinickendorf

Lübars shows us the rural Germany of yesteryear. A gentle village in the Berlin suburbs, it still reflects rural ways of living, with nearby fields and meandering rivers, plus a reassuringly traditional focus on equestrian transportation. Sites worth seeing include the late eighteenth-century village church, a vintage fire station and also a variety of beautifully ageing farmhouses. During the Cold War, the Berlin Wall actually ran through Lübars and featured the 'Checkpoint Qualitz', so-called because a local farmer, Helmut Qualitz, broke it with his tractor on 16 June 1990.

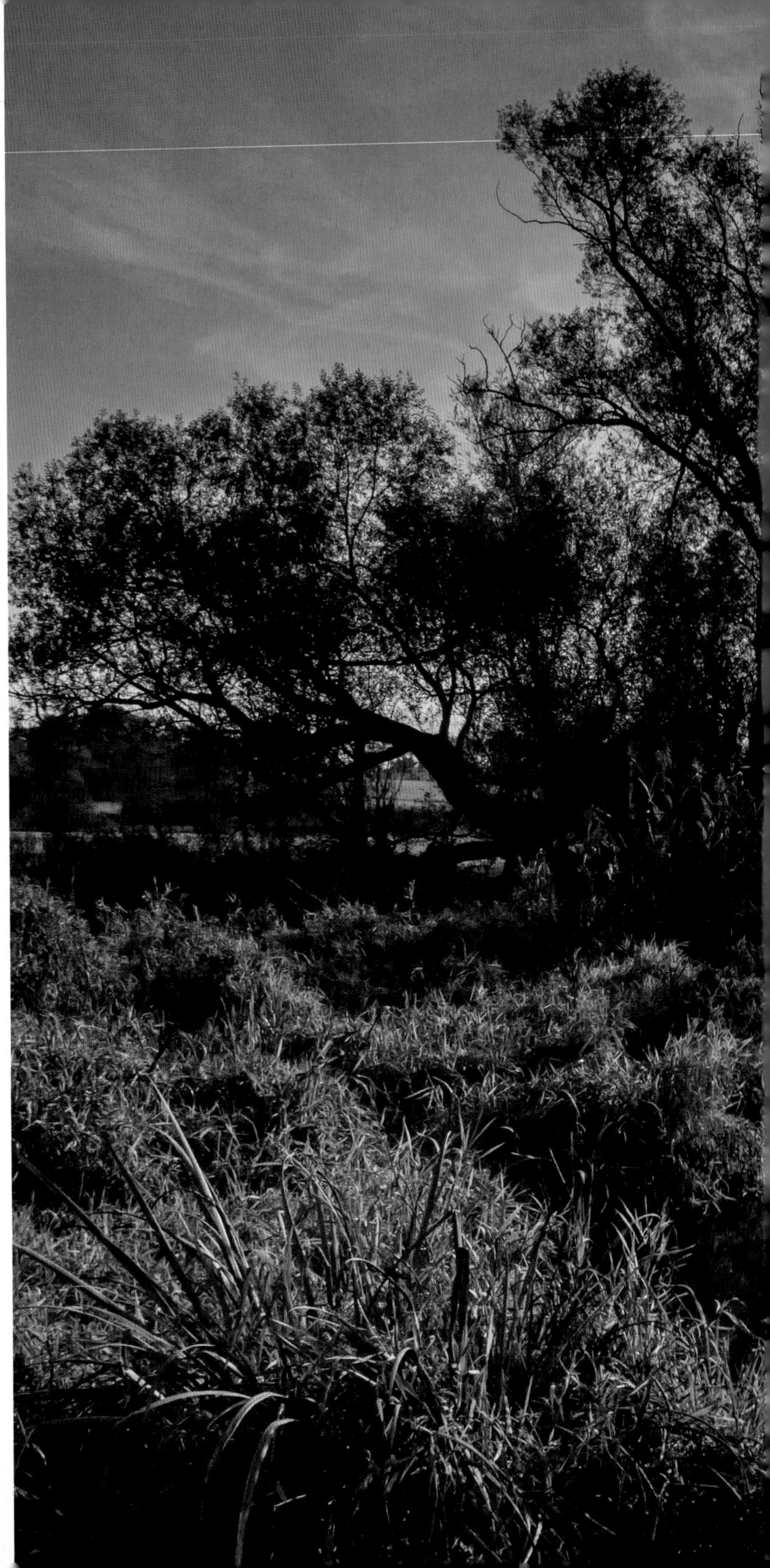

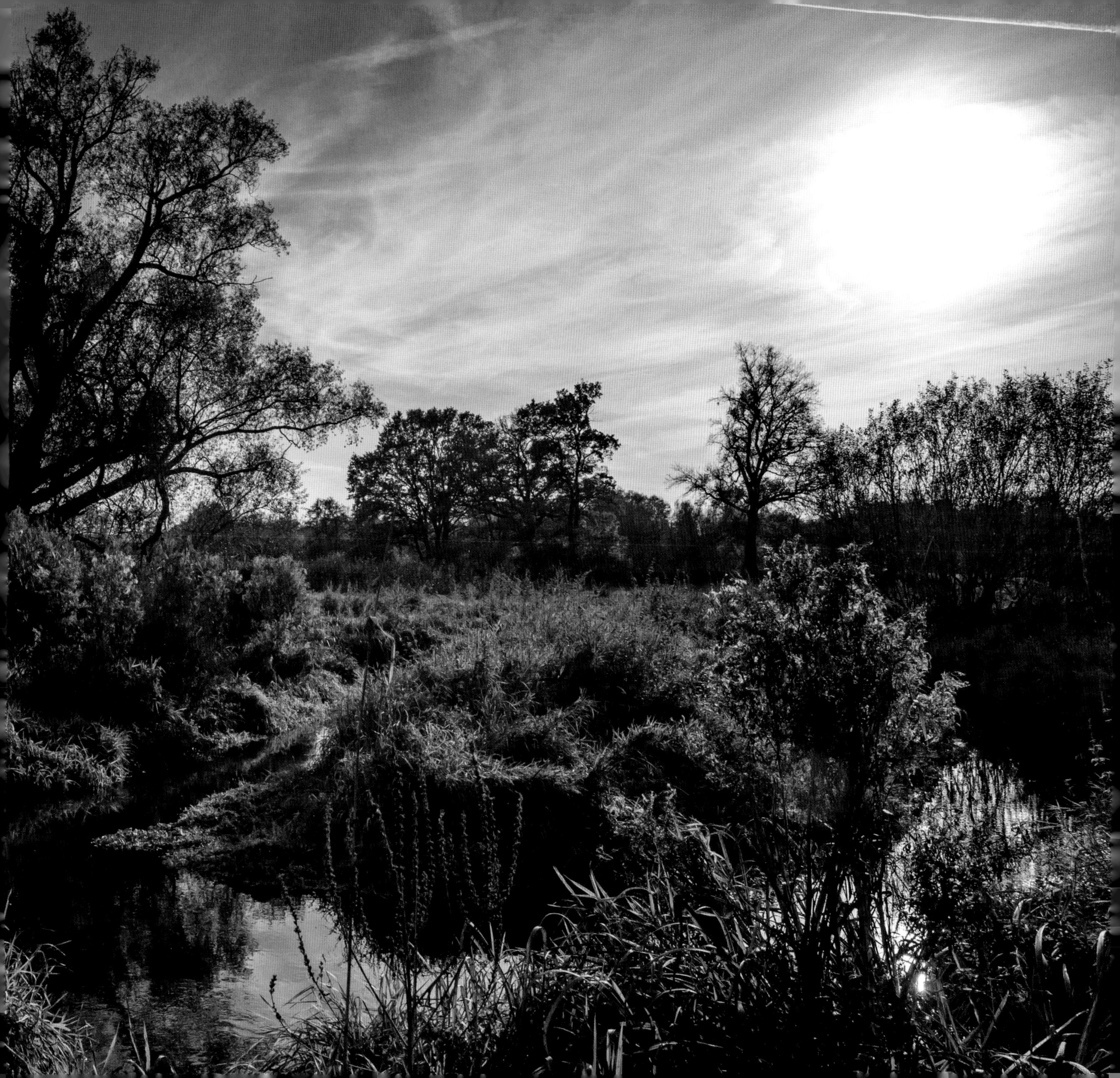

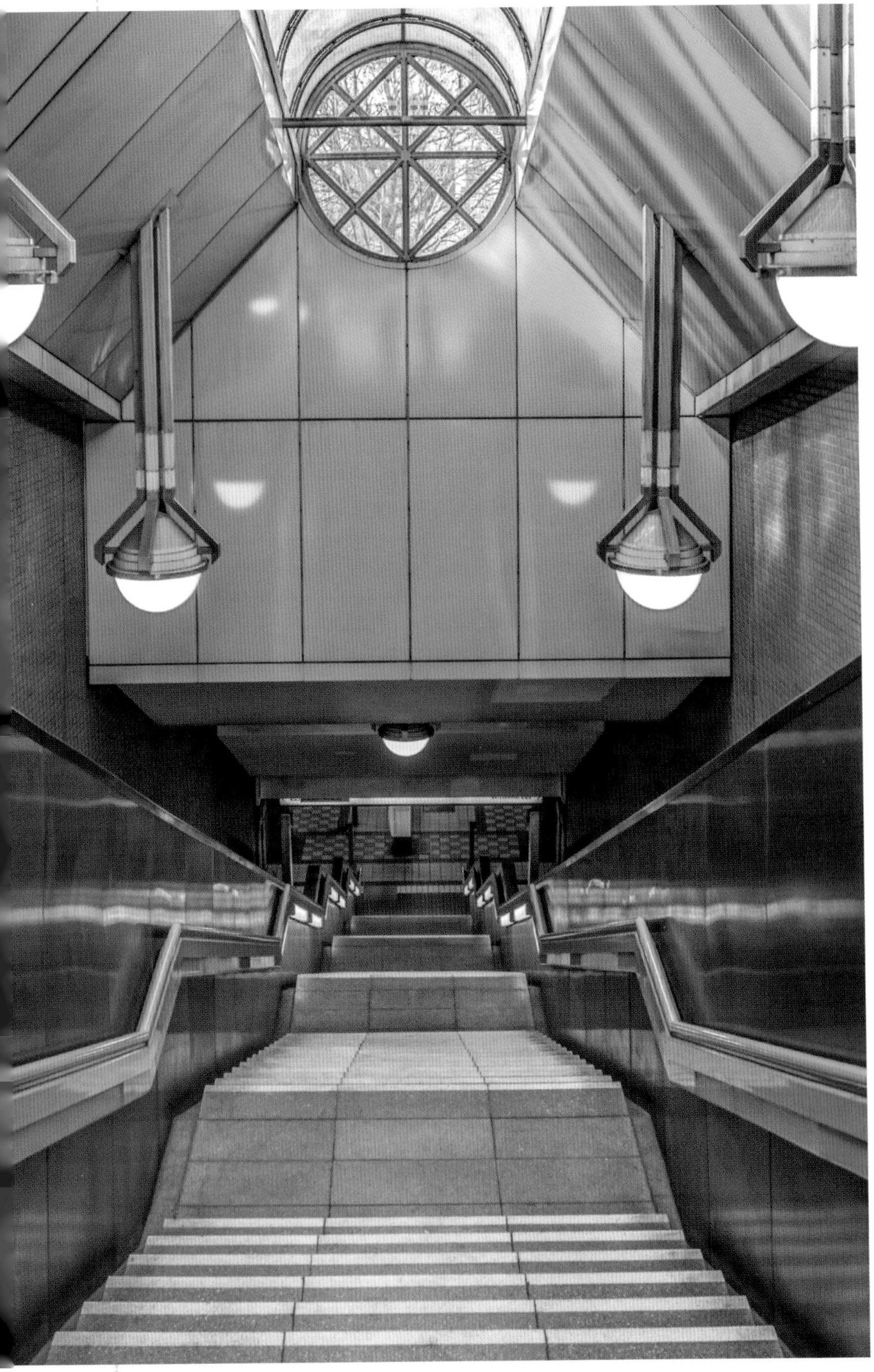

RATHAUS REINICKENDORF

Wittenau, Reinickendorf

Rathaus Reinickendorf (Reinickendorf Town Hall) is a U-Bahn station designed in 1994 by architect Rainer G. Rümmler (1929–2004), who designed other stations in the city. It is a working space of unusual beauty. Floors and walls are brightly patterned in colourful tile work with an Art Deco feel. Stairwells glow in strident blues (as seen here), with overhead glass delivering as much natural light as possible to the public areas below. Berlin's Untergrundbahn (U-Bahn; Underground Railway) has a total of 173 stations, many of which, like Rathaus Reinickendorf, are worth exploring for their architectural qualities.

DICKE MARIE

Tegel Forest, Reinickendorf

Dicke Marie is the name of a single venerable pedunculate oak in Tegel Forest. 'Venerable' is indeed something of an understatement, as the tree is thought to be in the region of 800–900 years old, which makes it older than Berlin itself. The name is said to have been granted by the famous Wilhelm and Alexander von Humboldt (1767–1835 and 1769–1859), who as boys played in the forest when they ventured out from the nearby Schloss Tegel; the name was the title of the cook in the palace.

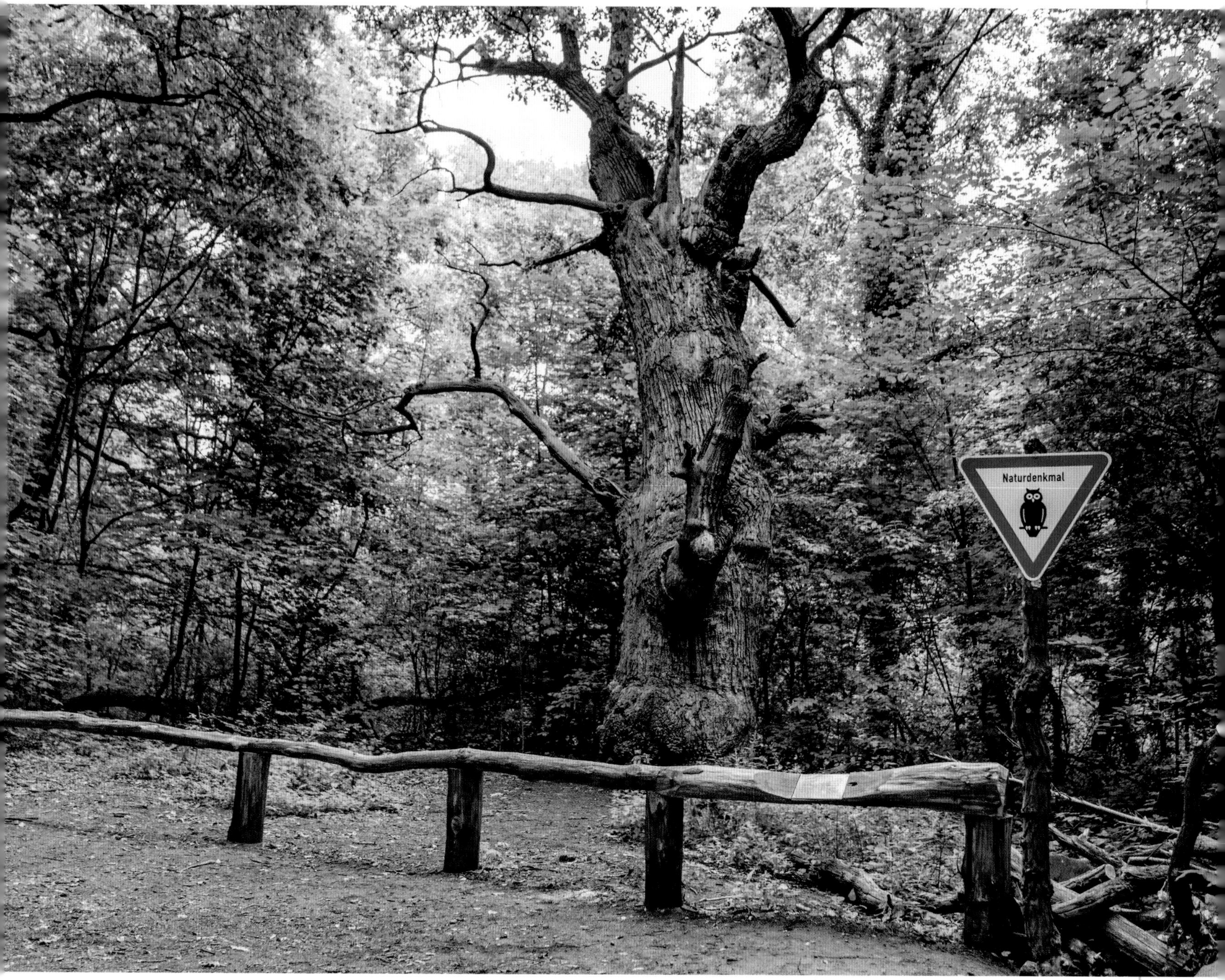
Naturdenkmal

SECHSERBRÜCKE

Tegel, Reinickendorf

Sechserbrücke (Six Bridge) is the popular name for the Tegeler Hafenbrücke, a pleasing steel, half-timbered pedestrian bridge that crosses the entrance of Tegel port. It was constructed in 1908–09 by the Berlin-based construction company Steffens & Nölle, who created a structure 91 m (299 ft) in overall length, with a main span of 65 m (213 ft). The Six Bridge name came from the toll of five pfennigs – a 'six' – that had to be paid to cross the bridge.

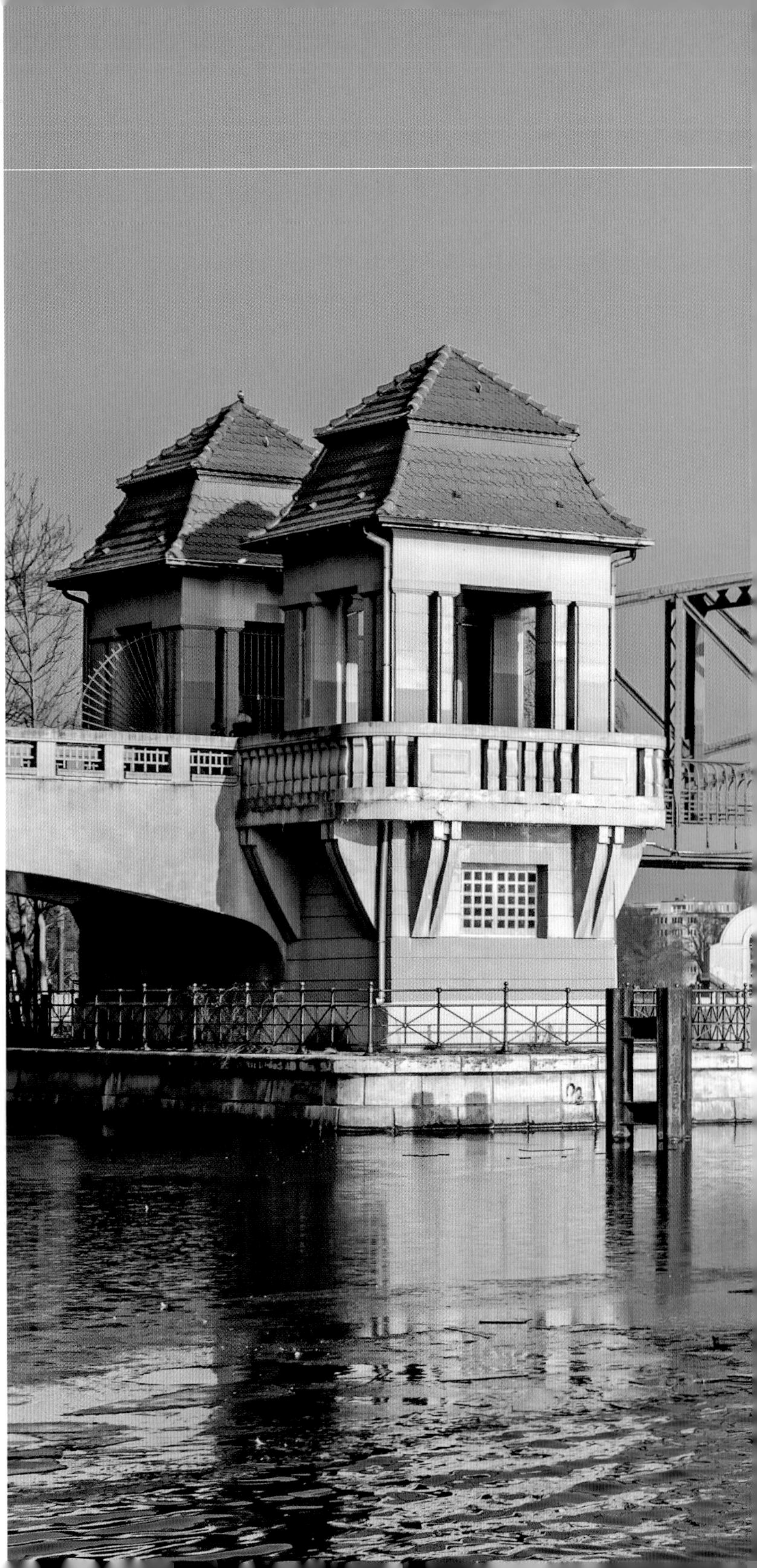

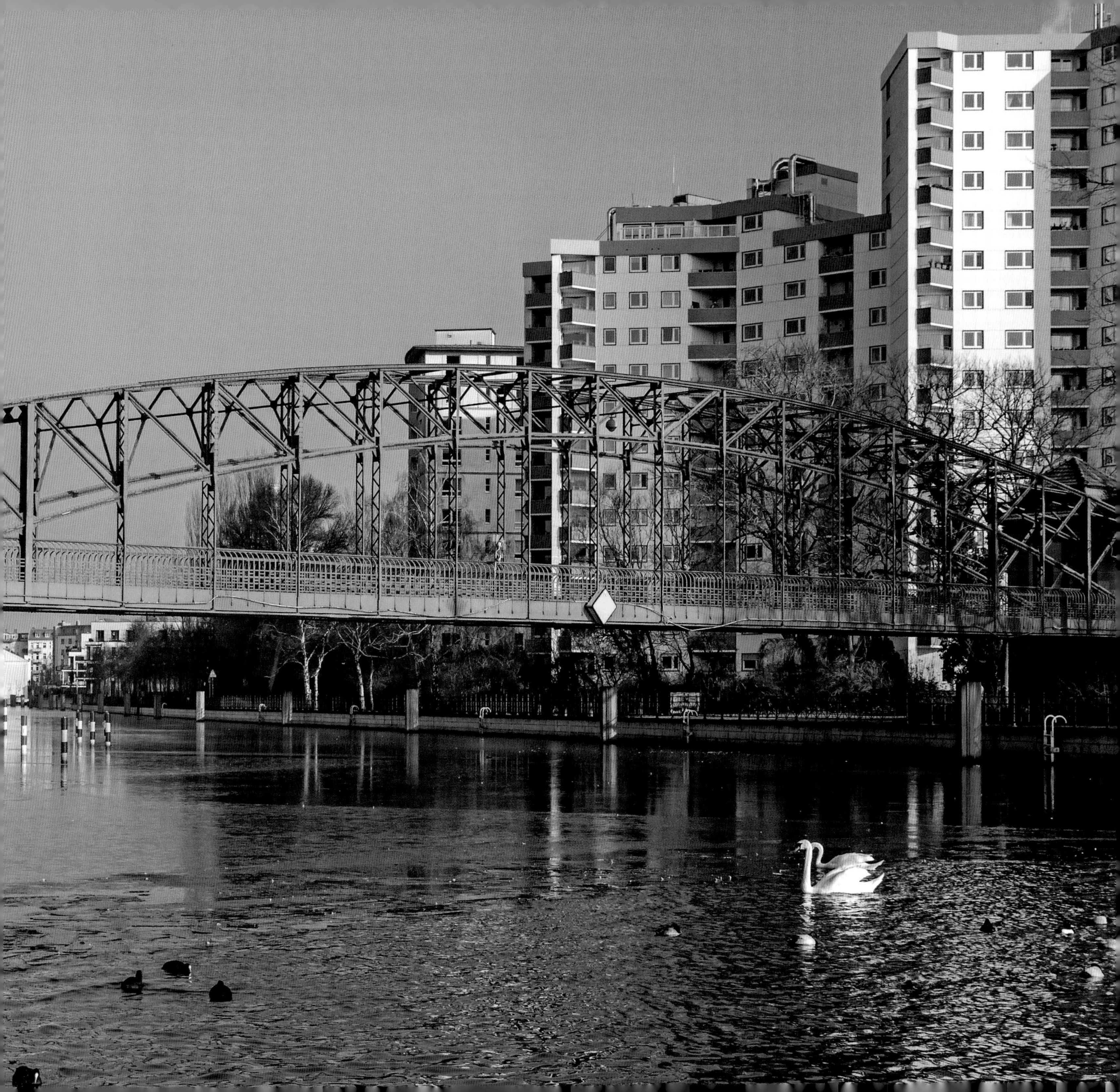

INDEX

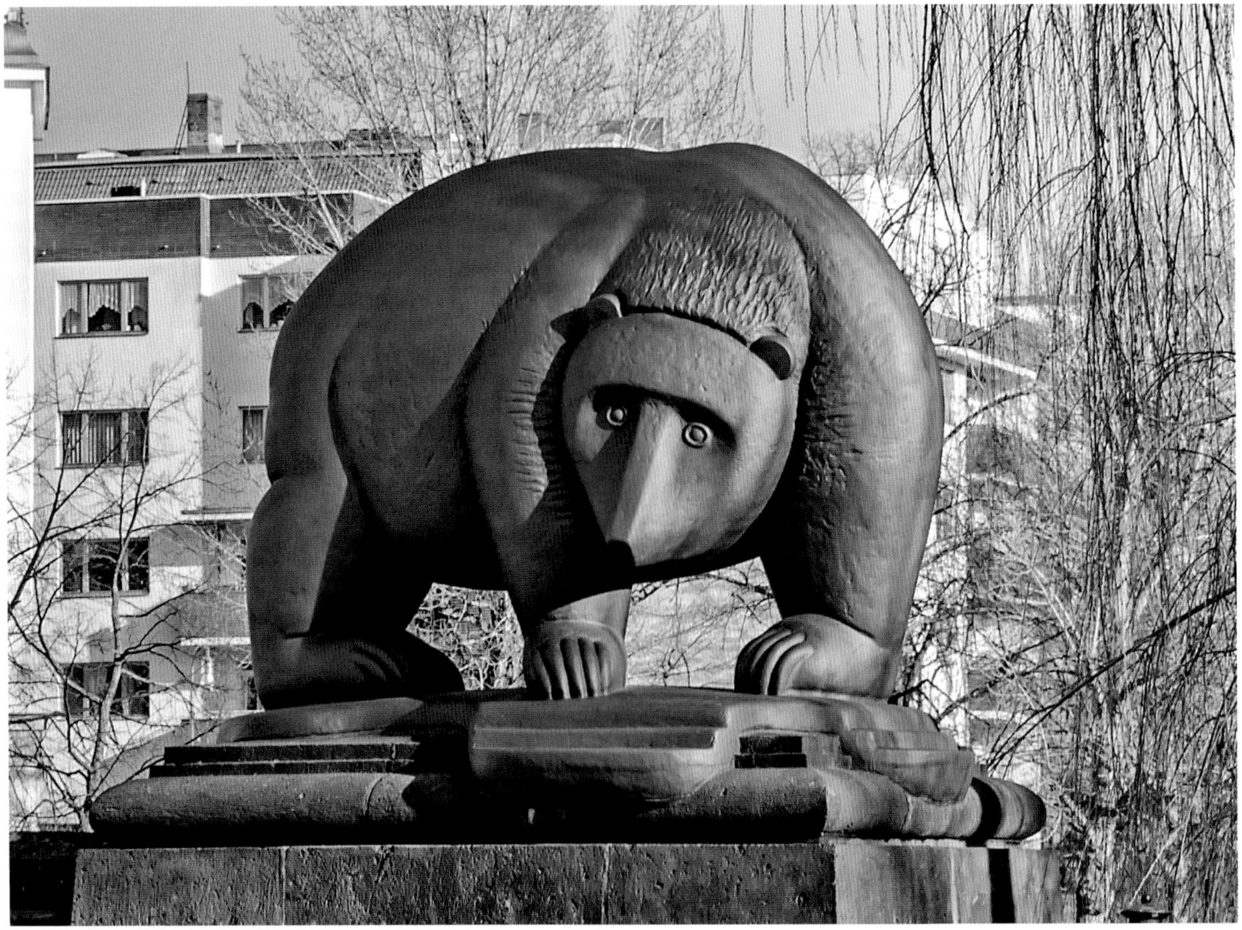